HEART *of the* BLACKHAWKS

HEART *of the* BLACKHAWKS

THE
PIERRE PILOTE
STORY

•

L. WAXY GREGOIRE
and
DAVID M. DUPUIS
with
PIERRE PILOTE

ECW Press

LIBRARY AND ARCHIVES CANADA CATALOGUING IN PUBLICATION

Gregoire, L. Waxy, 1951-, author
Heart of the Blackhawks : the Pierre Pilote story /
L. Waxy Gregoire, David M. Dupuis, Pierre Pilote.

ISBN 978-1-77041-136-4 (bound)
ALSO ISSUED AS: 978-1-77090-426-2 (PDF) | 978-1-77090-427-9 (EPUB)

1. Pilote, Pierre, 1931-. 2. Hockey players—Canada—Biography.
1. Dupuis, David Michael, 1958-, author II. Pilote, Pierre, 1931-, author
III. Title.

GV848.5.P49G74 2013   796.962092   C2013-902465-4

Editor for the press: Greg Oliver
Cover and text design: Tania Craan
Front cover photo courtesy Chicago Blackhawks
Author photo: Sharon Light
Printing: Friesens   5   4   3   2   1

Published by ECW Press
2120 Queen Street East, Suite 200,
Toronto, Ontario, Canada M4E 1E2
416-694-3348 | info@ecwpress.com

The publication of *Heart of the Blackhawks* has been generously supported by the Canada Council for the Arts which last year invested $20.1 million in writing and publishing throughout Canada, and by the Ontario Arts Council, an agency of the Government of Ontario. We also acknowledge the financial support of the Government of Canada through the Canada Book Fund for our publishing activities, and the contribution of the Government of Ontario through the Ontario Book Publishing Tax Credit. The marketing of this book was made possible with the support of the Ontario Media Development Corporation.

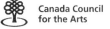

PRINTED AND BOUND IN CANADA

To Sue – DMD
To Joan – LWG
To Annie – P

TABLE OF CONTENTS

The Winter of His Youth

It was cold out this morning of January 20, 2012, bitter cold, like he remembered. The snow crunched under his feet as he got out of the car and walked towards the new arena. It was his first time seeing it, the Jonquière Sports Palace. He hadn't been back home in a very long time. His breath hung in the air like a heavy fog. Boy, it brought back memories, 80-year-old memories. Walking smartly into the arena's large lobby, he was received as a conquering hero.

When the moment came, he stood back smiling, excited, arms crossed. He pumped his fist as if to say, "Yeah, go-ahead, baby!" and watched Saguenay mayor Jean Tremblay and event chairman Réjean Laforest pull back the cloth sheet that unveiled a large bronze statue of himself created by artist Jérémie Giles. Soaking in appreciative applause, the moment was surreal and almost made him speechless—but he did have a few words to say.

"I can't tell you what a special feeling it is to be here with you and to come back home to the region of my youth where I spent many hours growing up on the other side of the tracks in Kénogami," he said in French, a language he had rarely used since moving away 66 years prior. Though he was a little rusty with some of the words of his mother tongue, his rolling pronunciation hadn't betrayed him.

"How often I crossed those tracks in the bitter cold to watch the men's senior hockey team from the snowbanks of the old Jonquière outdoor arena. My feet would be frozen by the time I walked all the way home. How appropriate that we are in an arena in Jonquière. To be honoured with such a special remembrance is warming to my soul on a cold Québec winter morning."

He thought of Annie and wished she were here. They had celebrated their 57th wedding anniversary the spring before. She was his soul mate. They had done everything together, through thick and thin. She wanted badly to come, but her health wouldn't permit her to make the 1,200-kilometre trek. But she was there with him in spirit.

"To all of you here, my French family, from the bottom of my heart, thank you! It is wonderful to be home, a place that holds special meaning for me. A part of me will remain here in stone for a very long time, but please know that a part of my heart will always be here.

"I have won Norris Trophies, a Stanley Cup, had my no. 3 retired to the rafters of the arena in Chicago, but this night and this honour is right up there with them. I am truly humbled. I stand proud and say: Thank you, Kénogami! Thank you, Jonquière! Thank you to the whole Saguenay region!"

The whooping cheers were thunderous from the people crowded into the arena lobby. Afterwards, they came up to him one by one, to shake his hand, to congratulate him, to tell him how proud they were that he was one of their own. He didn't know most of them, but they sure knew who he was.

Later that evening, before a major junior game in the same arena, the crowd was told of his legacy—a Stanley Cup with the Chicago Black Hawks in 1961, Norris Trophies as the NHL's best defenceman in 1963, 1964, and 1965, the retired no. 3 hanging in the rafters of Chicago's United Center in 2008, and the election to the Hockey Hall of Fame in 1975.[1] And he was one of theirs.

---

1 Though today they are known as the Chicago Blackhawks, during Pierre Pilote's hockey career and until 1985–86 the team's name was the Black Hawks and they are referred to in that way throughout this book.

As he came out onto the ice wearing his no. 3 Chicago sweater, a banner was unveiled in his honour and he dropped a ceremonial puck prior to the beginning of the game. They thought they knew him but they didn't. They only knew a little bit of his remarkable story; a journey too filled with memories, laughter, hurt, pain, and yes, glory, to completely tell in a Friday-night sound bite.

Only he knew what it had taken to overcome every obstacle, and there were many, in attaining his goals. He thought of the many miles he travelled, the personalities he met during his journey in becoming one of the greatest defencemen of all time.

No, they couldn't possibly know his life, and what a life it had been.

It was a remarkable journey. "I'll have to tell that story some day," Pierre Pilote often thought.

The Kénogami Kid

Today, the sprawling City of Saguenay is comprised of the amalgamated towns of Chicoutimi, Kénogami, Jonquière, and Arvida, but in the 1800s, they were all small, growing towns.

The vast pristine, virgin lands, abundant lakes, rivers, and forests of northern Québec were ideal for the lumber industry, and the Saguenay region had always relied on it. Powered by a 27,000-horsepower hydroelectric dam on the nearby Sable River, the pulp and paper industry ran the town at the start of the twentieth century.

The town of Jonquière, named after the Marquis de La Jonquière, governor of New France from 1749 to 1752, was founded in 1847. Kénogami, situated on the northern shore of the lake that bears its Innu name, meaning "Long Lake," was originally part of the town of Jonquière. Though detached in 1911, they were really joined at the hip.

In the late 1800s, young Albert Pilote moved with his family to the Saguenay region as his father looked for employment in the lumber industry. He grew up, met and fell in love with a local Innu girl named Madeleine Dallaire, who was born on the shores of Lac St. Jean at the Innu reserve near Roberval, north of Kénogami. Not not to be mistaken with the Inuit of the far north, this Innu band was also known as "les Montagnais," or the Inuatsh of Pekuakami.

After marrying in June 1906, the couple moved to Kénogami where Albert secured work at the paper mill. Though it appeared that they severed all ties with the band, his bride would be known as mystical, a medicine woman who informally carried on her many traditional herbal cures and practices.

From the beginning, Madeleine ruled while Albert, a quieter and meeker partner, succumbed to her direction and whims around the house. Their brood soon grew to six daughters and four sons, including one Paul Émile Pilote, born on April 4, 1908.

By the time he was 14, Paul began working at Price Brothers, as a log sorter and loader in the large holding area that surrounded the pulp and paper mill. The holding pond was fed by a mile-long, water-fed shoot that carried the cut logs or "pitoune" as the French called them, from as far away as Lac Saint Jean. Paul used a long gaff to sort and guide the logs onto a large conveyor belt which carried them into the mill to be ground into chips.

Paul eventually advanced in the mill, only to discover a situation within the company that was prevalent throughout industrial Québec in this time period: the English had better, higher paying jobs than the unskilled French labourers. Paul looked past his early frustrations. He needed the job and wouldn't make any waves, not just yet.

Paul met Maria Gagné, daughter of Adeos Gagné, a widowed lumberman from the Gaspé region who had moved his family to the Saguenay in search of steady work. Maria's mother had died when she was 12 years old and Maria became the instant surrogate mother to her other siblings and assumed the unpleasant task of cooking at her father's lumber camp.

English prejudice was a contributing factor in young Paul's becoming an accomplished boxer, soon earning the moniker "Kayo" Pilote. Though not a big man at 150 pounds, Paul's fists were fast and solid, and did some of his talking. His amateur fights in the region were well enough organized that he ran miles a day to prepare. He didn't lose many, as exhibited shortly after his marriage to Maria on April 3, 1928, when he knocked out a group of larger, drunken men who unwisely challenged him at a wedding reception, which only increased his local legend.

They moved into an apartment on the corner of rues Bergeron and Cabot in Kénogami and attempted to start a family, but two pregnancies resulted in stillbirths. When labour pains began on December 11, 1931, the third pregnancy threatened to have the same fate. Arriving from Jonquière, Dr. Ernest Marchand explained the dire situation to the worried husband.

"It's a pretty big baby in there, Mr. Pilote," Marchand told him. "I'm not sure it's even going to come out!" They both knew the consequences of that.

Working quickly to save the baby and the mother, the young doctor was able to turn the baby to just the right angle within the birth canal and, gently but firmly, pull the child out. After a few tense moments, Joseph Albert Pierre Paul Pilote came screaming healthily into the cold world.

This pregnancy was followed by another stillbirth, which ensured young Pierre would be nursed for an extra year. "I could almost walk and talk and I was still being breastfed!"—a situation that he would jokingly credit with his future good health and toughness.

A new world awaited little Pierre as he grew up in the barren, cold landscape around Kénogami. With busy parents, he was on his own to explore and survive in it. Though he grew wiser before his time, he was still a child at heart.

"Christmas only truly happened to me once—when I was six or seven," he recalled. "I was still sleeping and Dad walked into the house with snow on his boots, to make tracks like Santa. Then he quickly woke me up yelling, 'Pierre! Pierre! Santa's here! He's here in the house! Hurry out and you might still see him!'"

Pierre ran excitedly into the living room but was disappointed at only finding snowy footprints run rampant throughout the house. Still, his disappointment was tempered at the close encounter.

"I almost saw Santa!" Pierre laughed. "I just missed him!"

A few years later, Pierre and two friends decided to fetch their family's respective Christmas trees. The day was bitterly cold and things soon took an ominous turn as they had greatly underestimated the task and the weather conditions.

"We quickly became disoriented in the thick bush," recalled Pierre. "It took quite a while to find our way back, and with only one tree. One of the guys almost lost his foot because of frostbite. Our winters were bitterly cold! You had to respect them. It was a lesson learned."

Paul's house was in close proximity to Albert and Madeleine Pilote's, ensuring that young Pierre would be strongly influenced by his grandparents.

"My grandfather Pilote belonged to the Knights of Columbus," Pierre related. "In the summer evenings he would walk by our place to go play cards at their hall. There had been a shoeshine parlour up the street and I had thought to myself: 'Why can't I do that?' So, one evening, I got a box and put a chair on it, put it right at the corner of our property and waited for grandfather to walk to the K.C. Hall. Sure enough around six o'clock he was walking by on the other side of the street and I yelled to him: 'Hey Grandpapa! Can I shine your shoes?'"

Albert Pilote smiled and ambled on over to his seven-year-old entrepreneurial grandson and became Pierre's first customer. At the end of the exercise Albert gave him a dime. Pierre's eyes lit up like firecrackers. It was his first business transaction, one he would never forget.

"I often walked over to Grandmaman's. She was a hard-working lady who controlled everything, especially my grandfather. She was a great cook and fed me all the time. Grandmaman's tourtière at Christmas and New Year's was something else. I helped her with her chores. She liked me—the first Pilote grandchild. She was also a real gossipy type who didn't get along with my mother. She'd spy on my mother. Grandmaman sometimes tried to instill some warped ideas into my head but that was not a problem because I always thought for myself, but she did teach me things."

One day Madeleine was making soap and sent her grandson to the store to buy 10 pounds of salt. Little Pierre could barely carry it back the three blocks. When he arrived, spent, she smiled at him.

"Now Pierre?" she asked him, taking his load from him. "What's heavier . . . 10 pounds of salt or 10 pounds of feathers?" The answer seemed easy to him.

"Why, Grandmaman, 10 pounds of salt!" he proclaimed quickly without thinking. She laughed without saying a word, watching him think it over. He soon realized the answer and the lesson, one of many.

Pierre attended a French elementary school called École Sacré Coeur (Sacred Heart School), run by a denomination of Christian Brothers dedicated to Catholic education throughout Canada. Despite the Christian setting, animosity between the English and the French seemed to crystallize here.

"In class if you didn't use an English word you got a little cross. But if you used an English word, then a classmate could take your cross. So there was a lot of animosity between the English and us French kids right there! I didn't have to worry too much about losing crosses because I could never speak English, but my first English words were, 'Do you want to fight?' We used to taunt the English kids who lived on the other side of the railroad tracks."

In Kénogami, with a lot of big families around, a boy soon learned he had to defend himself. Pierre remembered one particular bully who was always pushing him around after school. One day, Pierre got fed up of the ritual and humiliation.

"I was afraid of him for sure but I just hauled off and hit him solid! Bang! He went down and I ran home! He never picked on me again. I didn't really like to fight at school, only if I had to."

Once, Pierre's tough tendencies directly affected his family. The Pilotes rented the basement of a duplex and Pierre played with the landlord's son.

"Rodé Coulombe had a wooden wagon with an emblem of a plane on the side," recalled Pierre. "I had a red steel wagon with an emblem of a fast train on the side and I could always push my wagon faster than he could. One day we got into an argument about what was faster: a plane or a train. Of course I said a train was faster, he said the plane. We finally asked his brother to decide and naturally his brother sided with him. I didn't like that answer.

"Having lost the intellectual argument, I decided to make it physical and I threw a stone and hit Rodé right in the head. He went home crying. Rodé's father, our landlord, was livid and got into an argument with Dad, who came back into the apartment steaming, saying, 'That's it! We're moving out!' I was never sure if we got evicted or if Dad decided but we were soon on the move— because of me!

"My grandparents had a big lot so Dad hired a contractor and built us a house right next door, on my grandparents' lot. Afterwards Dad said to me: 'If Rodé Coulombe comes on this property, you get 'em!' I never did and in fact we stayed good friends, even long after, but it was a lesson learned about the consequences of fighting."

In Pierre's early days in Kénogami, Knights of Columbus community picnics were common and baked beans were plentiful, with varying degrees of succulence.

"Some folks made great baked beans, and some were just awful, I mean really bad! You had to really know who made the best ones," Pierre explained. "We'd go around with Dad, because he knew the ones *not* to eat!"

At one such picnic, one of the Christian Brothers fell out of a truck, struck his head on the pavement and subsequently died from his injuries.

"A week later, the head of the Brothers got the whole school together, about six hundred of us," recalled Pierre. "We're all standing there and he talked about the death of the Brother and then said afterwards, very seriously: 'We will have to replace Brother so and so. One of you will have to decide one day to enter the order and replace him.' I looked around and thought to myself, it ain't gonna be me!"

From the beginning, the children were drilled to pray constantly, especially before going to bed, and attend church every Sunday. To not do so would guarantee one's place in hell. The scare tactic worked: "I said my six Hail Marys, six Our Fathers every night until I was 25, no kidding! I always went to church every Sunday. I thought of it as a good luck charm, but I didn't always agree with their rules. My aunt was refused communion once because she was attending a Protestant high school. I thought that was silly, but the church ruled by fear. They sure scared the heck out of me! But one good thing the church and school had—a rink.

"My first pair of skates were my mother's. I used to shove things in the toes so they would fit me," he remembered. "There were about 30 or 40 of us on the rink at school skating around. The Brothers were playing hockey with some of the older boys. We were just skating around, and I remember falling in front of the net on this one Brother's hockey stick. Sticks back then were rough and really full of slivers.

"This Brother didn't even think twice and just pulled on his stick and I ended up with a huge, huge sliver in my right buttock. Oh it hurt! I raced home crying and my mother tried for about three hours to pull it out without success. We finally walked to see Dr. Marchand, who froze it and got that sliver out. It was an injury that is sensitive to this day. I have a few of those—reminders of my past, and my first one connected to hockey!"

Though his parents were concerned about his physical health, they were certainly less worried about his academics, a sign of the times.

"My parents were never concerned about my homework or my marks," recalled Pierre. "It was normal not to worry about those things back then. Life out of school is what mattered."

Until his 11th birthday, life out of school was summertime, and for Pierre that meant only one thing—time spent at his uncles

Lionel and Maurice Pilote's 30-acre camp on the Shipshaw River. His father's two brothers had left home in their mid-teens and squatted on virgin land on the river north of Kénogami. Cutting trees and clearing the land, they eventually grew an assortment of vegetables, raised pigs, cows, horses, chickens, and other animals.

"My aunts Rosa and Violette would bring me up there in the summertime. My first chores were to feed the animals," he recalled. "Then I'd pick up the fresh cow's milk that had been collected every morning and put it in the stream to keep cold. I had to pick up the milk and bring it to my grandmother. She would spread the cream from the top of the milk on fresh homemade bread for me cooked from the outdoor oven—oh boy! That was good!"

The camp also presented its own dangers. One day, young Pierre was playing at the end of the dock on the water, when he suddenly slipped and fell into the water. Unable to swim, he screamed out as loud as he could, thrashing about in the cold water. Seemingly alone, he was a goner.

"I was lucky someone heard me! It was pure luck because I was often left to my own devices. I was just small. And I remember being scared a lot as a little guy because I had to always watch out for bears. There were always bears around. I would have been easy pickin'!"

While at the camp, Pierre's aunts also found time for courtship. One Saturday young Pierre's inquisitive, teasing nature and out-spokenness collided with his aunt Rosa's courtship ritual as Rosa's boyfriend and future husband, René, was bicycling the 15 miles that evening to court her. But first, she had to get ready.

"That afternoon my grandmother is picking lice out of my aunt Rosa's hair with a fine tooth comb. Wow!" Pierre remembers with a laugh. "Now I'm sitting there, quiet, watching, taking it all in when they suddenly realize that I'm there. They all look at me."

"Pierre!" said his aunt. "You don't say a damn word about this to anybody! Hear?"

"Oh no! I won't!" Pierre answered, shaking his head side-to-side.

Later that evening, after Rosa's boyfriend had arrived, they were all sitting around talking. Pierre had taken quite a liking to the young man who always teased and talked to him. Suddenly, a thought came to his head.

"Hey René!" Pierre declared with a big grin. "Guess what I saw this afternoon!"

"What?" René asked him.

To the horror of the ladies and before they could stop him, Pierre described the cleaning of the lice from his girlfriend's hair. The women, horrified, started screaming at Pierre and chased him from the room.

"Oh boy, did I put my big foot into my mouth and get into trouble with my grandmother and Aunt Rosa! Oh boy!" Pierre laughed. "The cabin had two big rooms, one of which had a row of bunk beds. I got sent to bed in that room. I didn't dare come out the rest of the night!"

Paul Pilote occasionally helped his brothers and earned money himself by picking up and selling their cords of wood back in Kénogami. First he enlisted Pierre and his friends to help.

"The truck had very high sides, and we'd fill it right to the top with wood. Then we'd ride right on top of the wood—right on top of the load of wood!" Pierre remembered, shaking his head. "When we'd come to an overpass or a covered bridge Dad would yell back for us, to put our heads down. We'd duck, sometimes just barely making it through! It's amazing that none of us kids ever got killed!"

As Pierre grew, he was joined by other siblings: Reine Marie, born in 1934; Florent in 1936; Paulette in 1937; Gilles in 1939; and Yolanda born in 1942. Pierre's Saturday nights were soon spent babysitting while his parents went dancing at a local hangout called the Valmeno.

Paul had steady work at the Price Brothers Mill during the depression years of the 1930s, and while many families suffered throughout North America, employment in Jonquière and Kénogami hummed along.

"We never went without food. I remember going to the butcher shop down the street, called Carrien's and the grocery store called Lavoid. We had an account at both places. It was a Friday ritual for me to go and pick up a big roast pork and some veal. Mom would cook them on Saturday to eat on Sunday, with browned potatoes. During the week we'd eat sausages or liver, but Fridays . . . well, that was something else!"

Like all Catholic families at the time, consumption of meat was forbidden on Fridays. Maria's solution was homemade crepes, pancakes that she made by mixing flour, baking soda, milk, fried in lard, and topped with brown sugar, corn syrup, or black molasses. Sometimes she made meatless spaghetti.

"Mom's meatless Italian spaghetti attempt was not very appetizing. She'd mix stewed tomatoes with onions, then she'd throw the spaghetti in there and slop it together. It looked like worms! We ate it but, ugh . . ."

By 1940, Paul Pilote grew frustrated with the constant English promotions at the Price Brothers Mill. Passed over time and again for jobs he was more than qualified for, his tolerance of the unfair situation finally snapped. With the support of the local parish priest, Paul attempted to organize a union. The attempt was squelched.

"The priests were always for the common people in those days, and had great influence on the workers," Pierre recalled of the situation that would affect his family. "Dad had the skills and seniority to be a foreman but they would advance the younger English guys. That angered him. Even though the paperwork, management stuff, was all done in English, Dad could speak, understand, and write it very well. Dad could be a hothead, and suddenly fed up, he quit!"

With a growing brood to feed, Paul quickly found temporary work in nearby Arvida. He next landed a full-time job with the local Canadian National Railway, where he soon became a fireman and, later, an engineer.

He was still at home often enough though and one day, he took a good look at the family's black-and-white cat that was six-year-old

Florent's pet. The cat's tail seemed to have become diseased with hair falling off it, replaced by large scabs.

"Boys, we got to fix that cat or he's going to die," he said to little Florent and Pierre. Florent was horrified at the prospect.

"What are we going to do, Pa?" Pierre asked.

"I'll show you what we're going to do," their father answered.

Like most men of the times, Paul smoked a pipe. Buying his own tobacco leaves, he cut them up with a small tobacco cutter—a piece of wood, on which swung a hinged blade.

"Pierre, you grab that cat's head, and Florent, you're going to hold the tail!" Paul instructed. The boys, still unsure, obeyed while Paul set up his tobacco cutter in the middle of the kitchen floor.

"We're holding onto Flo's cat," Pierre recalled. "Dad then placed the cat's tail on the tobacco cutter, and with the hinged blade, whack! He cut off the tail! That cat never moved like for three seconds because he couldn't get traction on the linoleum floor but when he did, poof, he was gone! There was blood all over the place!"

Hearing the screams of the cat, Maria ran in on the bloody aftermath of the operation that had just taken place in the middle of her kitchen. She looked at the mess and started screaming at her husband: "Paul! Why didn't you do that outside?"

Paul shrugged innocently, like he hadn't really thought about it. Young Florent held the tail, its blood dripping all over the floor.

"Maman, what should I do with this?" Florent yelled.

"Get rid of it!" she screamed at her younger son. It was like a scene out of a slapstick movie.

"That cat never came out for three days!" Pierre laughed. "Florent always talked about that cat. But hey, it worked. That cat survived. Dad did some crazy things but we were just an ordinary family, really."

Madeleine Pilote's habit of spying on her daughter-in-law next door finally caught up with her. The unceasing spying and judgment of his mother on his wife finally became intolerable for Paul. He went over to confront his mother about her prying. An argument ensued and Paul stormed out of her house and into his own house.

"That's it!" he screamed. "We're moving out!"

Paul sold his house to his brother Lionel and bought a three-bedroom house on nearby Rue Champlain. Pierre's visits to see his grandmother gradually decreased. Soon after this Madeleine Pilote developed an awful cough that expelled thick green phlegm. Pierre didn't know it at the time but the condition would later be diagnosed as tuberculosis.

Around 1943, with the Second World War raging in Europe, work became scarce at the CNR and Paul found himself working only two days a week. He needed something else but going back to the Price Mill was simply not an option. Paul heard that companies in Hamilton, the steel capital of Canada, were hiring. At the height of the war in 1944, 14,000 tanks were rolling off Canadian production lines and demand for tank parts was skyrocketing. Hamilton's steel production and workforce was the logical place to build tank parts.

So, Paul packed his bags and set off for Hamilton, accompanied by his buddy Bill Huard. With his father gone temporarily, 10-year-old Pierre assumed added responsibilities.

"I started the fire in the stove every morning and get the toast going on the top of it. The milk would get dropped off at the back door too, and I had to get it in quick before it froze. We managed okay. Dad used to send us a hundred-dollar money order every two weeks that I picked up at the post office."

During this time, Pierre managed to acquire his first bicycle, but shortly afterwards, the bike's wheels became wobbly, its spokes so loose that Pierre couldn't ride it anymore. The local bike shop owner told Pierre that he could fix the bike—for five dollars. Pierre didn't have the cash. Standing dejectedly around the bike shop, and not knowing what to do next, Pierre observed other bike spokes being straightened and tightened using a certain little tool. He was soon rushing home with an idea.

"I wrote Dad in Hamilton," Pierre related. "I described this certain tool that I wanted him to send me, so I could fix my own tire. After a few months, Dad sent me this little tool, a twenty-five-cent tool. I finally got my wheels straightened out. I was soon riding to my heart's delight again."

Pierre and his mother became closer during this time.

"I was kind of the man of the house, I guess. I was the oldest, so my mother would give me the biggest piece of pie or let me go to the movie theatre. My mother made me my first suit, one shoulder a little lower than the other but that was okay."

As time went by, Pierre found himself skating more and more.

"There was a rink behind the school. I didn't play hockey but I would help shovel off the ice, and then I could skate around. There was also an open-air rink in Jonquière and I'd walk the whole way there and back home. My toes would be just frozen! It was so cold! I would thaw my feet, do my homework, and go to bed. The next morning I'd get up and walk to school."

Though Pierre did not play any hockey while living in Kénogami, the sport was starting to pique his interest. He'd watch the local men's team at the Jonquière outdoor rink.

"I had no money to pay for admission, so I'd get there an hour and a half before the game and I'd watch the whole game on the snowbank. I learned an awful lot just watching these guys, studying them, their plays, blocking shots, taking passes. At eleven at night, I would walk the couple of miles home, frozen to the bone!"

Winter nights at the Pilote household were spent like most Québec households of the day—listening to the Montreal Canadiens games broadcast from the Montreal Forum.

"We had this big old RCA radio with a big round top," Pierre recalled. "We used to gather around and listen to the radio station in Chicoutimi, the only one we could get, and if it was a clear night, we could hear the Canadiens games. Even at that, the reception wasn't always clear."

With the war coming to an end in Europe, and tank parts less in demand, Paul Pilote found his factory hours in Hamilton starting to decrease. Again the CNR came to his rescue when he and his buddy were offered full-time positions down the road in Fort Erie. After only a few months on the job Paul realized that the job was secure. It was time to bring his family with him. In the summer of 1945, Paul got a few days off work and headed home to Kénogami. He arrived without fanfare and declared his motive upon arrival.

"Pack up, we're leaving!" he said. Pierre was flabbergasted.

"What? Where are we going?" Pierre asked him.

"Where we're going is going to be great!" Paul answered enthusiastically. "You're going to have grass! There are apple trees, pear and peach trees on the property!"

"Holy cow!" Pierre answered in shock. He had heard about grass, but the only fruit they had ever seen was in the grocery stores and too expensive to buy. Soon, the household was packing frantically, preparing for the trip.

"We packed up and the CNR gave us a full boxcar for all our stuff. If you're moving, that was part of the deal back then. When we got on the train Florent started asking about his cat. Dad told him the cat was in the caboose with our stuff but in actuality, Dad had decided to leave the cat behind."

Their train left Jonquière at eight o'clock in the evening, journeying through the night to Québec City, where it arrived in Montreal at 11 a.m. The family disembarked for the short layover before catching another train to Toronto, arriving there at five o'clock in the afternoon.

"In Montreal there were French people around us and even in Union Station in Toronto we were sitting together, so the loudspeaker announcements in English didn't bother me too much," explained Pierre. "On the train from Toronto to Niagara Falls, that still wasn't too bad because we sat together, but then the shocker came when we disembarked in Niagara Falls and we were waiting for a bus to Fort Erie. It was raining and we were in an outdoor gazebo-like bus shelter that had eight sides to it. There must have been a hundred people packed in there, and they were all talking English!"

At that moment, 13-year-old Pierre Pilote thought he was in a bizarre new country and environment. He couldn't understand the cacophony of languages that were exploding all around him at that bus stop. He almost panicked.

"I didn't understand them at all, the people around me! Not a word of French! I got scared and realized, 'Oh boy! I'm in trouble! Wow!'"

As he stood there with his family, huddled out of the pouring rain, in a foreign landscape, a strange city, amongst a sea of strangers and languages, and afraid, the young teenager wondered, "What has Dad gotten us into?'

Young Pierre Pilote, from Kénogami, Québec, would soon find out.

CHAPTER 2

Coming of Age in Fort Erie

The half-hour bus ride from Niagara Falls to Fort Erie that summer evening in 1945 was scary for Pierre Pilote, just 13. He was now in a new world, far removed from the familiar surroundings of Kénogami.

Situated on the shores of Lake Erie in south-central Ontario, Fort Erie was a town of 7,000 inhabitants that had once been a fort in the British quest to fend off American invasion during the war of 1812. Throughout the 1800s, Fort Erie was also safe crossing into Canada for African-Americans fleeing enslavement. The opening of the huge Peace Bridge between Fort Erie and Buffalo in 1927 marked the friendliness of the two nations.

But in 1945, Pierre saw many "war houses" along paved streets, something unheard of back home. Disembarking at a bus stop just before ten o'clock, the family stepped out into a thick fog. Thankfully the rain had stopped. Carrying their bags, they walked up a small hill on Lavinia Street towards their new house. Suddenly, Pierre heard a sound he'd never heard before: a deep, very loud fog horn, blasting from a ship nearby on the Erie Canal. It was a sound he would grow accustomed to.

"We finally got to the big house and yes, it had green grass, apple and pear trees like Dad had said," he recalled. "It was near 'Nigger Hill,' a coloured neighbourhood, which didn't matter to us at all. In fact a Mr. Bright, a real nice man, was negro and he lived right beside us. I remember getting into that house and wow . . . it was not a very nice house, old, with a lot of mice holes in the baseboards, but we made this a home, for a while."

That summer Pierre's grandfather, Albert Pilote, moved in with them. Paul had also gotten his father a job with the railroad, cleaning up the roundhouse. Albert wasn't there very long when sad news out of Kénogami sent him home—his wife had died from tuberculosis.

Later that same summer, familiarity came into their life when the Huard family from Jonquière moved only a mile away from them. Bill Huard had accompanied Paul to Hamilton and Fort Erie but it was a perpetual joke that Paul had seniority because he had handed in his registration papers only minutes before his friend. Their presence made the Pilotes feel a little better.

"They had four boys and a girl named Doris," noted Pierre. "The oldest was John Paul. He and I became good friends. They came over often which was nice. I didn't have any friends because I didn't speak English. I did become friends with a girl who lived across the road, but mostly we stuck together as a family that first summer in Fort Erie."

Upon Albert's return from his wife's funeral, he resumed work at the CNR roundhouse.

"That first summer Mother would prepare his hot lunch and I walked the mile or so and brought it to him every day," recalled Pierre. "While doing this, I used to walk by the softball field by the CNR tracks. There were some good baseball players who were brought in to work at Fleet Aircraft. Sometimes, I would watch their games from outside the fence. After the eighth inning, they'd open the gate and I'd go right in to watch the rest. I used to hope for a tie game so I could watch more innings. I started to like that game."

When September arrived, it was time for the Pilote kids to go to school. Paul enrolled his kids at an officially bilingual school nearby, Douglas Public School on Stanton Street, just three blocks away from their house. Their enrollment was feted in the local paper in a story titled: "French Pupils Put Teachers Back in Class."

The Pilote children were quite a challenge for the school and Principal William O. Robertson, who remarked to the press that it was the first time in the school's history that "French only" students had entered their halls. Most other students had at least been bilingual. Pierre, Gilles, Florent, Reine Marie, and Paulette's attendance forced their teachers to brush up on their French while giving their new students some English tutoring. Assigned to the children was a 12-year-old, fluently bilingual student named Collette Chaput. She asked Florent how he liked his new school.

"Oh fine, but I'll be happier when I can speak English," Flo replied to her in French. "Then I can talk with the other children and I will be able to understand what the teacher says."

"I went from Grade 7 in Kénogami to Grade 3 because I wasn't very good in English," Pierre recalled about his first few days. "In Grade 3, I sat right in the first row and was pretty big compared to the other kids. It felt a little out of sorts but my teacher, Mr. Jackson, was very nice. Then I moved quickly to Grade 6, 7, and 8 once I adjusted."

The move to an English community was even more difficult for Maria Pilote.

"As a stay-at-home housewife, my mother just couldn't adjust," Pierre remembered. "She didn't understand a word of English. Our first year in Fort Erie was very difficult for her, and especially my younger sister Yolanda. I had my troubles at school too. If I thought that I'd left fighting behind in Kénogami, I was sadly mistaken. There were always a couple of bullies there—Jack O'Brien and Jack Kennedy.

"When it rained out, we would go downstairs for recess, and O'Brien used to push my head against the school's stone basement wall and laugh. He was older but it wasn't long before I grew as big as he was and I fixed him."

One day the children complained to their father about their

mother's cooking. Paul nodded. That night at supper, the children were waiting for the customary call to the table but it wasn't coming.

"When's supper?" someone finally asked their father.

"We're expecting company," Paul said. "Mr. Lafaim is coming, so we're not eating until he comes."

Time clicked by and supper was very late. Finally, Paul called his brood to the table. They sat silently at the table, waiting. Paul saw that his troops were getting restless.

"Are you all hungry?" he asked. They nodded.

"Good and hungry?" he asked again, smiling.

"Yes!" the children all answered together.

"Good, because Mr. Lafaim has just arrived!"

The children looked around for a few confused moments until the point he was making finally sunk in.

"Ah, Mr. Lafaim?—in French, 'Mr. Hunger' had just arrived!" Pierre recalled of his father's statement. "Dad played on words but we finally got the point he was making. We never bitched about our mother's cooking ever again!"

But the culinary aspects of their young lives improved drastically.

"Soon, we met some Italians," added Pierre enthusiastically. "They showed Maman how to make real Italian spaghetti! Ah! What a transformation! We didn't want to eat no crepes on Fridays! No way! We wanted spaghetti! And I'd say to Mom with a wink, 'By the way, Maman, you can make the odd mistake on Fridays and put some meat in there too!'"

Their first Fort Erie winter had snow which made them feel at home, but their new town wasn't as enamoured.

"In those days I think Fort Erie had only one snowplow," noted Gilles Pilote. "They weren't used to snow. Course we were!"

As Pierre grew, he began to expand his interests and explored Fort Erie, but he still had responsibilities at home. "I babysat my brothers and sisters a lot. And Florent was like my dog, he followed me everywhere."

A year after their arrival, Paul purchased a larger, better wartime house in the west end, at 75 Kingsmill Street. This move necessitated Pierre moving to Our Lady of Victory Catholic School for Grade 7. The new school, accommodated in a former military building vacated at war's end, helped ease the educational demand created by the growing influx of baby boomers and their children to the area.

By 1947, still having trouble with his English and with only scant interest in academics, Pierre attributed his passing Grade 8 that year at Our Lady of Victory to a couple of smart, friendly girls who helped him in class.

And school helped to fuel his growing love of sports.

"There was this fella named Butch Fertinanti, an Italian guy, who used to come to the school and do physical fitness with us," recalled Pierre. "Then we'd play basketball. I didn't really like basketball—it didn't have any body contact! Exercising and sports were all new to me."

Despite his lack of sporting experience, 16-year-old Pierre showed he was a quick study as he amazingly won the 1948 Male Athlete of the Year Award that spring.

Father Frederick Lee, assigned as a parish priest at St. Michael's Parish in Fort Erie, believed that sports and particularly baseball were excellent means to keep youths busy, healthy, and out of trouble. The tall, friendly, spectacled Lee was instrumental in forming a baseball league that summer of 1948 and teams were formed throughout the city, sponsored by various service clubs. From the beginning, Pierre took up pitching.

"I played first, second, and third base, right field, everywhere, really, but I liked throwing the ball and I eventually became a pitcher."

Though Lee sparked Pierre's interest in baseball, he was also responsible for Pierre's first big-time hockey game—the NHL All-Star Game at Maple Leaf Gardens in October 1947. It was an experience Pierre would never forget.

After three years of living in a predominantly English

community, Pierre found his second-language skills improving. There was little discrimination amongst his peers because of his Native or French background.

"My English was coming along but in sports, you don't talk much," he explained. "I never felt handicapped or inferior, but I was wise enough to just listen, asking questions only if I didn't understand something. I was very wary that way. I didn't want to sound like a dummy so I would be quiet until it was safe for me to join in the conversation, unless of course if it was important and I had to know."

While Pierre denied any discrimination, his brother was not so lucky. "I'd get doors slammed in my face on Halloween as a kid because I was French," recalled Gilles Pilote. "I experienced a lot of bias growing up in Fort Erie. There were only a half-dozen French families in town. Pierre ignored it, but he was older."

By the summer of 1948, Pierre became so adept at throwing a baseball that he was chosen as one of two pitchers on the town's midget rep baseball team. One game, he walked only one batter while striking out eleven in seven innings to keep his team in first place. No one was more proud of his big brother than little Florent.

"Flo was still with me all the time and soon he became my practice catcher. I was rough on him," admitted Pierre. "I had read an article about hanging strings to make the strike zone more apparent, and so we'd hang these strings and I'd get mad at him to hold the mitt between the strings. He didn't like that. I used to pitch the ball pretty fast and I'd throw curves. For a young guy, he became a pretty good catcher."

Baseball success followed Pierre as his Fort Erie midget team was dominant in the playoffs and quickly eliminated Hagersville.

"We had a good team in midget. Vince Feltrin was our other pitcher. I remember Hagersville was tough for me to strike out in that first series because all their team members were little. I must have thrown two hundred pitches, and just about all of my pitches went over their heads!"

Paul Pilote, too busy working to feed his growing family to pay attention to his son's growing notoriety, was shocked when locals informed him of his son's on-field accomplishments. He soon started reading it for himself in the local papers.

"We were in the playoffs and all of a sudden Dad showed up to watch us play," remembered Pierre. "After eliminating this one team, the parents, kids, coaches, everyone, were gathered around and talking about the next series. The coach said, 'Look, we're going to need some drivers and some cars for the next game out of town.'

"Dad was there and I piped up right away: 'Yeah, my old man will drive us!' When we got home did I ever catch heck! Not for volunteering him but for calling him my 'old man.' I was just learning English you know and that's what everybody called their parents, right? Was he ever mad! He drove us to that game but I never called him 'old man' again—he was my dad!"

The team, managed by Frank Duranti, quickly disposed of Collingwood, Merrington, Langton, and Goderich on the way to the provincial finals. Their final opponent was supposed to be Prescott, but due to the travel distances and costs, Prescott defaulted.

"Besides, we were beating everybody very handily!" Pierre added.

To celebrate their success, the boys gathered in the auditorium at Our Lady of Victory Catholic School, where they were shown the 1947 World Series movie and were presented with new leather jackets by Fort Erie mayor Louis Ziff.

"We had a speaker by the name of Buddy Rosar, a catcher for the Philadelphia Athletics," Pierre remembered. "After he spoke, every-one's getting his autograph. I didn't even know what an autograph was but I remember standing right beside him, sizing myself up next to him, you know. I also remember looking at his World Series Championship ring, and thinking, 'I got to get myself one of those.'"

Following his summer baseball success, high school beckoned the young sporting hero. He attended it with tepid enthusiasm and after a few months he quit.

"I wanted to start working, make money and I walked a couple of miles to Hart & Cooley, a company that made warm-air registers. The boss was a nice gentleman. I told him that I wanted to apply for a job and he just hired me.

"My first job was as a dipping specialist. Warm-air registers had a backplate with a handle, like a baffle. Using a special glove I would dip them in paint, and hang them on a nail to dry. I made 40 bucks a week and I used to give my mother the money to support the family. After a couple of months, Hart & Cooley changed from an hourly wage to a production wage. I could do my job pretty quickly, so my salary jumped and I was now making an extra $10 to $15 a week! I used to give my mother my regular $40 and keep $15 for myself. She never knew."

Despite having severed his educational ties with his high school, its social aspect was another matter.

"I went to a lot of high school dances with the girls after I quit," Pierre recalled. "There was also a Catholic Youth Organization there, and I used to go to their dances every Friday night as well."

Despite his best intentions, Pierre's nervousness was still a factor in his developing social life.

"I'd practise dancing with my mother before going to these dances, then I'd drive Dad's car there. The music was provided by a piano player. I'd be too shy to dance and would wait until the last two songs before asking a girl to dance. I'd always ask the same girl to dance then give her a ride home after. She was a nice Chinese girl whose parents owned the hotel in front of where our family had originally gotten off the bus in 1945."

In spring 1949, having outgrown minor baseball, Pierre's ball skills benefitted his workmates in a new softball league. After an initial meeting was held at the Fort Erie Racetrack, a press picture showed a smiling Pierre sitting front row centre.

"I didn't play softball until I was 17 and working at Hart & Cooley. I was now playing with men 25 to 30 who could really play. That summer, I played both fastball and softball. In softball, I batted .500! It was a bigger ball, easier to hit."

With these men, Pierre was introduced to having an alcoholic beverage or two after games.

"We'd always go to the hotel for a few drinks," remembered Pierre. "I was only 17 years old. This one night in Fort Erie, this bartender wouldn't serve me because I was too young, so we went to the Legion. I overindulged: when I got home and went upstairs to my bed, I suddenly started feeling nauseous. It was a hot night. I knew I wasn't going to make it to the bathroom downstairs, so I ran to the window to vomit but Mom had put on the window screens that day and, oh boy, what a mess! Mother said, 'Don't worry, I won't tell your dad.' She always protected me."

In hardball, Pierre played with the St. Mike's team, also coached by Frank Duranti.

"Fort Erie Hurler Shows Promise," the local story went. "Pierre Pilote, youthful Fort Erie hurler, showed distinct promise of development into faster company tonight as he pitched St. Michael's to a 12-2 win."

Riding on his success, Pierre also made it as a starting pitcher with the Fort Erie juvenile rep team. The team met with the same playoff success as they had in midget.

"In one of the earlier series, Vince Feltrin and I beat Collingwood," remembered Pierre. "The game went 12 innings. I pitched eight innings and he went the rest of the way. There was an Indian kid from Collingwood who pitched the whole game and series for them. He was good! Then we eventually beat Cooksville and won it all."

Hockey was the farthest thing from Pierre's mind. He had never played the sport, had watched it occasionally, and had only been on his mother's skates recreationally. Fort Erie didn't even have a rink; its original arena closed in March 1939 when the roof collapsed during a snowstorm. Due to the rebuild cost, Fort Erie went without a rink until 1948, when the Fort Erie Memorial Arena opened to great fanfare.

"The arena, off Central Avenue, was not far from the Peace

Bridge," recalled Pierre. "It was your average small-town Ontario rink, built with blocks and big wood trusses. Everything inside—rooms, dressing rooms—were wood as well. Chicken wire was at the back and corners of the ice surface and seats lined each side. Over the offices and dressing rooms, where you entered the arena, were seats for another three to four hundred people. Mike McMahon, who had played with the Montreal Canadiens, was the first manager of the rink."

With the opening of the arena, talk at Hart & Cooley turned to forming a hockey team to play in a new men's industrial league.

"I remember one of the guys at work turned to me and said, 'Hey, you're French-Canadian! You should be able to play hockey!'" Pierre hadn't much thought about it, until he picked up a hockey magazine. Leafing through it he stopped at a story that ultimately changed his life.

"There was a story in there with pictures about Edgar Laprade, a centre with the New York Rangers," related Pierre these many years later. "He was French Canadian, with the same type of weight and body size I was. That article made an impression on me. I had chosen my hero! I thought, 'I want to be Edgar Laprade!'"

Now he just needed skates. Heading to the nearest Canadian Tire store, he tried on his first pair. Lacing them up, he was excited that the shiny pair of black skates seemed to fit. He paid $14 for them and other equipment and left.

"When I got on the ice, the skates were way too big for me. I was on my ankles, wobbling all over the place," he recalled. "So now what was I gonna do? Then this German guy at work asked me one day if I was playing hockey and said he was thinking of playing too, but he didn't have any skates. I asked him his size and then told him that I had bought a new pair for $25 but I was already thinking of upgrading, so I sold them to him for the same amount. I made a few dollars on the deal, went back to Canadian Tire, and bought a better pair of skates. This time I made sure they fit perfectly!"

To break in his new skates, Pierre went public skating at every opportunity. At one of the first events in the new arena, he was photographed sitting amongst a group of six hundred skaters. He was asked by a figure skater named Stella Yovatisch to be her skating partner for an upcoming ice carnival. Pierre agreed. Two thousand spectators came out to witness the carnival, and their picture appeared in the next day's paper.

"We were dressed up as a clown! A clown! I didn't look very happy in that picture. I ended up dating her sister for a while."

For the first time in his life, 17-year-old Pierre found himself on skates while holding a stick, a nice yellow-varnished CCM model he had paid $4.50 for at a local sports store. The industrial league played on Monday nights and the youngster was amongst men in their thirties and forties. His team was called the Hurst Butchers. He played centre like his hockey hero, Laprade.

"On our team was Sandy Bright, the coloured fella who lived across the street from us. It wasn't long before I knew where the penalty box was too. I made a lot of trips there! On one of the first plays, I went into the boards and my new stick shattered! After the game I took the pieces back to the sports shop and I went back to this Mr. Brooker, and I was really complaining, asking him to replace it. He didn't know what to say. Finally he said, 'Well, if you buy another one, I'll let you have it for $2.50.' Boy, I'll tell you I was careful going into the boards after that."

Since Pierre was now working full time, playing hockey with men, and having a few beers, Paul Pilote thought it was high time that his son be filled in on the finer points of life—as in the birds and the bees.

"In those days, sex education was nil; you got it on the street corner," recalled Pierre. "Dad started to drive me and Mom to the burlesque show in Buffalo most Sundays. The first time I went there, it was a crowded afternoon, and we sat way at the back. These girls came on stage and they're dancing and suddenly they're taking their clothes off! First time I had ever seen a naked breast!

I said, 'Holy shit! That's pretty good! I've got to remember this address!'

"From there, we'd go to the Buffalo Auditorium to watch a hockey game and we saw Ab DeMarco. It was standing room only for me. Dad and Mom had seats. I'd stand there and watch these games and I'd learn.

"A week or two later, I went to the burlesque show myself. I got there early and got a front row seat. Gypsy Rose Lee comes out and starts to dance and strip. What a disappointment! Her breasts were not bare at all, but were covered by a plastic see-through bra! It looked better from the back! That was my sex education from Dad. Later, Dad would keep going with my mom and then sometimes he'd bring my sister Reine Marie and we'd go to a bar that had a live band and my dad would say, 'She can sing!' and my sister Reine Marie would get up there and she'd sing a couple of songs, and in English too. That was our outing, our family time."

Buffalo would be an important part of Pierre's burgeoning hockey career. One of the teams in the industrial league was from Buffalo and an Indian named Maracle, a good hockey player, struck up a friendship with Pierre. He suggested that Pierre come over to the Aud to play on Sunday afternoons, which he did. One afternoon, Pierre overheard that the Niagara Falls Junior B Cataracts were practising in Fort Erie that afternoon.

"I somehow thought that I could just go see if we could make this club," explained Pierre. "Little did I know that's not how you made a hockey club, especially at the end of a season!"

Innocently, Pierre headed to the Fort Erie arena, walked straight up to coach Doug Boston, and asked if it was possible for him and his two friends to go out for a skate. To his surprise, coach Boston said, "Why not?"

"Maybe they didn't have the full team there, maybe they had a few players missing, I don't know but he let us go out," Pierre recalled.

Surprisingly, Pierre had a strong practice and during the ensuing scrimmage scored five goals. Feeling great and not knowing any better, he thought he'd made the team. He approached coach Boston after getting off the ice.

"Hey coach, what do you think?" Pierre asked.

"Well, you looked pretty good out there," the coach replied.

"So, what about it? Do I make the team?" Pierre asked him innocently, expectantly.

Boston tried not to laugh. "Well kid, you play centre and see, we're not looking for centres. We're looking for defencemen. But I'll keep you in mind for next year."

Pierre walked away disappointed but still buoyed by the experience. Back at his day job, he knew that he wasn't cut out for factory work, a job that had its fair share of perils.

"I remember guys losing their fingers on the presses," Pierre said. "I worked awhile longer, then they went on strike and that was the end of my job. It wasn't meant for me."

Remembering his Junior B tryout the previous spring and the reason for not making the team, Pierre was thinking ahead when Hurst Butchers called for him to join the team again.

"Sure, I'll play again this winter, but on one condition," Pierre answered. "I'll play if I can play defence." The condition was accepted.

Switching to defence, Pierre attracted the attention of the Junior B Cataracts. The season wasn't very old when Pierre found himself on the Junior B squad, amazingly in only his second year of playing hockey. The Niagara Falls Cataracts had some prolific players such as Benedict "Benny" Cardas, Bill Herrington, and goalie Bill Scott.

"We had some pretty good hockey players," recalled Pierre. "Jim McNulty was a few years older, but boy could he really snap that puck. We also played in a new arena."

The Niagara Falls Memorial Arena was officially opened on January 27, 1950, with a Cataracts game against Hamilton Aerovox. Though Pierre didn't make any of the game's headlines or noted plays in a 6-4 Niagara Falls loss, he stayed true to form in accumulating four penalties in the last two periods.

"I remember that first game in the new arena," Pierre recalled. "It looked like it had freshly laid cement on the walls—and it looked cold."

Pierre had a lot to learn, but he was a willing student. "The only real teaching I ever got was in Junior B," recalled Pierre. "Doug Boston, the coach, showed me that as a left defenceman, I was moving my feet the wrong way. He taught me how to turn my feet towards the boards and the player, which was important."

In the first round of the playoffs in the Cataracts' attempt to re-capture the Sutherland Cup, their opponents were the powerful Guelph Biltmores. Guelph handily defeated Niagara Falls in three straight games.

"Guelph had a pretty good club. I once tried to go through two players and I got sandwiched. Dad was at the game and he really got upset."

"Coming back on the bus after losing to Guelph, we stopped at a restaurant in Burlington. We always stopped there," Pierre remembered. "While eating, word got around that big Jim McNulty was getting married. He didn't have much, so we stole some plates and cutlery to help him out, to get started. That was his wedding gift from the team!"

By summer 1950, word had started to spread in the hockey world about the talents of a young Fort Erie defenceman named Pilote. Busy with work and playing softball and baseball that summer, Pierre was caught off guard when he heard that the New York Rangers had been inquiring about his availability. After one baseball game, a representative of the Galt Junior A Black Hawks approached Pierre and asked him if he'd be interested in attending the Galt training camp that September. Unsure, Pierre said he'd think about it. It was heady stuff, but it got even headier when a knock on the front door of the house on Kingsmill was answered.

"All of a sudden, Rudy Pilous showed up at the door," recalled Pierre like it had just happened yesterday. "He introduced himself and asked if he could come in. Once in, he started talking about how he had just gotten appointed as general manager of the St. Catharines Junior A Teepees. Mom and Dad were sitting there and Pilous was giving us his spiel, his sell. We felt really good about that."

Pilous understood if the Pilotes couldn't give him an immediate answer but said to call him when ready. He left his card, shook hands with everyone, and walked out the front door. As Rudy drove away, Paul gave immediate advice to his son.

"St. Catharines is where you should go, Pierre," he said. "It's only 30 miles away and I could go see you play there. Then after that, you would belong to Buffalo. You would play in St. Catharines for two years and then you would go to Buffalo to play. You could stay at home and go back and forth. But most of all, I think this Rudy Pilous is a good guy, a good French-Canadian guy. He'll treat you right." (Pilous was in fact Polish.)

Pierre called Pilous and started jogging and exercising to be ready for camp.

Paul Pilote drove his son to the Teepees training camp that September morning. Over 60 players lined up outside the St. Catharines Memorial Arena to register and sign an obligatory "A" Form, which allowed a club to pay a player's expenses while at training camp, without committing either the club or the player to a contract, nor threatening the player's amateur status. Paul stayed at rinkside that first day.

Looking around, Pierre wondered what his chances were to make the team, knowing he had raw guts and steely determination. At 5'10" and 170 pounds, he was not one of the biggest players at camp.

"Every day the team's getting smaller and smaller and I'm wondering when I'm going to get cut. I was in shape, was rested, and went to bed early. I was rough around the edges, but I wanted to make the club."

Pierre worked and skated hard, doing whatever it took to make the grade, even if it meant hitting players, many bigger than him, at every opportunity. It was a challenge he took up with relish.

"There was not a lot of fighting in training camp, but I know there were a few guys that had to be carried off the ice after I hit them and I soon learned who was and who was not chicken. The coaches could see it too, and soon I was eliminating a lot of players on my own, or so I thought."

The coach of the St. Catharines Teepees was Arthur Morris Jackson, brother of hockey icon Harvey "Busher" Jackson. Art Jackson had won two Stanley Cups as a centre with the Boston Bruins in 1941 and the Toronto Maple Leafs in 1945. After each Teepees session, Jackson would sit with Pilous and select the next round of cuts. Most of the time, the two men were on the same wavelength.

Then they got to Pilote.

CHAPTER

3

Flight of the Teepee

"We have to cut Pilote!" argued Teepees coach Art Jackson. General manager Rudy Pilous looked at Jackson like he was from Mars.

"You can't be serious, Art?"

"I am, Rudy. He's gotta go!"

Pilous shook his head again. The power play was on.

"Pilote stays!" Pilous vowed.

"I say he doesn't!" Jackson retorted.

"Well, we'll see about that!" Pilous said with a huff and walked away.

The brief exchange would have major repercussions for all involved, and moving forward, Pilous's future hockey endeavours would be inextricably entwined with Pierre Pilote's.

Rudy Pilous was born in Winnipeg, Manitoba, on August 11, 1914. After an unremarkable junior and minor pro hockey career, Rudy took a job in St. Catharines, Ontario, in 1938. Playing as a left-winger for the city's Senior A Chiefs, it wasn't until he attended a thrilling Memorial Cup Junior A hockey game at Maple Leaf Gardens in May 1943, that he got the organizational bug. After extensively lobbying the Ontario Hockey Association, the league awarded Pilous and friend Jay MacDonald a Junior A franchise for St. Catharines with the 28-year-old Pilous as coach, Ted Graves as the GM, and MacDonald as the team's secretary-treasurer.

The St. Catharines Falcons played their first game in fall 1943. Going further afield, Pilous also scouted for the AHL Buffalo Bisons. When the Falcons fell into financial difficulty, the team was bought by George Stauffer of Thompson Products, who changed the team's name to Teepees, after the company's initials—"TPs." Former NHL player Art Jackson became the team's coach.

In 1950, Stauffer, at Pilous's urging, signed a Junior A affiliation agreement with the Bisons. Stauffer then made Pilous the Teepees GM with Jackson still the coach. One of Pilous's first moves was to visit the Pilote household in Fort Erie.

After his argument with Jackson over Pilote's talents, Pilous conferred with Stauffer, who then fired Jackson as coach and gave him an unrelated job at Thompson Products. "Art was a good player, but he wasn't a great coach," Stauffer said later.

At the next Teepees practice, Pilous was coach and GM. With full control he signed Pilote.

As training camp broke, Chuck Wurzer of the *Buffalo Evening News* wrote about Pilote: "A Buffalo area product stood out as future Buffalo hockey timber. Pierre Pilote, 18, 170 pound Ft. Erie defenceman, finished the week of training camp . . . with Bisons farm club, by sending his teammates sprawling with soulful bodychecks.

"Then, the Fort Erie youngster shook the perspiration from his black hair, looked at general manager Rudy Pilous, and said: 'So, maybe pretty soon I play with Bisons, eh? Me and Art Lessard make great pair some time, no?'

"Pilous said, 'Yes, maybe soon.' Pilote, who played with Niagara Falls last season, looks like sure future Bison backline material!"

Pierre's basic "A" contract paid him $35 a week, minus room and board, which left him with $17 a week. The contract also ensured Pierre a $120 a week job in some capacity at Thompson Products. After training camp, Pierre moved out of the New Murray Hotel and into a boarding house. The initial arrangement didn't suit him very well.

"The first place I stayed at had five guys and was noisy, and the landlady was a terrible cook!" recalled Pierre. "Maybe we got steak once in a while but ughh!" Conferring with Pilous, Pilote moved to a boarding house on Duke Street owned by a Mrs. Kemp. "She lived with her husband and son. I roomed with two other guys, one of which was Charlie Marshall," said Pierre. "Mrs. Kemp always served the food on our plates herself. If there were seven of us for supper, she cooked eight pork chops. Nobody dared ask for the extra. It was her way of controlling costs. She knew that Charlie and I could have devoured 25 pork chops if she'd served them!"

At Thompson Products, Pierre worked the dayshift, which included hockey practices.

"I worked in the packaging-shipping room. Thompson made auto parts. We were there because we played hockey and the catch was, if you went to practice in the morning and went back to work in the afternoon, you got paid for the whole day. But if you didn't show up for work after practice, you didn't get paid for that day. I always went to work after practice."

"I had to learn an awful lot that first year, especially how to properly give and take a pass while skating at full speed," he recalled of those early practices. "It was a basic skill that young hockey players would have been taught but I had never played and had never been taught."

The team provided minimal perks—CCM sticks and one pair of Tackleberry skates. "Some equipment would be new, some second-hand. The skates used to get wet and would be stiff as a board the next day. Some of us got a new pair after Christmas, but only if you really needed them."

By Christmas, Pierre was proud that he had saved over $300 between the team allotment and his job, mostly because he didn't do much to spend his money.

"That first year, I was quiet, hung around with Charlie Marshall. He was a church-going guy, brother of American League ballplayer Willie Marshall. I'd also periodically take the bus and go see my parents as I didn't have a car. We'd hang out at the Crystal

Restaurant but I'd be home for 11. It was a short walk. Sometimes Rudy would call at 11 to check up on you, you never knew. If you broke curfew, especially on a Saturday night before a Sunday game, he fined you $5. Sometimes he'd dress but not play you the next day—which was worse than the fine."

By the sixth game of the season on October 27, 1950, the team travelled to Windsor, Ontario, across from Detroit, to play the Spitfires.

"We always travelled on Niagara Region bus number 38, always with this driver, Stan. The bus had terrible brakes. Boy, was that a long drive! In Windsor, we faced Glenn Hall too. Glenn told me later that one of my shots had cut him for 10 stitches. It was a tough rink to win in."

With 10 minutes remaining in the game and Windsor leading 5-2, referee Len Loree called a bench minor against St. Catharines. Pilous was incensed and refused to send a player into the penalty box. Loree then slapped a 10-minute misconduct onto it. When Pilous refused a second time to send a player off his bench, arguing ensued between Pilous, players, and referees Loree and Frank Udvari. After a two-minute stalemate, the referees invoked rule 77 and awarded the game to Windsor.

"Rudy was a very animated, outspoken coach," recalled Pierre. "He was very expressive with his hands and could really get upset at referees!"

Pilous was slapped with a 10-game suspension by the league, his coaching duties filled in by St. Catharines juvenile coach Vic Teal, Buffalo Bisons coach Leroy Goldsworthy, and Bisons GM Art Chapman. Banned from entering arenas during his sentence, Pilous remained with the team, but sat outside listening to Rex Stimers's description of the game on St. Catharines radio station CKTB. During Pilous's absence, Pierre's play was solid and his performances improving.

"In my first year, everything was a learning experience. I remember going into Guelph and getting into a shoving match with Ron Murphy and Harry Howell. Murphy got behind me on his knees and then Howell pushed me and I fell backwards. I was lucky I didn't crack my head!"

With a break in the schedule, Pierre decided to pack a suitcase, catch a bus and head to a Leafs game at the Gardens. Getting off at Union Station in the early afternoon, he walked excitedly to Maple Leaf Gardens, only to be informed that the game was sold out. Seeing his disappointment, the teller informed him that there would be standing room only tickets available shortly, but that he'd have to wait in a line.

Buoyed, Pierre rushed to a nearby rooming house on Jarvis Street, deposited his suitcase and headed back to the Gardens. Standing happily in line, he heard someone yelling: "Tickets for sale!" Unsure, Pierre gave up his spot and approached the scalper. Five dollars later, he was the proud owner of his first NHL ticket. Pierre's excitement turned to trepidation when he wondered if the ticket was stolen. Shoving the thought from his mind, he got a bite to eat before re-entering the Gardens. The excellent centre ice seat was right behind the penalty box.

"I'm watching the game but the whole time, I'm watching over my shoulder to see if I'm in somebody else's seat. By the third period I relaxed," he related. "It was a great seat to watch and learn. Bill Ezenicki hit this player from New York and the stretcher came out afterwards. He used to swing around when the guys cut in on him and whack! Could he hit and hurt you!"

The Leafs, led by scoring wizard Max Bentley, also played a tight checking game so Pierre saw both strategies at work, but the hitting impressed him the most, especially when a defensive lesson unfolded before him.

"I could see guys trying to cut through the middle of the Toronto defence," Pierre recalled. "Suddenly, this one guy came through and Toronto's Bill Barilko was crouched down, waiting for him. Barilko swirled into him, stuck out his butt, and the guy went flying! I said to myself, 'Holy shit! I've got to practise doing that!'"

Inspired, Pierre took the bus home the next day and at Monday practice he tried out his new weapon—the "Barilko Bump." After a week of perfecting it, he felt ready for the Saturday tilt against the visiting Marlies. The game proceeded along smoothly until Pierre's moment of truth arrived. Eric Nesterenko, a star centre called up by Toronto, rushed towards him at centre ice and tried to go around him. Pierre was waiting.

"I lined Eric up perfectly and gave him my 'Barilko Bump.' They carried him off on a stretcher! I was so proud of myself! The trip to Toronto had been worth it! That ticket really paid for itself—I had a new weapon!"

"I was at that game and I remember that hit on Eric Nesterenko," recalled a young St. Catharines fan at the time, Anne Greshchyshyn. Though she hadn't attended a lot of Teepee games to that point in her life, that particular game made an impression on her. "Pierre hit Eric Nesterenko and the stretcher came out! Oh I remember that!"

For the first time in his career, Pierre was also becoming familiar with the importance of trainers to a team. If there were any small perks to playing for this Junior A team, trainer Jimmy Joy provided them.

"Jimmy was just a short but special guy. The night before a game you could go to the rink and Jimmy would be there. He'd give you a rubdown and get rid of knots in your back, arm, leg, or shoulder. He used this liniment and you came out of there smelling like a medicine cabinet but, boy, it felt great! Jimmy hung our equipment, did a lot for us."

Much to the team's growing consternation, Pierre's defence partner Orrin Gould superstitiously never washed his underwear, fearing it would cancel his good luck. It was tolerable until Christmas, when Gould's underwear finally looked and smelled like a brown, rotten pretzel. The team took matters into their own hands and threw the offensive undergarment into the shower.

"Boy, was he mad! Nobody fessed up to doing it but we just had to wash that thing," recalled Pierre. "It was gross and started to affect our mental state!"

While the team was starting to come together under the watchful eye of Pilous, Pierre liked to share the hitting glory.

"Orrin Gould was my defence partner," Pierre noted. "One time against the Oshawa Generals at home, there was a guy who played with Alex Delvecchio, a dipsy-doodler, and he's going down Orrin's side. Now Orrin wasn't a big hitter. I did the hitting. Orrin always stayed back and covered my butt, but this guy from Oshawa is dancing all over the place and going towards Orrin's corner. Really, I shouldn't have been in that corner, but I flew in from my side and nailed him. The guy went down like a ton of bricks but Orrin was right there too, you know, and we kind of hit him at the same time. After the hit, Orrin said excitedly, 'Pierre! Pierre! I got 'em!' I said, 'Yeah, Orrin you did! Yeah! That one was yours!' That made his day and made him feel real good."

Pierre's family was always supportive. "The whole family jumped into Dad's car to see him play hockey," recalled Pierre's brother Gilles, eight years younger. "It didn't matter the weather, Dad would give 'er! He was from Québec, eh? What's a little bit of Ontario snow? Nothing!"

Pierre, still impressionable, chose his next NHL hero to emulate. "Kenny Reardon of the Canadiens was at one of our games. He was a suave, well-dressed fellow in a black suit, white shirt and tie, nice overcoat. After the game I saw him outside our arena. I'm sizing him up and I was starting to play like him. He was a hitting defenceman and I wanted to be just like him."

Pilote's first-year left-winger, Jim Robertson, described Pierre as "running on skates." The young defenceman took it as a compliment.

"No doubt my skating was not yet as smooth. Jimmy was a smooth skater but Kenny Reardon used to run on his skates too, so maybe I ran on my skates—to be like him."

The Teepees finished in sixth place in the 10-team league and Pierre amassed 13 goals and 13 assists in 54 games. His rough, no-holds-barred play also earned him a league-leading 230 minutes in the penalty box—over 4.25 minutes per game, double his nearest teammate. The reality is that 200 of those minutes had been served by the season's halfway mark and, after some suggestions from Pilous, Pierre was able to significantly cut his trips to "the hoosegow" for the remaining games.

"I still really didn't know how to skate backwards well or turn properly," Pierre recalled. "Guys were getting around me, but I'd do whatever was necessary to stop them. I was very aggressive and raw. I would hook or grab them. I earned my penalties, but I thought they were good penalties."

"In his first year of Junior A hockey, Pierre Pilote is easily the leading contender for the 'Bad Man of the League' trophy," went a story in the local press. "With only one year of organized hockey to his background . . . Mr. Pilote has come a long way and although he still has lots to learn, his desire to play makes him one of the most colourful performers in this season's Junior circuit."

In the playoffs, the Teepees were underdogs against the Guelph Biltmores. The Teepees got bombed in the first game of the best-of-five quarter final 7-3, but surprisingly stormed back to defeat Guelph 4-1 to tie the series. After the teams exchanged victories, the stage was set for the fifth and deciding game. Backed by the superlative goaltending of Don Simmons, St. Catharines defeated Guelph 1-0 in a thrilling series finale. It was on to the semis for a date with the powerful Toronto Marlies.

"Maple Leaf Gardens was always tough to play in," Pierre related. "It was a big, hot rink. In St. Catharines, I could really nail guys, they couldn't get away from me, but at the Gardens, there was a lot more room. I probably got more penalties there just trying to catch guys."

The Teepees were eliminated three games to one in the best-of-five-game series. True to form, Pierre garnered two goals and two assists in nine playoff games but sat in the penalty box for 23 minutes—almost 2.55 minutes per game.

Still working at Thompson Products in the off-season, Pierre opted to stay at his rooming house with Mrs. Kemp. On his off days, he took the bus home to Fort Erie for a weekend visit with his family or went to the beach. And he wanted to start going out on the town, dancing, but to do that Pierre needed clothes.

"I bought my suits in Hamilton then brought them to Harold Nash's in St. Catharines to get hemmed," recalled Pierre. "A team-mate, Ted Powers, and I would go to a bar in Niagara Falls, New York, on Sundays, all decked out. The legal drinking age was lower on the other side of the border. Ted's father was an RCMP officer and Ted acted like one too, sometimes, though at 6'2" he wasn't of a 'tough' nature.

"One time, we started dancing with these girls, these guys' girls I guess. We ended up getting into a fight outside. I've got my one and only suit on. Holy shit! We cleaned that up in a hurry but I never wore my suit there again."

Archie Katzman was a St. Catharines cab driver who often drove the Teepees players around town during the season, even purchasing the under-age players the occasional case of Cincinnati Cream beer. Whenever they were dancing late in Niagara Falls and missed the bus back, Pierre and his buddies always had a back-up plan.

"Archie, we missed the bus again!" Pierre would say in his late night call to Katzman, who happily drove over the border to pick up "his" boys.

By the third week of training camp in September 1951, Pierre was amongst the last 30 players still vying for a starting spot.

"Teepees will have a team to be reckoned with in OHA Junior action this year," reported the *St. Catharines Standard*. "Buddy Boone, a star of last year's team, returned on Thursday from Sault Ste. Marie, where he attended the Detroit Red Wings training camp. Pierre Pilote and Orrin Gould, two outstanding defencemen from last year's team, will be catching the eye of professional scouts if they continue as they are presently going. Fast and tricky, they are good puck carriers and know their defence job well."

As training camp closed, and having easily made the squad again, Pierre figured he wanted a raise. After all, he was now a veteran and he felt $35 a week was a pittance after room and board was subtracted. Besides, the Teepees were drawing large crowds, especially in the playoffs. Surely, Pierre thought he should be able to get a larger slice of that pie. As further ammunition, he knew some of his teammates were getting $75. Why shouldn't he?

"When it came time to sign my contract, I was ready. So was Rudy," recalled Pierre. "I had to argue like hell with him. I was making more money working than playing hockey. We went back and forth until he upped my pay to $55 a week—a $20 a week raise! At least I got something and with working at Thompson Products, it still wasn't such a bad deal."

The 1951–52 Teepees were a vastly different squad.

The team's second campaign with Pilous at the helm started poorly with a 6-3 loss in Guelph. Their home opener wasn't any better as 3,333 fans saw their "Kitts" edged out 3-2 by Barrie—an ominous start. They didn't win at home until their seventh game, a 6-2 victory over the Galt Black Hawks on December 12. Pierre led the way by rushing with the puck into the opposition end and scoring in the opening period against Galt goaltender Les Binkley.

"Now I'm starting to get more confident in moving the puck, making better plays," Pierre remembered of this second year with the Teepees. "Guys weren't beating me or getting around me anymore."

Pierre was having a good season, and it was clear that his raw hockey skills were improving daily, so much so that on December 30, 1951, he was called up to Buffalo to help shore up the Bisons shorthanded blue line. The local paper heralded his call up: "20 yr. old Pierre Pilote has been brought up from the St. Catharines Teepees to bolster the defence corps. A resident of Fort Erie, Pierre is built along the lines of Ray Gariepy and plays the same style hockey, a rock 'em, sock 'em brand that is pleasing to the fans. Up on a 'look-see' basis, he will be permitted to play three games with the Bisons without losing his amateur status. If he makes the grade, as expected, he will then be signed to a regular pro contract with Buffalo."

The local paper noted in its sports pages after Pierre's appearance: "Buffalo drew a heavy gate from St. Catharines and this area, mostly to see Pierre Pilote of Teepees, who fared well in his pro trial. Nor were they disappointed and Rudy Pilous was as tickled as punch with the showing of the TP rearguard. Pilote saw his share of action and those who saw him were surprised when the TP went through the tilt without a penalty.

"Pilote played cautiously, yet strongly and insofar as railbirds saw, did not make a bad play. This being his last year of junior, he won't have far to scamper next season if the Bisons pick him up, since he lists his home town as Fort Erie now. Pilote has the steel-wire build that lasts long and Pilous predicts Pilote could make the NHL in two terms. At that, he fits like a 'T' on Canadiens French club."

In the second game with Buffalo in Syracuse, Pierre injured his shoulder but still tallied an assist. "We were really shorthanded going into Syracuse for a game we needed to make the playoffs," Bisons coach Fred Hunt said a few years later. "We called up Pierre, Brian Cullen, and Orrin Gould from St. Kitts for the game and the kids so fired up the old pros by their all-out play that we beat Syracuse in that key game. Pilote, while he was still crude, showed that ability to step into an opponent and had the Syracuse players coming down the ice with their heads up before the night was over."

Pierre was scheduled to play a third game for Buffalo but his shoulder was still sore, so he returned to St. Catharines.

At the two-thirds point of the 54-game Junior A schedule, nine of the 10 league coaches selected their six-man All-Star team, and Pilote was the top defenceman.

Pierre's tough reputation was spreading. Before the Teepees travelled to Guelph on January 18, local sports columnist Clayton Browne wrote that Andy Bathgate might be in the lineup against the Teepees, but added: "Wonder what the Guelph club will think, if Pilote steps into Bathgate and sends him back to sick bay again?"

The Teepees grew with faith and confidence and moved up the standings.

On February 5, they pounded the Waterloo Hurricanes 11-1, with defenceman turned centre Frank Martin notching five goals. Afterwards, Pierre and teammate Allan Kellogg decided to hit their favourite hangout, the Crystal Restaurant. Sitting down at a booth, Pierre noticed a blond girl with her back to him. He also noticed her friend was watching them while whispering to this girl.

"One day, a friend called me saying she had something exciting to show me. She wouldn't tell me on the phone," recalled Anne Greshchyshyn, a local St. Catharines girl. "So I met her at the restaurant and she showed me her new diamond engagement ring. He was a guy I had introduced her to. I was around 18 years old at the time. Then some hockey players walked in and sat behind me.

"So my friend was looking towards them (I had my back to them) then she says, 'Annie, do you know that Pierre Pilote?' She knew their names better than I did. I said, 'No not really. He's a hockey player, right?' So I turned around to look at him and just then he was looking at me and my heart went pitter patter. It really did! As soon as I looked at him, our eyes met and I felt something, and I thought, 'Wow! I guess I'd better meet that guy sometime.'"

It didn't happen that night but their paths would cross again.

As the season wound down, St. Catharines ended up in a fifth-place tie with the Kitchener Greenshirts. League rules indicated that in the event of a tie, goals scored decided which team finished ahead, but both teams were tied in that department. The impasse was solved the old fashioned way: a toss of the coin. To Pilous's dismay, his St. Kitts crew lost the toss, ending the regular season in sixth spot. His protest fell on deaf ears.

Pierre's growing offensive contributions were evident, and he finished with 21 goals, 32 assists for 53 points, fourth in team scoring. His penalty minutes dropped dramatically to 139 minutes, without having compromised his hard-hitting style.

The Teepees faced Kitchener in the first round of the playoffs and lost the opener 5-1, but rebounded to take the next three games by scores of 2-1, 6-1, and 5-1. Their next playoff opponents were the Toronto St. Mike's Majors.

"During the series with Kitchener, they had a defenceman who cross-checked me on the arm," recalled Pierre. "He didn't break it, but did he ever hit me. I still have the mark on my arm. There were a lot of tough fights and I used to get a lot of cuts in the face, mouth, around the eyes, a lot of high-sticking."

In this playoff season, the Toronto Maple Leafs practised in St. Catharines, and Pierre often noted the fancy hats Leaf icons Cal Gardner and Harry Watson wore when they ate at the Crystal Restaurant.

"Those are nice hats! Where do we get those hats?" Pierre asked his defence partner Orrin Gould one day.

"In Toronto, at a place called Sammy Taft's on Spadina Avenue," Orrin answered. Pierre decided to get one when the team resumed their series with St. Mike's in Toronto. Orrin wanted one too.

"I waited for Orrin at the corner of Spadina and Queen Street," Pierre related. "Finally, we walk into Sammy Taft's hat shop. A hat place, what an experience! On the walls were pictures of all the famous hockey players wearing a Sammy Taft hat. So I got a hat. I was so proud wearing that hat! I'd puff it out. All the hockey players in the '40s and '50s wore Taft hats."

St. Catharines came out flying in the opening game of the series in Toronto. "Teepees had the hustle, dash, and desire and, as a consequence, completely overpowered St. Michaels by a 6-2 margin," reported the *Standard*.

More than 4,089 fans crammed into the Phelps Street arena and many more were turned away for the first time in the team's history but the luck of the Irish was certainly working for the St. Mike's squad during the second game in St. Catharines on St. Patrick's

Day in 1952. With only 17 seconds gone in the game, Pierre was sent off for holding, which set up the first St. Mike's power play goal. The game was a seesaw battle with St. Catharines goalie Marv Edwards making some amazing saves, but it was the lack of scoring punch of a third period Teepee power play when Pilote, Gould, Martin, Haas, and Young couldn't get the equalizer that cost them a 3-1 defeat. Still, Pilote and Martin were singled out for their defensive play.

The teams next exchanged victories and the semifinal series was tied at two games apiece going into the fifth and deciding game at Maple Leaf Gardens in Toronto, witnessed by 12,904 screaming fans.

Ten minutes into the game, the Teepees opened the scoring and 56 seconds later rookie Brian Cullen scored a goal assisted by Chuck Marshall and Pierre that made it 2-0. The teams exchanged goals before the period ended with St. Catharines leading 3-1. As the second period unfolded, the Teepees played kitty-bar-the-door hockey as the Majors went eight minutes without a shot on net. At 10:30, Foley fired a rebound behind the Majors goalie Ed Chadwick, making it 4-1 for St. Catharines. The onslaught continued as the Teepees built up a 6-1 lead on a tip-in shot from a Pierre point blast that ended the second.

Going into the third period, the Teepees thought they had it in the bag and seemed to relax while the St. Mike's squad poured it on, scoring in the very first minute. At the five-minute mark, Pierre lost his stick and drew a holding penalty. During the ensuing power play, a Murray Costello shot "wicked" in off Bill Lee, making the score 6-3. Now the Teepees were scrambling to hold back the St. Mike's onslaught.

When both Allan Kellogg and Pierre drew penalties 33 seconds apart, it took the Majors only 28 seconds to pot another, making the score a tenuous 6-4. The Majors netted their fifth goal 43 seconds later. St. Mike's was piping hot while the curse of penalties had struck Pilous's crew and they scrambled to keep their heads above water. But a reprieve was coming, and from an unlikely source.

After St. Mike's giddy fifth goal, the jubilant Toronto fans showered the ice with programs and drinks that forced a long delay as the Gardens maintenance crew cleaned the ice. Many of the St. Mike's players sat on the ice in front of their bench to relax. The break cooled off the Majors, while the Teepees regrouped and found their legs.

Buddy Boone was hauled down by Bob Sabourin, giving the Teepees the man advantage with 2:07 to play, and they leveraged the situation. A power play goal by Marshall reversed the tide, putting Pierre's crew up 7-5. Only a minute remained when Gerry Foley added an insurance marker to win the game 8-5. A victory photo of the Teepees dressing room after the game showed a jubilant gang surrounded by a smiling and sombreroed Pilous.

For the first time in the 10-year history of Junior A hockey, St. Catharines was now in a best-of-seven OHA final against their archrivals, the Guelph Biltmores. The team knew what they were up against.

"Guelph was a good team," Pierre recalled. "They had Andy Bathgate, Dean Prentice, and Kenny Laufman, who was the best junior I ever played against and led the league in goals and points. He was really good. They had Lou Fontinato, Ron Murphy, Ron Stewart, all these guys, good hockey players."

In the opener in Guelph, the Teepees stormed out of the gate and surprised their hosts by stealing a 4-3 win. But the strain of playing 14 playoff games in 23 days took its toll on the club.

Back in St. Catharines, Pierre found himself short extra tickets for family and friends who wanted to attend. At the Crystal Restaurant, he was told of someone who had some to sell and that person approached him.

"We have some tickets for tonight's game if you want them," piped up the slim, pretty blond girl who had caught his eye a few weeks before. They quickly completed the transaction.

"The girls I was with had decided not to go to the game. We were going to go somewhere else, to a dance or something," Anne recalled. "Pierre bought the tickets off of us that night. By this time I certainly knew who he was. I also remembered that earlier pitter patter of my heart moment, but I was talking business. I wanted him to buy the tickets and that was that."

Pierre left contentedly, but for some reason this particular girl piqued his interest. It marked the first time they had actually met and spoken. He knew her name was Anne.

Guelph won the next game in enemy territory by a lopsided 8-4 score and outlasted St. Catharines back on home ice by a 5-3 score. The series shifted back to St. Catharines for Game 4 with the Teepees down two games to one.

"In those '52 playoffs, we had played a lot of games in a short span," remembered Pierre. "I had a good playoff and I was just starting to figure the game out. There were scouts there and I thought I was ready but really I wasn't. I was just starting to know how to make plays, realizing there was some thought to hockey."

Guelph was on a roll and they handily defeated the Teepees 8-6 before the series shifted back to the Royal City. Pilous, always an innovator, decided on a new course of action.

"Rudy thought he had a great idea, and he brought us in to Guelph the night before the game," recalled Pierre. "He put us in a hotel, in Guelph, right on the main drag. First time it had ever been done. It was springtime, warm in the rooms, so our windows were all open. It was on a hill, there was construction. Trucks were going all night. I never slept all night and neither did anybody else! We were tired. Rudy's big idea backfired."

Guelph won the final game, 5-4, on March 31, 1952, taking the series. Despite the loss, the Teepees were feted at a testimonial dinner.

"I want to thank the Teepees and coach Rudy Pilous for the best hockey season St. Catharines has ever experienced," Mayor John Franklin remarked. Attendance had jumped to 84,235 in 1951–52 compared to 67,090 the year before.

Pierre Pilote was pleased with his personal stats for the playoffs: three goals and 12 assists in 14 games, and 50 penalty minutes.

He was looking forward to trying out with the Buffalo Bisons next fall. "At the end of my second year with the Teepees, I'm thinking, 'I want to stay in this game. I've gotta make Buffalo now!' I wasn't thinking about anything else."

But before that could happen, there was a summer of playing ball and going to dances. Little did he know that his "ticket girl" had become enamoured with him.

Anne recalled, "I went to a function by myself and I was all dressed up, in high heels and everything and I had to walk to the bus stop. I was by myself, and walking by another local hangout, the Diana Sweets Restaurant. There were some guys there who whistled at me and I waved at them as I walked by to catch the bus. Pierre was there too. I certainly noticed him as I walked by.

"I would later see Pierre at a YMCA dance. I was wearing a white blouse and a velvet skirt. He asked me to dance. My blouse was somewhat of a see-through blouse, and when we were dancing Pierre kept looking down my blouse. It was rather funny! We only danced together and then parted."

Ending his playing days with the Teepees, Pierre continued to work at Thompson Products and boarding at Mrs. Kemp's. He purchased his first vehicle, a green 1939 Buick, from his uncle Ernest Gagné. It helped him get around, especially to baseball games.

That summer of 1952, Pierre tried out for the St. Catharines Stags, a senior county ball team. At batting practice a couple of home runs ensured he had made the team. They offered to pay him $15 a game. He agreed. The team played area rivals such as Welland, Niagara Falls, and Oshawa. He rotated between playing right and centre field or second base.

He quickly discovered that he was playing with real ball players. "That summer, I wasn't hitting a .300 average anymore, more like the high .200s. These guys could really pitch," Pierre noted. "Some of them played semi-pro you know. My style of hitting was too aggressive and I often swung too early. I should've been sitting back, waiting a little longer. I didn't get struck out too often but I wasn't connecting with the entire baseball. I needed someone to teach me. I was a solid hitter and I had a few flaws, yet I was holding my own and playing pretty good."

Anne hoped to meet Pierre again. "Pierre was playing baseball a couple of months after the ticket purchase and we had a lot of mutual friends. I knew some of the guys and we'd go watch the baseball games too. I knew Pierre was playing, I was curious about him. I'd seen him play. So, we left this one particular game early and I rode my bike back to the Crystal Restaurant. I was standing outside, a bunch of us talking, and there was one guy who was really interested in me and was trying to latch onto me and wanted to walk me home. I had my bike hidden, in a nearby alley, but I didn't say anything.

"Suddenly, Pierre came wheeling around Jane Street in his car, his big Buick. He parked on the far side of the street, got out of his car and, in his baseball uniform, came up to me, put his arm around me, and said, 'Remember you're going home with me.'

"Pierre whispered about the ride in my ear. Right there and then I knew. This other guy persisted later, wanted to walk me home, but I said, 'Oh no, Pierre is giving me a ride home.' When Pierre drove me home that night, he said, 'We'll have to see each other again.' I agreed. I liked him and wanted to go out with him. We went to a movie later, I think, and things just naturally fell into place and I was soon dating him."

Pierre had found his girl, which brightened up his summer considerably, but his mundane job was getting to him. "I was working the afternoon shift at Thompson Products on a machine that would grind up pistons. It was steady work but it was boring. It was a great place to work and they had insurance and getting time off to play baseball during the summer wasn't a problem. In the fall I'm about to try out with Buffalo so I was going to quit Thompson, I was tired of the job. I had had it!"

One game in early August changed his summer. "I hit a double into right field. I didn't have very good spikes on my feet back then.

I'm running hard past first into second base, when I'm starting to put on the brakes while looking out into right field. All of a sudden I hear a pop and a sharp pain shot up my left ankle!"

Pierre stood on second base as the ball was thrown in from right field and back to the pitcher. His left foot was throbbing. Pierre attempted to step off second base as the play was about to resume when the pain shot through his foot again. He yelled for a time out. The coach ran out.

"Holy shit!" Pierre said. "My ankle is really sore on the right side near my little toe! I don't think I can run anymore."

The coach nodded and put in a pinch runner. Pierre hobbled to the bench. He was out of the game. He then got dressed and left the ballpark that night with Annie, as he'd come to calling her. He could hardly walk, the foot hurt so much.

When he awoke the next morning at Mrs. Kemp's, the foot was really throbbing, hurting more than the night before. He headed to the medical clinic located at Thompson Products, to see the Teepees doctor who also worked for the company, and he ordered X-rays. Pierre was in the waiting room when Dr. Michael Zaritsky came over with a grim look on his face.

"Pierre, you've got a broken foot," the doctor told him. "I have to put it into a cast. You'll have the cast for at least six weeks."

"Six weeks!" Pierre said, at a loss for words.

When he later emerged from the clinic hobbling on crutches, a heavy cast on his foot, he didn't know what to think. He was despondent. Was his hockey career over after showing so much early promise?

One thing he knew for certain: the Buffalo Bisons training camp in Montreal, Québec, was just eight weeks away and here he was, in a cast for six of them!

It was a good thing he didn't know that interests were conspiring behind the scenes to derail his Buffalo hockey plans as well.

CHAPTER 4

Joining the Herd

As Pierre drove home from the Thompson clinic that summer day in 1952, his left foot in a cast, he was disheartened. Only eight weeks away from his first professional training camp, would word of his injury leak out to Rudy Pilous and the Bisons?

There was a silver lining to his situation—he hadn't quit Thompson Products, so he was on sick leave at three-quarters pay. "They were very good to their workers that way. That helped a lot," Pierre said.

He checked out of Mrs. Kemp's boarding house and returned home to his parents' place in Fort Erie. He took it easy that summer, often went to Crystal Beach to lay in the sun with Annie, helped his parents around the house with light chores, but the injury and its implications worried him.

"Because of the foot, I couldn't get in shape or train and the Bisons camp was coming up," Pierre said. "It was a tough summer, mentally."

His hockey fate rested in the tangled hands of three strangers: Art Chapman, the embattled general manager of the Buffalo Bisons; Eddie Shore, the cantankerous and oft disliked owner of the Springfield Indians; and powerful NHL president Clarence Campbell. Like the Art Jackson scenario a few years before, Pierre would have no knowledge of events until later.

After playing with the Boston Bruins and the New York Americans, Art "Chappie" Chapman had finished his career by winning a Calder Cup with Shore and the Bisons in 1944. After coaching them to another championship two years later, Chapman was made Bisons GM by the Jacobs brothers, owners of the team. In February 1952, Chapman hired former Bisons player Fred Hunt to coach the remaining games.

The plot thickened that summer when Bisons president Edgar Danaby clashed with Chapman and resigned. Chapman knew his days were numbered, so he contacted Shore and offered him the top Bisons defensive prospect—Pierre Pilote. Shore jumped at the chance. Chapman secretly dropped Pilote from the Bisons protected list and Shore picked him up. It would be Chapman's final snub to the Bisons organization. Pilote would be a Springfield Indian—or so Chapman and Shore covertly thought.

When Chapman suddenly resigned his Bisons position and hopped a bus out of Buffalo, the Jacobs brothers suspected something was amiss. They appointed Hunt as the new GM. Hunt and Pilous looked over Chapman's recent dealings, and they soon discovered his dirty work.

The Bisons took their case right to the top—NHL boss Campbell, as the unfair situation ultimately involved NHL farm systems. Campbell quickly established Chapman's underhanded and vindictive actions. No fan of the collusive Shore, Campbell ruled that Springfield had officially picked up young Pilote at 11:55 p.m., "five minutes BEFORE" Chapman had officially released him from the Bisons protected list at 12:00 a.m. therefore the deal null and void. Pilote was still a Bison.

With that situation taken care of, Hunt hired Frankie Eddolls, formerly of the Canadiens and Rangers, as his playing-coach.

After six weeks of lazing around, a nervous Pilote returned to see Dr. Zaritsky at the employee health clinic. The doctor removed his cast and declared the foot healed enough to return to work in a week. Relieved, Pilote hobbled to his boss, thanked him for the job, but informed him that he had to quit as he had a pro tryout with the Bisons in a few weeks.

The foot was still sore but at least he was no longer wearing the cast. Hoping it would get better with each passing day, Pierre started gingerly skating a few days later at the Stamford Arena outside of Niagara Falls. It still hurt but he didn't let it bother him.

On the evening of September 5, Pierre met with Pilous and Hunt to talk contract. "I kept quiet about my foot," Pierre said. "There had been a small press story that had gone under the radar, so nobody knew about my injury, which was fine by me. I also recall what they offered me and how stupid I was in accepting it."

Hunt offered Pierre $5,000 and asked him how he wanted it divided up between playing salary and signing bonus. Craftily, Hunt informed Pierre that he would receive the bonus immediately upon signing, which sounded appealing.

"I took a $1,500 signing bonus and a one year $3,500 salary. I got thinking about it later and realized how stupid I had been because the next year, I would be starting my salary negotiations at $3,500. If I would've taken a $200 signing bonus that first year, the next year I would have been negotiating from a starting point of $4,800, not $3,500. Salaries were low and raises hard to get. Perhaps I was thinking of getting a new car!"

The signing gave him some security heading into the Bisons training camp and he was happy to be making more than the $130 per week that he had been getting previously from the combined Teepees ($55) and Thompson Products ($75). Or was he? Subtracting the $1,500 signing bonus and dividing 26 weeks of hockey into his remaining $3,500 salary, his pay worked out to $135 a week: a mere $5 more!

On September 14, he took the train to Montreal where the Bisons held a joint camp with the Canadiens.

"I was worried about my foot, especially when we had to walk every day from the Queen's Hotel over to the Forum," he recalled. "It was a bit of a walk. I had a slight limp, but I didn't let on and nobody noticed. In my first practice Elmer Lach soon had me forgetting about my foot. I went to check him, not too hard, but his stick came right up and crosschecked me right in the nose. Whack! Did that ever hurt! 'Welcome to the NHL, kid!' He was a tough little guy. From that moment on, my stick was held pretty high for protection. It was every man for himself!"

Pierre was in awe at first, being on the same ice as these hockey icons, and soon realized that his passes and stickhandling were not as smooth as these NHLers. To size up the rookies, they were often thrown on the same line with a Rocket Richard, Lach, or other veterans, a situation that boosted Pierre's naivety.

"I was actually thinking I had a chance to make the Canadiens: I was on the same lines, right? But then all of a sudden in the last week, I'm practising solely with Buffalo."

The Bisons players worked out at the nearby Verdun Auditorium under the watchful eye of Eddolls.

In an afternoon scrimmage against Sam Pollock's Montreal Junior Canadiens on September 15, Pierre got a goal in a 4-1 win. Later against the Québec Aces, he garnered an assist in a 4-2 loss. In a game against St. Jerome, he suffered two broken bones in his right hand when he got slashed. The injury kept him out of the lineup for a week as did a later broken nose sustained in another game. It was a rough fall.

"You'd think I would've learned from the Elmer Lach incident! But I figured I had a good shot at making the team," recalled Pierre. "The only thing that worried me was I was a defenceman, and Montreal's farm system had loads of defencemen."

By the time "the Herd" returned by train to Ontario to resume training camp, Pierre had survived the cuts. He missed Annie and she had missed him.

"During these years, the Toronto Maple Leafs had their camp in St. Catharines," she explained. "I was single and had let one of these Toronto players walk me home but I didn't trust him, and it never went any further than that. Then the year Pierre went to training camp in Montreal, there were a bunch of guys around our hangout, the Crystal Restaurant. I had to fight off all these guys. I missed Pierre enormously! I remember Eric Nesterenko being there in St. Catharines too but he knew I was with the Frenchman. Soon, Pierre was back, thank goodness."

Back on home turf, the Bisons practised in Fort Erie and at the Buffalo Arena. The arena, city, and franchise had a storied past.

Situated in New York State directly across from Fort Erie, Buffalo had become a major railroad and shipping hub. In a bid to get out of the Great Depression in the late 1930s the federal government funded many public works programs throughout the United States, and Buffalo Memorial Auditorium or "The Aud" was one of them, fuelled by Buffalo's decades-long love affair with hockey. When it opened during the war on October 14, 1940, the arena was dedicated as a memorial to those soldiers who had died in combat.

Early praise in the press had Pilote as a defenceman who will be "ranking with the best this city has ever had." When the Canadiens called up some Bisons forwards, Pilote played forward for the season opener.

Eddolls, at 31 one of the youngest coaches ever to guide an AHL team, told Buffalo sports columnist Cy Kritzer that he expected Cleveland, Pittsburgh, Hershey, and Providence to be the toughest teams to beat. And he liked Pierre.

"If we can fortify the right wing and centre position, we'll shoot for third place and with the breaks, be ready to strike higher. We'll be stronger later. . . . Centremen are hard to find, but there's a good crop of fine wings and defencemen. That's one of the reasons we're using Pierre Pilote, the rookie from Ft. Erie, at forward. He's an excellent stick and a skilled puck-handler. He'll go back to defence as soon as we get enough forwards. Pierre will be one of the top rookies of the year!"

The club opened the season on the road with Pierre playing left wing on a line with Eldy Kobussen and Ken Davies. By the third game, he still hadn't scored a goal, but neither had his linemates.

For their November 11 tilt in St. Louis, the *Buffalo Evening News* reported that the Bisons would be "fixing to see if they can't get young Pierre Pilote in position for a goal."

Coach Eddolls stated that he was just waiting for that line to come to life and help the team win its first game. "Pilote has been doing well up front," he said. "He has handled the position in good style and is only missing that first goal to get started."

Pierre didn't score that night in a 3-1 loss, nor did he score at home the next night when the Bisons were embarrassed 8-3 by the Providence Reds, though he did get an assist and two penalties in the match. Towards the end of the third period, a discouraged Hunt put his head down, unable to watch anymore. When Providence scored their eighth goal with just under a minute left, Hunt wearily raised his head and asked to those sitting around him: "Is it over yet?"

With the Bisons now one point out of last place, Hunt vowed in print that it would be the end for some of his underperforming players. He brought up centre Billy Young from the Teepees to play centre on Pierre's line. That didn't work. When he put out an S.O.S. to the Canadiens, he was sent Gene "Ack-Ack" Achtymichuck, who would be the next centre on Pierre's line with Ken Davies for a November 19 home game against Pittsburgh.

In their eighth game in Syracuse on November 21, Pierre finally scored his first goal in an 8-2 loss. As the now last-place Herd limped home for a couple of home stands, the team was clearly lacking in scoring punch and good goaltending.

Despite the tough times on the ice, there was always time to initiate a rookie. "Ross Lowe was the leader there," Pierre recalled. "They grabbed you, got the shaving cream out, and 'hazed' you, shaved your family jewels. 'Welcome to the pros, kid!'"

If his initiation was a bad memory, so was his old car. "I hadn't used my bonus money yet, I still had the '39 Buick from my Uncle Ernest, with its leaking radiator," Pierre recalled. "I couldn't put antifreeze in the damn rad so if I went to Buffalo overnight, I had to dump the water out. Coming home to Fort Erie, I'd have to put water in it to drive over the Peace Bridge or the damn engine would heat up!"

By mid-December the Bisons had only 11 points after 18 games. In a game against Syracuse, Pierre's frustrations came out. "We're in this game against Syracuse and the puck got shot into their end, so I went in to check. The puck was shot back out to centre ice and Ross Lowe fired it back in just when I was coming out to get onside, with my head down. The puck hit me right in the nose!"

In the dressing room, the team doctor looked at Pierre and offered to straighten it out. The doctor grabbed the crooked nose and cracked it back into place. Pierre got off the table, looked in the mirror, and nodded approvingly. The doctor taped it up and sent him back out. No sooner had Pierre returned to the ice than he was forced to play defence because Eddolls sustained a knee injury and had to leave the game. Things looked bleak for the Bisons, with a record of only eight wins, 20 losses, and two ties by January 1. Little did they know that help was on the way in the form of a "Snake."

Jacques Plante had been a hot goaltending prospect in the Canadiens system for a few years and had just been signed to a $10,000 pro contract in the middle of the season by Canadiens GM Frank Selke. Since veteran Gerry McNeil held the main goaltending spot in Montreal, Selke sent Plante and Dickie Moore to help Buffalo.

"I remember Dickie Moore came down to us with a sore knee," said Pierre. "He came down for only a few games. He was a big-league guy with a big-league attitude towards us minor leaguers, but that was alright because we got Plante."

Plante won his first game in Cleveland, 2-1. The next day, January 4, in the friendly confines of the Aud, Plante stunned the visiting Pittsburgh team with a shutout. Suddenly, the Bisons were believers. On January 7, Pierre suffered a four-stitch cut to the back of his neck during an intense practice scrimmage. Their next game was another Plante shutout victory.

The largest crowd in three years came to the Aud on January

11 to see the new star goalie, dubbed "Jake the Snake," take on the first-place Cleveland Barons. The goalie, with the penchant for leaving his crease to snare and pass errant pucks, was playing on a sore ankle, but didn't disappoint. Pierre, back up to left wing, took a pass from Jim Conacher in the slot and beat the Barons' Johnny Bower for the game's first goal. In the second period, Pierre was crunched into the left goal post at the Cleveland net by Glenn Sonmor, and sustained a leg injury that forced him from the game.

"I was trying to go around Sonmor and he came at me and hit me right on top of the knee," recalled Pierre. "I got a charley horse. Sonmor had a tough reputation."

Sonmor incurred a penalty, and the Bisons scored on the ensuing power play. Plante's shutout streak of 198:34 minutes was finally broken at 8:52 of the third period. Still, the most important thing was that the Bisons hung on to win 2-1 and clinch their fifth straight victory.

Annie was now a regular at the Bisons home games. "Pierre and I were very serious by then," she said. "Only a storm would keep me away. I'd take the bus over and he would drive me home after the game or if they were leaving town after the game, he would wait with me for the bus. Sometimes, if they had to really leave quickly after a game I wouldn't go at all."

Was she worried about her boyfriend's rough style of play? "Pierre was a rough player and watching him, I naturally didn't want him to get hurt. But I was glad he was able to handle himself. I really took it all in stride. It was part of the game. I soon got used to the roughness."

"That was quite an experience," Plante observed of his first year in Buffalo. "We were in last place, 11 points behind the team in front of us when I got there. We had very few good players, though one of the best was Pierre Pilote. We reeled off five victories in a row and attendance in Buffalo jumped from 1,000 a game to 9,000. They started calling me 'Jake the Snake.' I loved all this publicity!"

"Plante showing up had an immediate impact," Pierre recalled.

"We started winning more. He was a funny guy, a real loner. I talked to him a lot in French because he didn't speak English very well."

After Plante's first seven games, the winning streak couldn't last with six players on the injury list, not counting Plante himself, who played through his sore ankle. Pierre, still hurting from the Sonmor crunch, missed a few games and played hurt when he did return. In a game on February 14, in Pittsburgh, the legend of the rough, tough Pilote was about to be eloquently cemented.

"Pierre Pilote, playing his first season of pro, apparently is determined not to be shoved around by anyone, when things started popping in Pittsburgh," wrote Jack Laing of the *Buffalo Courier Express*. "Ray Timgren took a swing at the young defenceman . . . Pierre bopped him right on the button and down went Mr. Timgren as cold as a cucumber.

"Out of the corner of his eye, Pierre saw Elliott Chorley headed in his direction and with mayhem in his heart, out lashed that Pilote fist once more, and down went Mr. Chorley . . . two punches, and two Hornets decked . . . he was handed one of the season's stiffest penalties of 22 consecutive minutes when two five-minute majors, a 10-minute misconduct, and a minor were given him in a single severe crackdown by referee Red Storey."

"I've seen a lot of fights, or so called fights, in hockey, but I never saw two settled so quickly and with so much authority as Pierre settled those," coach Eddolls later commented. "That little guy sure put Timgren and Chorley, who are a lot bigger than he is, down in a hurry."

The team's winning ways subsided but the team remained competitive, backed by Plante's excellent play. In one of the last games of the season, a 4-2 home win over the visiting Syracuse Warriors, Pierre got into a dandy scrap with veteran Bep Guidolin at the 2:50 mark of the third period. The moment was another lesson for the young defenceman.

"Guidolin was muscular, 32 or 33, a tough guy, on the way down from Boston. I didn't think he was that tough when I went at him but we had a fight in a corner and boom, he hit me! He got the first one in. He was quick—boom, boom, boom! Boy, I knew I had picked a dandy! He cut me right above the eye. If he would have gotten me on the jaw, I would've been done. I said to myself, 'Okay, I won't call on that guy again!' That's how you came to know."

The last-place Bisons—22 wins, 39 losses—were lauded for their never-say-die approach and work ethic. For rookie Pilote, the lessons from his first pro year were invaluable.

"I was just learning and there were a lot of smart hockey players in Buffalo and the whole AHL," recalled Pierre. "They didn't skate as fast as they once did, they may have gotten hurt or had bad knees, were on the way down, but man oh man, they were smart hockey players!"

In 61 games played, Pierre amassed two goals, 14 assists, and was second on the team (to left-winger Vern Kaiser) with 85 penalty minutes.

With the arrival of spring, Pierre turned his attention to buying that new car—a maroon 1952 Ford Monarch, four-door sedan with automatic transmission. His purchase was timely.

"After that first year, we were having a team party," recalled Pierre. "The team president, Mr. William Joseph, was there. He had taken over the team and he liked me. He was also a fighter so we had a certain affinity. Joseph was a little guy. But, he also ran Sports Services, one of the biggest companies in North America."

Sports Services Inc. owned and operated concession stands in many hockey arenas, baseball parks, and racetracks. When an interested party put forward a bid to buy a sports team, Sports Services often stepped up to provide the necessary loan for the acquisition, but always on the condition that it have the sole rights to run the lucrative concessions for an extended period of time.

At the party, Joseph queried Pilote about his summer plans. Pierre answered that he didn't have any.

"Look, why don't you come and work for us?" Joseph asked.

Pierre was taken by surprise, but smiled and accepted.

The following week, Pierre went to see Joseph at his office, and after an initial chat, his hockey boss smiled.

"Pierre, how would you like to go to Ottawa? We have the baseball and football concessions there and we want you to be the assistant manager of them."

"Sure, but how do I do this?" Pierre asked.

"Well, first, you'll train two weeks here in the office. The pay is $100 a week," William Joseph said. Pierre agreed and was soon on his way to the nation's capital.

"I take off for Ottawa in my new Monarch," Pierre recalled. "I got into a boarding house right across from Lansdowne Park. The guy who I worked with was Fred Curry. He's the manager, I'm the assistant manager. He ran the whole thing. My first task was to sell a few ads for the programs. Then I opened up the stores and the vendors, checking everything. I learned a lot, had a good time, especially when Annie came to visit me once in a while.

"Next thing you know, I was also in charge of the concessions at the Brockville Arena, which hosted Friday night summer wrestling shows, western shows, and concerts. I had two or three people under me. We sold popcorn, hot dogs, and hamburgers, and whatever. I'd take the cash, freeze the leftovers, and clean up."

Until training camp opened in the fall, Pierre bounced from Ottawa and Brockville, to Annie in St. Catharines, to his parents in Fort Erie.

The Bisons were rebuilding. The glaring humiliation of having finished in last place did not sit well with GM Hunt and he was determined it wouldn't happen again in the 1953-54 season.

"That year, none of the Canadiens were being signed, not until Jean Béliveau would be signed to a big five-year, $100,000 contract—$20,000 per year!" recalled Pierre of the joint Bisons-Canadiens camp at the Forum. "It was huge money, headline news! I remember after he signed, then they signed everybody else."

When the Bisons broke from camp, they were a totally revamped squad with only Plante, Eddolls, Pilote, and centre Gord Pennell returning to anchor a team that Hunt would eventually spend $175,000 to rebuild. Eddolls referred to Plante and Pilote as "our blue chip kids."

"I never worried about making the team. I thought I was good enough, not the best, but good enough," related Pierre. "I always looked at guys who were better than I was and they gave me something to shoot for. When I caught up with them, then I would look for someone else to try to catch."

The Canadiens had sent the Bisons a good array of talent in Gaye Stewart, Eddie Slowinski, Ross Kowalchuck, Pete Babando, Donnie Marshall, and Rollie Rousseau. From the folded St. Louis Flyers, Hunt acquired Harry Taylor, Ken Hayden, and goalie Red Almas, who was assigned to the WHL Victoria Cougars. Next, he bought Joe Lund from the Montreal Royals and drafted Pete Wright from Sherbrooke. The moves paid off as the team lost its first game of the season but then catapulted to the front of the AHL pack.

"Marshall was a big addition that second year," recalled Pierre. "He was a very smooth skater, talented at play making. Gaye Stewart was good. He was in his early thirties then. Boy, could he skate and stickhandle! Man, he had a big heavy stick. He had class, confidence."

Another major change for Pierre was moving back to defence where he had always wanted to be. Paired with Eddolls, Pierre had to make an adjustment to play on the right side, as Eddolls played the left. Pierre told his coach outright that he didn't want to play on the right side.

"I shoot left, Frankie!" Pierre pleaded. "I've never played on the right side!"

"Well, you've got to learn to now!" responded Eddolls.

"But, I don't know how!" Pierre shot back. Eddolls thought a moment and then looked at his young protégé.

Eddolls pointed out that Doug Harvey played the right side and he shot left; the impressionable Pilote, wanting to be like him, agreed.

He quickly saw the advantages of the move. "Eddolls was older, slowing down, and I had the speed so when the puck was shot in, I went back and got it," recalled Pierre. "I soon realized that when I carried the puck up ice, I could see the whole ice so much better. For an offensive blueliner it was a good trick. Even the Rocket played on the wrong side, and when he came around from the right side, he could see the whole net a lot better. I hadn't thought about it until then, so in the end, it was better for me. Frankie had done me a favour."

Eddolls had no favourites, though, and once when Pilote was late for a meeting at the Buffalo train station, the coach fined him $50.

"You know, it was a lesson learned," Pierre observed. "I was never late again, in Buffalo or anywhere!"

Against the Pittsburgh Hornets, Pierre scored on a 45-foot slapshot that beat Hornets goalie Ed Chadwick, but they still lost 5-4, which pushed them temporarily out of first place. While Pierre's play was heralded in the press, apparently his spot on the club had been tenuous.

"In training camp, I was frankly disappointed in Pierre," Eddolls said. "He was still making the same mistakes he made when he came out of junior. I was afraid he wasn't going to supply the strength we needed back on defence.

"But Pierre, who has worlds of heart, didn't give up on himself and just worked that much harder to prove he had the necessary ability. Today, he's undoubtedly the most improved player on the team. Pierre isn't too big for a defenceman, but he always could hit hard and catch his man in mid-ice and not depend upon nailing him along the boards."

"I only fight when the other fellow is out looking for trouble!" Pierre added.

By the fall of 1953, Annie Greshchyshyn consumed much of his thoughts.

"The season before, I had roomed with Sam Lavitt, and so I mentioned to him one day that I was starting to get serious about Annie and Sammy introduced me to a jeweller in Cleveland. So this season, we're in Cleveland, and I go see that jeweller. I picked out a ring but he said he had to mount the diamond first.

"Okay, so on our next trip there, I brought the $500 and picked up the diamond. Now I've got to take this ring back to Buffalo without losing it. I was paranoid, so I unclasped this small chain around my chain, and hung it around my neck for the trip home. I was ready to pop the question!"

"I knew we were serious and I wanted to marry him," Anne recalled. "We were at his parents' place in Fort Erie at Christmas when I opened up one of my presents and there was the diamond! Oh my god! It was quite a diamond! I loved it! I said 'yes' of course! I loved it! And I loved him!"

"When I gave the ring to Annie she needed sunglasses because the ring sparkled!" boasted Pierre. They discussed a spring nuptial, as marriage in the middle of a hockey season was taboo. They would have to wait.

By January 2, the Bisons had a league-leading 48 points, thanks to a 6-4 victory against the Hershey Bears. Pierre picked up a goal, an assist, and a penalty, and his play was starting to be noticed.

"Pierre Pilote is the most improved player in the American Hockey League, and if he continues along that line, he'll someday reach the National Hockey League," praised Hershey coach Murray Henderson. "About the only thing that impressed me about Pilote a year ago was his ability to bodycheck well for a fellow his size. Now the fellow is beginning to show some of the makings of a top prospect. You catch him out of position less often. He makes fewer mistakes when clearing the puck from his own end and is more dangerous on the point."

Pierre attributed his improvement to a mid-season Bisons move. "I got paired with Rollie Rousseau," Pierre recalled of the Canadiens prospect who had played with the Montreal Royals the season before. "They kept saying Rollie was better than I was, so I had something to shoot for. He was a nice little player, definitely smarter and better at handling the puck than I was, so I watched and learned from Rollie."

After 48 games, the first-place Bisons were leading the league in goals with 186, and their first-place lead swelled to 10 points.

"Pierre's willingness to work and his ruggedness alone are strong recommendations," observed the Bisons ice boss to the press after a workout in the Fort Erie Arena. "The way he and Rollie Rousseau are fast developing as a team, they'll be the best 'little man' defence in the league before the season is over."

Plante continued to anchor a team that was humming along nicely. Pierre could also see that their goalie had more talent than just playing goal. An avid knitter, Plante could often be found on road trips knitting his own underwear, socks, and tuques. And the man could paint.

"Jacques and I got along well. I spoke French so we had a cultural connection. One day he had bought a TV in Buffalo and brought it across the border, so I kept it at my parents' place until he could ship it to Montreal," Pierre remembered. "I knew he was a good portrait painter too, so for keeping the TV at my place, I gave him a photo of Annie and he did a beautiful oil painting of her. I don't think very many people have a Jacques Plante painting of their wife, eh?"

"Jacques Plante? Oh I liked him! We were buddies. He was fun!" recalled Annie. "I remember seeing that painting and thinking, 'Oh my god! That's such a big painting of me!' I didn't know it was coming!"

In mid-February, Pierre and company played host to Cleveland and their star goalie Emile "The Cat" Francis, who had been unilaterally picked to the league's All-Star team over Plante, despite the fact that Jake the Snake boasted the league's best goals against average. The snub was raw to Plante and Bisons boosters.

As 9,332 fans cheered, the Bisons edged out a tough 2-1 victory, their fifth win in a row. It was Plante's last game as a Bison because on February 11, Canadiens goalie Gerry McNeil hurt his ankle and Plante was called up.

"When Plante got called up by Montreal with only 15 games left to go before the playoffs, we went downhill," remembered Pierre. "We still ended up in first place, and we had a good club but it seemed like a big letdown. Plante had been a big part of the club."

With the playoffs looming, goalie Charlie Hodge was dispatched to the Bisons as a fill-in. The Bisons stretched their lead over Cleveland to 14 points with a 6-2 victory over Hershey in which action got a little tense after Pierre nailed Bears right-winger Norm Corcoran with a right to the jaw during a mêlée.

"Corcoran used to be a lacrosse player, eh, so he always had his stick up to protect himself," recalled Pierre. "He high-sticked me and boom, I let him have it! You had to let these guys know, 'Hey, I'm not going to screw around with you.'"

Hodge won two of his three games, but unsatisfied, GM Hunt went searching for a more experienced goalie for the playoffs. He acquired Red Almas for $40,000. Almas, Hunt hoped, would be the man to anchor the Bisons down the stretch, with the offence still running at full steam. In one game, the Bisons peppered the visiting Barons and Francis with four goals in the first three minutes en route to a 9-2 shellacking before a deliriously happy crowd of 6,821 fans at the Aud. Pierre added two assists while Almas stopped 48 of 50 shots.

Three games later, they trounced Syracuse 13-3 to stretch their first place lead to 16 points. On excellent help from teammates Stewart and Slowinski, Marshall notched his 84th point, an AHL single-season record for rookies. Pierre picked up four assists in the game. On March 9, with two weeks left in the season, the Bisons huddled at 71 Linwood Ave. in Buffalo, where five of the Bisons shared a house, and listened to the radio as Hershey defeated Pittsburgh.

"Everybody was happy. We had clinched first place!" Pierre recalled. "We got a ring that year for that too. I still have it."

The Bisons had gone from last to first in one season. But things were still tenuous. Almas allowed 45 goals in his nine-game stint.

"Red Almas didn't pan out. It seemed like all of a sudden we didn't have a goaltender," said Pilote. "We were scrambling and everything was going in. We fell apart. We just lost our confidence with Plante leaving. We changed our style to protect the goalie more but when you change your style, everything can go wrong. Plante used to come out of the net, handle the puck but suddenly we're hesitating and the opposition were on our back. It changed our style completely."

For the third last game of the season, Almas was replaced by Jean Renaud, a 32-year-old veteran who had seen limited action the previous year with the Montreal Royals. In the final two games, Renaud allowed seven goals, hardly the numbers to boost confidence in his abilities.

On the bright side, the Bisons had won the Teddy Oke Trophy as regular season champs. Marshall was named rookie of the year and Eddolls received the *Hockey News* Award as the AHL's top coach. Pierre ended with two goals and 28 assists in 67 games, and his 108 penalty minutes were second to teammate Pete Wright.

As the playoffs loomed, the Bisons were reminded again about their misfortunes when Plante, despite his ascent to the NHL, was chosen as the AHL's best goaltender with a 2.69 goals-against average. It was a sore point, made worse when a season of such promise came crashing down in the playoffs as the Bisons lost the first two games of the series to Cleveland by scores of 7-2 and 5-3. Clearly Renaud wasn't up to the task despite the Bisons defence battening down the hatches, and Cleveland had some good, tough players.

"Andy Bathgate was a great player with a hell of a shot," Pierre recalled. "Tommy Williams was an All-Star defenceman, one of the best defencemen I ever saw in the American League. Fred Glover was a tough guy who could score. If you were going to hit him, you had to go through a lot of wood. If you got him, he would get you back. He took no prisoners! Bob Bailey was a tough, crazy guy you had to always watch because he could really hurt you and intentionally. "

The Barons went for the kill in the third game of the best-of-five series, but the Bisons weren't about to roll over and die, and had a 4-3 lead with minutes remaining. Cleveland scored two quick goals to squeak out a 5-4 win that eliminated the disheartened Bisons.

"We had a great team that year, don't kid yourself," Pierre reflected. "We should have done better, but you can't win in playoff hockey without good goaltending!"

Putting the loss behind him, Pierre had a summer job to look forward to, and an impending wedding. In March 1954, he went back to the Sports Services office to see William Joseph about summer employment. They were waiting for him.

"Look, Pierre," Joseph said immediately. "We want you to go down to Lancaster, Pennsylvania. There's a baseball team there, and we want you to go run that concession stand down there. We think it's just the fit for you."

Pierre accepted the assignment. He was unsure from the outset about moving so far away for the summer with his approaching wedding to Annie, but he needed the work and so he went, reluctantly.

"In Lancaster, I opened the concession up and got it going but soon got really lonesome," Pierre remembered. "It was hot in Pennsylvania too. I didn't like the place."

Pierre found himself merely going through the motions. He was always one who put his heart and soul into anything he did, on and off the ice, but he was miserable and unhappy. After three weeks, he'd had enough. He called Joseph in Buffalo.

"Look, Mr. Joseph, I'm not feeling good. I've got problems at home," Pierre explained matter-of-factly, of which the latter part of his plea was a small white lie. "You've got to send a new manager here."

There was silence on the other end of the line.

"Please, sir, I want to come home. Besides, I'm getting married soon."

As Pierre waited for the answer, he wondered if it was the end of the line for him and Sports Services, maybe even with the Bisons— after all, they owned the team. Here he was about to get married and it looked like he could be unemployed, both off and on the ice.

On that spring day in 1954, with his immediate future hanging in the air of a suddenly silent telephone line, Pierre wondered if his days as a Bison were over.

Wedding Bells and Insights

Pierre waited on the phone with bated breath when the tension was cut by William Joseph.

"Okay sure, Pierre, I understand," Joseph answered. "We'll send someone to take over. When you get back, we'll see about a new assignment for you."

Pierre breathed a sigh of relief. He and Joseph had always had a good relationship. When he arrived home, Pierre was elated to see the woman he was about to marry.

Anne Greshchyshyn often reminisced about how she had arrived at this moment.

In the shadow of the Great Depression, Anne was born in Winnipeg, Manitoba, on July 21, 1931, to Ukrainian parents John and Anne Greshchyshyn. Looking for work, John moved his small family to the growing village of Bonnyville, Alberta. They weren't there long before tragedy struck in 1933 when Annie's mother died before the little girl was even two years old.

"I can still see them taking her to the hospital, wrapped in a grey blanket," she recalled.

John and Annie boarded a freight train back to Winnipeg where the widower hoped to enlist support from the local Ukrainian community. Realizing he couldn't work and take care of his daughter at the same time, John temporarily placed Annie in a Catholic orphanage.

"I was cared for by the nuns until they told my father one day that another couple was interested in adopting me," remembered Annie. "These people were coming to meet me, and take me out for a ride. Suddenly, my father showed up at the orphanage to take me home with a lady, who would turn out to be my stepmother. Her name was Nelly and she was a very nice lady.

"This lady became my mother, really. We soon moved to Toronto, where we stayed in a little apartment that had a Murphy bed while she worked at the Royal York Hotel. Really, I had two mothers! My father was a carpenter and work was hard to find so we eventually moved to St. Catharines, where my dad found a job. I was very close to Nelly. She was such a beautiful person. I was very lucky. Some people have wicked stepmothers, but mine was so special."

As the Second World War dawned, her parents secured work making ammunition at Thompson Products, which was just down the street from the new house John had built them on Churchill Street. The company's outdoor skating rink was also just down the hill from the Greshchyshyn homestead. Annie frequented it often.

"Happy but tired, I would walk all the way back up the hill with my skates on!" she said. "I'd be frozen! My parents would have lukewarm water ready for me to thaw my feet."

When she turned 14, Annie was enrolled at Edith Cavell High School, in the city's west end.

"Growing up in St. Catharines, I was not really a hockey fan, but everybody hung out at the Crystal Restaurant, and the Diana Sweets Restaurant. The hockey players hung out there too. The Crystal Restaurant was newer and that's where I first noticed Pierre, and the rest, as they say, is history."

Saturday, May 29, 1954, was a beautiful, sunny day as a large contingent of family, friends, teammates, and Bisons head scout Rudy Pilous gathered at St. Mary's Church in St. Catharines for the Pilote wedding.

"So many people came to the house to see me that it took forever to get from the house out to the car, to the church," chuckled

Annie. "I was very, very late for my wedding. The priest who married us, was mad, pacing back and forth!"

As per Ukrainian custom, there was lots of food. "We sat down to eat three times—we Ukrainians are like that," Anne reminisced. "We had cabbage rolls and stuff and we danced and ate! All my girlfriends were there of course. It was a happy occasion!"

For their honeymoon, Pierre took his new bride back to his hometown of Kénogami. He hadn't been there since leaving when he was 14.

"I saw where Pierre was born, where he grew up," said Annie. "It had changed a bit since he had left but I remember the long covered bridge was still there. His relatives welcomed us with open arms. We went for a week or so, took our time, drove there in Pierre's new Monarch."

The newlyweds rented an older upstairs apartment at 527 Niagara Blvd., near the river in Fort Erie. Annie didn't work, at Pierre's insistence, and they painted and changed the flooring in their new abode. Annie used the nearby laundromat and also spent time with Pierre's mother. Within a few months, she was pregnant with their first child; that was alright because Pierre was working again.

"Mr. Joseph sent me to work at the Fort Erie Racetrack that summer, which was great because I was near Annie," recalled Pierre. "I was in charge of the concessions there that summer along with the Turf Club. It was a lot of responsibility but it was great."

Having just won his third Stanley Cup with the Detroit Red Wings, coach Tommy Ivan was about to change his own responsibilities when he left the Red Wings to assume the general manager duties of the cellar-dwelling Chicago Black Hawks. It seemed a perilous move, and the new GM's monumental challenge would be to lead a woeful franchise out of the hockey wilderness.

After Pierre and Bisons GM Fred Hunt negotiated a slightly larger contract, Hunt noted Pilote's extra 10 pounds and declared that "the youngster has reached his full growth, and should be a solid threat on our back line this season!"

Changes were in the air though in September 1954 when Bisons owner Louis Jacobs ended a 10-year association with the Canadiens, opting to operate the Bisons independently with no NHL ties, spurning a $125,000 offer from Toronto. The Bisons and Canadiens did continue their training camp arrangement together in Montreal however.

Another big change was the appointment of Bisons forward Gaye Stewart as the new playing-coach, replacing Frankie Eddolls, who had been promoted to coach the Black Hawks. The Eddolls-Bisons connection and influence in Buffalo, St. Catharines, and Chicago would soon become clearer.

Pierre again sputtered at training camp, so much so in fact that Hunt entertained trade offers for him, but held off making a deal. "I'm awfully glad I waited," Hunt confessed later. "I couldn't quite convince myself that Pierre wouldn't settle down on the ice to become consistently good."

To team observers, it soon became clear why Pierre had suffered from self doubt. "If defenceman Tony Schneider and Pierre Pilote hit opposing forwards as hard and often as they hit each other in practice, the Buffalo Bisons will come up with the most feared defence combination in the American League this season," a story in the *Buffalo Evening News* explained.

"In training camp, I don't think Tony liked me," Pierre recalled of his run-ins with the rookie. "Schneider and I were always going at each other, almost dropped the gloves once! He was a pretty big, tough guy. He was trying to make the club through me, but he wasn't going to make the club on my back! Then Stewart put us together and the next thing you know, Tony's buying me a coffee, which was alright! He would be my defence partner for that third year."

In a testy exhibition game against the Black Hawks on September 28, three fights broke out that demonstrated the seriousness of players wanting to make their respective teams. Two newcomers made good first impressions for the Bisons as goalie Hank Bassen allowed only two Chicago goals while centre Kenny Wharram set up the first Buffalo goal and played a strong game. With the Hawks leading 2-1, Pierre fired a 35-footer into the Hawks cage to tie the game at two, where it remained.

"Last year . . . our defencemen lacked size for the rugged going," coach Stewart wrote in a column for the *Buffalo Evening News*. "This was apparent in the playoffs against Cleveland. We just couldn't match bodychecks with them. Now, we're a match for any club. Frank Sullivan and Pierre Pilote, both of whom stand at 5'10" and hover near the 180 pound mark, are our little guys.

"Pierre is just about ready to make a name for himself. He is one of the most solid bodycheckers in the league and while this is his third year with the club, it's his first year at playing his normal left defence."

On Halloween night the Bisons were behind 4-1 against the Springfield Indians, and Hunt and Stewart, dumbfounded by the team's lackluster performance, asked team president William Joseph if he'd like to say something to the players before the third period began. Joseph obliged and gave them an emotional speech. Inspired, the Bisons marched out of their room shouting and notched seven goals for an 8-7 come-from-behind victory.

Despite this performance, it was a tough year for them as exemplified by a very rough November 20 4-1 loss in Hershey that deposited them in a tie for last place after 17 games. "Snarling and scrapping like bobcats, the Hershey Bears and the Buffalo Bisons tangled in a rough and tumble contest here tonight," declared the *Reading Eagle*.

In a six-team league, they faced each other 10 times, a schedule that created intense team and personal rivalries, and ample opportunities to settle old scores. In a November 27 game in Cleveland, the Bisons were handed a 3-1 defeat highlighted by a third period brawl that was one for the AHL history books. When Barons right-winger and tough guy Fred Glover invaded his territory, Bassen grabbed his stick. Glover then slashed Bassen, and within seconds, Bassen and Glover were swinging at each other before Buffalo defenceman

Schneider jumped on Glover. Then, Cleveland goalie Emile Francis skated the full length of the ice and started swinging at Bassen.

A slew of major and minor penalties were handed out by referee Bill Chadwick. Amazingly, Pierre, not involved in the fracas, used the four-on-four's more open ice in his favour when he spoiled the Cat's shutout bid with an unassisted goal with just 44 seconds left in the game. It marked the second time in a week that Pierre had spoiled a Francis shutout bid in the last minute of a game.

It was clear that while he was still a tough and mean hombre unafraid to mix it up, Pierre was becoming a confident offensive threat in his own right. In a Thanksgiving Day re-match against the Cleveland Barons, reporter Tony Wurzer was completely enthralled by a Pilote performance in a Bisons 6-1 rout that clearly demonstrated Pierre's growing offensive abilities.

"The Pilote goal was a masterpiece," the scribe penned. "The young, black-haired guy picked up a loose puck at mid-ice, headed down along the Main Street boards, north towards Emile (The Cat) Francis, the Baron goalie. Glen Sonmor engaged him at the Cleveland line, but from there on he clung to Pilote and the flying Bison defenceman held the chunky Sonmor off with one hand, while with the other, he steered the puck ahead of him, curved finally in front of Francis, and let fly with a close, vicious shot that the Cat had to duck, rather than try to save!

"It was one those goals that you automatically call sensational and this time the crowd forgot its turkey filling and howled. Happening as it did at the three minute mark of the final period, it appeared to break whatever resistance was left in the Barons, and the game quickly turned into a 6-1 rout."

Pierre enjoyed playing Pittsburgh for one main reason—Frank Mathers. "He was my idol in the AHL!" Pierre said enthusiastically of the Hornets defenceman. "He played just like Doug Harvey. I loved watching how he controlled the puck. Could he make great plays! He was probably the best defenceman that ever played in the American Hockey League that never made the NHL."

In an article published by Jack Horrigan halfway through the season, GM Hunt was singing Pierre's praises. "For a fellow his size, Pierre is exceptionally strong and hard to take the puck from once he's underway. . . . He is now the hockey player I had looked for him to eventually be after that first game with us four years ago. His slap shot is deadly from the point, and he has become a fine blocker of shots in addition to maintaining his effectiveness as a hitter. And very seldom does he get outsmarted or outfought in the corners."

Pierre himself attributed his success to something else: "I feel confident that I can really do the job for the first time since I turned pro, and of course, since I got married last spring, I have a great deal more incentive to go to the top in this game."

Jack Laing of the *Courier Express* wrote that Pierre had "learned to curb his temper; his bodychecking has picked up finesse and he carries a puck well. One of these days you'll see his name in the lineup of an NHL team, possibly the Chicago Black Hawks."

Perhaps writer Laing had inside information in making the Chicago connection because a few days later, on January 7, it was announced that Louis Jacobs had sold the Buffalo Bisons and their farm team, the St. Catharines Teepees, to the Chicago Black Hawks for $150,000. The Hawks and Tommy Ivan were well aware of the talent goldmine they had just purchased. Chicago now held the keys to the Bisons and Teepees, thanks to the Rudy Pilous/Frankie Eddolls/Tommy Ivan connection. The deal turned out to be the lifesaver for a struggling Chicago franchise envisioning a steady pipeline of future talent.

To one budding superstar, Bobby Hull, there was only one reason the deal was made. "In 1955, the Hawks bought the flippin' Buffalo franchise just to get Pierre," recalled the Golden Jet. "It wasn't me! In the mid-1950s when Chicago was really down, Ivan bought the Buffalo franchise because Pilote was there!"

In an article published by Tony Wurzer later that month, the writer observed that Pilote used to fight at the drop of a hat, but now his play had begun to take on polish. "Last spring Pierre got married . . . then came the tempering of the steel," Wurzer wrote. "He began to walk away from fights. Not because he was afraid. He isn't. But he had learned diplomacy."

"You're no good to your team in the penalty box," Pierre admitted to Wurzer. "I married. I found out that things don't have to go my way. Sometimes I have to knuckle down. Then I found out that this is sometimes a good thing for a man . . . it makes him see things from somebody else's viewpoint. It makes him think of being part of a team. Now I am part of two teams, one at home . . . one on the ice. It's better like that."

Pierre finished the season with a healthy 38 points but still led his team in penalty minutes with 120. Buffalo and Springfield edged out Hershey for the last playoff spot, both tied for third. Cleveland would face Buffalo.

As in previous years, the Herd had to go into the playoffs with less than stellar goaltending, with Bassen having been called up to the big team after playing 37 games. Ray Frederick, who had played five games for the Hawks that season, filled in for the last 22 for the Herd, winning 15. Not bad, but for the Bisons to have a chance, he'd have to improve on his less than stellar 3.77 goals against average.

Buffalo won Game 1, 3-2, lost the second game, 6-3, then rebounded to take Game 3, 8-0. They finished the Barons with a 6-4 win, taking the series. After so many years of elimination at the hands of Cleveland, the Bisons had finally enacted a thorough and sweet revenge. But they couldn't rest on their laurels as they now had to face the league champion Pittsburgh Hornets, who had knocked off Springfield. It was Buffalo's first Calder Cup appearance in four years.

The Bisons lost the opening game in Pittsburgh by a slim 5-4 score but bounced back to beat the Hornets 3-1 at the Aud. The Hornets squeaked out two slim victories in Buffalo to take a commanding 3-1 series lead. The Bisons' backs were against the wall as the series shifted back to Pittsburgh. In a tight checking game on April 9, the Bisons scored at 1:17 of the second overtime period to win the game 5-4 and send the series back to Buffalo. The powerful Hornets were not to be denied though as they beat Buffalo 4-2 to capture the Calder Cup.

It was a disappointing time for Pierre but the loss was soon tempered by a new arrival. One afternoon, Annie and Pierre had just gotten to his parents' home for supper when Annie started feeling labour pains. Trying not to panic, Pierre drove her to the hospital.

"The first baby was much harder on Annie than me," Pierre recalled. "I took her to the hospital and I hung around in the waiting room until seven o'clock or eight o'clock when the doctor came in and suggested I go home. In those days, you didn't stick around. And so I went and had a few beers at the Barney House, went home, and eventually went to bed. We were still living on Niagara Street.

"At around 6:30 Mrs. Jackson, the landlady, yelled up to me, 'There's a call for you, Pierre!' We didn't have a phone so I went downstairs and it was Dr. Whiting. 'Hey Pierre, you're the proud father of a baby girl!' I yelled back: 'How is he?' Guys are always thinking of a boy first. 'How is he?' A slip of the tongue! Our Denise, our first child had arrived. Oh, I was so proud and happy!" It was May 3, 1955.

Not long afterwards, mom and baby were home, and Pierre was again with Sports Services.

"I worked as assistant manager of the concessions in Toronto at the old Woodbine Racetrack that summer," Pierre recalled. "Then, in August, when the races moved to Fort Erie, I ran Woodbine by myself: the bar, the concessions, and the restaurant. I had a manager for the restaurant but I still oversaw everything."

Next he turned his attention to finding better living arrangements to accommodate his growing family. "That summer of 1955, we bought a wartime house in Fort Erie for $3,800," Pierre related. "I got a mortgage with Central Mortgage. My monthly payment was $37 a month, interest, principal, and property taxes included! Wasn't that something!"

On August 1, a letter from Chicago GM Tommy Ivan notified him that the Chicago training camp would open September 12 at the Memorial Arena in Welland, Ontario.

He stayed at the Reeta Hotel, along with his 19-year-old brother Florent, or "Flo," who was also trying out for the team. Flo had played the previous season with the Junior A Galt Black Hawks. Chicago had three sets of brothers try out for the team that fall: Larry and Johnny Wilson, Fred and Sandy Hucul, and the Pilote brothers.

"Flo was a good skater and could really hit," Pierre recalled. "It was kind of neat having him there and I was hoping he'd stick but guys were getting around him. At a certain level, watching these guys, you could tell."

Returning to the Junior A Guelph Biltmores, for Flo it was the first of a few Chicago camps. In the end, only the Wilsons cracked the Chicago lineup through training camp, with Larry sent down to the Bisons after a few games. His brother Johnny played in all 70 games for the Hawks under new coach Dick Irvin, who replaced Frankie Eddolls. Eddolls's stint behind the Hawks bench the previous year had been disastrous as Chicago had won a miserable 13 games and finished 52 points out of first place. Eddolls was reassigned to the Bisons where he had earned so much success, his return heralded in the Buffalo press.

Pierre was looking better with each Hawks camp he had attended but again was relegated to Buffalo, under his old coach, who had retired from the "playing" part.

"Frankie Eddolls was great," recalled Pierre. "He told and taught me so many things." Years later, Pierre told the *Hockey News* that "Frank Eddolls showed me how to block pucks . . . and he showed me how to go down with my stick too."

In the season opener on October 8, 1955, in Pittsburgh, the Hornets pulled out a 5-2 win. Pierre had many memories of his

AHL years. Once in Cleveland, while walking towards his hotel room, Pierre spotted young referee Scotty Morrison entering a room with his new bride. To Pierre's surprise, Morrison was refereeing the next night's game against Cleveland. In the game, the Indians were giving the Bisons all they could handle and Morrison handed Pierre a penalty. Later in the game when he handed him another penalty Pierre's frustration boiled over.

"Hey Scotty, what do you think this is, a honeymoon?" Pierre yelled on his way to the penalty box. Morrison glared back and tacked on a 10-minute misconduct. After the game Morrison recommended that Pierre be given a further $25 fine. He was.

"I earned that one," Pierre observed. "But I liked playing in Hershey. I always played well there. Hershey was clean, and they had a nice museum to explore and a nice hotel also owned by the chocolate company. Back then of course we always took the train, got off at Harrisburg, and from there we'd bus in, about five hours in all.

"One game in Hershey, they're losing by one goal and they pull their goaltender. I've got the puck in our end and Larry Wilson is breaking out, and I had to wait until he was open, but Ray Gariepy was coming at me. He was going to crunch me, but I didn't care, I was making that pass no matter what! I made the pass alright but Ray crushed me, knocked the wind right out of me! I just barely crawled to our bench, but we scored the goal. I can still feel that hit!"

"A Boston writer once labelled me 'Rockabye' when I was up with the Bruins because I supposedly hit like a rock," recalled Ray Gariepy of the days when he used to lay out his opponents. "I used to rock them I guess. But I remember Pierre. He was a good puck handler, a good skater, a good, rushing defenceman and I did whatever I had to do to stop him."

Back in Buffalo, Anne Pilote loved going to the Aud. "It was like a big party. I met a lot of great fans and they loved Pierre," Annie remembered. "There were some very loyal fans. There was one elderly couple who went to all the games. They knew exactly where I sat, close to the boards. I grew close to them. A lot of fans belonged to the booster club and I got to know a lot of people there and they were so good to us. The peanut guy knew me well too, because I loved peanuts. We were invited to a lot of restaurants after a game. We ate well and had a lot of fun.

"Most of the other Buffalo hockey players rented places in Fort Erie, so I used to go and visit their wives and if I had the car, I would take them out. I hung out quite a bit with Kenny Wharram's wife, Jeannie, that year."

For Pilote, the AHL was a continual learning experience. "Junior hockey was fast in my time, but we scrambled all over the place, out of position," Pierre remembered. "Then in the American Hockey League, it's more structured but there were more crazy guys who could hurt you. Then there were the Willie Marshalls and Topazzinnis, fast guys who kept you on your toes. Willie Marshall was quick and often fooled you. There were many talented guys whose primary sin was their inability or refusal to stay in shape for an NHL season. There were many gifted players who were just slowing down, but good. The AHL changed in my four years because it seemed to get easier as I got better, no kidding! And of course there was my 'Eureka moment!'"

Pierre described his awakening, during a Bisons practice, as almost mystical. "We're practising and the puck came to a spot at centre ice and I'm racing somebody else for it," Pierre recalled. "Prior to this moment, I would have gotten to that puck first, grabbed it, and passed it to somebody else right away. My thinking was in a block, a Rubik's cube, turning over the same combinations all the time. But all of a sudden, at that precise moment, I realized that my picking up the puck was not the best play. I eased up and let this other player have the puck and he went with it and right at that moment it came to me—'That's how you play this game! That was the best play!'

"I couldn't and still can't describe what happened that day but I could suddenly think ahead, see it all develop in my mind, envision the play unfolding before me almost before it happened! I could see everything and everyone around me, what the play was going to be. It was a moment when all of the games I had watched, the plays I had seen, plays I was part of, the guys I played against, just came to me. Yes, it was very weird, but it was the start of my new hockey career. No kidding! Everything jelled in my mind. It was in that fourth season. I call it 'a moment' like somebody threw water on me. From that point on, I really improved my game, I mean really improved!"

The awakening of his sixth hockey sense of sorts, an uncanny ability that only the very best players have, to see and feel both team-mates and opposition players on the ice, to know the plays, almost before they happen, held Pierre in good stead and clearly elevated his game to the next level. Proof came with the announcement of the AHL All-Stars in January, picked by the league's coaches. Pierre made the AHL First All-Star team, cracking its complete domi-nance by Providence and Pittsburgh players.

He didn't have long to enjoy the moment. On the morning of January 25, 1956, the phone rang at Pierre and Anne's house. It was Buffalo trainer Frank Christie.

"Pierre, we just got contacted by the Black Hawks. They want you to play for them in Toronto tonight. You're to meet them there, nice and early."

"You're kidding?"

"No, I'm not."

"Holy shit!" was all Pierre could say.

"Look, Pierre, I know it'll be unnerving for you, your first time and all. It's a long enough drive. If you want, the wife and I'll drive you. That is if you want?"

"Okay, Frank. Yeah, that'd be great!"

Pierre got off the phone and told Annie. It was a shock to both of them.

"It was exciting when Pierre got called up to Chicago! Oh boy!" Annie recalled. "That's what he was aiming for, right, to go up there? We were both happy. Wow!"

Next, Pierre phoned his parents. Paul was proud of his son and immediately wanted to drive him to Maple Leaf Gardens himself, to see his son play.

Pierre shook his head. "No Dad, don't get too excited. I'll be lucky to see one minute of ice time and that'll be if the game is out of hand. You'd be wasting a trip. I'm sure I'll just ride the bench. I don't want you and Mom to come for nothing."

Paul reluctantly agreed not to go.

Around noon Christie and his wife picked up Pierre for the two-hour drive into Toronto. Feeling the young man's nervousness, Christie kept reassuring him throughout the trip that he'd be fine.

"Relax, Pierre. Don't worry," Christie told the young defenceman. "You'll do great, kid. No problem!"

"Yeah Frank, that's easy for you to say!" Pierre answered with a nervous smile.

Arriving in Toronto with plenty of time to spare, Christie dropped Pierre off at the hotel to register and brought his equipment to the Gardens. Pierre deposited his clothes off in his room, then walked over to the Gardens to hang around. He had played there as a junior but had never really looked around before. When Frank Martin came into the room while Pierre was nervously getting dressed, Pierre felt relieved to see a familiar face. Then Hawks coach Dick Irvin walked into the room.

"Starting lineup," Irvin bellowed. "On defence, Martin and Pilote!"

"Holy shit!" Pierre thought, full of trepidation. He wondered if he had been hearing things, but no, he had heard correctly as Martin looked over at him and winked. Once out on the ice, butterflies filled his stomach. He later took position on the blue line and took a deep breath. This was it, his big chance. He was in his first NHL game!

Leafs centreman Todd Sloan readied himself for the faceoff and when the puck was dropped by the referee, Sloan quickly pushed the puck through the Chicago centre's legs and rushed towards Pierre.

"The puck was about six feet away from me and I hesitated, wondering should I go for it or not?" remembered Pierre. "Suddenly Sloan got the puck, and he skated around me so quickly I didn't know what had happened. He was gone by me on a clearcut breakaway! I turned around and started chasing him but he was already five or 10 feet in front of me. I didn't have a prayer of catching him. I was skating with my head down, praying, 'God, I hope our goalie can stop him. Please stop him.' I figured if Sloan scored, I'd be toast, I'd never see the ice again.

"Sloan came in cleanly and tried to put a few moves on our goalie, Hank Bassen, but Bassen wasn't buying it and made one heck of a save! Oh boy! My goalie bailed me out! Finally, after rushing back, I was able to catch up to Sloan and take him out of the play. I picked up the puck and away we went the other way."

At the whistle, Irvin sent out a complete line change. Skating to the bench, Pierre was met with a cool look from Irvin. Sitting down on the bench, catching his breath, the silence from the stern bench boss behind him was almost deafening.

Pierre's mind envisioned the *Globe and Mail* sports page the next morning showing various players' ice time: "Pilote—45 seconds!"

"Holy shit," Pierre thought, sitting quietly on the Chicago bench. "I think I've just blown it!"

The only time Pierre seemed to have curls, which he outgrew.
PILOTE FAMILY COLLECTION

Pierre with his mother and siblings Paulette and Florent. Pierre's father was selling the wood piled on the right for his two brothers, Maurice and Lionel, who owned a farm on the Slipshaw River.
PILOTE FAMILY COLLECTION

Taken on his grandmother's porch, Pierre is proudly wearing his new suit made by his mother—it had one arm slightly shorter than the other.
PILOTE FAMILY COLLECTION

Albert gave Pierre his first business transaction: a dime for shining his shoes. This picture of Albert dancing with his daughter-in-law, Pierre's mother Maria, shows his muscular frame.
PILOTE FAMILY COLLECTION

Pierre with his Teepees teammates. *From left to right:* Allan Kellogg, Pierre, Brian Cullen, Charlie Marshall, and Teepees trainer Jimmy Joy. PILOTE FAMILY COLLECTION

The 1951–52 St. Catharines Teepees. Pierre (back row, third from the left): "Rudy Pilous, the coach and GM, was the reason I made the team. We had some great players but only Frank Martin (no. 2), our goalie Don 'Dippy' Simmons (in dark pads), and I would see real action in the NHL." PILOTE FAMILY COLLECTION

Pierre (front row with arms crossed beside bat boy) was one of two pitchers on the Fort Erie Juvenile B All-Ontario Champs baseball team. He credits the community for supporting the team throughout its run to winning the provincial crown. PILOTE FAMILY COLLECTION

Pierre's dad's 1939 Monarch in front of their Fort Erie wartime house at 75 Kingsmill one evening before Pierre would take it to a dance at Crystal Beach in Fort Erie.

PILOTE FAMILY COLLECTION

Here is Pierre wearing his first pro sweater, no. 16, with the Buffalo Bisons. Pierre: "I'm smiling, but not about my first contract." He realized when he went to negotiate his next year's salary, he began with the previous year's salary, not including the bonus. "Oh well, I had made the pros!"

PILOTE FAMILY COLLECTION

In his second year with the Bisons, Pierre got paired with fellow defenceman Rollie Rousseau (left), from whom he learned a great deal by just watching his style. PILOTE FAMILY COLLECTION

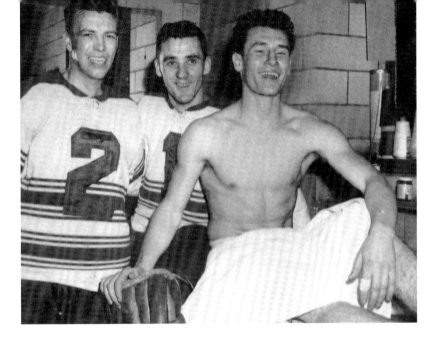

Playing coach Frankie Eddolls (left) taught Pierre the finer points of playing defence while goalie Jacques Plante (centre) would help catapult the Bisons to first place before being called up permanently to the Canadiens. PILOTE FAMILY COLLECTION

Pierre's brother Florent Pilote, or "Flo," was as tough as they came. He didn't quite crack an NHL lineup, but he would go on to have a major Eastern Hockey League career with the Charlotte Checkers and the Nashville Dixie Flyers. IMPERIAL OIL-TUROFSKY / HOCKEY HALL OF FAME

Appearing radiant at the time of their courtship and wedding, Annie Greshchyshyn looked like a movie star. This photograph was the basis of the portrait that Jacques Plante later painted of her.

PILOTE FAMILY COLLECTION

May 29, 1954. The happy couple exiting St. Mary's Church in St. Catharines.

PILOTE FAMILY COLLECTION

Annie and Pierre in his 1954 Monarch just as they were about to drive back to Pierre's hometown of Kénogami, Québec, on their honeymoon.

PILOTE FAMILY COLLECTION

Despite the crowd of people in front of him, Glenn Hall, "Mr. Goalie,"
made this stop. Pierre always called Hall the greatest goalie he ever saw.
JOE RIZZUTO

Pierre: "The Moose and me! Elmer 'Moose' Vasko was so dubbed because of his huge size. A 'stay-at-home defenceman,' he was my best friend and defence partner. Moose was a Tower of Power and the crowds loved his periodic end-to-end rushes!" LE STUDIO DU HOCKEY / HOCKEY HALL OF FAME

An innocent-looking Pierre in his first year of Junior hockey in St. Catharines. If he looks unsure, it is probably because it was heady stuff playing Major Junior A in only his third year of playing organized hockey— and for a whopping $17 a week, after room and board were deducted. IMPERIAL OIL-TUROFSKY / HOCKEY HALL OF FAME

Here is Pierre posing with Annie along the boards at the Chicago Stadium after he had been made captain of the Hawks. His greatest supporter, Annie would miss a home game for only one reason: if they couldn't find a babysitter. PILOTE FAMILY COLLECTION

Signing his new Bisons contract with GM Fred Hunt looking on in the fall of 1955. The Hawks had won first place the year before and despite their playoff loss, things were looking up.

Pierre, Reggie Fleming, Stan Mikita, and Moose Vasko pose in boxing gloves during the 1960–61 season. The reputation of the rough and tough Hawks was realized that season when they won the Stanley Cup and became the most penalized team in NHL hockey history.
LE STUDIO DU HOCKEY / HOCKEY HALL OF FAME

Two captains, Montreal's Jean Béliveau and Pierre, battle in front of the Chicago net in the Montreal Forum. "Le Gros Bill," as Béliveau was dubbed, was one of the hardest players to defend against in front of the net. LE STUDIO DU HOCKEY / HOCKEY HALL OF FAME

In this classic photo, Pierre is upending Toronto's Gerry James. Pierre:
"It was a great check, but I had to keep my head away from him as his
skate came within a whisker of cutting me very badly. It was actually
scary for a second there!" IMPERIAL OIL-TUROFSKY / HOCKEY HALL OF FAME

Pierre, You're Up!

"Okay, change 'em up! Defence too!" bellowed Dick Irvin at the next stoppage of play. Pierre didn't move, figuring he was benched for the rest of the game.

"Pilote, that's you! Get back out there!" Irvin hollered. Shocked, Pierre jumped sheepishly over the boards but once he stepped onto the ice, a steely determination came over him. He wasn't going to make any more mistakes that night, and he didn't. In fact he played every second shift.

"That was a big surprise," Pierre recalled. "Irvin kept putting me back out there. He never said a word to me about that first mistake. As it turned out, I ended up playing 25 or 30 minutes that night."

Despite Pierre's solid play, the Hawks lost the game 3-1. Still, he personally felt good about his debut. After the game, he went back with Christie to Fort Erie. He had an irate Paul Pilote to deal with the next day.

"Oh, was Dad ever mad when he found out how much I had played in that game!" remembered Pierre. "He missed it. He had wanted to drive me. But how was I supposed to know how much I was going to play that night? I really wasn't expecting it."

Pierre was called up on three separate occasions and then sent back down for reasons he didn't understand. But his first experience playing in the Chicago Stadium would be with him for a lifetime.

"My first game in Chicago was great. I looked around, the organist was playing," he recalled. "It was just amazing, fabulous!"

But trying to crack an NHL lineup in the 1950s was exactly that, trying. After one game in Detroit, where he had played very well, he thought he would be staying, but he was told to catch a late-night train back to Buffalo. With time to kill, Pierre headed to a Detroit bar. That night's referees walked in and Pierre said hello to them. They returned the greeting just as Carl Voss, the referee-in-chief arrived.

"He apparently fined them each $25 just for saying hello to me," Pierre related. "But I had to wait until three in the morning to catch this train back to Buffalo. It was an all-around long night that I never really understood."

A week later, the Hawks called him up again—with instructions to bring more clothes—for a game in Toronto on February 4, 1956. This time his father drove him.

On his second shift, Pierre let his presence be known when Hank Ciesla stole the puck away from Leaf defender Tim Horton. Pierre saw the play develop and raced towards the front of the net where his old Teepee teammate fed him a perfect pass. Pierre fired the puck behind Gil Mayer.

"For Pilote, a fearless, capable little defenceman, it was his first National Hockey League goal," wrote Rex MacLeod the next day. Pierre got almost 33 minutes of ice time that night and yet he couldn't rest on his laurels as the teams had a return match in Chicago the next day.

With the rematch tied at one apiece in the second period, Pierre rushed into the Toronto end. "Pilote put on a fancy skating exhibition, and a real piece of sharp shooting to put the Hawks ahead," penned MacLeod. "He eluded the Toronto defencemen until he got clear then sailed a 30-foot screened shot into the corner of the net, making the score 2-1."

Two goals in two games! His defence partner Gus Mortson made it 3-1 Chicago in the third period but Toronto then applied the pressure. In a four-minute span, the Hawks were a man short and two men short for 24 seconds. The Hawks defence scrambled everywhere and Al Rollins kept it out for a 3-2 victory.

Chicago Sun-Times noted that Pilote had sparked the team. "Coach Dick Irvin was going around Monday in a state of mind of a man who drilled for water and struck oil," wrote Jack R. Griffin. "Pressed desperately for a defenceman, he brought up Pierre Pilote from the Buffalo farm club over the weekend. Pilote not only turned in a stellar defence show, he also teamed up with Gus Mortson to provide the offensive spark in the 3-2 win Sunday night over Toronto.

"The victory, second over Toronto in two nights, moved the Hawks into fourth place, one point ahead of the Leafs. Pilote also scored in the Saturday game against Toronto. He, Mortson, and some brilliant goaltending by returnee Al Rollins were the difference in the Sunday game."

Pierre was quickly becoming a familiar face around the league, and his aboriginal background helped him stand out.

During a game in the Olympia against the Red Wings, Gordie Howe leaned towards his teammate Ted Lindsay on the Detroit bench while watching Pierre make a good play.

"I think that Pilote kid is going to be a great one," Howe observed.

"Oh? Why's that?" Lindsay asked him.

"Because, they've already put his picture on the front of their sweaters!" Howe remarked wryly. Lindsay laughed at the jest, which in no way was meant to be discriminatory.

Pierre stayed up with the Hawks through February and into March, but the Hawks needed more help than Pierre could provide, and their skid to the league cellar was inevitable.

"The Hawks were not a good team at the time," Pierre remembered. "Our only strength was goalie Al Rollins, who played great every night, but we had some older players coming to the end of their careers."

In the 14 seasons of the Original Six era since 1942-43, Chicago had made the playoffs only three times, and had finished dead-last seven times. But Pilote's call up for the 19 games that season was impressionable, especially a nasty incident in Montreal on February 10. Lee Fogolin was chasing the Rocket when Maurice Richard's high kick back struck Fogolin in the mouth. Blood was everywhere as Fogolin was taken off in distress. The next day at practice, Fogolin came into the room, his face and jaw a swollen mess.

"What happened to you?" Pierre asked him.

"I'm in bad trouble! I'm done!" Fogolin answered, barely.

"Apparently, when the dentist went to fix his jaw and teeth, Lee's whole top palate moved," Pierre said. "His mouth would forever be sensitive to the cold, especially at ice level. I never forgot that!"

A few weeks later, again at the Forum, Pilote and Mortson attempted to intercept a determined looking Richard heading toward the Chicago net. The three collided in a heap. Rocket slid into the Chicago net, striking his head on the post. The collision not only knocked the net off its moorings, and Richard unconscious, it put Richard out of the lineup for the remainder of the regular season.

When asked later by the press which Canadien gave him the most trouble, Pierre surprisingly said it was Kenny Mosdell. "Mosdell is real cute at dumping the puck between your skates and he got around me a couple of times so that I looked bad."

The Hawks missed the playoffs for the third year in a row with a dismal 19 wins, 39 losses, and 12 ties, for 50 points and last place, exactly 50 points behind first-place Montreal. Rookie Pilote was pleased with his three goals and five assists in his short stint.

The Hawks ensured that Pierre only played in enough games to enable him to return to the Bisons for their playoff run. In his absence the Bisons had brought up a Teepee defenceman who would have a strong impact on Pierre's life and career.

Dubbed "Moose" because of his 6'4" and 220-pound physique, Elmer Vasko from Duparquet, Québec, was one of the largest players in professional hockey at the time. Elevated to the Bisons in the final week of the season as they battled Cleveland for third place, Vasko played the team's last four games. Pierre, briefly down with Buffalo, fondly recalled Elmer's signing.

"I didn't know anything about Moose except that he was big. He earned his name well. Anyways, he's just got called up and he's having a shit in our washroom when they barged in on him: 'Here, sign this.' Moose signed his first pro contract sitting on a toilet! I'll never forget it!" Pierre laughed. "There was no big announcement, no negotiation and certainly no photo op. Everybody was yelling, 'What the hell's going on in there?'"

Once Pierre returned to Buffalo for the playoffs, he and Vasko were teamed to make a strong and formidable defensive force.

The Bisons faced the first-place Providence Reds in playoffs, who had All-Stars in goalie Johnny Bower, and wingers Zellio Toppazzini and Camille Henry.

"Zellio was a big, strong skater," Pierre recalled. "He was a real nice player, not rough. Camille Henry was small and thin but he was a master at tip-ins. He could score goals! And of course the China Wall was tough to score on. He was the best in the AHL. We had our hands full going into that series!"

The return of Pierre was trumpeted in the Buffalo papers but the Reds easily won the first game of the series in Providence on March 27 by a 5-1 score. The game was costly for the Bisons as Vasko suffered a deep gash above his left ankle and had to leave the game. The injury was supposed to keep him out of the series indefinitely or "at least two weeks."

In the second game, back in Providence, the game was going the Bisons' way when winger Sam Bettio was viciously speared in the mouth by a Reds defenceman. There was blood everywhere. Bettio was helped from the ice in pure agony and taken to the clinic by GM Fred Hunt and defensive scratch Vic Dzurko. Dzurko, a big, tall, blond kid, was one of the toughest players on the Bisons. Once Sam got to the first aid room, the doctor opened his mouth.

"Apparently, when the doctor opened up Sam's mouth, all 16

of his teeth came out in a pool of blood!" recalled Pierre. "And big tough guy Dzurko fainted right there on the spot! Right out! Imagine getting that many teeth knocked out in one swipe!"

Despite losing Bettio, the Bisons handily beat the Reds 5-1.

Back in Buffalo, Bettio's teammates vowed revenge.

"The dressing rooms in Buffalo were real small," Pierre remembered. "We're all sitting there and in walked Sam Bettio with his mouth massively swollen. He was in bad shape. All the players were looking at him with big eyes. Holy shit! It wasn't pretty. It was the worst thing the coaches could have done—let him come into the dressing room. All the guys became chickenshits that night. Bettio scared the shit out of everybody!"

The suddenly traumatized Bisons went out and lost 8-2 in a Reds romp.

"Al Dewsbury and I, we played well regardless," Pierre recalled. "Bettio's appearance didn't bother us. I played like a son of a bitch. Al was so upset too, he swore, 'Those sons a bitches! Look at that!' But the rest were all chickenshits! Who could blame them."

With the Reds ahead 2-1 in the series, things looked gloomy as injuries to Al Dewsbury and Clare "Rags" Raglan severely depleted the Bisons defence core. Panicking, coach Eddolls asked Moose to try to play and he did. The Bisons regrouped and took it 4-1, with Vasko scoring the first goal of his pro career. After the game, when he removed a blood-soaked bandage from his ankle in front of reporters, Eddolls praised Vasko: "That's what you call the will to win . . . a real effort for the team!"

In Providence for the deciding game, the Reds poured on the offence and smashed the injury-ridden Herd by a 6-3 score to eliminate them. The powerful Reds swept the Cleveland Barons to win the 1956 Calder Cup, outscoring Cleveland 23-8.

An article about Pilote and Vasko in *Blueline* predicted the pair were bound for the Windy City. "They're both ready for the National Hockey League and I'm sure Dick Irvin will be glad to have them in Chicago's lineup next season," said Eddolls.

"I often think of Pierre's play that first season," the coach continued philosophically to Jack Horrigan. "He's come a long way since. He couldn't skate, was always falling down when he tried to get back on defence, and was easy to go around. The only compensating factors were his desire and he handed out a mean bodycheck when he lined up his man."

"Pilote looks like a pug too," the article continued, with the first published description of his features. "His near-pallid skin is drawn tight over a well-boned face. Deep-set eyes almost touch the sides of his broad, slightly askew nose, a full-lipped mouth rounds out the pattern, while a stitched scar cuts a furrow through his right eyebrow, accentuating the ruggedness of the countenance. Pilote's 165 pounds are distributed over a muscular frame. His shoulders are those of a weight lifter, although he prefers manual labour to barbells for off-season conditioning. His chest is deep and legs sturdy!"

"I think they are two of the finest boys I've ever coached," said Pilous in the article. "No one will be happier to see them succeed. Pierre was little more than a rough kid when he came to St. Kitts. Through application, he's improved just about every phase of his game. Vasko has the potential for greatness. He's young and inexperienced."

Regardless of the accolades, hockey was done for another season. With the approaching summer it was back to Sports Services.

Pierre went to Toronto's Woodbine Racetrack, until a newer, identically named Woodbine Racetrack was opened. "That was a hell of a job! I was working hard, handling all of these things, so I went to my boss for a raise."

William Joseph looked at Pilote carefully, and asked, "Pierre, what do you know about running a bar?"

"A bar? Not very much," Pierre answered honestly. "I've never run one before."

"Well, since you don't know much, you'll learn about it then, you'll be the assistant bar manager."

"My job was basically to make sure the bar manager was putting all the money in the till!" Pierre laughed. "In a way, I was the manager. I was writing the cheques, so they gave me the same salary as a manager. Sports Services was really a great place to learn business. Then that summer of 1956, my last hurrah, I was the complete manager of the Fort Erie Racetrack—concessions, restaurant, the whole thing. I was close to home, Annie, and Denise, which was good that way but I didn't seem to make a lot more money."

"That first summer when we had Denise," recalled Annie, "I would pack us a picnic and we'd go down by the waterfront. On days when Pierre couldn't come, he'd drop me and the baby off in the morning and pick us up in the afternoon. Then we would have supper together."

With the summer of '56 nearly over, the familiar letter arrived from Chicago GM Tommy Ivan instructing Pierre to report to training camp in St. Catharines on September 17. As former Teepees, a press picture showed Moose and Pierre were photographed getting dressed at the Garden City Arena amongst 59 other hopefuls. The players soon learned that coach Dick Irvin, diagnosed with bone cancer a few years before, would be too ill to attend. He died of the disease at age 64 on May 15, 1957.

"I seldom had a good training camp, even though this year's, I think, was about my best," Pierre told the *Hockey News* months later. "I usually show up at camp several days behind the others in conditioning. It's because I can't keep in as good physical shape during the off season in my job as concessions manager at Fort Erie Racetrack."

As Ivan, the GM and new coach, assessed his troops it was plain for him to see that Pilote and Vasko were his present and future investment. They would mature and grow to be the cornerstone of a revamped Chicago defence. Pilote may have been a little out of shape but his determination more than made up for it, and besides, Ivan now knew what Pilote could do, he had seen it first-hand. From his experience in Detroit, Ivan knew that a good defence was the key to winning Stanley Cups.

Thomas Nathaniel Ivan was born on January 31, 1911, in Toronto,

Ontario. While playing senior hockey, a fractured cheekbone led into refereeing and then coaching. In the Detroit farm system, he coached in Omaha and Indianapolis through the late 1940s. By 1947, Ivan was appointed coach of the Red Wings, making him the first NHL coach to never have played in the league. He coached Detroit to Stanley Cups in 1950, '52, and '54.

In the process, Ivan witnessed the manner in which Wings GM Jack Adams effectively engineered and built a farm system to supply the big team with budding stars, and he brought this knowledge with him when he moved to Chicago in 1954. Ivan was the brains behind the purchase of the Bisons and Teepees by Hawks owners Arthur Wirtz and Jim Norris.

Despite having finished in last place, Ivan opted to keep the bulwark of last year's team intact. To start the rebuild from the blue line out, he had young Pilote and Vasko.

"Tommy called me into the office," recalled Pierre. "I signed a basic NHL contract. As a rookie, I was just happy to make the team and be getting more money than in the American League. It was a big move. It was basically, 'Here it is, take it or leave it.' I took it! It was just an NHL contract, not a two-way contract like some guys had, so Tommy was pretty sure that I'd be in the NHL.

"A rookie had nothing to gauge his worth in the NHL. The Buffalo years didn't matter. They also made their contract offer during training camp, even to the veterans, as a way to scare them into signing with everyone all trying to make the team, but it was worse for a rookie."

Ivan opted to keep goalie Al Rollins and veterans Ed Litzenberger, Johnny Wilson, and Glen Skov but he traded Wally Hergesheimer to the Leafs in exchange for young Eric Nesterenko, who would strengthen the Hawks franchise.

As training camp broke and Pierre left for Chicago, his success was tinged with temporary sadness as he and Annie had decided that, with her second pregnancy, she would remain home. "In fall 1956, I stayed back in Fort Erie to keep seeing my own family doctor, because I knew it was going to be a big baby," recalled Annie. "There might be complications and I didn't want to deliver with a new doctor at a strange hospital in another country; so little Denise and I would still go to visit Pierre whenever they came into Toronto to play during the season."

For Pierre, the move was not easy. "I had to find a place to stay without a car; I had left it for Annie. I had to concentrate on playing hockey, but a part of me was always worried about how she was, what was going on at home. I knew my parents and family were there to support her, so I knew she was in good hands but, still, I always wondered."

In Chicago, Pierre's first order of business was to find a place to stay. "Right off the bat, I had an apartment with Elmer Vasko and Hank Ciesla at the Château," Pierre related. "The Château had cooking facilities. It was close to the elevated train that we could get onto with a short walk, and then when we got off it, a short 10-minute walk to the rink. It was a good spot for us to live.

"My first impression was that Chicago was big, and had a lot of different nationalities, more than I was used to. I made friends, learned where we were to shop, bank, get clothes cleaned, all the little things in a strange city."

Pierre had other difficulties. "In that first year, my hay fever acted up quite a bit. I couldn't do anything outside. Luckily, when I got on the ice, the hay fever went away. Then I started getting shots for it and my hay fever was much better."

Pierre knew sticking in an NHL lineup was difficult during the six-team era. "I got my chance, but it was tough," he admitted. "You had to carve yourself a job. I played with a lot of enthusiasm. It took me four or five months to finally settle down and play smart hockey in that first year."

Chicago struggled at first with only two wins after the first 14 games; and by the halfway point in the season Chicago was moored firmly in last place, nine points lower than Toronto. Team cohesion and spirit were one problem that the 1956–57 Chicago team had to contend with.

"Our team wasn't close in my first year," Pierre recalled. "We were a few young guys with quite a few older players who went up and down, from Chicago to Buffalo, so it was hard to be close, especially when you didn't win very often."

On January 5, 1956, the Hawks were part of hockey history as they travelled to New York to face the Rangers in the first televised hockey game carried on a U.S. national network. Fans on CBS saw the Rangers win 4-1.

"I remember my friends from Fort Erie were happy that Saturday afternoon because they could watch the game on the Buffalo station," said Pierre. "The fellow that did that the colour commentary—I think his name was Bud. He came in the room to do an interview, to kind of educate the American audience."

The interviewer asked the Hawks players to explain fighting to him. "You know if you're boxing, in the ring, wouldn't you want your gloves on, so it doesn't hurt your hand when you're hitting somebody? Why do you guys all throw your gloves on the ice?"

"Well, to tell you the truth," someone yelled, "it's because we're all looking for a better pair of gloves to keep for the rest of the game!" The team tried hard not to laugh.

Things weren't all dismal for Pierre in his inaugural season as he was featured for the first time in the January 12 edition of the *Hockey News*, dubbed a "Bantam Bouncer" in the headline.

Writer Bud Booth used the anglicized "Pete" for Pierre's nick-name, and heralded Pilote's rough play despite his small size. "In addition to his passing and playmaking talents and the ability to solidly check opponents of all sizes and speeds, Pilote has developed into a very valuable man around the Black Hawk goal," went the article. "His work this year has been a definite aiding factor to the excellence of netminder Al Rollins.

"When burly Lee Fogolin was dispatched westward . . . there

were those who began wondering if Chicago would be able to come up with anyone as fearless in going down in front of pucks bulleted at the Hawks cage. 'Pete' seemed to fall into the spot almost immediately and has had Rollins as one of his appreciators ever since. He professes no fear of going down and . . . he recently blocked three successive shots aimed at the Chicago cage and displayed a bruised forearm to mark one of the deflections. It didn't bother him in the least, however, in view of the result, which saved the hard working Rollins from a dive or sprawl."

With his French background, Pierre seemed "a natural for les Canadiens" but he was too small, continued Booth. "The mistake of this verdict is now painfully accepted every time Pilote skates into an attacking Canuck. . . . The Hawks also have Pierre's younger brother Florent under their wing. . . . Pilotes might conceivably be plummeting Canadiens and all other opponents for the next 15 years. Oh yes, and then there's Pierre's hopes for a son next month."

The Canadiens came into Chicago and Pierre fired the winner in a rare 4-2 victory. Pierre was described as "fast coming into his own."

It was heady stuff for Pierre. "In Chicago we got crowds of 5,000 to 6,000, but when Toronto or Montreal visited, there'd be 12,000, 13,000. There was a lot of excitement."

He knew the Hawks were not a good team. "You know, I remember sitting there, looking around at the talent we had and thinking, 'We aren't going to make the playoffs.' We didn't have the horses. You could tell."

On February 16, the Hawks participated in another American televised game and the results were better this time as Glen Skov's goal with less than three minutes remaining in the game lifted Chicago to a 6-5 victory over Boston.

"Yeah, that game was a funny one," recalled Pierre of the television arrangements. "We didn't get a lot of fans that year in Chicago, so they had all the spectators sit on one side of the arena, opposite to where the cameras were, so the cameras would pan the crowd, to make it look like it was a full house."

"When the team wasn't doing so good, I still thought I was playing good. I just worried about the next game," noted Pierre. "There were guys though who weren't putting out, guys near the end of their careers. We were not making the playoffs. I just wanted to play."

As Pierre readied himself the morning of February 23 to leave the Château to head to the Chicago Stadium for an afternoon game, a phone call from Paul Pilote in Fort Erie elated and concerned him.

"Pierre, you're the proud father of a baby boy!" said his father.

"Is that right? Is everybody okay, the baby and Annie?" Pierre asked.

"Yeah, everybody's okay."

"That's great!"

Relieved, Pierre boarded the train with Moose and Hank to head to the game. The schedule did not permit Pierre to see his new son, Pierre Jr., until the end of the season, which was slowly and mercifully drawing to a close. On March 9, the Stadium witnessed a rollicking game as the Hawks and Canadiens resumed their rivalry. Pierre and goalie Al Rollins were involved in a four-man free-for-all with the Richard brothers. All were given major penalties except the goalie. Montreal won the match 6-4.

"I really got into an argument with Henri, right in the corner," Pierre remembered. "Then the Rocket came in, and then I got into a tussle with him, then Harry Watson came over and took care of the Rocket, not fighting him but took him off me. I could boast afterwards: 'I had a fight with the two Richard brothers!'"

When the dust settled over Chicago's season, the Black Hawks finished last again with only 16 wins. Pierre played in all 70 games and registered three goals and 14 assists while getting 117 minutes in penalties, a far cry from teammate Gus Mortson's 147 minutes in the sin bin.

Ivan surveyed the results and was not happy. With a reliable but ageing goaltender and team, he now had to look to the farm system to inject some new life.

The Teepees had a blond kid named Bobby Hull, who was

blossoming into a goal scorer in his second year. There were also rumblings that Detroit had grown sour on young Glenn Hall, who Ivan knew was a great goalie. Could he somehow get him?

The formation of the NHL Players' Association in February changed the landscape considerably. Ted Lindsay of the Red Wings and Doug Harvey of the Canadiens had spearheaded the organization, and forced the league into action.

The NHL Board of Governors announced they were creating a 5% levy, or special fund, from the net gate receipts to help boost the weak Chicago club. In reality, the funds would be used to combat the player's public battle. The owners also privately agreed that something had to be done about Lindsay and "the troublemakers."

The first domino fell on July 24, 1957, when Detroit's GM, Jack Adams, sent Lindsay, his superstar and second best point getter, and Lindsay's friend, "the young pest" Glenn Hall, to the Hawks. Adams described Lindsay as being "over the hill." At 33, Lindsay had just finished the best scoring season of his career, and he and Hall were First Team All-Stars.

Ivan was beside himself with glee having only given up minor league goalie Hank Bassen, Bill Preston, Forbes Kennedy, and Johnny Wilson. Other teams decimated and weakened their rosters by 25% except the Stanley Cup champions. Keeping their roster completely intact ensured the strong Montreal Canadiens more champagne drinking in the years to come at the expense of a weakened league.

Pierre, who delivered beer in Fort Erie that summer of 1957, knew that winds of change were blowing through every NHL city as the Hawks were sent the league's perceived troublemakers, with rumours of more to come. He knew many players who were banished to the minors for good, and rumours and roster changes seemed to be announced every few days.

As he slogged his beer, Pierre wondered like many: was he about to meet the same fate?

CHAPTER 7

This Could Get Interesting, Chicago!

The reverberations of the Ted Lindsay and Glenn Hall trade to Chicago on July 24 rippled through the league, and Pierre wondered if it could happen to him. When his Chicago training camp invite came in August, he breathed easier.

Tommy Ivan was excited as he watched the first workouts with Lindsay, Hall, and veteran defenceman Jim Thomson, obtained from Toronto. Then there was Robert Marvin Hull, making his third appearance at a Hawks camp after another stellar year with the Junior A Teepees. The 18-year-old left-winger seemed to be ready.

Making his final appearance at Hawks training camp was Florent Pilote. "Flo's training camp unfortunately didn't last very long," recalled big brother Pierre. "He went to check Ted Lindsay in the corner, Ted fell backwards and his skate came up and caught Flo right between the right eye and his nose! Oh boy, I thought he'd lost his eye! There was a lot of blood. I rushed over, I was really worried. Amazingly, our trainer stitched him up. He had to get 15 or 16 stitches. That was the end of his camp though. I felt sorry for him but at least his eye was okay."

The injury ended Flo's season and his Chicago association. He wouldn't play hockey again until the following season when he played a few games with the Indianapolis Chiefs of the IHL, then Senior A in Sudbury, Ontario.

Pierre had some challenges at the camp. "As I looked around in that second year, I saw these guys I had played against who were now with us," recalled Pierre. "There was competition from these guys now and so I went to training camp to give my 100% every time I went on the ice."

During the second week of camp, a message was scrawled on the dressing room blackboard: "Pierre Pilote, see me in my office after practice." He knew it was from Tommy Ivan, as that was often how he communicated. Pierre undressed, showered, and headed to the Queensway Hotel. He knocked on the door of Ivan's temporary office and entered.

They discussed Flo's injury and chitchatted about the summer and family until Ivan got to the point.

"Look Pierre, we want to sign you. You're looking good at camp. You had a good year last year so we're prepared to offer you the same salary this year."

Pierre hesitated, unsure what to say next.

"The same? Look, ah, Tommy, I think I played very well last year. I think I'm entitled to some kind of raise."

"Sorry, Pierre but that's our offer, in light of everything that's going on. You know?"

Pierre nodded at the unspoken nuance—the Players' Association. It was Ivan's silent trump card this year and the fear that it instilled was prevalent throughout the league. The other GMs were probably using the same card. Ivan pushed the offer over towards Pierre where the salary of $6,500, the league's unofficial minimum, was written on a piece of paper in pencil under his pencilled name. Pierre looked at the figure long and hard, then at Ivan, who also had a hard, serious look. Pierre finally reached for the pencil and signed the paper. Ivan stood, smiled, and reached across the table to shake Pierre's hand.

"Thanks, Pierre. Nice doing business with you. The formal

contract will be ready for you to sign when we get to Chicago. I'm looking forward to you having a good year for us again. And remember this is between us."

Pierre nodded and could only smile wanly in partial relief. As he left the office, there were a few other players waiting outside for their turn. They looked at Pierre for a sign of his successful negotiation. He wasn't giving any.

"We never talked about salaries amongst each other, nobody did," he recalled. "This is the amazing thing, we were either ashamed of it or we thought we were making more than the other guy. Sometimes, we were just relieved with Tommy's civility because we'd heard horror stories about Adams in Detroit and especially Muzz Patrick in New York, who used to scream and pound his fists on the table to scare guys into signing."

Amidst the player signings and training camps throughout the league, the owners signed another television deal with CBS to broadcast 21 U.S. games for the coming season. The players would see none of the financial windfall.

"We were only happy that our families could watch us more at home on TV," laughed Pierre. "No kidding. We weren't thinking about the money and who was making it. I was making the most money I had ever made. We all thought that way. We didn't have agents negotiating, getting us more money."

As camp broke, Pierre had to get his family out of his Fort Erie house, which they had rented to a Bisons player for the winter. He'd bought a second-hand, two-door Mercury hardtop for the family's long drive to Chicago. On top of the roof was a large carrier for whatever couldn't fit in the car.

"I had a big brown trunk that Pierre also shipped beforehand from Fort Erie to Chicago by train for some of our heavier stuff," related Anne. "You could put a lot of stuff in those big trunks. We tried not to bring too much because the apartment was fully furnished."

Their first Chicago home was a one-bedroom apartment on Laramie Street. Two-year-old Denise and one-year-old Pierre Jr.

slept in the bedroom while their parents slept every night on the Murphy bed that opened from the living room wall.

"The apartment was small but I was used to small places. Our wartime house in Fort Erie was not very big, but it was certainly bigger than this apartment," recalled Anne. "But there were nice people in the three-storey building, and the landlady was extremely nice and pleasant. It didn't take long to settle in."

The new look Hawks opened the 1957 season at home in fine style on October 8, against Toronto, as new goalie Glenn Hall made 26 saves in a 1-0 win in front of a small but appreciative crowd of 6,000. Lindsay scored the only goal of the game. The latest Hawk sparkplugs were installed and working.

Glenn Henry Hall, born in Humbolt, Saskatchewan, on October 3, 1931, had a quick rise through the ranks of the Detroit Red Wings farm system. Playing net for the Indianapolis Capitals of the AHL, then Edmonton Flyers of the WHL, he was brought up to the NHL permanently in the fall of 1955 to replace the traded Terry Sawchuk. Hall had two eccentricities: his butterfly style that was slowly accepted due to his fine play, and his penchant for throwing up before each game, a habit that became legendary.

"I liked our Detroit captain Ted Lindsay . . . Jack Adams told me not to talk to Ted because of the players' union thing and I told Adams I would talk to whomever I wanted to," Hall remarked. "Jack Adams was everything I disliked in a person. I certainly didn't abide by the rule never to say certain things to the general manager. I'll talk to whomever I want to talk to. Don't be putting any ideas into my head."

When Stanley Cups failed to materialize the last two years, Hall was unfairly blamed by Adams and because of his friendship with Lindsay, the two were sent to Chicago.

Detroit's loss was Chicago's gain. "Glenn Hall's impact was immediate," remembered Pierre. "He was young, energetic, and good! He had a swagger-like confidence. You could tell he wanted to be number one."

Ted Lindsay, born in Renfrew, Ontario, on July 29, 1929, grew up playing hockey in Kirkland Lake. At 5'8" and 165 pounds, he was not a big man but he was fearless, a trait that held him in good stead as captain of the Red Wings and in forming the Players' Association. Having won the NHL scoring title in 1947-48, last year's output of 85 points was his best ever and only four shy of league leader Gordie Howe.

At the apartment, Anne was adjusting to the city and her new surroundings. "I was really scared at first in Chicago," she said. "I'd heard about the crime, the mobsters, Al Capone and stuff. Whenever I took the kids out, I kept them real close to me. We would walk to a nearby schoolyard. The yard had a big gated fence so I felt safe.

"In our first few weeks in Chicago, Pierre had to catch a flight out of the airport. He drove to the airport and I remember trying to watch and landmark the route, you know, so I could find my way back without him. I was so nervous, my first real drive in this big, strange city! I managed to get the kids and I home, and after that I was never nervous driving around again.

"Once settled, I liked Chicago a lot. We got a good babysitter named JoAnn Curphey, whom Pierre had met at his laundromat the year before so we could go out or I could attend games. Ian Cusheman, a defenceman with Pierre on the Hawks, used to come over often with his wife, Jean. Bobby Hull used to come over for a few meals and ride with Pierre to the rink. He was a nice, pleasant young fella."

In Pierre, rookie Hull had a natural friend, leader, and teacher. "Pierre knew me as a rookie in training camp in St. Catharines, and I had met him and the family through his brother Florent, who had been a teammate of mine," Hull recalled. "Litzenberger may have been the captain when I arrived, but Pierre was the big cheese in '57. He and I hit it off from the very beginning. I enjoyed my rookie year with Pierre because he was so candid in explaining the game and showing me what it was all about, and living life. Things would come up and we'd chat about it. Most of all, Pierre was a guy who came to play every flippin' game! You could always count on him. He had grit, tenacity, and wanted to be the best on the ice. I liked him for that."

On October 19 the Hawks travelled to the Forum to face the Canadiens. In the third period, Maurice Richard was fed a pass in the high slot from Jean Béliveau and fired it in the net for the 500th goal of his career, making him the first ever to attain the milestone. Bedlam ensued as the all-time goal-scoring leader was mobbed by his teammates and triumphantly skated around the rink to the roar and adulation of the 14,000 fans present and in his province.

"The night the Rocket got his 500th, I was on the ice!" recalled Pierre. "It was historic, like it or not, and an honour to have been there, really. When he scored, the atmosphere was like a game-winning overtime goal. Everything stopped for five minutes. Wasn't much we could do about it but sit on our bench and take it all in. We were part of history. We didn't congratulate him, I can tell you that, but we admired him, a great feat that Glenn Hall was definitely on the ice for too!"

Pierre roomed with Vasko. "When we checked into a room, Moose always walked in first, looked at the bed and turned on the TV," remembered Pierre. "If it had clear stations, then we stayed in that room; if it didn't, we went to another room. And thank goodness the big guy didn't snore! We liked each other, respected each other's habits. We'd play crib to relax and bet—I always made sandwich money off Elmer. We seldom talked hockey, usually what was happening in the world, you know. He was quiet, the perfect roommate, and the perfect defence partner on the ice. We shared the same birthday too—December 11."

On October 28, *Sports Illustrated* published a hard-hitting article by writer Dan Parker that highlighted the NHL Players' Association fight and exposed the owners' shady ways. The story gave a complete history of the owners' monopoly down through the years and was not favourable to them in the least. It certainly buoyed the mood of the players and their representatives, and highlighted the fact that the NHL was skating on thin ice.

Despite the new additions, a team is not turned around overnight. Through November, the team sputtered, registering only three wins, and the fans' waning support showed.

"I remember sitting there some nights, tears just rolling down my cheeks," recalled Annie. "The arena was empty and I felt so bad for the players who were playing their hearts out on the ice with no fans to cheer them on! We made as much noise as we could, but it was tough to be there and watch some nights."

The crowds did sporadically show up. On November 10, 15,400 packed the Chicago Stadium to see the Hawks spread their wings as Pilote, Vasko, and Hull scored goals in a rare 3-1 win over Toronto. A week later, Vasko showed that he could motor when he scored the winning goal in Detroit.

"Oh, big no. 4! Moose was a Tower of Power!" Pierre laughed. "Elmer usually stayed back and I was all over the place. It was a perfect match. Moose was my back-up for sure, but when the Moose wanted to take off with the puck and get up a head of steam, look out, the freight train was coming! Everyone loved it!"

In the league basement after a 7-2 loss to Toronto on December 1, Lindsay tried to make them a stronger unit. "In that first year Ted Lindsay tried to get more togetherness with the hockey team," related Pierre. "We would go bowling and we often went to a place like Eddie's Bar."

"Eddie's Bar was just an ordinary restaurant and bar," recalled Annie. "But we'd get there, with the other wives and our friends, in the back room, and have our own little party. Sometimes we went to the Cottage, which was a pretty classy place downtown. This is how I got to know some of the players and their wives, which was important. I grew to really like Doreen Litzenberger and Pauleen Hall."

It soon became apparent that support for the trust suit amongst other players, especially in Detroit, was getting shaky. Lindsay's old teammates, no doubt harassed by Adams, informed him that fall that they were dropping their support.

"We were the last in the Association to hear any details," remembered Detroit's Marcel Pronovost. "We were not totally convinced of all the facts, so Red Kelly got us our own lawyer who contacted the Association's lawyer, but he wouldn't give us the information we wanted to know. We wanted more information, but it was too late in coming."

"The Red Wings withdrawal certainly didn't help our cause," Lindsay commented.

In later years, both Kelly and Howe stated that the option of a player's strike is what drove them to part with the Association. The other players in the league were furious at Howe, Kelly, and the Wings.

"I remember going into Detroit for a game right after that and all of us being so mad at them!" recalled Pierre. "I saw Red Kelly on the ice and I really wanted to hit him, a little harder than normally! Oh I was mad!"

The saga was not done.

With his team in the cellar, Ivan sent Hector Lalonde, Jack McIntyre, Bob Bailey, and Nick Mickoski to Detroit in exchange for Bill Dineen, Billy Dea, Lorne Ferguson, and Earl Reibel.

"The trade that Christmas of '57 was really just an exchange of players, about the same calibre. We didn't pick up an Alex Delvecchio, I can tell you that," said Pierre. "It was just to kind of shake up the club, scare people a little bit. It made you step up a little bit."

The Hawks picked up five points in their next three games, which included a 2-1 home victory on December 29 against the Leafs, where they skated like demons and checked relentlessly at both ends of the ice. Though he didn't figure in the goals, Pierre's growing defensive abilities were singled out after the victory.

"The real hero of the night was Pierre Pilote," stated the *Chicago Tribune*. "Pete enjoyed the biggest night of his career during these 60 minutes. Goalie Hall was credited with 21 stops, with only three in the final period. Pilote made almost that many by himself, halting hot Leaf blasts with his knees, elbows, middle and, one time, almost with his noggin, a headlong dive that thwarted the bright Brian Cullen.

"Pete's performance reached peak level in the early minutes of the second period when the Hawks were left two hands shy, almost simultaneously. Thus only three Hawks were left to protect Hall (Skov, Thomson, and Pilote). Pete took over like he was a combination of such Chicago rear guards as Lionel Conacher, Taffy Abel, Earl Siebert, and Johnny Mariucci."

With seven assists, Pierre finally got his first goal on December 31 in a 3-2 loss to Detroit.

Ivan shook things up further by stepping down as coach and bringing in Rudy Pilous from St. Catharines.

It worked, especially for Pierre. "I instantly felt good when Rudy came on board. He was the guy that scouted me, was always in my corner. Rudy worked the summer at the Fort Erie Racetrack and so I saw him quite a few times. We were very friendly."

With Pilous at the helm a few days into the New Year, Pierre and the Hawks responded with a 4-2 win over Toronto and a 4-3 win over the Bruins. His old coach seemed a tonic for Pierre. Things were looking up, that was until their next visit to Montreal on January 9, where 12 Habs made the scoresheet in an 11-3 win.

The humbled Hawks travelled to Detroit on January 11, where Gus Mortson sent Howe to hospital with a vicious check that reinjured no. 9's shoulder. Still, the Hawks lost 4-1. Pierre picked up an assist on Glen Skov's goal.

Chicago then beat the Canadiens 7-1 in Montreal's worst defeat in three years. It somewhat avenged the drubbing the Habs had inflicted on them a few days before. A picture in the *Tribune* showed Pierre going down to block a Donnie Marshall shot. Chicago fans were starting to appreciate Pierre's defensive work.

The arena was a big part of playing in Chicago. Big and cavernous, Chicago Stadium was completed on March 28, 1929.

Modelled after the Detroit Olympia, and situated at 1800 West Madison Street, bordering Wood, Warren, and Wolcott streets, it was the largest arena of its kind when it first opened at a cost of $9.5 million. The imposingly large, grey structure filled a city block and was a hockey cathedral.

The Stadium could accommodate 15,000 fans at the time of its opening, but this number illegally swelled during playoff games—in the odd years there were some. Yet after 35 games, there had been a dismal 140,000 less fans than at the same time the year before. To those loyal fans, who occupied the three tiers of seats—with the highest seemingly overhanging the ice surface—the arena was home, with its own familiar and unique eccentricities.

The 3,663 pipes of the Barton organ played throughout the game, and two features made the arena the stuff of legends—the steps leading down to the dressing rooms and the centre-ice clock. The dressing rooms in the arena were located under the seats in the basement, so the only way to and from the ice surface was down a series of 22 steps.

"Up and down, there were a lot of steps, cement steps covered by rubber matting," Pierre said. "The whole stadium was cement. The other team had 22 steps on the other side as well. In the dressing room, we could not hear anybody or anything. It took getting used to, but soon it was old hat and familiar. It was one of the things that made our home unique, along with that infamous clock!"

Other arenas in the league had similar four-sided Bulova scoreboards but Chicago's was unique and confusing. Installed in the Stadium in 1943, its large analog dial anchored each side of the four-sided scoreboard over smaller clocks that kept track of penalties.

"The old clock was hard to read and sometimes even we couldn't figure it out. I got to know the official in the penalty box, Chris Everest, because I was in there a lot. We'd golf together. During the game, he'd be reading the *Hockey News*, but he knew just when it was time to open the door and away I'd go. The old clock didn't usually affect us, but the opposition and their coach didn't like it. An advantage for us? Sometimes near the end of a game!"

It was also ironic that such an expensive Stadium was surrounded by one of the worst slums in the city. "Around the stadium was run down, subsidized housing," recalled Pierre. "There were some good neighbourhoods, a Polish section where I used to go to church, but black unemployment was prevalent around there, an unfair situation for them really, and eventually their good homes became run down. These coloured folks certainly had a tougher time making ends meet, and at that time, it was not a nice place to live. It was not Chicago nor America at its best."

On the ice, subsequent wins against Detroit and Toronto had Pilous giddy.

"Why shouldn't I smile," the GM told reporter Bud Booth. "We've got the makings of a great team here. The players are high-spirited and they're young."

In the weeks since his old coach had joined the Hawks, Pierre was on fire. "Little Pete Pilote has been roaring along on the hottest scoring and point-getting spree of any Black Hawk to date this season and may still be continuing," Booth wrote. "It is a streak that started with 1958 and found the Chicago rearguard averaging better than a point per game . . . he had moved into the scoring lead among Hawk defencemen and was ahead of several regular forwards as well with an admirable five goals and six assists in 10 games. . . . he has also shone brightly all season on the defensive side to earn a rating as the steadiest performer out front of goaler Glenn Hall . . . he doesn't hesitate to check the biggest of aggressive opponents . . . his particular value however is most apparent when he goes down to block shots before they ever get to the Chicago net." The Hawks won five out of nine games in that time span.

"I guess I stepped it up," said Pierre. "During my hot streak I was pretty well doing everything on the power play. Bobby [Hull] was starting to score then and he was put on the power play as well.

He and I had this give-and-go play almost from the start, that's how he liked to play. We could read each other perfectly."

The Chicago season trudged along as Hall registered his seventh shutout of the campaign in the Hawks 20th win, a 4-0 whitewashing of the Habs at the Stadium. "Mr. Goalie" was having a great season, despite the team's standings.

On March 8, Pierre appeared in a television interview where he talked about the team, his play, and heaped praise on his old Buffalo coach Frank Eddolls for having taught him the defensive aspects of the game. Eddolls must have been watching because a week later, Pierre received a letter from the Bisons hockey club.

"Dear Pierre, please accept my congratulations on your fine TV interview . . . and also my sincerest thanks for the kind words you said about me. Naturally, it gives me a great personal satisfaction to hear a former player of mine pay me such a tribute. Let me assure you the small part I had in your success was a pleasure indeed," wrote Eddolls.

"The hard work you have put into hockey has started to pay rich dividends. I only hope you will keep this up as you are only a year away from becoming an All-Star defenceman in the National Hockey League. This is the goal I would like to see you reach, so keep up the hard work! Kindest personal regards . . . Frank."

As the season wound down, a three-game winning streak lifted the Hawks out of the basement. They finished two points above Toronto, but still out of the playoffs.

"In the years we never made the playoffs, we seemed to always finish the season in Boston or New York," recalled Pierre. "Then we'd have to take the long train ride back. Some guys had already packed their bags and headed home right from there, not going back to Chicago. That always seemed to be the longest train ride of the year, back home after not having made the playoffs—again!"

But for the Hawks, things were moving in the right direction. Though they lost 39 games—the same number as the year before—they had tied eight fewer games and had put those into the win column. It was apparent the Hawks were protecting a lead better. The best statistic was the 23 fewer goals the team had allowed over the season, thanks to Hall and the defence.

Ivan was pleased with the new players.

Eric Paul Nesterenko was born in Flin Flon, Manitoba, on October 31, 1933. Acquired from the Leafs, Nesterenko had developed into a defensive forward, while still garnering 38 points in 70 games, and had finished fourth in team scoring. The 6'2", 197-pound Nesterenko could check at both ends of the ice, using his height and elbows to full advantage, especially in the corners.

"Eric was a complete player," Pierre remembered. "He was a real thinker, an intellectual. Bobby and I were intensely competitive but Eric never gave you that impression. He was easy-going. But oh, he could check the big guys, and could he skate!"

Ed Litzenberger had been traded from Montreal to Chicago in the 1954-55 season. As Chicago's scoring leader for the second year in a row, he had accumulated 62 points. Born in Neudorf, Saskatchewan, the 6'2", gentlemanly, and highly respected right-winger was one of the team's guiding lights in a year where there had been no official captain.

"Ed Litzenberger was a leader. He talked it up in the room and he delivered," Pierre observed. "He was not a smooth skater. He had long, choppy strides, but he had a hard, low shot that could pick the corners. He scored us a lot of goals in those early years."

Bobby Hull, not yet known as "The Golden Jet," finished the season with an impressive 13 goals and 47 points, but was edged out of winning the Calder Trophy as the rookie of the year by Frank Mahovlich of the Leafs, who had 11 fewer points. Hawks supporters cried foul at the snub.

"Bobby losing the Calder Trophy was a Toronto public-relations job number one," complained Pierre. "Toronto and Montreal were the centre of the hockey world and publicity. Bobby didn't get the exposure and publicity. Our public relations department in Chicago at that time was not the best. Bobby was a strong guy, a great guy, a lot of fun, always had a smile, right from the beginning. He was a very confident rookie and had a strong first year.

"But hey, Frank Mahovlich was a great hockey player too! On a better club, he might have looked more impressive. He was a big, lanky guy. I don't think Bobby really cared. The choice took place after the season and we'd all gone home."

Though Lindsay's points fell off drastically with 38, his leadership both with the Hawks and with the Players' Association could not be overstated.

"In Ted's first year with us, he had the chances but missed a lot of goals," recalled Pierre. "He had a lot on his mind with the Players' Association fight and his family back in Detroit. He used to drive back and forth. He had pressure and for goal scorers to be successful, they had to relax. Ted's numbers went down but it was understandable. He was at the centre of the storm. And besides, he's not playing with a top notch club anymore."

Hall played in all 70 games and his exciting butterfly style attracted rave reviews. His excellent 2.89 goals against average helped too, despite being outshot in most games. This later fact vaulted him to the First All-Star team ahead of Montreal's Jacques Plante, whose team captured their third straight Stanley Cup.

Pierre also played in all 70 games, with 30 points to place sixth in Hawk scoring, and his penalty minute total was 91, third on the team behind Lindsay and Nesterenko. But most importantly, it was the accolades he was starting to receive for his defensive work in front of Hall that were starting to make the rest of the league take notice.

As Pierre looked back on the 1957-58 season, the first one in Chicago with Annie in their rented apartment with two kids, he was extremely pleased with how it had gone and how she made his home life as stress free as possible.

"Annie was no. 1 for being behind me, which was a big thing," admitted Pierre. "Taking care of the kids, she was a pro at being the wife of a career hockey player. Like the old saying goes: 'She was not in front of me, she was behind me, pushing.' For me hockey was extremely mental and Annie enabled me to always be in that right frame of mind. She made sure from that everything ran smoothly at home."

And on the ice, his team was also getting smoother. "We still didn't make the playoffs," recalled Pierre. "I looked at the other teams and I looked at the guys on our team, and I thought, 'If this or that guy made our club, then we're not good enough. Not yet!'

"I'd been in the AHL and now the NHL and I came to the conclusion that making the playoffs and playoff success boiled down to the strength of the third line. Everybody had a good first and second line but the third line determined the strength and depth of a team. If they're weaker, the team was weaker. If you put a weak player on a strong line, it weakens the line. In the first few years you could tell, we were weaker—but we were getting better! We had a strong core and with a little bit more maturing and a bit more tinkering, I thought, 'Yeah, this could get interesting, Chicago!'"

The Son Rises in Chicago

In summer 1958, Tommy Ivan and Rudy Pilous knew they had a fabulous goaltender in Glenn Hall, and a great defensive tandem in Pierre Pilote and Moose Vasko. But any successful team had to have more than one solid defensive unit so Ivan acquired Dollard St. Laurent from Montreal, Jack Evans from New York, and Al Arbour from Detroit.

Looking to spruce up his offence, Ivan got Earl Balfour and Tod Sloan from Toronto. They helped Ed Litzenberger, Bobby Hull, Ted Lindsay, Eric Nesterenko, and Glen Skov incite some offensive spark. Pierre's growing ability to move the puck up, thus creating a lot more Hawk chances in the opponent's end, was an unexpected bonus. With Pierre's career-high 30 points the previous year, Ivan was counting on him again.

As training camp opened on September 15 within the familiar confines of the St. Catharines Arena, a newfound optimism was evident.

Arbour thought that Lady Luck had finally shined on him. "I was glad to get out of Detroit," recalled Arbour. "Chicago hadn't won in years, but they were getting good players. I could see that Pierre was there; Moose Vasko, Ted Lindsay, Glenn Hall had been sent there. I thought, 'We've got the makings of a good team.'"

When it was time for contract negotiations, Arbour felt like he was still back in Motor City. "Tommy Ivan learned a lot from Jack Adams in Detroit," Arbour continued. "Tommy called me in and was talking . . . he had papers and books strewn all over his desk and I wondered, 'What's he looking at? What's he reading?' When Tommy left the room momentarily, I got up and I looked at all the books and they were blank, nothing in them! 'What the hell?' I thought. In the end, he offered me a $200 raise. That's the way it was in those days. You wouldn't dare say anything."

Alger Joseph Arbour was born in Sudbury, Ontario, on November 1, 1932. The 6' defenceman learned his trade with the junior Spitfires in Windsor alongside Hall. One of the few players to ever wear glasses while playing, "Radar" became especially adept at blocking shots. Having played in four partial seasons for the Red Wings, Arbour had played every game last season before Adams angrily shipped him to the Edmonton Flyers of the Western Hockey League. Left unprotected, Chicago gladly picked him up.

Adams and other owners boasted of sending Chicago their players "to help their poor cousins out of the cellar," but there is no doubt that it was also meant as punishment. With Lindsay, Hall, and now Arbour, the Hawks gained at Detroit's expense.

"That's not the sign of a good hockey man," recalled Lindsay of Adams's stupid moves. "Jack Adams weakened his team out of spite. He lost all his perspective. Montreal certainly didn't weaken their team. Jack's vengeful moves, like the other owners', would only help Montreal's future Stanley Cups."

As the Hawks broke camp, another piece of the puzzle fell into place with the addition of speedy junior star, Kenny Wharram.

Kenneth Malcolm Wharram was born on July 2, 1933, in Ferris, Ontario, near North Bay. Having played for the North Bay Black Hawks of the Eastern Canada Senior Hockey League and then Junior A for the Galt Black Hawks, he joined the AHL Buffalo Bisons in fall 1954. His speed and improved puck handling ability ensured he would finally stay with the big club.

"Kenny had come up three times before but didn't play with

the right players," recalled Pierre of Wharram's earlier promotions. "Kenny was one guy who could really backcheck. He had a lot of speed and big forearms like Popeye. He didn't weigh much, maybe 160 or so, but he could keep up with any opposition player. He was an all-around great addition."

The Pilote home this season was a larger apartment in the same building where they had rented the year prior. "The kids still slept in one bedroom, which was a little bigger and we still slept on the Murphy bed in the living room," noted Annie. "To tell you the truth, I found it very comfortable. Murphy beds were the thing back then. It was a way to make a one-bedroom apartment into two."

As the season began, Litzenberger was named the team's captain. Assistant captains were Ron Murphy and Pilote.

"Ed Litzenberger was a real talker in the room, a leader, and he delivered his 30 goals a season," recalled Pierre. "He had long legs and a choppy stride but he was fast."

Ten thousand fans showed up at the Stadium for the October 8 home opener, a 1-1 tie with New York. In the closing minutes of the opening period, Pierre took matters into his own hands and scored the first goal of the season and the only Hawks goal of the game. Three nights later, Sloan enacted some sweet revenge against his old team when he scored twice in Maple Leaf Gardens in a 3-1 Hawks victory.

"Tod Sloan was a good player, a quiet guy, a good addition to the team," recalled Pierre. "Tod, Ron Murphy, and Earl Balfour all stayed in the same apartment building and they used to ride together in Tod's old car. The floor was rusted through and it often wouldn't start. There was always a problem with that old car. Oh, we really teased him!"

When the Hawks then defeated the Leafs at home and the Red Wings at the Olympia, heads were turning—was it all for real? It wasn't. Chicago came down to earth with a thud, losing games to Detroit and then Boston before travelling to Montreal for an October 23 game at the Forum.

"Montreal Canadiens are boss once more in the NHL," went the Canadian Press story. "There's little question after the 9-1 pasting they gave Chicago Black Hawks Thursday night. Hawks looked like the team that wanted a share of first place with Canadiens for just one period, holding the score to a 1-1 tie; then they fell apart. Their offence stumbled, their defence collapsed, and goalie Glenn Hall was hopelessly outnumbered."

"That was a shellacking in Montreal! Oh boy!" recalled Pierre. "I didn't play well. None of us did. A very angry Tommy Ivan came into the dressing room afterwards and fined us all $100 for 'indifferent play.' It's the only time we ever got fined. He was not happy. Neither were we." The fine didn't seem to have much effect on the team as Chicago next got pasted 6-2 in New York.

The Hawks were sputtering and things weren't looking any better when the cocky Canadiens returned to the Stadium five nights after the Forum slaughter. The Hawks were losing 5-2 with only six minutes remaining, and boos rained down from the upper galleries. The abuse worked as the Hawks suddenly came to life, and they clawed their way back to make the score 5-4 with just enough time remaining to make the end interesting. The overconfident Canadiens were reeling and the Hawks pressing when Hull netted the tying goal. The tie ended their four-game losing streak. It was like a victory.

Through November Chicago played better than .500 hockey before heading to Toronto for a Saturday night game on the 29th where they faced Toronto GM Punch Imlach in his first game behind the Leafs bench after he had fired coach Billy Reay. With just over a minute and a half to go in the game, Pierre rushed into the Toronto end and spoiled Imlach's debut by firing a 20-footer behind Leafs goalie Johnny Bower for a hard-fought 2-1 Hawks victory. Outshot 26-14, the win moved Chicago within a point of fourth-place New York.

When the Hawks tied the Leafs 2-2 at the Stadium on December 10, the crowds were still sparse. Attendance had slipped, with 4,000 fewer patrons at the same point as the year before. The team was clearly not generating a lot of fan excitement in Chicago—yet.

When they lost 4-2 in Boston on Christmas Day of 1958, Pierre and company only had 11 wins in 32 games. Things were dismal.

Rebounding with two ties and two wins in their next four, things seemed to be looking up. Sloan, laid up with a knee injury, saw positives. "These guys can be the best team in the league . . . except for Montreal," he told Toronto writer Jim Proudfoot. "Any time they're at full strength and they all feel like playing, they can beat anybody by five goals—except Montreal. No kidding! I'm sold on this club! It's got everything—an All-Star goalie in Glenn Hall, an All-Star defenceman in Pierre Pilote, and two good, solid forward lines. I think we'll be real tough from here in."

Six more victories lifted them in the standings. Nobody was more pleased than Pilous, whose job security was shaky in his first full year behind the bench.

Pierre attributed the team's improvement to a newcomer. "Dollard St. Laurent was the type of guy who liked to get together: 'Where are we going tonight? What are we doing?' Dollard was always happy-go-lucky and when he'd host the team, everyone showed up. He was a natural talker, friendly with everybody. He brought the team closer together. His wife, Jessie, was very sociable and nice too. Dollard built team spirit."

Pierre was gaining in notoriety. Marcel Bourassa wrote an extensive piece on him in *Le Soleil* and described for the first time his Kénogami roots, his growing up in Québec, his move to Fort Erie, and his ascent in the hockey world.

A few days, later, another French column called "Le Soleil au Saguenay" (Sun on the Saguenay) described a campaign from the Kénogami-Saguenay region to "officially" celebrate Pierre's career in a ceremony planned for the March 14 Chicago-Montreal game at the Montreal Forum. Seems odd today, but the Forum and the Canadiens were accustomed to the occasional public celebration of Québec-born players on other teams.

In thumping the Rangers, 7-1, on January 18, Pierre notched his 18th assist of the campaign on a goal by Balfour. The win increased Chicago's second-place lead over New York to three until a three-game losing streak by the Hawks saw them tied again. Back at Madison Square Garden 10 days later, Pierre got a goal and an assist in a 3-1 victory that edged them back in second place again.

"It is the proof of the pudding that this club isn't going to fade," Pilous vowed. "Winning that game proves that our players can see the edge of the forest! After losing three straight, it shows they have the thoroughbred's heart to win, the desire. They played inspired hockey. They have the winning complex."

When the mid-season All-Star teams were announced a few days later, Hawks fans were crying foul when Pierre was left off it. "Chicago fans are still at a loss to figure out why Pilote, now 27 . . . was neglected in the first half selections for he has been among the top three rearguard scorers right from the start of the season," wrote Bud Booth.

After tying the Canadiens in Montreal one Saturday night, the two teams took the all-night train to Chicago for the next day's return match. In the late '50s, train travel was still prevalent for the NHL. Teams often took the same train but stayed in separate passenger cars and ate in the dining car at separate times.

"Teams didn't mix at all in those days," recalled Arbour. "We couldn't talk to anyone. . . . We would walk on one side of the street, they would walk on the other!"

"When we got on the train, we would be assigned a porter, a person who served us drinks or food, if we needed something," related Pierre. "Sometimes we got very friendly porters, sometimes real grumpy ones. When we got off the train, the porter would be at the bottom of the stairs, with a stool for us to step onto the platform and he would stand there with his hand out, waiting for his tip. In those days, it was customary to tip a good porter fifty cents, but if the porter was bad or rude, we'd tip him 'a Chinese half'—a quarter and a nickel! Many a porter got the latter!

"What I recall most about travelling on the trains was I always looked forward to going into the dining car to eat. You know the train would be going clickety-clack, swaying from side to side, but the coloured waiters could really balance their trays of drinks and food, go with the train you know. They were amazing and the tables had cloths. The meal was fancy and it was always good. And we would get a food allowance of twelve bucks instead of 10. Things cost more on the train."

On February 1, the Stadium was packed with 16,988 fans, the largest home crowd since 1949. The Hawks didn't disappoint their growing faithful as they battled the Stanley Cup Champion Canadiens to a 3-3 draw.

Four nights later in a packed, raucous Boston Garden, Bruins rookie Gordon Redahl scored what appeared to be the go-ahead goal on Hall, but referee Dalton MacArthur signalled otherwise to send the crowd into a frenzy. The score remained tied at a goal apiece until a few minutes later when Pierre carried the puck over centre ice.

"It took one of the craziest shots the National Hockey League has seen since Rocket Richard was a peewee . . . Chicago defenceman Pierre Pilote uncorked his 11th goal of the season, a shot he may not duplicate if he plays until he draws old-age pension," read the Canadian Press story. The puck bounced crazily off the corner boards towards the Boston net and, before goalie Don Simmons could react, went through him into the Bruins cage. The Hawks won 2-1, which kept them tied with the Rangers for second place.

On February 18, the Hawks beat New York again by a 4-2 score with Pierre notching his 25th assist of the season in grand style as he carried the puck into the Ranger zone and stickhandled the puck for a full minute before feeding a pass to Sloan, who fired in the insurance marker. A few nights later in Toronto, Pilote and Litzenberger helped Lindsay score one of his three goals of the night in what was described by the Chicago press as one of the best plays of the season and helped the Hawks win 5-1.

In a letter dated March 6, 1959, Pierre's upcoming tribute was confirmed. "My dear Pierre," the letter began from the "Pierre Pilote Night" Organization. "You are undoubtedly aware that a group of your admirers from the towns of Jonquière and Kénogami are organizing a demonstration of esteem that will take place during the Chicago-Canadiens game next Saturday, March 14, at the Montreal Forum. This has been made possible thanks to your manager Mr. Ivan and that of the Forum, Mr. Frank Selke. This demonstration of our esteem should be interpreted as a measure of admiration on behalf of the sportsmen of our two towns who rejoice in your success."

The event was organized by Dr. Ernest Marchand, the very man who had delivered Pierre screaming into the world in 1931. The recognition campaign kicked off during a February junior game between the Saguenay Sagueneens and the Lions from Trois-Rivières. The doctor put up the first $25 and over 500 supporters bought Pierre Pilote ribbons. The bursary grew.

On March 14, a large contingent of family, friends, and admirers from Jonquière-Kénogami made its way on an overnight train to Montreal for the celebration. Pierre was feted at an afternoon reception at the Queen's Hotel, attended by his parents, his 75-year-old grandfather Albert Pilote, aunts, uncles, and other family, as well as residents of his home region.

"I remember walking into the room and there was a great cheer," recalled Pierre. "It was nice, really. There were a lot of people. There were some schoolmates there, Rodé Coulombe was there, but of course, we were all grown up and looked so different, but it was nice."

Pierre gave a speech in French, and when he finished, the crowd cheered again.

Prior to the start of the third period, a ceremony took place at centre ice. Pierre, his father standing proudly beside him, was presented with a $250 bursary in his honour by Dr. Marchand. Pierre's durability was noted as well: "Pierre has not missed a single game since his debut in the NHL, and as he nears the end of the present regular season, he will have played his 230th game in a row with the Hawks."

"He possesses three grand qualities: ardour, determination, and enthusiasm," the *Jonquière-Kénogami Reveil* newspaper reported. "He doesn't have the reputation of a Harvey or a Johnson but he is already recognized as an ace. He will be victim to injustice if he is not chosen for one of the All-Star teams at the end of the season!"

The Canadiens were not very good hosts that night, delivering an 8-4 drubbing. The loss also sent Chicago on a four-game losing streak that was only curtailed in the last game of the regular season, a 4-1 victory in Boston that helped them stay in third place.

Pierre had again played in all 70 games, which kept his playing streak intact while garnering 37 points and 79 minutes in penalties on the season, still far behind the scrappy "Terrible Ted" Lindsay, who earned 184 minutes in the sin bin.

"In my first few years in Chicago, nobody ever told me to stop my aggressive play, to stop getting penalties," said Pilote. "You had to be aggressive on defence. When these guys came at you, you had to take them out. Most guys who made it to the NHL got penalties. Penalties were a natural thing."

The Hawks were in the playoffs for the first time in six years and, as their reward, they had to face the first-place Canadiens, who had finished 19 points ahead of them. Montreal was listed as 5-1 favourites despite Rocket Richard being sidelined with an ankle injury. Still, Habs coach Toe Blake had his team watch films of their previous Stanley Cup win as a reminder of what it would take to do it again.

"Toe Blake had to win," recalled former Habs defenceman Dollard St. Laurent. "In Montreal, that was the motto. On the ice, you have got to win the game!"

A phone call from New York general manager Muzz Patrick caught Pierre completely off guard as he looked forward to his first postseason play in the NHL.

"Pierre?" Muzz said. "How would you like to come to Europe with the Rangers at the end of the playoffs?"

"Rangers? Europe?"

"Yeah! We're heading to Europe after the playoffs to play a series of 23 exhibition games in 30 days against the Bruins. A few of our guys can't make it. You'll be getting $1,000. We could sure use your help. I've cleared it with Ivan. Interested?"

"Yeah sure!" Pierre answered enthusiastically.

But the playoffs were his first priority.

Heading into the series, a reporter asked Pilous what his strategy was going to be against the Canadiens. He answered right away, laughing: "Beer on the bench, rubber sticks, and no back-checking!" Perhaps it was his way of alleviating the stress of the impending Herculean task before his team.

"Rudy Pilous was a real character, a real talkative guy," recalled Arbour of his coach's attitude on the bench. "He didn't know what was going on in the game sometimes. The guys would change by themselves, because he would be arguing with the fans behind the bench, but that was Rudy. Still, he was a good coach though."

Pilous wasn't the only one to have difficulty with fans, so Chicago made a move to protect opposing players.

"The penalty box in Chicago was completely enclosed by a wire screen," noted an article in the *Hockey News*. "It was completed just prior to the start of the playoffs and is a very progressive move. It would be nice to see the penalty boxes enclosed in some fashion in every rink."

Prior to the series' opening games in Montreal, the Hawks brain trust decided on three courses of action to help them gain an advantage over the Canadiens. For the first time in their history, they chartered a plane to take them to and from Montreal. The cut in travel time didn't help in the opener, nor did the two goals scored by Sloan, as the Canadiens outshot the Hawks 46-13 on their way to a decisive 4-2 win. The score would have been even more lopsided had it not been for Hall. "Their goaltender was real hot," admitted Toe Blake.

The second idea was to fly the wives and friends in to Montreal just in time for the second game as extra incentive for the players. The third idea was that after the first game in Montreal, the Hawks retreated to a secluded hideaway in the Laurentian mountains north of the city. There, Pilous handed out miniature Stanley Cups to motivate his team. For Pierre, the next turn of events must have been déja-vu from his junior days with Rudy. This time, a terrible thing happened on the way to the Forum.

"First of all, we're ready to go and we're waiting, waiting, and waiting for Rudy Pilous to get on the bus," Pierre recalled. "We finally get going and then we get caught in hectic Montreal traffic. We are stuck, dead stop! It was stressful!"

The Hawks arrived so late they had to forgo the normal pre-game skate, which was disastrous.

"We weren't ready at all! The game wasn't 15 seconds old," remembered Pierre. "They had, for some unknown reason, a warm, unfrozen puck to begin the game. I got the puck, and passed it to Kenny Wharram. He went to carry it up ice but the puck stuck to the ice. He skated right by it. Montreal scooted in, picked it up, went in, and scored! After everything we'd just gone through, it was a hell of a way to start the game!"

Before the Hawks could get into the game, Montreal had piled up a big cushion, coasting to an easy 5-1 win and a 2-0 series lead. Pilous was furious with his team and refused to take any blame.

"We lost two games in Montreal . . . and it was the second game that hurt most," said Pilous. "It was humiliating to be associated with a team that was just standing around. There won't be any more of that if I can help it!"

"We didn't look too bad in the first game, but we weren't even skating in the second," lamented Hawks owner James D. Norris as he arrived at Chicago Stadium to watch his troops work out prior to Game 3. "They seemed to lack desire. We were playing the greatest team in hockey and we helped them prove it!"

As motivation, Norris handed each player an unsigned check worth $3,350. "Bring them back to me after you win the Cup and I'll sign them!" he declared with gusto to the players. (The amount merely totalled a Cup win paid out by the league.)

Chicago came out hitting in front of a wild crowd of 14,723. Arbour scored his first goal of the playoffs and the rough play saw the Canadiens lose the services of Jean Béliveau, who received two cracked vertebrae in a third period collision with Glen Skov. Vasko, who already wore a shoulder brace to keep his arm down, had his shoulder separated for the third time this season when Dickie Moore lifted Moose's arm in a third-period attempt to get at Pierre, who was involved in a skirmish with two other Canadiens. The Hawks powered their way to a 4-2 win and no longer saw themselves as underdogs.

"We're going to play it straight away and we're not fooling," said Pilous prior to Game 4. "We'll keep on hitting them and if the boys are skating as well as they did Saturday, things will be alright."

Montreal coach Toe Blake was having none of it. "We're not going to be chased out of the rink no matter what Pilous thinks!" spat Blake. "This is my fourth season coaching the Canadiens and we have met rough teams before in Stanley Cup play. We can handle them alright and we're not getting panicky. Of course Béliveau's loss will hurt . . . but I think our replacement strength will measure up and we will be going back to Montreal with a 3-1 lead in games."

Blake went on to call Saturday's game "the worst refereed I have ever seen, either in the NHL or in Stanley Cup games! Referee Red Storey was letting everything go. He didn't even call a penalty on Skov when Béliveau was slammed into the boards!"

Coach Pilous shook his head over Toe's claim. "We played a hard, solid-checking game and we're going to do it again!" predicted the Chicago coach.

Backed by excellent goalkeeping by Hall, who stopped 30 of 31 shots, and a determined Vasko, who signed himself out of hospital to suit up, the Hawks evened the series with a convincing 3-1 victory. It was the first time in seven years that Montreal was forced to play six games in a semi-final.

Back in Montreal, the Canadiens regrouped, scoring four times in the first 16 minutes and held on to beat Chicago 4-2 to take a 3-2 series lead. Pilous was critical of referee Frank Udvari's work and as the series shifted back to the noisy confines of the Chicago Stadium, he requested Storey to officiate the game. Pilous knew his choice of Storey would get under Blake's skin and it did. He could not know of the repercussions of his fateful choice. Pierre certainly liked the choice of Storey for a referee.

"Red Storey refereed our games often," recalled Pilote. "I got along so good with him. He was like my angel, always behind me and the play. Sometimes he'd whisper to me, 'Hey Pierre, watch it, there's somebody behind you.' He would actually say that! He was one of those referees who would talk to certain guys all the time."

Playoff fever gripped Chicago as fans lined up for blocks at the Stadium and a downtown clothing store that served as the only ticket-buying locations.

The atmosphere in the Stadium for Game 6 was electric, and the crowd of 18,521 was the largest for an NHL game anywhere in 12 seasons. Extra policemen were brought in to search the crowd prior to the start. Almost a ton of garbage was confiscated, which included fruit and vegetables, eggs, and bottles—but they didn't find everything, as referee Storey later found out.

As he was skating around the ice, a fan caught his attention and Storey stopped to look. The man opened his coat to reveal a pistol in a holster.

"I'm gonna blow your brains out!" the fan yelled.

"Well, I hope you have good aim. I don't want to be wounded or a cripple!" Storey yelled back, before waving for security. Pierre came over to see what all the fuss was about. Storey wrote in his memoirs that when the police escorted the man away, they just brought him to a higher seat and gave him his gun back.

From the first stirring sounds of the Barton organ belting out the national anthems to start the game, the screaming crowds belied the fact that the first two periods were relatively calm and close. The Hawks came from behind twice to tie it up and with seven minutes to go in the third period, the air became tense with the score tied at three.

As Litzenberger broke out of his own end, he collided with Marcel Bonin and fell. It looked like a trip and all eyes in the arena zeroed in on Storey who kept his whistle by his side. When the continuing play resulted in a Montreal goal by Moore, the mood in the arena began to turn foul. Litzenberger was livid and raced at Storey screaming: "You're nothing but a goddamned homer!"

Storey looked at him, trying not to laugh. "What rink do you think we're playing in, Litz?" Storey retorted. The ice was littered with fruit and bottles. The mood eased somewhat when Lindsay tied the game minutes later, but trouble was in the air.

With just under two minutes remaining in the period, Hull was checked by Junior Langlois and sent flying. The hip check looked like a miss and a trip—all in one. Again, all eyes turned to Storey, who refused to call a penalty. The crowd was incensed and the tense situation was further compounded seconds later when Claude Provost scored for Montreal on the same play.

"I slid from the goddamned blue line to the red line, tripped right up. All our guys quit because they thought it was a penalty," recalled a still emotional Hull of the series-ending play. "How bad was it? I got up and was the first man back trying to catch Provost, before he put the puck behind Hall in our net. Everyone had quit, thinking for sure it was going to be a penalty because Storey had let one go just before that! After the goal, that's when it started; the stuff was coming over the boards."

The crowd was screaming for Storey's head. Cans, bottles, wooden chairs, programs, shoes, cushions, and seat parts rained down on the referee, who stood at centre ice with his bewildered linesmen. Players took cover at the side of the boards. Pilous, steaming behind the bench, gave the choke sign at Storey, which encouraged even more mayhem.

Two spectators jumped the boards and raced towards the referee. One threw a cup of beer in Storey's face. Incensed, the referee grabbed the spectator and was about to punch him when Canadiens defenceman Doug Harvey yelled at him: "Red! You can't hit a fan!" Harvey grabbed the spectator instead and punched him, sending the fellow flying.

Things were happening fast and Storey was unsure where to turn next. Seeing Harvey mouth "Watch out!" over the screaming crowd, Storey turned and flipped the other attacker over his back. Before Storey could belt the second attacker, Harvey slashed him with his stick, which made a large gash. The sight of the two bleeding aggressors groggily leaving the ice deterred others from trying the same thing.

"Harvey's actions that night, I think, might have stopped a flippin' riot!" recalled Hull.

For 25 minutes the game was delayed as police tried to restore order and officials picked up the debris. NHL president Clarence Campbell, who was in attendance, refused to come down from his seat to give guidance to the officials, who thought maybe the game should be called.

The tension eased slightly by the delay, the game resumed. With mere seconds remaining, a final desperate dash in the dying seconds by Pilote and Lorne Ferguson at the Canadiens net was smothered by a diving Jacques Plante.

The *Chicago Tribune* wryly noted the next day: "Provost, Langlois and Storey . . . settled the Hawks' fate for the 1958-59 season!"

Storey and the other two officials needed to be escorted off the ice by police and secreted out of the arena to their hotel. Lucky to be alive, Storey later heard Campbell's public criticism of the two missed penalty calls. Livid, his reputation sullied and feeling betrayed, Storey hung up his whistle and never refereed another game. Montreal easily captured their fourth straight Stanley Cup weeks later by defeating Toronto in five games.

Though the sting of the playoff loss lingered for the Hawks, the series had shown a newfound swagger, confidence, and even real, deep-rooted anger at the loss to Montreal. That was good. That they had the support of growing and very vocal crowds was also good.

Things were also looking bright for Pierre. He had had a good season, and the team had made the playoffs and pushed the Canadiens further than anyone had expected.

Despite the disappointment of the early playoff exit, Pierre had some upcoming excitement to look forward to as he and Annie packed up the apartment and the kids for Fort Erie for the summer.

Pierre was headed to New York and from there it was on to Europe for a month, to do something he absolutely loved to do— play more hockey!

A Hawk and a Jet Take Flight

After the two-day drive to Fort Erie from Chicago, and settling Annie and the two kids into their Aberbeen Court home, Pierre turned his attention to Europe. He took a flight from Buffalo to New York City for an overnight stay and met up with his Hawk buddies, Bobby Hull, Eric Nesterenko, and Ed Litzenberger, who bolstered the Rangers lineup.

The exhibition tour of 1959 marked the second time NHL teams had toured Europe, the first being the Canadiens and Red Wings, with a nine-game stint in spring 1938.

This current tour, organized by Swiss hockey player Othmar Delnon and sponsored by a Swiss winemaker, had the Rangers and Bruins scheduled to play each other 23 times in 26 days in 10 cities in six countries. Both teams flew 16 hours to London on a Lockheed Constellation on April 27.

"It was a prop plane and the wings bounced up and down," recalled Pierre. "I remember the sun coming up over Ireland, and seeing its pretty plush green hills and valleys.

"In London, we played the first two games. Phil Watson was the coach and we had Eddie Shack and Gump Worsley was our goalie. Oh boy, we had a good time with Gump. He was a nice guy. We played Boston every night and sometimes after Shack hit a few guys it got rough. It was supposed to be an exhibition series, but he would put on a good show.

"We stayed in the Hyde Park Hotel in London, near Buckingham Palace. Their steaks were small, like the palm of your hand, with little servings on the side, like a high-class joint."

The teams travelled to games in Geneva, Paris, Antwerp, Zurich, Dortmund, Essen, Krefeld, Berlin, and Vienna. For Pierre, his first trip abroad meant taking as many 8mm home movies as he could, so he could show Annie back home.

"I took a trip to go see East Berlin, the Berlin Wall, the Russian soldiers, and I saw an old lady pushing a wheelbarrow around picking up bricks—many places had been destroyed during the war and this was not long after really. In Geneva, Switzerland, I never ate so well. We had white asparagus! I had never seen that before! And they had nice trout too.

"During that time I think I lost five pounds. We played a lot of hockey. When they paid us the $1,000, I didn't know what to do with it. I didn't want to carry around that much cash, so I mailed seven or eight envelopes home to Annie with $100 in each one."

But the highlight of the trip for Pierre was watching Hull emerge as a goal scorer. The large hockey rinks of Europe were suitable for a flying superstar and Hull used it to full advantage.

"You should've seen Bobby: he was tearing up the ice, just flying!" Pierre recalled. "That's when I saw him come out and blossom, full of confidence and style. Phil Watson would shake his head and say, 'Man oh man, I wish you guys were playing for us!'"

"On that trip, Pierre and I raised our games," Hull remembered. "We got to really know one another as we were together all the time. I think we were the big cheese on that team. We were the backbone of that New York team. Phil Watson loved Pierre because of his French connection, plus we were winning the games for him. We had seven and a half extra feet on either side, so we could skate a little bit.

"I played with Litzenberger as my right-winger and I was still playing centre. They still hadn't figured out that I was too dumb to be a centreman! And I had Eddie Shack on my left side. That goddamned Shack, you had to tell him every shift: 'Now, Eddie, stay wide, lay it out there in the slot and I'll make sure the biscuit gets in the basket!' Well, every shift, if you didn't tell him that, Shack was liable to be all over the goddammed place. He also was as likely to hit you as anybody on the other team! It was just as dangerous to be on his side! He had talent though, if you could harness it.

"It was a fabulous trip! Every night we clashed on the ice with 'The Battering Ram' Dick Meissner, who played for the Bruins. He had thighs as big as our waists. He was built and thought he was tough, but his shots were like golf putts because he always shot off the wrong foot, off balance. But that trip is where I learned how to play, I mean really play! Pierre and I played a lot and so well together because he understood me and I, of course, understood him. That really came together in Europe."

Like all NHLers of his day, once back home, Pierre turned his attention to making money to support his family during the summer.

"I had seen a laundromat in Chicago and so I contacted Westinghouse, who made washers and dryers, and opened a laundromat near the arena in St. Catharines, near the Queensway Hotel," recalled Pierre. "It was called the Westinghouse Laundromat. Boy was it ever busy! It was the first one in the Niagara region and I couldn't keep up."

As a change of pace, the Hawks training camp convened in fall 1959 in Sault Ste. Marie, Michigan. A week into camp Pierre was called in for contract negotiations. He had been thinking all summer about what he might ask for.

After the usual small talk Ivan slid the offer towards Pierre. The offer was a scant increase, very scant. Pierre didn't have to look at it very long.

"No, Tommy, this just won't do."

"Well, Pierre, we're giving you a raise."

"Hardly. Look, Tommy, I think I played very well last year."

"Yeah, well, what did you do well last year?"

"You know what I did. I had a good year. Should have made the All-Star team."

"But you didn't."

"But I should have and I've been invited to the game anyways, you know that, though I know I'm not going without signing."

"Well, you have to go, to represent the Black Hawks."

"Tommy, I have to represent my family too," Pierre answered coolly.

"Well, Pierre, that's our offer. Take it or leave it."

"I'm sorry, Mr. Ivan, but I've got to leave it. I want $12,000." Pierre pencilled in the number and pushed it towards his manager.

Ivan stared at the paper. "Gee, Pierre, I'll have to think about that."

"You do that, Mr. Ivan, you just do that!" Pierre walked out of the room, leaving Ivan staring at the piece of paper.

He was not alone in his negotiating restlessness. Tod Sloan and Hull did not sign through training camp either. If Ivan thought that the three stars would capitulate, he guessed wrong. In Toronto, Conn Smythe was having the same difficulties penning Tim Horton, Dick Duff, and Bob Pulford. The Annual All-Star Game was slated for Montreal and all had been named to participate.

"All named as members of the team to oppose Montreal, and [all] are among the missing," wrote the *Windsor Daily Star* on October 3, 1959. "Their absence could tarnish slightly the honours attached to playing in the annual classic."

The cat and mouse game of contract negotiating continued. "One day before the All-Star Game, Tommy Ivan ran into me in the elevator of the hotel," recalled Pierre. "We're both standing there silently waiting for it to reach our floor when he turned to me, saying he had the train ticket to the All-Star Game in his pocket. He asked me if I wanted it. I said, 'No, I'm not going. Not until I sign a contract for what I want!' And so I didn't go."

The impasse continued until the team returned to Chicago. Pierre and Ivan met a few more times. "I stuck to my guns and then we were $1,000 apart. Then we agreed to meet halfway and I signed for $11,500, $500 less than what I had wanted. I got close to what I wanted, but you had to stand your ground."

Hull, another hold-out, could relate. "Tommy had said to me, 'Bobby, if you don't sign, you're not going to the All-Star Game!' I said, 'Tommy, if this is going to be the only All-Star Game that I ever play in, it won't make a rat's piss of difference. I'm not signing my contract and I'm not going to the All-Star Game!' So I stayed home along with Pierre. Ivan and I came to terms before the season started. There weren't a lot of differences in the raises back then. I agreed to $12,000 but you had to have a pretty decent year in order to get a raise."

For the home and season opener on October 7, the Chicago fans were still upset at Red Storey. A mannequin dressed up as a referee with black pants, striped shirt, and a mop of red hair appeared with a sign above it that read, "Rest in Peace!" They knew Storey had quit refereeing.

"If the fans in this city aren't the most enthusiastic in the world, which I think they are, they must be the noisiest," reporter Ken McKenzie wrote in the *Hockey News*. "It was a great crowd on hand to cheer the Black Hawks . . . and the game must rate as one of the most successful openers in Chicago history."

Rudy Pilous tried Hull on left wing, centred by newcomer Stan Mikita and Nesterenko on the right. It worked as both Hull and Mikita scored goals in the impressive 5-2 win over the New York Rangers.

Stanislav Guoth was born on May 20, 1940, in Sokolce, Czechoslovakia, eventually renamed the Republic of Slovakia. He was eight when he was sent by his parents to live with his aunt and uncle in St. Catharines, Ontario, in 1948. He was adopted by them and took his uncle's surname, Mikita. Stan started playing hockey and made the hometown Junior A Teepees, where he spent three years. In his last season, he led the OHA with 97 points. He was now ready for the NHL.

Another playing ace joining the Black Hawks that season was a big redhead named Bill Hay. Born December 8, 1940, in Saskatoon, Saskatchewan, "Red" played junior in Regina for the Pats for two seasons before joining the Colorado College Tigers in 1957-58, where he led the WCHA in points with 116. In fall 1958 he played for the Calgary Stampeders of the Western Hockey League, a Hawks farm team. Bill notched an impressive 54 points in 53 games during the 1958-59 season. In this first fall tryout with the Hawks, he easily made the club. Another brick in the Hawks rebuild was in place.

For Pierre and Anne, pregnant with their third child, renting the small apartment was no longer an option. Instead, they rented the house that Ed and Doreen Litzenberger had stayed in the season previous, as the Litzenbergers had moved further north.

"Doreen told me the previous spring that they were moving out of their rented house, a duplex, in Berwyn. It was close to a laundromat and the hospital, and was very clean and nice," recalled Annie. "This house was furnished, had a nice TV, which really mattered back then. So we rented the house. Glenn and Pauline Hall lived nearby, so she and I grew close as well."

Despite the season-opening win, the Black Hawks had only two ties and four points to show after 12 games. The team played hard but kept coming up short and frustration set in. During this extended skid, Pierre inadvertently developed one of his pre-game superstitious habits, which he maintained for the duration of his career.

"In this one particular game that year, we were warming up, and I was the last player on the ice to touch the puck," related Pierre. "On the first play of the game, the other team went down and scored right away. I didn't like that! From that moment on, I ensured that I was never the last one to touch the puck before we went off the ice before its resurfacing. I made sure!

"Another little habit I had was getting to the rink just before the game and always timing it so that I was tying my skates when the coach came in to say a few words. I'd tie them while the coach was talking to us, then I'd immediately get up and go right out onto the ice."

On the ice things were not good, nor were they kosher in the Hawks dressing room as evidenced when coach Pilous told Nesterenko and Litzenberger to stay home as the team travelled to Montreal shorthanded for a November 7 game. According to Pilous, they had become "a little confused in their thinking."

The Hawks, without the two scratches and Lindsay, who was recovering from a concussion, went with only three forward lines. The strategy worked, as the undermanned Chicagoans spotted the Canadiens two goals by Bernie "Boom Boom" Geoffrion and Doug Harvey but stormed back to earn a 2-2 tie on goals by Mikita, set up by Hull, and a short-handed goal by Elmer Vasko assisted by Ron Murphy. Penalties determined the game's outcome with all goals either scored on power plays or short-handed. At one point the penalty box had Pilote, Mikita, Ab McDonald, and Dollard St. Laurent in it, joined by same number of Canadiens, all sitting side by side. Hall was especially strong in the last few minutes as the Canadiens pressed in the Hawks end trying to eke out the win, but to no avail. The Hawks were elated in their dressing room after the game.

"Leaving those guys [Nesterenko and Litzenberger] at home was a good idea," said Pilous. "The others decided to work a little harder!"

On November 8, the high-flying second-place Bruins hosted the Hawks in the hostile confines of the Garden. Led by the hot goal-tending of Harry Lumley and the league's leading scorer, Bronco Horvath, the Bruins also had the helmeted Charlie Burns in their lineup. Burns wore a special helmet to protect his head, in which a steel plate had been inserted because of a double skull fracture suffered in junior hockey. Doctors had cleared him to resume his hockey career.

The game turned ominous in the third when Pierre and Burns collided heavily at centre ice, leaving Burns lying on the ice in a pool of blood and having to be assisted from the ice.

"Burns wore a big black helmet, thick. I didn't know why he had it," Pierre remembered. "I hit him clean with my shoulder. He had his head down looking at the puck. I wasn't going fast, he was. If he'd have looked up he could have easily avoided me. I never got a penalty and no Boston player came after me. What was I gonna do, get out of his way?"

A rare penalty shot was awarded to Boston when Hawks defenceman Al Arbour threw his stick to stop a Horvath breakaway. In a strange twist of fate, Chicago was given the choice of picking the Boston shooter. The Bruins protested the ruling vehemently, and produced an old rule book that indicated the captain of the non-offending team had the choice of picking who could take the shot. Referee Dalton MacArthur disagreed and allowed Chicago to pick Larry Leach to take the shot. Hall stopped him, but Leach scored a later goal on the way to the Bruins 5-3 victory, stretching the Hawks' winless skid to 12 games.

After the game, the Hawks, who stayed overnight, went to their usual Boston bar. Pierre was sitting with the team when Bobby Hull noticed Pierre sitting there, quiet.

"What the hell's the matter with you, Pierre?" Hull piped up. "You're not drinking!"

"Aw, I feel bad about that hit on Charlie Burns," Pierre answered sheepishly.

"Why?" Hull asked again.

"Well, I'm worried about how he is, his wife and kids and . . ."

"Pierre," Hull replied with a laugh, "Burns isn't married."

"Oh, is that right?" Pierre answered in pure relief. He suddenly smiled. "Well okay then, in that case, get me a beer!"

Burns was diagnosed with only a minor concussion, and played 10 more helmeted seasons in the NHL.

Some plays never made game reports, such as Pierre handing

the puck off to his partner Vasko. With that look in his eye, Moose took off at full speed into the opposing zone as the crowd vocalized its approval with "MOOOOOOSE!"

A win, the team's second, mercifully came in their 16th game on November 15, as they clipped the visiting Red Wings 5-3.

A post-game story in the *Tribune* after the Hawks hosted the Canadiens on November 22 summed up the season thus far. "What happened this time?" Charles Bartlett wrote. "You're kidding! You mean you don't know that the Canadiens won another, and the Black Hawks lost another? Alas, folks that's the straight of it— Montreal 3; Chicago 1."

With their blossoming talent, the Hawks started to pull things together as November flipped into December. On December 16, Hall registered his first shutout when they beat Boston 4-0. The victory hauled them out of the cellar by one point over New York.

Three more wins in December lifted their Christmas spirits, helped no doubt by the great play of Hall and Hull, whose three December hat tricks gave the team a shot in the arm. By January 5, 1960, Hull had amassed 24 goals and 25 assists in 40 games and led the league in scoring. A cautiously jubilant coach Pilous told John Kuenster of the *Chicago Daily News* that he felt Hull was just starting to come into his own. "But he's got to learn to control his shot," exclaimed Pilous. "Half his shots aren't on the net, and he'd be more effective if he'd keep the puck down low."

"My first two years in the NHL, I really hadn't figured it out yet," Hull said. "Twenty goals was the yardstick then. Then in my third year, they put me on left wing, which I didn't like as much because a centre can go anywhere, but I had good centres."

Centre Hay and right-winger Balfour gave Hull the puck often as did a defenceman named Pilote. Many observers in the league began comparing Hull with his similar physique and style of play to the great Howie Morenz of the Canadiens.

"He hadn't been labelled it yet, but to me, that's when he became 'The Golden Jet,'" Pierre remembered of Hull's new free-wheeling rushes that season. "I used to love getting in on a give-and-go play with Bobby. He was starting to score then and he was put on the power play with me. We would take off and we could read each other's moves perfectly."

On January 15, the *Tribune*'s Bartlett wrote a piece on 12 Hawks wives and their 22 children. The article broached the subject of getting babysitters so that the wives could watch their husbands play in person.

"The rivalry for babysitters is such that Pauline Patrick Hall, petite, dark-haired wife of the Hawks great goalie Glenn, recently chided Anne Pilote on 'stealing' the lady who had been minding Pat Hall, 4, and his sister Leslie, 2." Anne Pilote admitted with a good-natured smile that she did so because she wanted to "indoctrinate the sitter for the imminent advent of a brother or sister for Denise, 4, and Pierre Jr., 2."

The story included pictures of Pauline Hall, Jessie St. Laurent, and Annie with their children, but it is a shot with Doreen Litzenberger and her two-and-a-half-year-old son, Dean, that is particularly poignant. Playing on the floor with her son, the beautiful, well-dressed, dark-haired mother explained that she had just missed a home game because she couldn't find a sitter.

The Rangers came to town on January 17 for a game won 3-1 by the tribe. Three nights later, the Hawks hosted the Bruins. As usual, the wives sat together to cheer on their boys, a habit no different than any other time, except that for Anne, something was very different this night.

"I couldn't explain it except that for some reason, Doreen Litzenberger looked very different that night at the game, there was just something about her. She looked really pretty, radiant," recalled Annie. "I don't know what it was but I couldn't take my eyes off her as we all kibitzed in the lobby between periods. Of course, I shrugged it off later and didn't think anything of it."

Later that night, Doreen Litzenberger was killed when the car she was driving skidded off the icy road and struck a viaduct. Her husband, a passenger in the car, sustained broken ribs, contusion of the liver, and a concussion and remained in hospital for several days.

"We had a friend named Bob Gaymey who called me that night at three o'clock in the morning," Pierre remembered. "He said, 'Pierre, I just got a call from the hospital. . . . Ed Litzenberger and his wife have been in a car accident. They want to know who to contact.' The Litzenbergers had his card on them. Bob didn't know what to do so I told him I would handle it and I called Rudy Pilous. He and Tommy Ivan took care of things. It was a tough, sad time."

"Doreen's death was such a shock to me," recalled Annie softly. "We were close; the wives were all close. We had a lot of fun together. Doreen was so pretty and she was a very good mother to little Dean. I felt close to her. We all did. We were all upset. We had lost one of our own. We had lost a dear friend.

"I was pregnant and before the wake and funeral, some of the other wives came over to our place to see me, and advised me not to go to the funeral or the wake, not to upset myself, to remember her as she was, that she would understand. So I didn't go. And we were now staying in the very house she had lived in and the others wondered if I felt funny about that. I said no, that I felt honoured to be in the house she had stayed in the year before. I felt close to her now. It took quite a while to get over it."

The team played on. An extended homestand enabled them to visit Litzenberger in hospital, attend the wake and funeral, and come to grips with the tragedy that had befallen their captain. It wasn't easy.

"We were definitely shook up," Pierre observed. "Our minds were not on the games for some time. Doreen had been a very popular, nice lady. Our wives were upset, which naturally upset the husbands. It was a tough stretch of time."

The tragedy affected the whole team, but especially young Mikita, who was staying with the recuperating Litzenberger. Mikita's level of play suffered as he tended to his captain and friend. Mikita asked Hull what was wrong with his play on the way to practice one day.

"I told him, 'Stan, you have to get out of that house and concentrate on yourself,'" Hull recalled. "'You have to pull yourself together. There's nothing wrong with your play, except you have to concentrate on being the best you can, get in better shape, stay fit and healthy.'"

Mikita took Hull's words at face value and started to pull himself out of his slump and live up to his potential. He also had to improve some parts of his game.

"In that first year, I used to call Mikita a trampoline artist," Pierre explained. "He could skate, handle the puck well, but he was always trying to go through the two opposing defencemen, and would always end up being flipped, tumbling all over the place. He finally got smart and started going around the defencemen. He had the speed and soon got on track."

The Hawks tied the Leafs twice and lost to the Canadiens before heading to Boston on February 4, where they took out their frustrations by pasting the Bruins 7-2. The two teams were now tied for fourth place in the standings.

In their next six games, the Hawks really came to life and won five of them. The dreary season finally had some light at the end of a dark tunnel. It continued on Valentine's Day as Hull got out of his scoring drought in a 2-0 Hall shutout over the Canadiens.

On February 21, Hull really broke out, notching four goals and an assist as the Hawks outscored the Leafs 7-5 at the Stadium. After a win against the Wings, Pierre banged in his sixth goal of the season and his 37th point, equalling his output of the season before. He was the top point-getter in the league for defencemen, with nine games to go.

Hall and the defence blanked New York 5-0 in an NHL weekly televised game on March 5, their second consecutive shutout, and things were really looking rosy as the win, their 26th game of the year, increased their hold on the final playoff spot by six points over

Boston. Hull netted his 37th goal and an assist boosted his league-leading points to 77. Litzenberger, recovered from his traumatic loss and injuries, returned to the lineup that night. He and Pierre scored during the rugged game in which referee MacArthur called 24 penalties.

When the Hawks extended their winning string with a 4-2 victory over the Canadiens on March 6, many were calling goalie Hall a strong contender for the league's MVP award with his 2.58 goals-against average in 64 games, despite the team's terrible start, and being outshot in most games.

"I have always said that Glenn Hall was the greatest goalie," recalled Pierre. "He was invaluable to our team's success."

There was a growing chorus in the media singing the praises of Pilote. "One of the biggest 'robbery' cries heard hereabouts in a long time will roar forth within a few weeks if Black Hawk Pierre Pilote doesn't get All-Star recognition," wrote Bud Booth. "The stocky underrated rearguard has this season seemingly concentrated on doing just about everything that can be expected of a hockey backliner . . . especially in the last-half of the schedule, his work has ranged continually from very good to excellent."

While Pierre was away playing in Detroit, labour pains forced Pauline Hall to drive an expectant Annie to hospital, where on March 16 she gave birth to daughter Renee Anne. Pierre would see his third child upon his return.

In a game on March 19, 1960, against the Leafs at Maple Leaf Gardens, Pierre was captured flipping Leafs forward Gerry James onto his head in a timeless photograph taken by famed photographer Leon Turofsky. While the shot was an all-time classic, the check didn't help the Hawks cause in a 1-0 loss.

For the final six games, the Hawks, marred by injuries, limped towards the post-season. In winning only one game, and tying three, they battled to try to stay ahead of the Red Wings for third place, but the real excitement for Chicago as the season closed also lay in Hull and Hall both going for individual awards—Hull for the scoring title, tied with Boston's Horvath, and Hall, tied with Montreal's Jacques Plante in the goals-against Vezina race.

How does a team play defensively to help their goalie win the Vezina, while trying to go for broke in getting their leading scorer the Art Ross scoring title? The fate of Hull and Hall's season came down to the last game against Boston on March 20, 1960. Mr. Goalie's fate also rested in the results of the Canadiens-Rangers game that night.

"Horvath and I are tied with 39 goals," recalled Hull. "It came down to the last game of the season and we were playing against each other!"

In typical Hawks style, the game was wide open to the detriment of their goalie, and Hull's 81 points beat Horvath by a single point for the scoring title. The 5-5 tie meant that Hall again lost the Vezina race to Plante on the last weekend of the season—Montreal had only given up three goals against New York.

"Oh, poor Bronco," remembered Pierre. "He was going for the scoring title against Bobby and we had a guy on him all night. He couldn't get much."

Pierre, whose offensive style often left Mr. Goalie alone with the stay-at-home Vasko, felt for Hall.

"We were not a defensive club, we were offensive minded," Pierre recalled. "We were outshot a lot and I used to wonder, 'Where the heck is everybody?' Ya gotta be backchecking. Not taking anything away from Plante, but Montreal was first and foremost a defensive-minded checking team with an explosive offence. This is why Glenn was so great. Imagine, being outshot in most games and still having a shot at a Vezina against the Canadiens and Plante! But we let him down."

Hull's Art Ross Trophy secured him a place on the First All-Star Team. Hall was chosen for the First All-Star Team ahead of Plante, which didn't sit well with Canadiens coach Toe Blake. "We win first place, Plante wins the Vezina for the fourth time and he's not the (First) All-Star goalie!" Blake complained.

"My guy was the best!" answered Pilous in the press. "And he played without a mask!" alluding to Plante's historic wearing of the mask for the first time that season. The Hawks weren't finished, as Hay was named top rookie.

"Bill had an impressive rookie year," recalled Pierre. "He had the size, was confident, a great skater, and a real finesse player. He complemented Hull and Murray Balfour on that line."

Pilote, with 45 points and again playing in all 70 games, took his place on the Second All-Star Team in his third NHL season.

"I was climbing, working harder, always trying to better myself. I got $500 for being an All-Star at the first half, the same for the second half, and the team matched it. That was big money back then!"

The Hawks finished in third, and had to face first-place Montreal in the semifinal—again. There was no doubt the Hawks were improved but if the regular season was the yardstick, the Canadiens had seven victories to Chicago's three, with four ties. All the Hawks wins had come at home. It didn't bode well.

The Hawks, soured by the Laurentians experience the year before, registered in a downtown hotel.

"We also wanted to have the players where we could keep an eye on them and be closer to the centre of things," Ivan explained.

After a 75-minute workout the day before the first game, Ivan said that the team was in good spirits. "They know they're capable of playing the type of hockey they need to win. If we stay healthy we're going to give them a hell of a fight."

But the Hawks weren't healthy. Arbour was nursing a bad ankle and Mikita had just been discharged from hospital with a fractured cheekbone.

"Mikita has difficulty seeing, so we'll rest him for the first game," said Pilous. Wharram also had a fractured jaw but was fitted with a special helmet to protect his face. Hull missed the opening game due to a tonsillitis infection that had spread into his ear, causing a high fever.

Montreal had its share of problems too, with Doug Harvey

suffering from a leg injury and Marcel Bonin nursing a broken toe. Blake said he was feeling confident but not cocky. "All I can tell you is we are expecting a pretty tough time," he predicted.

In Game 1, played on March 24, the Canadiens continued their Forum dominance over an undermanned Hawks team in a surprisingly close 4-3 win. Hull and Mikita returned for Game 2 of the series and, though Hull netted the first Chicago goal of the night, and goals by Balfour and Wharram sent the game into overtime, the Canadiens again prevailed when Harvey slammed a 55-foot shot behind a screened Hall at 8:38 of the extra stanza to steal another 4-3 victory.

Despite the two losses, Chicago had put up a battle at the Forum and had reason for optimism as they headed home. "We're beginning to treat them like just another bunch of hockey players, not like supermen," exclaimed Pilous.

Blake gave credit to the growing Hawks determination and improved play: "No doubt about it, the Hawks are playing great. We expected a tough series with them and that's what we sure are getting. They're checking fiercely."

As per usual, Pilous had his team workout lightly the morning of Game 3. It was a habit that did not sit well with some of the players.

"Pilous was the idiot who started the day-of morning skates!" recalled Hull with clear disdain. "The guys needed their rest. Let them sleep in but no, we had these day-of-game skates because Rudy couldn't sleep in! A team meeting was one thing, but don't send guys out to take a chance that they might work up a lather, go back to bed, and then lose their edge. It was one thing that I detested him for!"

Though now at full strength, the Hawks were still hurting. As the *Tribune*'s Bartlett reported, "The Black Hawks dressing room—or should it be hospital—revealed a hockey team under whose aches, pains, bandages, and patches . . . you sensed a collective mood of anger. These Hawks are mad to get back at the mighty Montrealers."

Trainer Nick Garen was a busy man prior to Game 3, as he was treating new injuries—Pierre for a strained back, Hull now with a charley horse to add to his ear infection, Sloan with a bad cut on his forehead, and Wharram continued to slurp milkshakes through a straw.

Game 3 was a fierce, unruly affair and the first period saw ferocious checking and rugged play from the opening faceoff. Chicago twice caught Plante out of his crease and nailed him with bodychecks. The period took over 50 minutes to play because of stitches required to Plante's head from a Murray Balfour shot and delays caused by fans raining debris on the ice. The Hawks had come out flying and out-shot the Habs by a 12-10 advantage, but had nothing to show for it.

During the game, Pilous was so steamed up that he reached over and grabbed one of the linesmen after what he thought was a missed offside call. During a fight between Henri Richard and Murray Balfour, a fan threw a giant firecracker that landed at Rocket Richard's feet. Just before the game ended, another giant firecracker exploded at the back of Plante's net.

Despite the determined effort, injuries proved too much for the tribe to overcome as the Canadiens easily shut them out 4-0 in front of a bitterly disappointed home crowd that included Mayor Richard Daley. With their backs to the wall and down 3-0 in the series, the Hawks played hard against Plante three nights later in Game 4, but the Montreal goalie wouldn't budge, playing some of the best hockey of his career. Into the third period with a 2-0 lead, Chicago came at Plante with everything they could muster, but it wasn't enough as he completed the four-game sweep with a 2-0 shutout. It was a bitter end to a promising season.

Back in Fort Erie for the off-season, Pierre turned his attention to running his laundromat. The sting of the playoff loss was soothed somewhat by the fact that he personally had a pretty good year.

Soon after arriving home, he was informed that there was going to be a "Pierre Pilote Appreciation Night" organized by Terry Evans and the local Knights of Columbus.

"Like many young Catholic men, when I turned 18, I had become a Knight along with Dad," recalled Pierre. "I had gotten my third degree. But I was no longer active because obviously hockey and business had taken me away. But I was still a member in the Fort Erie Knights of Columbus, in spirit."

In attendance at the special dinner were Fort Erie mayor Herbert T. Guess, Port Colbourne mayor R. Knoll, Buffalo Bisons GM Fred Hunt, Bisons coach Frankie Eddolls, Chicago coach Rudy Pilous, and Pierre's defence partner Moose Vasko. Of course a proud Paul Pilote was also at the all-male dinner.

"Pierre Pilote is considered by many top professional hockey players to be the best defenceman on ice," boasted the night's guest speaker, Scott Young of the *Globe and Mail*. "And there are some who claim he is the best of any position. There are three All-Stars on the Chicago Black Hawks and this is unusual, but I would say that Pierre, who is also the team's prankster and the one who is able to keep up the spirits on the team when things are not going good, is still holding back on what he can do. We have not yet seen the best of Pierre but we will and we look forward to it. He is an outstanding hockey player and an outstanding personality!"

Moose, introduced as Pierre's "partner-in-crime," even got up and spoke briefly on how pleased he was to be present, honouring "one of the best guys to work with."

"It was no surprise to me that Pierre was named to the Second All-Star Team last year," Eddolls told the assembled crowd. "I freely predict that he will make the First All-Star Team this season, and that the Black Hawks will end up on top of the NHL."

The prediction made the crowd cheer, but as Pierre sat there taking in the accolades coming his way, he started to feel slightly uncomfortable, especially when his coach next rose to speak. As Pilous grabbed the edges of the lectern, he looked at Pierre.

"I think I am privileged to criticize him, being his coach," Pilous started off. Pierre smiled wanly, gulping slightly. The crowd laughed.

"That, plus the fact that I signed him to his first 'A' contract," Pilous continued. "I still don't think he has reached his potential yet!" In his seat, Pierre squirmed. "He is an excellent player and is well-liked by all other players. Pierre enjoys the tough going. The tougher the play, the more he likes it."

Pierre and the crowd laughed. Then Pilous looked straight at his young defenceman and said, "I look for great things from this young man in the years to come!"

As he stood to respond after a standing ovation, Pierre gulped from the weight of Pilous's challenge: "I look for great things from this young man in the years to come . . ."

CHAPTER 10

Coming Together

The annual dance in St. Catharines was on.

"The first week of camp was tough, after eight to 10 days, you're just starting to get in gear, hit your peak, you're like a duck starting to fly, then you have to fight for your contract," moaned Pilote.

He did have a new advantage, though. "Having been an All-Star the year before was an ace in my pocket," recalled Pierre. "Still, Tommy's thinking all summer how he can keep you down. Negotiating yearly contracts was not easy. Players didn't discuss them, so we had no salary yardstick, only your own performance the year before. But mine had been pretty good."

Rumour had it that Rocket Richard had always been the highest paid player in the league, his salary not offered to him by the Canadiens until all players in the league had been signed by their respective clubs and then, after the annual courtesy call to league president Clarence Campbell revealed the highest paid player signed, Frank Selke would sign Rocket for a couple of hundred more. Now the Rocket was retired.

"You have to remember, the average teacher, coalminer, our fathers and brothers back home in Sudbury, or Kirkland Lake, Selkirk, Saskatchewan, or wherever in small-town Canada, wasn't making very much money then," recalled Ted Lindsay, who had retired from the Hawks before the start of this 1960–61 season.

"And we were getting better money, having fun playing a great game for six months of the year. It was hard not to judge ourselves that way and see; the owners and managers knew that too."

Tommy Ivan seemed to negotiate differently with each player who came into his office. With Al Arbour, he rifled through books on his desk, with Pierre he looked him straight in the eye. Ivan was searching through drawers as Bobby Hull waited. Hull walked out, insulted.

"In fall 1960, after I had won the scoring title, I told Tommy Ivan I wanted $25,000 to sign," related Bobby Hull. Ivan reacted like he'd been shot.

"No way!" Ivan answered. Hull, incredulous at the immediate rejection, didn't take to it kindly, but he was ready.

"To hell with you then," replied Hull. "I'm going to see Mr. Norris!" He stood and stormed out the door. Hull knew owner Jim Norris loved his hockey players.

"Jim Norris was a real sportsman," Hull recalled of the 1960 impasse. "He was fabulous, the greatest damn guy! I went to him and got my raise."

Pierre bargained hard too, as he and Ivan exchanged offers. Ivan could not doubt Pilote's talent. After multiple sessions, Pierre received just about what he wanted, which was slightly below Hull's salary. It put him into a great state of mind as he headed to Montreal for the annual All-Star Game.

"I hit the ice really happy that fall," he remembered. "I had bargained for myself and my family, and I felt really good about the results. It gave you such a lift."

An exuberant Pierre was enjoying this camp, and after an exhibition game at the Aud in Buffalo, he received permission from Ivan to drive to his parents' in Fort Erie and to take Jack Evans, Kenny Wharram, and Arbour with him. Paul and Maria Pilote were happy to see Pierre and his teammates. The men sat down to a few beers, talked shop, training camp, and life, when the conversation turned to a clear liqueur Paul always bought in Québec called "liqueurs des îles de St. Pierre et Miquelon." The little islands, owned by France in the Gulf of St. Lawrence off Newfoundland, were well known for their special liqueurs. That sounded interesting, the boys thought. Paul walked to the cupboard and grabbed a bottle.

Maria pulled out the glasses and mixed combinations of clear liqueur, hot water, and sugar then passed them out. The drinks went down smoothly and the rounds continued. Everyone was smiling sweetly, but before they knew it, it was one o'clock in the morning

"Holy shit, boys," Pierre suddenly said while looking at the clock. "We'd better get back to St. Catharines!" Evans, Wharram, and Arbour attempted to stand.

"The first thing that happens after you drink that stuff is your knees give out," Pierre laughed. "The boys were all staggering. I wasn't. I'm laughing at them. I was used to it—I thought."

The three guests stumbled to Pierre's car and fell in while Pierre opened the driver's door. A concerned Paul asked his son if he was okay to drive.

"Oh sure, Dad! Look at me, I'm fine. I feel great!" Pierre said with a laugh. "I can handle that stuff. No problem!" Maria approached the car as it was about to pull away. Pierre rolled down his window.

"Look, Pierre, you can brag in front of them all you want," she whispered in her son's ear. "But just so you know, I put almost no liqueur in yours; yours were all water and sugar."

Pierre laughed as he drove away, watching his mother smile.

"She protected me. She knew I had to drive back," he laughed. "I never told the boys. They were impressed that I could really hold my liquor! They never knew!"

At the All-Star Game dinner in Montreal's Sheraton Mount Royal the night prior to the contest, Pierre received recognition for his Second All-Star Team placing. The next morning he represented the Hawks at the Pension Society meeting where NHL president Clarence Campbell boasted that night's game would add another $30,000 to the Players Pension Fund and bring its total assets to just under $2,470,960.

"We sat there and listened. They told us how good our pension fund was," Pierre recalled. "But really, who knew? Who were we to say otherwise? It sounded good at the time."

As the season began, the Hawks now had former Canadiens Ab McDonald and Reg Fleming in their lineup. The 6'2" McDonald played left wing for Stan Mikita and Wharram while defenceman Fleming provided some much needed brawn.

"Ah, the initiation of Reggie Fleming. He was strong and smart," recalled Pierre. "We had to be real smart to fool him first. He used to room with Murray Balfour, who was very strong too, and one day we told Reggie that Murray could lift three guys off the floor. Reggie didn't believe us. Ha! So we we're sitting around and of course Reggie was gullible a little bit. So Murray gets on the floor and we're trying different guys, sitting on his arms, trying to balance, and somehow Reggie is in there.

"Next thing you know, the guys start wrestling and we're battling, and we've got Reggie all screwed up. Everybody's all entwined, legs over legs, and arms locked in arms. Reggie suddenly finds himself tied up, backwards, and all exposed. I happened to look up at the trainer's room door and Nick Garen was standing there smiling, holding a Gillette shaver with a little cream. Reggie suddenly realized he was the victim. So we got Reggie that way. Poor guy. He was upset. But he was not a hairy guy. It didn't take long!"

A confident tribe tied the Red Wings 1-1 in the home and season opener on October 5, and then beat them 4-2 the next night at the Olympia. The team—and especially Hull—were firing on all cylinders.

The tribe was rolling as they went into New York on October 19 for quite the encounter. Fleming entered the game without a single penalty in the season, but that changed in the second period when he squared off against Dean Prentice in his first fight. In the third,

Fleming showed his true brawn when he took on Prentice, John Hanna, and Eddie Shack. After the donnybrook, Reggie had a two-minute minor, three five-minute majors, an automatic 10-minute misconduct, and a game misconduct for a total of 37 minutes on the night. In one fell swoop, he became the league penalty leader.

"In that game in New York, Reggie was fighting everybody," recalled Pierre. "I wasn't involved but I sat back and enjoyed the show. Reggie and Shack really went at it, at the instigation of the two coaches."

Goalie Glenn Hall had unruly fan behaviour to contend with on October 23 in Boston Garden when he was struck in the head with a light bulb in the final minute just as Bruin winger Don McKenny was speeding towards him. The bulb fell to the ice, shattered in front of a stunned and distracted Hall, and McKenney fired the game-tying goal. The game ended in chaotic fashion with Chicago players swinging sticks at the catcalling, unruly Boston fans.

"It's tough enough trying to play the puck without having to play that damned thing," Hall spewed angrily after the game.

"The fans were so close to us in Boston," related Pierre. "It was a very small rink and when the Bruins dumped the puck in your corner, they were right on top of you—and the fans were too."

An odd thing happened to Pierre that night in Beantown. "I had a great game! I was really flying!" recalled Pierre. "But afterwards, I started thinking of my contract. I'm playing so well, hadn't missed any games, and now I realize, I didn't get enough money! 'I'll be a son of a bitch! They got me too cheap!' I suddenly had that feeling!"

When the Hawks crushed the Stanley Cup champion Canadiens 8-4 at home, they were hot, having lost only once in their first nine contests. They had also outscored the opposition 30-17. The addition of big McDonald and tough Fleming was having a positive effect.

"Ab McDonald was a talkative team player," recalled Pierre. "He fit in with Stan right away. He liked to have people around him. He really created team togetherness, a team effort, like Dollard.

Reggie was a happy-go-lucky, friendly guy off the ice. On the ice, he'd kill penalties, but he would often be sent out to shake us up and the other team too! He could sure do that! There were no enforcers then, but Reggie was."

At this time, Ivan got into the public relations game, by naming the Hull-Balfour-Hay line the"Million Dollar Line" with its fine balance of scoring, checking, and play making. He next dubbed the Mikita-McDonald-Wharram line the "Scooter Line" due to its all-around speed.

"Those stupid names!" laughed Hull. "I told Tommy that if we were really the goddamn Million Dollar Line, then I'd gladly take my $333,333.33 share, and Murray and Billy can divvy up the rest!"

In the first three weeks of November, the Hawks lost five and tied one on the road, but their eight-game home undefeated streak was on the line when they hosted the Bruins on November 17. What was notable about this particular game was not so much the 4-2 Hawks win but coach Pilous calling Hall to the bench for an extra attacker during a delayed penalty call against Boston. When Balfour scored on the play, other coaches took note and the strategy slowly caught on.

After a Christmas Eve 3-1 loss to Montreal at home, rumours had Pilous being relieved, but then Hall gave Rudy a shutout against the Wings in Detroit and the team won its next two, bringing him relief.

A Canadian Press article at the end of the year labelled the Hawks the most penalized team in the league, Pierre leading the way with 76 minutes, and Nesterenko just behind. "An old hockey maxim is that a team can't win games from the penalty box. The Hawks, a team almost everybody figured would give Montreal Canadiens a run for first place, is struggling along in fourth at the season's halfway mark," went the article.

"That year, I played tough, Reggie played tough. Stan, Bobby, Eric, everybody played tough," recalled Pierre. "We followed through our checks. We weren't afraid of anybody!"

Hull had his own theories about his and the team's lack of success at this time. "All of a sudden, Billy Hay stopped giving me the puck because some goddamned sports writers told him he should shoot more," remembered an angry Hull. "I was going up my wing quacking like a decoy, honest to God! Billy would wind up and shoot it anyways. I stopped getting the puck and I stopped scoring goals.

"And Pierre stopped getting the puck. The most important play for a team is the first pass out of your own end; if you screw up that first pass you're back-peddling all night. Pierre could move the puck out just like a Doug Harvey and I would think, 'Someone please just give the flippin' puck to Pierre! He'll get us moving.'"

They eventually did because Chicago started on a five-game winning streak, including a 3-2 win over the Rangers in New York, as Hull notched his first goal in 11 games. Andy Hebenton's power play goal for New York snapped Hall's shutout streak at 202:55. Mikita had a hot hand, scoring his eighth goal in six games on a pass from McDonald and Pilote as the Hawks won their sixth in a row in Boston on January 5, 1961. The win tied a club record and salvaged Pilous's job.

As the tribe arrived at the hotel the evening before a February 4 clash against the Canadiens, the boys had time to kill.

"In Montreal, we'd check into the hotel and then head to the Green Door," remembered Hull with a hearty laugh. "It was an old Irish Mansfield pub near the Royal Hotel. We went down this alley, opened one door, went down two or three other steps, opened another door, and wham . . . the cigarette and cigar smoke would hit you right in the face!

"We'd go in there, all 15 or so of us, put three or four tables together, and the flippin' beer would come out, 'les gros Molsons'— in quarts! We drank those flippin' quarts like they were pints. Now there were a bunch of these old buggers in there and they'd be watching us. By the time we left there we were as drunk as they were—well, six or seven of these quarts are like 12 pints! These folks were regulars and shit, so were we because we played in Montreal seven times a year! At the end of the night, they'd stumble over to our table, and say very drunkenly, 'I know who I'm going to be bettin' on tomorrow night, and it sure as hell ain't gonna be you Hawks!' So guess what? We waxed Montreal the next night!" Indeed, the Hawks handily beat the Canadiens 4-1.

"Oh the Green Door was always an experience!" Pierre added. "Those quarts were Black Horse and they kicked like a horse too. Another thing I enjoyed about going to Montreal was the Forum had great hot dogs! 'Chiens chaud' they were called. They had this great mustard and cooked cabbage on this special bread, not a bun. The whole thing was pressed or toasted. I would get four or five of these big hot dogs to take on the train or plane. Man, they were good!"

In mid-February, 15,789 Stadium fans saw Pierre put on a defensive and offensive show against the Canadiens. While both he and Moose were singled out for their excellent defensive play, Pierre shone offensively by constantly moving the puck up. In the first period, he fired a shot at Plante that was deflected into the net by Ron Murphy, and three minutes later, rushed into the opposing end after a give-and-go play with Sloan, circled the Montreal net and fired in a backhander that put the Hawks up for good.

"The good thing about those backhanders," Pierre said to reporter John Kuenster, "is that the goalie doesn't know where the shot is going to be because you're moving your stick in front of you and he can't see it."

"I'd say that was a pretty good team effort," added Pilous. "And you've got to give credit to Pilote; he played it smart on that second goal."

Two weeks later, on February 25, 1961, the visiting Hawks again went to the Green Door the eve of a Forum game.

"It's now two weeks after our last visit and we come streaming into the Green Door again!" recalled Hull. "And here are these same flippin' old buggers, these derelicts, the same ones sitting at the same tables, and they see us pour in. They come over to our table and say sheepishly, 'How the hell did you guys do it, clean the Canadiens two weeks ago?'

"But see, they'd seen us pour ourselves out of the Green Door tighter than a buzzard's ass in a power dive! But what they didn't know was that after we left the pub, we headed to Joe's Steakhouse or the Blue Silvery Moon or Ben's for a sandwich. Ben's had great smoked meats! We would eat well before going to bed . . . despite our paltry meal money! We got a measly $9 dollars a day for meal allowance—$9 a day! Do you believe that? If we were on the road for eight or nine days, we'd be into our own pockets by the third or fourth day!"

The next night, they held the powerful Canadiens to a 1-1 tie. The Green Door boys must have been shaking their heads in disbelief, but Hull had another theory for their Montreal success.

"If you're out having a few pints the night before a game, you damn well played guilty and smarter," continued Hull. "You knew, 'Holy cow, I gotta crank up my game tonight!' And we flippin' did! I played my share of tough games."

The Hawks had the wind in their sails heading to Toronto on March 11 to battle the Leafs.

From the outset, referee Frank Udvari sensed the foul mood on the ice and called 14 penalties in the first period alone, hoping the players would stick to hockey. With only four penalties called in the second, Chicago went into the third with a 2-1 lead. What had been a hockey game turned into "Fight Night at the Gardens." Udvari tried desperately to overlook infractions against both teams in a bid to keep the teams even, but his tactic soon backfired. At the 14:31 mark Pierre, already with two penalties in the game, turned and swung his stick at the head of Eddie Shack.

"I was just coming across and Eddie came from behind and speared me," recalled Pierre. "So, as he was going by, I just wanted to give him a little haircut, and then all of a sudden, all hell broke loose."

Bert Olmstead moved in and grabbed Pierre. Both men started

swinging but before Pierre knew it, Olmstead had him pinned to the ice.

"I shouldn't have gotten involved with that Olmstead," Pierre observed. "He was a tough hombre. I got a couple in and he got a couple. He didn't hit me too hard. He was about 6'2" and had a long reach. We both fell and he fell on top of me and had me by the neck. He was squeezing hard and I thought, 'I'd better not move, or he'll crack my neck.' That didn't bother me; it was round one for him!"

Larry Hillman took on Fleming while Shack started swinging at Mikita. Shack turned his attention to Fleming, who in turn fractured Shack's nose with what Eddie later called "a sneak punch."

"That was Reggie's game, to keep them on their toes, their heads up," added Pierre. "His rough play rubbed off on some of our usually less aggressive players."

Not done, the scene shifted to the Chicago bench where Sloan and Hay threw their sticks at Shack before Nesterenko reached over the boards at him. Hay then jumped on the ice, followed by 10 Hawks, which was answered by Toronto's Dick Duff leading a charge of Leafs off their bench.

"Dick Duff was a tough little guy," said Pierre. "He didn't take a back seat to anybody. Not a fighter but, boy, he could stand his ground."

When the dust had cleared, the Leafs ended up tying the game on a goal by Bob Nevin with a minute and a half to go. Afterwards, 21 players were assessed $725 in fines by Clarence Campbell. Most of the $25 fines went to the 21 players—11 Hawks and 10 Leafs—who left the bench to join the fray. Eight misconducts added another round of $200 fines to Pilote, Fleming, Mikita, Sloan, and Hay, and Toronto's Shack, Olmstead, and Hillman. In the hard-nosed hockey of the early 1960s, establishing a team's toughness on the ice was paramount.

"We didn't go looking for trouble," recalled Pierre. "Fighting is tough, it's tiring. And if you fight one guy, there's another watching, then you've got two guys out for you. But you have to stand up for yourself and your teammates. We weren't afraid of anybody."

Returning home for the second last week of the season, Chicago lost to the Canadiens 6-2 and tied the Red Wings 2-2, but it was now clear that the Hawks were united. They won, lost, and fought as a team. At home, that togetherness was helped on a few fronts.

"Paul Gardenia, an Italian fellow, carried our sticks across the ice to the bench. He had a garage on Chicago Avenue," noted Hull. "His wife's name was Ruth. We used to stop in there after practice and hang out, sometimes with our wives. He'd feed us at the back of the garage! He was a great old guy with black, greasy hands. I'd swear his salad dressing had 10W30 in it! He fed us these magnificent salads, fresh buns, cooked rabbit, squirrel, moose, venison, pork, and beef. It was amazing! Lunches at his garage brought us together and built team spirit.

"Eddie and Joanne would host us at the Monarch Café, at the corner of Konard and Augusta. They loved us and they'd put us in the back room and supply us with tons of food and beer. That started the bonding. It was just a flippin' hole in the wall but it kept us together and the wives together and happy. You keep the wives happy and you have a happy group. That was the most important thing really."

The tribe ended the season losing to Boston 4-3 and though they were still in third place, they had finished the season hot, losing only five games of their last 19.

Bring on the Canadiens, their first-round opponents—again! In 14 matches, the season's series against them had been even, but in the last five match-ups, Chicago had three wins, a tie, and only one loss. The tribe felt Montreal, who was gunning for its sixth straight Stanley Cup, was ready for the taking.

"We felt good going into the playoffs," noted Pierre, the Black Hawks assistant captain for the third year running. "We had confidence."

"We had Glenn Hall in net, a great defence corps, with Dollard,

Al Arbour, Jack Evans, and especially Pierre," recalled Hull. "We had some older guys, Tod Sloan and Ron Murphy, who knew how to play the game too, to play defensively. We had strong lines, ours, Mikita's. We were ready, as was little no. 3, where a lot of Hawks plays originated from."

It was clear in a team full of great players and superstars that Pierre Pilote was making his mark. His aggressive play, exemplified by his 165 penalty minutes, led the NHL. Despite this, he had accumulated 35 points in 70 games again, and most importantly, he had been selected to the Second All-Star Team for the second year in a row. He was clearly the catalyst of the Hawks attack.

Now to answer his coach's challenge at the Knights of Columbus dinner eight months earlier.

CHAPTER 11

Beware the Habs of March

For the third-place Hawks, the 1961 Stanley Cup playoffs had a familiar theme as they faced the first-place Canadiens for the third year in a row. Montreal had been in the Stanley Cup final 10 consecutive years and were shooting for a record sixth-straight Cup.

Though the Habs were favoured, as they had bounced Chicago in four games the previous year, it had been a very injury-laden Hawks squad. Chicago hadn't forgotten that, especially in light of their recent success against Montreal.

"We felt that we could beat them," Litzenberger said years later. "Like I said to the guys, 'Hey, they're human, just a bunch of guys like we are.' All we had to do, as a player, was to win each shift."

"Heading into that first series against Montreal, we really, really, wanted to win," recalled Pierre. "Montreal, who I do think were a better team, could skate, and by the third period, you were always tuckered, so our game plan would be to check, check, check, and hit everything in sight. We had to slow them down."

In the first game at the Forum on March 21, the Hawks skated with the Habs and hit them at every opportunity, even outshooting the Canadiens 12-4 in the first period. But Jacques Plante in the Montreal net was sensational and kept the score 1-1. The plan also worked for the second period as the teams exchanged goals, but in the third, the Hawks seemed to run out of gas when quick goals by

Dickie Moore and Phil Goyette sealed Chicago's fate in an eventual 6-2 Montreal victory.

Despite the loss, Chicago's tough play paid dividends. Jack Evans' hit on Jean Béliveau left "Le Gros Bill" dazed for the duration of the game, Dollard St. Laurent's check sent Montreal forward Bill Hicke to hospital with a slight concussion, and Donnie Marshall sustained a knee injury. The verbal sparring between the two opposing coaches started immediately.

"Dirty hockey!" fumed Montreal coach Toe Blake after the game. "Chicago should play this game with tomahawks!"

Blake next alleged that St. Laurent had deliberately tripped Hicke.

"Hicke came right into me," answered St. Laurent. "His head struck me on the shoulder as he hit me on the side, then fell."

Rudy Pilous defended his team. "We use our weight legitimately! Canadiens were the ones doing a war dance. They were getting away with all kinds of interference. The Canadiens are the champs when it comes to interference."

Pilous abandoned his "lucky" green suit two nights later as the Hawks returned to the Forum and outshot the Canadiens 9-8 in a rough, scoreless first period which saw seven minor penalties called. Montreal outshot Chicago 11-4 in the second, but Glenn Hall was sensational. His team responded on goals by Stan Mikita and Kenny Wharram to put the Hawks up 2-0. But the champs roared back, tying it up. The Canadiens came out flying in the third period, but Hall answered the challenge as he stopped Béliveau cold. Later, with Montreal's Doug Harvey in the penalty box, Plante made great stops on Pilote and Wharram before Bobby Hull stuffed it in to put the tribe up 3-2. Then Phil Goyette tied it up yet again.

With time winding down, Montreal's Jean-Guy Gendron was about to break in on Hall when linesman Matt Pavelich whistled the play offside. The Hawks bench breathed a sigh of relief while the Montreal bench went berserk. With three minutes to go, Litzenberger tipped in a point shot on a give-and-go play from

Pierre and Eric Nesterenko to put the Hawks ahead 4-3. With a minute left, Blake pulled Plante but the Hawks and Hall were able to fend off the Montreal attack. Pilous, a white fedora on his head, pumped the air with his fist at the final buzzer.

"This was a big one . . . one we had to win!" Rudy exclaimed with a sense of relief in a euphoric Hawks dressing room afterwards.

"We got very few breaks," Blake said afterwards without a comment about the rough play. "The puck wasn't bouncing our way. What can you do when it's not?" Already looking ahead to the series shifting to Chicago Stadium, he added, "but if we can't win on the road . . . then we don't deserve to win the Cup!"

The Canadiens practised at the Forum before heading to Chicago and Blake finally complained to *Montreal Matin* reporter Jacques Beauchamp about the unfair offside call by Pavelich, but still added they had lost Game 2 because "they committed some monumental errors at critical moments."

A cartoon in the same paper depicted Pilous dressed as an Indian chief telling Blake, "Now you come play in my territory!" and Hawks players dancing around a burning fire. The caricature of the rough play and Blake's references to tomahawks was bolstered when seven Chicago players were photographed wearing Indian headdresses from the Koda Indian Reservation. The drawing of Indian Sac Chief "Black Hawk" on the crest of the Chicago sweaters and Pierre's aboriginal background made the headgear fit him especially.

"We used to laugh about the crest!" chortled Hull. "The older Pierre got, the more he looked like Chief Black Hawk on our sweaters! We didn't make any bones about it! We weren't making fun of his aboriginal background, he was proud of it and so were we."

When the Hawks were forced to practise at the Rainbo Arena, some of them spent the time recuperating. Mikita received treatments from trainer Nick Garen for a sore right ankle and Ab McDonald reentered the hospital in Chicago with a violent case of hives derived from an allergic reaction to an antibiotic for a wrist infection and was expected to miss the entire series.

An "official" standing-room-only crowd of 16,666 patrons crammed Chicago Stadium for Game 3 on March 26, 1961, but 4,000 were rumoured to have snuck in. They witnessed one of the most dramatic Stanley Cup playoff games ever.

"Chicago Stadium was like a volcano waiting to erupt," wrote Boom Boom Geoffrion years later. "And it stayed that way throughout as bodies crunched bodies."

The heat made the ice terrible. Toe Blake stated the ice was soft and sloppy. "The Hawks deliberately did this to slow down my players because they know that we could outskate Chicago. The conditions were a disgrace."

In the first four minutes, Chicago swarmed the Montreal net but the Habs came back and forced Hall to make great saves on Marcel Bonin and Al Langlois. When he next robbed a wide open Claude Provost the roof lifted off the building. Montreal outshot the Hawks 13-7 in a scoreless but rough first period that saw Reg Fleming level Henri Richard with a well-aimed elbow, Red Hay tangle with Jean-Guy Gendron, Mikita square off against Moore, and St. Laurent fight Montreal's Ralph Backstrom.

Early in the second period, the Hawks received penalties against Murray Balfour and St. Laurent 25 seconds apart that forced Chicago to play a minute and a half while two men short. Pilous sent out Pierre, Moose Vasko, and Nesterenko to thwart the awesome Montreal power play. Holding their position in a defensive triangle, the Chicago trio kept Montreal to a lone, long shot by Béliveau.

"Killing off that five on three was key," recalled Pierre. "In a way, it's easy to defend because you're just moving the triangle around, not rushing, not going into the corners, just holding your ground. You block a shot, then hold your place, trying to slow things down, keep them outside."

When the penalties ended, the crowd went wild and the penalty kill boosted the Hawks. With barely a minute to go in the second, Hull blasted a slapshot off Plante's chest and Balfour fired in the rebound from 10 feet out to put Chicago in front 1-0. The defensiveness of the period showed in Hall facing only five shots and Plante, four.

The third period was emotional as Mikita fought Hicke on the ice and in the penalty box. When Jean-Guy Talbot tried to get Mikita, Fleming grabbed Talbot. Chicago continued to defend its tenuous 1-0 lead and, with 80 seconds left, referee Dalton MacArthur sent Hay to the sin bin. Montreal saw its chance as Blake pulled Plante for the extra attacker. Swarming the Hawks net, the Canadiens were able to get a faceoff in the Hawks end to the right of Hall.

"In those days, defenceman often took the defending end faceoff," recalled Pierre. "I often took them, except in the penalty kill. For some reason I took that one in that key situation that night." He'd wish he hadn't.

Goyette cleanly beat Pierre on the draw, fed the puck over to Richard, whose shot beat Hall to tie the game with 36 seconds left. A hush fell over the crowd as the Canadiens rejoiced. The game was going into overtime.

Halfway into the first overtime, Montreal's Marshall took a pass from Goyette and slammed the winning goal behind Hall, but referee MacArthur signalled a high-stick no-goal. The Montreal bench instantly went from delirium to outrage. Both goalies continued to play flawlessly through the first overtime, each facing eight shots.

In the second overtime, Chicago threw 13 shots at Plante while Hall faced 19. Hall drove the fans into a frenzy with breakaway stops on Richard and Provost. Power plays created by penalties to Talbot and Langlois of the Canadiens and St. Laurent of Chicago brought no results.

During the extra-long game, it is amazing to note that most of the players didn't drink any water to hydrate themselves and between periods only sucked on sliced oranges. "Not drinking water might not have been good for us but we didn't know any better," said Hull. "Only Dollard St. Laurent drank copious amounts of water during a game, which we actually found weird. If I drank water, I just wanted more and more. The only nourishment we had that night was Tommy Ivan coming to our bench in Chicago during the third overtime with drops of brandy on sugar cubes."

As the teams started a sixth nerve-wracking period, tension wafted through the air like steam. Play see-sawed back and forth and the Stadium crowd held its collective breath until 11:44 of the period when MacArthur's hand went into the air to send Moore to the penalty box for tripping Litzenberger. Blake was screaming and gesturing wildly at MacArthur.

On the power play, the Hawks moved the puck into the Montreal end. Pierre passed the puck to Mikita, who shot it towards the crowded net. In the slot, Balfour got his stick on the rebound and shot through a melee of players and into the Montreal net. The place erupted after 112 minutes and 12 seconds of tough, hard-fought hockey.

An enraged Blake jumped onto the ice and weaved through the littered ice to the referee at the timekeeper's box. As his players tried to hold him back, Blake got to MacArthur, whose back was turned to him. Swinging, Blake's punch deflected off the unsuspecting referee's shoulder and hit his jaw. In shock, MacArthur turned around to see Blake lunging at him again while yelling profanities. His players grabbed Blake and pulled him off the ice as he continued screaming at MacArthur.

As he later pushed his way through to the dressing room, he stopped only long enough to tell reporters: "I haven't got a thing to say!"

From his place in the stands that night, NHL president Clarence Campbell saw everything and the next day slapped Blake with a whopping $2,000 fine for hitting MacArthur, which represented 11% of his $18,000 salary—the most severe punishment ever given to a coach at that time. When asked whether it was awkward to be fining a coach in the middle of a big series, Campbell answered tartly: "Blake is a coach and is subject to the rules just as anybody else in the league!" Campbell added that Blake was saved from suspension because of his past good record and the fact that "no injury was sustained."

Prior to Game 4, Blake had calmed down and talked openly of the incident. "I did something wrong," he apologized. "I shouldn't have. A guy can't go around doing things like that. It could have been worse . . . I could have been suspended."

He paused and smiled. "My wife went shopping in the Loop before it all happened. Now, maybe she'll have to go back tomorrow and return all those things she bought."

Thirteen minutes into Game 4 in Chicago on March 28, Bonin fell on top of Vasko and started punching the big Chicago defencemen, who didn't take kindly to the tactic and swung back. Within seconds, every player on the ice except the goalies were paired up. Referee Ed Powers thought he had finally restored order when Bonin started swinging at Vasko again. This time, Moose responded and got the better of him to the roar of the crowd.

"Poor Moose, he didn't throw punches like a real fighter," recalled Pierre with a smile. "The crowd was cheering, but Elmer was not a mean guy. He scared people because he was so big; he wasn't a fighter. But he wasn't a pussycat either and he wouldn't back down if pushed."

When Pilote and Backstrom each received spearing penalties, retired Canadiens legend Maurice Richard commented it was "the dirtiest hockey I've ever seen! I'm not talking about a rough series. I've played in plenty of rough ones but this one is the dirtiest!"

Champions do not go gently into the night and the Canadiens proved that handily as they turned on the heat to fire 26 shots at the Chicago net in the first period alone and didn't let up en route to a 60-shot, 5-2 victory that evened the rough series at two games apiece.

Going back to the Forum for Game 5, Montreal was a hurting squad. Béliveau was nursing a concussion, Geoffrion had torn knee ligaments, and Plante was nursing a sore knee.

"The Black Hawks were kicking the stuffing out of us,"

Geoffrion wrote in his memoirs. "Their tough defence had practically nullified our offence. And . . . we didn't have an antidote for their roughhousing!"

The tribe had its fair share of injuries as well but the return of big McDonald bolstered the physical game. In his pre-game pep talk, Pilous blasted the lack of defensive play by the forwards.

"I want one guy backchecking all the time!" Pilous boomed. "We'd better play defensive hockey or they're gonna outscore us again. I don't want you to score goals, I want you to come back. We've got enough goal scorers, they'll bide their time. I want you to backcheck!"

The talk was not lost and both teams played a cautious first period with no goals scored and, even more amazing, not a single penalty was called by referee Frank Udvari. In the second period, the Hawks' defensive play allowed only two Canadiens shots with Murphy in the penalty box. Having killed that time, Montreal's Talbot then tripped Pierre and was sent to the sin bin. The Hawks power play swung into gear.

Hull and Pilote pushed the play into the Montreal end, throwing the puck around in a give-and-go play that had their opponents flustered. Pierre threw the puck back to Vasko, whose high-screened shot bounced out of the net so quickly that Blake argued it hadn't entered the net; Udvari disagreed and the goal lifted the Hawks and quieted the Montreal bench and crowd.

"After that first goal, you could just feel it," recalled Litzenberger years later. "The guys knew we were just as good as they were."

The defensive Hawks allowed the Canadiens only 15 shots over two periods and their confidence was building. Behind 1-0 going into the third period, the Canadiens threw caution to the wind in an attempt to push the play into the tribe's end as the Chicagoans went into a defensive shell. The Hawks pounced on a Montreal mistake and counterattacked as Pierre got the puck up to McDonald, who fired the puck behind Plante to put the Hawks ahead 2-0.

Now in a panic, the Canadiens fired 17 shots at Hall from

every conceivable angle, especially with the man advantage during a Wharram penalty, but to no avail. A few minutes later, Mikita tipped in a McDonald shot from the right short side that sealed the deal. Henri Richard was so upset on the play that he pushed Udvari and drew a 10-minute and game misconduct.

"That was a big one!" shouted Hall as he walked in the jubilant Hawks dressing room after his first career playoff shutout having stopped all 32 shots the Canadiens threw at him.

"They'll have to start respecting us now!" yelled Pilous. "That was a clutch game."

"Game 5 in Montreal, you've got to really give that one to Glenn," said Pierre of the win. "Glenn really played well. It was amazing really. But we were checking too!"

In the Canadiens dressing room, things were bleak and angry. "You can't score goals holding onto the puck!" screamed Montreal GM Frank Selke. "You've got to shoot it into the net and if you don't, you're going to have trouble with me next year [at contract signing time]. It's obvious these boys aren't interested in money the way those other guys are!"

"They outplayed us and outskated us," was Blake's simple explanation.

The Hawks were given another boost at 3 a.m. on Easter morning when they arrived at O'Hare International Airport, where they were welcomed home by a large crowd.

"What a difference in the years when we started flying," recalled Pierre. "The transition from trains to planes was great! The meal was always filet mignon. The flight was an hour, hour and a half. What a speed up from those long train rides to New York or Montreal. We had more free time and it was more restful.

"In those early years, the plane's landing gear was very noisy when dropping, so before it would drop I'd say to a new rookie, 'This plane doesn't sound right,' and they'd look at me concerned, then when the loud roar occurred beneath us it would scare the shit out of them. Oh, I laughed!"

The Hawks were confident as they worked out the day before Game 6.

"They're a tough team anytime," cautioned Litzenberger. "They're the defending world champions with their backs to the wall. It's a game they must win. Now is the time for us to pour it on!"

"I've been excited about my horse races . . . the Kentucky Derby. I've been worked up over championship fights . . . but it's hard for anyone to understand my thinking about the Black Hawks," a nervous Jim Norris told columnist David Condon. "You don't have an idea how I've suffered with this club. You don't know how I worry that we might blow the semifinal if we don't clinch it in the big one here tomorrow night! The boys know they can win it . . . the goal's right there for 'em to grab! This thing is as personal as a kiss!"

As the Canadiens boarded the train for the 22-hour trip to Chicago, Blake was still feeling confident that his team could rise to the occasion as they had so often in the past. Clouding their efforts was the fact that Béliveau was still not fully recovered from the Game 1 hit and Geoffrion had a cast on his left leg.

Knowing Geoffrion's importance on the Habs power play, team captain Harvey crazily removed the cast from Boom Boom's leg, so that by the time the team arrived in Chicago, a cast-less Geoffrion hobbled off the train, in pain but ready to play. It was an indication of the panic the Habs felt about the do-or-die game.

The Madhouse on Madison was in a frenzy for the sixth game on April 5 as a standing-room-only crowd of 18,000-plus jammed in. Warm weather and an ice show a few days earlier had made the ice rough and slushy, which the Hawks figured could work to their advantage in slowing down the flying Frenchmen.

Desperate, Montreal came at the Hawks with everything they had, and made many four-man rushes into the Chicago zone in a bid to get the all-important first goal, but the Hawks defence stood tall while the forwards backchecked furiously. Chicago counter-attacked as well when Sloan and Murphy had partial breakaways but were stopped by Plante.

The bleak Montreal situation was epitomized by Geoffrion's falling twice on his bad knee. He was ineffective in the little bit he played in the game. Matters became worse for Montreal when goalie Plante hooked Mikita, who was swarming around his net at the 16:15 mark, and the Hawks power play was poised to strike.

It almost backfired. With the Hawks pressing, Canadiens speedster Marshall suddenly nabbed the puck and broke in alone on Hall at the other end. Marshall tried to stuff the puck under Hall but Mr. Goalie made a kick save that brought the house down.

"I don't think Don got off the kind of shot he's capable of," Hall said of the Marshall breakaway after the game. "That ice was pretty bad and he didn't get in his best lick."

Mr. Goalie's great play kept the first period scoreless as Montreal outshot the tribe 12-7, which included a Hab two-man advantage at one point.

The Hawks charged out of the gate in the second period when, after a give-and-go passing play with Hull and Balfour, Red Hay stuffed the puck behind Plante in a play that broke the ice and the Canadiens spirit. Four minutes later with Langlois in the penalty box, the Hawks pressed again. Balfour passed the puck to Pierre on the point and his hard shot was tipped in by Hull to put the Hawks up 2-0.

"Pierre and I played so well together," recalled Hull of that playoff year. "I was always giving him the puck. He knew what to do with it!"

The Hawks went into a tight-checking shell to protect their lead but pounced on a Montreal mistake and moved the puck into the Canadiens end. Hull, whose backchecking was turning heads in the series, took a bad angle shot from the left side that Plante stopped but Nesterenko popped in the rebound to put the Chicagoans up 3-0. The goal was met by a thunderous ovation as firecrackers popped.

Seizing the opportunity, the third period was all Chicago as they checked and backchecked the undermanned Canadiens into the ice in an attempt to preserve the lead and the shutout.

"Our philosophy as a team was, 'If we had the puck, then they couldn't do anything with it!'" related Hull. "A good defence is a good offence."

With four minutes left in the game, they indeed had the puck, and the crowd was on its feet, roaring. They wanted not only the victory, but another Hall shutout. They got it as the tribe outshot the Habs 12-7 in the final frame. At the final buzzer, pandemonium reigned. The Hawks had stopped a sixth straight Canadiens' Stanley Cup, eliminating them four games to two.

In the exuberant Chicago dressing room afterwards, Mr. Goalie extolled the virtues of the whole team. "I don't think you could say that any one player was a bit better than anyone else," Hall said. "This was strictly a team performance, the greatest one I ever have had anything to do with!"

"The size and the condition of our guys helped a lot in the soggy going," added Pilous. "It took less out of us and we were better able to keep control late in the game. We had to be because we beat a hell of a hockey team to get this far. This was far and away our best game. Unquestionably, the Canadiens missed Boom Boom Geoffrion."

Blake gallantly made his way to the happy Chicago dressing room and personally congratulated every Chicago player.

"I still thought we had a good chance of winning because we have a great team," Blake said to reporters. "But we had those injuries and some of the fellows looked tired. The Hawks had too much desire for us . . . they have three well-balanced lines, and they are the biggest team in hockey."

As the Hawks looked ahead to the Stanley Cup Final against the rampaging Red Wings who had easily eliminated the Maple Leafs four games to one, it was left to Pilous to ensure that his Hawks stayed focused.

"We'll have to be just as good against Detroit!" Pilous told reporters. "The Wings have a hot hand too."

"When we put out Montreal, it was a big boost," recalled Pierre.

"Having beat the previous champions was like having three hands on the Stanley Cup. It sure gave us confidence. But, now, we had to move on, put Montreal behind us, and quickly focus on Detroit."

The Hawks were going to the Stanley Cup final for the first time in 17 years. And if that wasn't pressure enough, the Windy City hadn't won a Stanley Cup since 1938.

Dancing with Stanley

The 1961 Detroit Red Wings were not the powerhouse they had been in the early 1950s but they were still a formidable force that was playing well. After losing the first game to Toronto in the other semifinal, the fourth-place Red Wings had roared back to defeat the second-place Leafs in four straight games. Allowing only five goals in the four wins, they were getting stellar goaltending from the legendary Terry Sawchuk, who had been named one of three stars in all five games. "Terry is the Terry of old, playing like he did when we were winning Stanley Cups and he was the greatest!" exclaimed Gordie Howe.

With a strong lineup, the Wings had to be taken just as seriously as the Canadiens.

Hockey fever in Chicago was at an all-time high in April 1961 as fans started lining up four abreast at the Stadium box office for Stanley Cup final tickets at 6 a.m. the day before Game 1. The ticket line stretched clear around the parking lot.

The same day, Pilous held a practice to "look into their eyes following a well-earned victory celebration," and was pleased that "all the players were able to follow the puck!"

"Hawks 13 to 10 Favourites Over Wings," was the headline heading into the first all-U.S. Cup final since 1950, which assured a

Norris would win the Cup since Jim's Hawks were facing a Detroit team owned by his siblings, Bruce and Marguerite.

The Hawks were healthy, with only captain Ed Litzenberger in Henrotin Hospital fighting a bad flu. Ronald "Chico" Maki was flown in from Buffalo to replace him. The Wings were hurting with Sawchuk nursing a sore shoulder and bruised hip while his defence buddy Marcel Pronovost had a cracked fibula in his foot. With the chips on the line, nothing was going to keep the big Red Wings defenceman out of the lineup.

"I wore a removable cast, hobbled to the arena on crutches. Five minutes prior to the national anthem, the doctors came in with the needles and froze the ankle," recalled Pronovost. "I'd lace up the skates, tape the ankle, and out I would go. That's how I began that series with Chicago."

It was a scalper's dream with box seats going for $20 instead of the usual $6, mezzanines for $12 instead of $4.50, and first balcony tickets for $8.00 instead of $3.50. The capacity crowd roared as the Hawks took to the ice.

The tribe came with the same physical game that had worked against Montreal and Sawchuk quickly bore the brunt of it. Four minutes into the game, Murray Balfour's collision with the Detroit goalie after a chase for a loose puck left Sawchuk writhing on the ice with a painful left shoulder. After a five-minute delay, Sawchuk continued.

Detroit's Warren Godfrey and Howie Young tried their own physical game against the Hawks, but the move backfired when Young went off for boarding and Bobby Hull connected on the ensuing power play. A minute later, the Scooter Line brought the puck right back into the Detroit zone. Ab McDonald's shot was stopped by Sawchuk, but Kenny Wharram batted in the rebound to make it 2-0 Chicago at the 10:10 mark of the first period.

The Hawks kept coming. Three minutes later, Pierre deftly carried the puck out of his own end and his cross-ice pass inside the

Red Wing blue line caught his favourite target, Hull, in full flight. The left-winger swung in towards Sawchuk and fired a bullet behind the netminder just as he crashed into him. The goalie was left writhing in pain for the second time. Sawchuk again recovered and finished out the period but his backup, Hank Bassen, was in the net to start the second period with Chicago up 3-0.

The Hawks continued the physical game and it cost them. Referee Frank Udvari penalized Jack Evans for tripping and then 28 seconds later, he sent Reg Fleming to the box for boarding. For the third time in these playoffs, the Hawks would be two men short for almost two minutes.

Rudy Pilous sent Pilote, Moose Vasko, and Eric Nesterenko out again. It was nail-biting time. The Wings tried valiantly to find an open man but Pierre managed to clear the puck out of the zone three times. Another time, Howe was taking dead aim from 25 feet directly in front of Hall when Pierre fell to his knees and knocked the puck down the ice just as Fleming came out of the penalty box. The Hawks were called for icing. The penalties had been killed and Pierre received a roar of approval from the crowd and pats of appreciation from his teammates as he went to the bench.

A holding penalty against Red Hay at 15:42 of the second period gave Detroit another power play and they capitalized when Len Lunde beat Hall to end Mr. Goalie's amazing playoff shutout streak at 171 minutes and 50 seconds, which had stretched back to the third period of the fourth game against Montreal.

The Hawks lead carried into the third period as the Wings pressed, outshooting the Hawks by a 13-8 margin. A tip-in goal by Allan Johnson with 43 seconds left made the 3-2 lead tenuous. The crowd and its team held its collective breath. The Wings immediately pulled Bassen and swarmed the Chicago net but were unable to get the equalizer before time expired.

Though his team had won, Pilous was not happy about the win. "Too close for comfort! Instead of firing the puck out of there, our boys got tricky and tried to skate it out. Well, the first thing you know, Howe's got the puck and they've got a goal. You can't get tricky with Gordie Howe!" said Pilous.

"We'll get 'em!" vowed the usually quiet Howe. "This will give us a real lift because we didn't fold up!"

"This is a game hockey club," boasted Detroit GM Jack Adams. "We had a perfect chance to quit . . . but we didn't. I'm well pleased everything considered! It'll be tough, but I'll assure you one thing— this Chicago club isn't going to out-rough us."

Detroit fans must have heard Adams's declaration because after the game a fight broke out inside the Billy Goat Tavern across from the Stadium on West Madison Street. It took 30 police officers to restore order, with four of them hospitalized, while seven persons were jailed overnight.

Game 2 of the series was uncharacteristically shifted to Detroit's Olympia due to a skating show at the Stadium. The Hawks' chartered flight touched down in Detroit without Litzenberger, who was still in hospital.

Sawchuk and Pronovost didn't dress but the rest of the Wings picked up the slack, led by the temperamental Young. Not only did Young belt out bodychecks, delighting the 14,000 fans, but he also scored the game's first goal, assisted by Alex Delvecchio. With Dollard St. Laurent in the penalty box, Delvecchio gave the Wings a two-goal lead just before the first period ended. The Hawks mustered a mere two shots on Bassen in the Detroit net.

Pierre took matters into his own hands in the second period when he intercepted a Detroit clearing pass out of their zone and his quick backhand shot from the right point landed behind a surprised and screened Bassen to bring the Hawks to within one.

The Wings threw up a blanket of checking in front of Bassen as Chicago pressed in the third before Delvecchio popped in the empty netter in the last minute of the game to seal a 3-1 victory and tie the series.

In Chicago for Game 3, Pilous changed strategy and relieved winger Ron Murphy from checking Howe, giving that task to

Hull. Not only did Pilous figure a freed-up Murphy could spark the attack but the coach reckoned with Hull playing a solid two-way game thus far, he'd be able to blanket Howe and still break free offensively when opportunity knocked. Pilous was right.

The Hawks put on the pressure from the puck drop, but brilliant goaltending by Bassen kept the Chicagoans goalless in the first period. Stan Mikita ended the scoring impasse by scoring from Hull at the 11:54 mark. Less than three minutes later, Murphy made it 2-0 after a three-way passing play with Litzenberger and Pilote. Chicago continued to press and after Bassen had kicked out a Hull shot, Balfour tucked in the rebound past the sprawled goaltender to make it 3-0.

The teams stuck to playing hockey as referee Ed Powers didn't call a single penalty in the second period, but the two teams had him blowing his whistle early in the third. Hall's shutout was broken when Howe eluded Hull and beat him from the slot. Howe's first goal of the series wasn't enough, and the Hawks won handily, 3-1, to take the series lead.

When Pierre, who had assisted on the first two Hawks goals, walked into the dressing room he yelled excitedly: "We're halfway home, gang!"

"Yeah! We'll wrap it up in two more!" someone else screamed back.

The next day, Pilous said his team had more than enough incentive to finish the job.

"I'm not worried about keeping them up," Pilous said. "They're mature men and they know what they have to do." When asked to comment on Howe, Pilous answered: "Hell! Howe's just another hockey player! We're going to use our weight to good advantage from here on in."

On April 11, Montreal sports columnist Red Fisher praised Pierre: "Pilote has his own rooting section, which has come up with a sign that reads, 'There's none so fair as our Pierre!' Pilote has been all of that during the playoffs against the Canadiens and the Red Wings. He has been the most consistent man on defence although there has been little to choose between any of the Chicago defencemen, but he's in a class by himself going both ways."

The Pilote accolades continued in a story filed the day of Game 4 by W.R. Wheatley of the Canadian Press. "Despite a remarkable record in the post-season," Wheatley wrote, "Pilote has been almost overlooked in the wild acclaim for goal-scoring forwards and the brilliance of goaltenders."

The same day, Detroit coach Sid Abel said the Chicago ice in Game 3 was "the worst ice I have ever seen!" He also took a shot back at Pilous's remarks that the Hawks were hungrier. "They're not any hungrier than we are! They just grabbed control of the game in Chicago. We certainly didn't want them to control the game but they did."

The good news for Detroit was that Game 4 was back in the friendly confines of the Olympia, and Pronovost and Sawchuk were back. It was clear that Detroit came to play as they outshot the listless Hawks 14-6 in the first period, but Hall was again superlative in keeping it scoreless.

The Hawks came to life in the second when Hay fired a high shot over Sawchuk's arm to put the Hawks up by one at the seven-minute mark. The lead was short-lived though, as 36 seconds later Hull was in the penalty box for high-sticking Young. Half a minute into the power play Delvecchio took a slapshot that hit Fleming's butt and bounced in the air. Delvecchio knocked it down with his glove and fired a 40-footer under Hall's left leg to tie the game and brought a roar from the Olympia crowd. The Hawks outshot the Wings 10-9 in the second but the score stayed 1-1.

It was an unruly affair both on and off the ice and the game was delayed several times by Red Wings fans littering the playing surface with debris that included a bottle of ink, an octopus, and even a live hamster.

Play see-sawed back and forth in the third period and with less than seven minutes left, rookie Bruce MacGregor took a shot from the slot that squeezed through a screened and falling Hall into the net. The Hawks bench screamed at Udvari about MacGregor and Young's interference on Hall in the crease, but to no avail. The goal stood. As time wound down, the Wings threw a blanket around Sawchuk, who faced 10 third-period shots against Hall's five, to close out the victory and even the series.

In the Chicago dressing room, Pilous was livid at Udvari, and called the game the worst-officiated of the series.

"Glover was committing a penalty when the winning goal was scored," added Pilous. "And that penalty on Murray Balfour— Howe held his stick and held him down. Howe just gets away with too much! He's a helluva hockey player but of all the infractions in the book, he invented half of them. If [Udvari] wants to watch a game he should buy a ticket and stay in the stands!"

General manager Tommy Ivan, not one to generally comment, was even angrier. "Adams put out the statement late in the season that Udvari was picking on Howie Young and apparently it took!" Ivan began. "Udvari let the game get out of hand and never caught up with it. He let Howe clutch and grab sticks all night. Hull may have had a penalty coming—I never complain against penalties called against my guys—but if Hull can get nailed for an infraction, why can't Howe? Finally, in the last half minute of the game, when we had Hall out of the goal, Stasiuk interfered with Hull all the way down the ice . . . but Udvari just skated along! I don't care if there are 15 minutes or 15 seconds to go, a penalty is a penalty!"

When Udvari was leaving the Olympia that night at the same time as Fleming, the Hawk launched a verbal tirade at him. Udvari was having none of it.

"If you want to stay in the league you'd better get on back there with your teammates," the referee shot back.

Back in his office at the Stadium the next day, Ivan wouldn't let it go. "That call against Hull was a disgrace! He was 15 feet away from anybody! His stick got caught in the boards and as he yanked it loose it lifted into the air. I don't think Udvari knew what happened. He just guessed."

Ivan must have known that his statements would not go over well with the league. NHL president Clarence Campbell fined him $300 and Pilous $200 "for making statements that had the effect of impugning the courage and integrity of the game officials. They were entirely unwarranted and in violation of league bylaws."

"Udvari was the best NHL referee," recalled Pierre of the controversial refereeing. "For the most part, I found him fair. Only once or twice did I really get upset. Eddie Powers was good too. Udvari was a nice guy, always trying to be above the crowd. You're talking about the Stanley Cup. In the playoffs, referees put the whistle away for 50% more of the infractions. You knew if you got a cheap call against you, you'd get it back later. The problem would be if they didn't call obvious penalties against just one team, then that wasn't good! Penalties can decide things."

Heading back to Chicago for Game 5, the series now tied, the Hawks had an emotional chip on their shoulder and they were angry.

When Udvari stepped onto the ice on April 14, he was roundly booed by a standing-room-only crowd and even had a few oranges tossed at him.

"The atmosphere of the Chicago Stadium was electric and amazing," reminisced Hull. "When the national anthem started, the greatest fans in the world started that great crescendo, which followed through until they dropped the puck. What a lift!"

The Wings had come to play. With Sawchuk in net again, Detroit had Chicago penned in their zone within two minutes. As the Hawks scrambled, Detroit's Allan Johnson grabbed a loose puck and skated towards Hall. His shot was stopped by Mr. Goalie, but Leo Labine stuffed home the rebound at the 2:14 mark to put Detroit on the board. The Hawks were being so thoroughly checked that they didn't get a shot on Sawchuk for nearly six minutes.

The Chicagoans, scrambling to hold back the rampaging

Wings, wouldn't get their second shot on Sawchuk until the 10-minute mark but it counted, as Balfour took a pass from Hay and beat Sawchuk at the goalmouth to bring the crowd to its feet. Twenty-eight seconds later, Murphy knocked down a shoulder-high pass with his glove in the Detroit end and shot the puck into the Detroit net to make it 2-1. As the Stadium crowd roared, the Wings bench exploded, claiming that Murphy had knocked the puck in with his glove, but Udvari disagreed and the goal stood. Undeterred, Detroit tied the game with Vasko in the penalty box at the 15:35 mark of the first.

The second period was even until Pierre took a shot at Sawchuk and Balfour knocked in the rebound for his second goal of the night, making it 3-2. Minutes later, the stubborn Wings tied it on a Vic Stasiuk goal before the period was out.

As Pilous headed to the Hawks dressing room he was seething. Having blown leads twice in the game, he knew his team had to win this one. Deep in the bowels of Chicago Stadium, his roaring criticism was scathing. His voice rising in fury, he asked them to dig deeper, reminding them they didn't want to lose at home and risk heading back to Detroit with the Cup on the line.

"I gave 'em hell!" Pilous later said. "I just wanted to find out if this is an honest hockey team or not."

"They took the criticism like thoroughbreds," added Ivan.

The tactic worked. The Hawks came out flying in the third, led by the Million Dollar Line, Mikita, and Pilote. As Hull and company pushed immediately into the Detroit end, Young tripped Balfour, who fell heavily into the goalpost. The play resulted in a Hawks power play, but Balfour was lost for good with a broken arm.

Seizing the moment, Pierre and company came at Detroit. Just after 30 seconds with the man advantage, Pierre fired a point shot that Sawchuk stopped but Mikita poked in the rebound to send the West Madison Street crowd crazy as the Hawks went ahead 3-2. The Hawks continued to press, and five minutes later, Pierre fired the puck at the Detroit net when Wings defenceman Godfrey deflected the puck into his own net. The place exploded in mayhem. Chicago smelled blood and didn't let up as the Wings scrambled. When Mikita scored the sixth and final goal from Murphy at 13:27 of the final period, it capped a wild finish as they pelted 24 third-period shots at Sawchuk. At the final buzzer, the jubilant Hawks clambered down the 22 steps and into their dressing room to the chants of: "Just one more! Just one more!"

Pilous was asked to comment on the officiating. Choosing his words carefully, he indicated that he still wasn't entirely happy about the officiating, but before he could say anything of substance, some of his players piped up: "Watch it, Rudy or you'll get fined again." He smiled and paused.

"Well, they finally got Gordie Howe with a penalty," he remarked sarcastically.

When asked the same question about Udvari's officiating, Detroit coach Sid Abel had no comment.

Pierre's contribution to the Hawks playoff success was gaining notice as demonstrated by a piece written by Charley Barton, who pointed out that Pierre was leading all playoff point-getters with three goals and 11 assists for 14 points, unheard of for a defenceman. When asked about the fact that he hadn't missed a game in his four years with Chicago, Pierre answered: "I've been fortunate to keep away from any serious injuries."

"We were confident going into Detroit, but not overconfident," recalled Pierre. "I personally was having fun. I think that's why I was playing so well."

Fretful owner Jim Norris was not having fun. He was a bundle of nerves and he wasn't about to jinx his team's hopes so he barred Johnny Gottselig, the team's public relations man, from buying or icing any champagne for a dressing room celebration should they win it all.

The team left Detroit's Leland Hotel at 5:30 p.m., except room-mates Hall and Litzenberger. When the two gentlemen calmly emerged from their room on the 21st floor a half hour later to go for a walk, they met sportswriter Red Fisher in the hallway as they all waited for the elevator. Fisher was surprised to see the two men.

"You're not giving yourselves much time," quipped the writer to the two hockey players.

"What do you mean?" they answered. "It's only 6:05."

"Yeah, that's what I've got too," answered Fisher. "But the game starts at seven."

The teammates looked at each other calmly, trying not to laugh.

"Aw, he's just pulling our leg!" Litzenberger said to Hall with a wan smile.

"Yeah," said Hall, grinning nervously. "It's an eight o'clock game."

"The game starts at seven o'clock!" the scribe answered dead seriously as the elevator doors opened.

"You're *not* kidding!" Litzenberger suddenly realized.

"No, I'm not kidding," the Montrealer answered, which sent the two men into a sudden panic. Needless to say, the elevator couldn't get down the 21 storeys fast enough and when its doors opened to the lobby, the *Montreal Star* writer saw the two men fly out of the front doors yelling frantically for a taxi.

On April 16, the Stanley Cup, shipped by rail from Montreal, was in the Olympia for the sixth game.

In North Carolina, a very interested person was frantically trying to keep tabs on the series. Flo Pilote had just finished playing 64 games for the Charlotte Checkers of the Eastern Hockey League. The team hadn't made the playoffs, and Flo was trying to eke out a living during the off-season.

"I was doing my best to keep tabs on my brother Pierre," recalled Flo. "They were on the verge of winning the Cup. Jesus Christ, I had to somehow hear this game, you know! I was living in a small trailer in Charlotte, North Carolina, on a high hill. I got into my little '49 Ford, got some wire, and hooked it up to the car antenna, to make it extra long. Somehow I made that radio work, and I could hear it! The sound was fading in and out. I got a six-pack of beer and I could hear the game! The teams were coming onto the ice! Jesus it was exciting!"

The Wings were confident as each team had won at home. With Bassen back in the Detroit net, the Wings took it to the Hawks from the opening faceoff. The Hawks seemed frazzled, disorganized from the get-go.

Perhaps thrown off their game by the very late arrival of Hall and Litzenberger, the Hawks were scrambling and badly outplayed, but Mr. Goalie kept them in it. An early penalty to Arbour handed the Detroiters a power play and they pressed. Howe's 40-foot shot was stopped by Hall, but Parker McDonald banged home the rebound through Hall's legs at the 15:24 mark of the first period to give the Wings the lead. With its victim reeling, Detroit continued to press but Hall, Pilote, and company scrambled to stave off more damage despite being outshot badly as the period ended.

Watching his team's woeful performance from the door of his bench, Pilous couldn't understand his team's performance.

In the dressing room, his voice started out loud but then softened, which got their attention.

"You all know that was not your best! You all know that Glenn saved us in that period, again. I don't have to tell you that! You all know what's at stake. Over $1,000 is riding on this game for you guys! If you don't start skating out there, you may as well forget it!"

He looked around, took a deep breath and chose his next words carefully. "Look, it's too late for me to do any more hollering. You've come this far . . . it's all up to you now." He turned and walked out.

Early in the second period a Hawks power play was totally listless. What was going to wake them up, Pilous wondered? Then, at the six-minute mark, Chicago rookie Wayne Hicks took a penalty. The Hawks were in even deeper trouble. The Detroit power play pressed but barely 20 seconds into their advantage, penalty-killer Fleming stole the puck at his blue line and carried it through centre ice into the opposing zone. Losing the puck to Stasiuk, Fleming took it back and fired a shot behind a surprised Bassen to tie the game and stun the crowd. The Hawks had life.

"Bassen thought I was going to cut over to centre ice," explained Fleming after the game. "I just flipped it in on the short side."

The goal jolted Detroit and they pressed into the Chicago end again, but Mr. Goalie was up to the task, with a little help from Lady Luck. Hall stopped a long shot with his glove but the puck wobbled straight up into the air, hit the crossbar, and plopped back into his outstretched glove. On another power play later in the period, Howe's shot from the blue line had Hall desperately kicking while falling and his catching glove snared the puck just before it crossed the goal line. The Wings argued vehemently that the puck had crossed the line, but referee Powers, standing nearby, immediately shook his head sideways.

Play went back and forth as the Chicagoans finally found their legs. With a little more than a minute left in the second, Mikita sent Hull into the Detroit zone with a perfectly timed pass. The blond superstar carried the puck around the defence and went crashing in on Bassen as he shot. Bassen made the stop, but was taken out by Hull and the rebound was left wide open for McDonald to tap in the go-ahead goal. Amidst the celebrations, Detroit's Young cross-checked an unsuspecting Mikita, who fell into a heap on the ice. Seeing the vicious and late check, Pilote and Hull raced towards Young. Pierre won the race but, at the last second, merely swung his stick to graze Young's head.

"I was mad when I took that swing, but I guess I held back a bit," Pilote confessed after the game. "I guess I didn't try too hard."

"I was going to hit him right in the head, I was so mad!" recalled Pierre as if it was yesterday. "Young's crazy! I was gonna get him. At the last moment I changed my mind. Sometimes, you remain a human being and not an animal. I was glad I didn't, because there would have been a suspension. I could have been out of the series. I was glad I didn't. I had other ways of getting him back."

In Charlotte, Flo was listening with intensity and eagerness.

"They were playing—I could hear it!" recalled Flo Pilote. "The sound was coming in and out; Jesus, but I can hear, 'Pierre Pilote, Pierre Pilote!' The announcer's saying his name quite a bit, 'Pierre Pilote has the puck,' 'Pilote moves up,' 'Passes the puck to Bobby Hull; Hull shoots, he scores!' Ah, that's what it sounded like! I was broke, didn't have much, but I had it all that night."

The McDonald goal and Mikita incident galvanized the Hawks and they suddenly came at the Wings with renewed fire. Bassen kept it close. A minute into the third period, Pierre exacted his revenge by assisting on Nesterenko's third Chicago goal. Pierre's 12th playoff assist was a record for defencemen, breaking Doug Harvey's mark.

The desperate Wings opened things up, which left them exposed, and at the 6:27 mark Hawks defencemen Evans grabbed the puck, split the Detroit defence, and beat Bassen with a slider along the ice. It was his first goal in two years.

"That goddamned Jack Evans," Hull said with gusto. "He took the puck, went up the middle, and scored a goal, like a Pierre Pilote! Just like an All-Star defenceman!"

Then Wharram broke free, split the Wings defence, and fired a low shot that beat Bassen and sealed the deal. When the game ended, the Hawks poured over the boards and mobbed Hall. As the two teams lined up for the customary handshakes on a hard-fought series, the animosity evaporated as Young apologized to Mikita for the cross-check. Mikita told him there were no hard feelings.

MacDonald, Mikita, and Vasko temporarily hoisted Mr. Goalie onto their shoulders to hail their conquering hero. Team supporters flooded onto the ice, and when the Cup was wheeled out and presented to captain Litzenberger, Flo Pilote was still sitting in his car listening to his radio, overcome with tears of joy at his brother's success. "It was so emotional! Pierre, my brother, had won the Stanley Cup! Wow! I was all alone, but that didn't matter. I had one of my beers in a toast! I was so happy and proud!"

The Stanley Cup sat on a table at centre ice as the team gathered around it for a picture. When Pilous took his hat off and placed it on the table, Pierre grabbed the hat and laughingly placed it on the Cup, then flung the hat high into the air with the exuberance of a child. The Cup was carried into the dressing room by Litzenberger. Fleming was the first player to reach the dressing room and appropriately, he let out a whoop like an Indian.

"Whew! Yes sir!" he yelled. "We won the big one!"

An exuberant Jim Norris stood at the door congratulating each player as he entered. Soon the room was a cacophony of celebration and yelling.

"That was the biggest goal of my life!" Fleming shouted above the din. "How about that? My first year in the league, we get in the finals, and win the Stanley Cup! What else can you ask for?"

"Fleming was the spark plug," commented Pilous. "His goal in the second period gave us the lift we needed, the turning point! It was a terrific series with Detroit, just as it was with Montreal. We finished a little stronger than the Wings. Maybe our little added weight helped us. It was a great season!"

Amidst the hugs, backslapping, and hoopla dawned the realization that there was something missing from the celebrations.

Litzenberger approached Pilous.

"Rudy, the boys are complaining," Litzenberger.

"Complaining? Why?" asked the coach, surprised.

"There's no champagne for the Cup!"

A few bottles of ginger ale found their way into the room to fill in for champagne. Bruce Norris, owner of the Wings, came in to congratulate his brother, Jim, who was taking a swig out of the Stanley Cup.

"Leave a little in the bottom, Jim," said Bruce.

"We didn't want to jinx the boys," explained Norris later. "They'll get all the champagne they want at our victory celebrations when we get back to Chicago."

Jack Adams came into the room to offer his congratulations. "They had too many big guns and muscle for us," said the Wings

GM. "We gave it a real good shot but that goal by Fleming while we had a man advantage killed us."

Wing players Howe and Sawchuk also came in, and Sawchuk headed straight to an exhausted Hall to offer his congratulations. The two men smiled at each other as they shook hands.

The small dressing room became especially crowded when members of the 1938 Stanley Cup–winning Hawks came in, including goalies Mike Karakas and Alfie Moore, players Carl Voss and John Gottselig, and coach Bill Stewart.

For Pierre the moment was surreal. "I never realized how good that Stanley Cup looked until I had my picture taken with it!" Pierre said to the assembled press.

"I used to think money was the most important thing in hockey," Hall said. "But winning that Cup proved how wrong I was."

Then Paul Pilote, who had driven with Maria from Fort Erie to Detroit, squeezed his way into the dressing room.

"It was special having Dad come into the dressing room afterwards to be with the team," recalled Pierre. "I have a picture of him and me with the Stanley Cup. Mom couldn't come into the room in those days, so I went and saw her in the hallway. She was happy. I was kind of in a trance about the whole thing. I didn't know how to enjoy the moment. I was not the kind of guy to jump around and stuff. I was quietly happy."

When Adams returned to the tomb-like Red Wings dressing room, he couldn't resist taking a final shot at the new champions. "The league built them up. Let's face it—we gave them a lot. All the teams in the league gave them players in trades and drafts or they wouldn't be in the league now. It was a high price for the league to pay, but it was worth it to create balance."

When told of Adams's comments about his team being built by the league, Norris bristled. "We spent a million dollars since 1957 to build the team that won this championship! If you look through the trades and switches we made, you'll see that we traded away plenty of talent. And study our roster—we produced our own stars such as Elmer Vasko, Pierre Pilote, Stan Mikita, and Bobby Hull."

After the accolades and celebrations in the dressing room were done, the team rushed to shower and dress, and catch the flight home. A blinding snowstorm had them sitting and waiting at the airport, the status of their flight uncertain.

"We were having a few beers at the airport bar, we couldn't take off," Pierre recalled. "Bobby had filled up Mike Wirtz's hat and we were drinking champagne out of that hat. I think Bobby later was sick!"

The flight was officially cancelled after two hours, and the team bused back to the Leland Hotel, where Norris reserved two full floors for his team and supporters to stay and party. There turned out to be one minor problem: someone had forgotten to tell Pierre and Moose about the party because they headed back to their room.

"Big Elmer had been really uptight during the playoffs, hadn't slept well," remembered Pierre. "So he finally unwound and had a quite a few beers at the airport. Back in our room, he called his wife, Claudette, and I called Annie and the next thing I know, big Elmer is flaked out on the bed, snoring away. He's gone for the night. I think he just collapsed from sheer relief and exhaustion.

"So then I thought, 'Boy what am I going to do now?' I walked two blocks to a nearby bar and had a couple of beers, alone in my thoughts. When I went back up to the room, Elmer was sleeping away. I got into bed and went to sleep. I didn't know they were celebrating somewhere in the hotel. That's how stupid I was! They had a big party and everybody was asking where Pierre and Moose were. That was Moose and my big Stanley Cup night celebration!"

The next day a large crowd greeted the returning champions at O'Hare Field, and they were given a police escort to City Hall, where a seven-piece Dixieland band played "Chicago." When the heroes walked into council chambers the band then broke into a rendition of "When the Saints Go Marching In."

"The greatest hockey team ever put together anywhere!" boasted

Mayor Richard Daley to loud applause from the gathered crowd. "No team can surpass them for ability and agility!"

Daley then presented Litzenberger with certificates of merit for the whole team, while Pierre came forward to accept the Mayor Richard J. Daley Trophy.

From there, the team, wives, and officials headed to the Bismark Hotel, owned by Wirtz, for an official victory celebration. The Stanley Cup was the guest of honour, and everyone took turns having their picture taken with it or drinking champagne out of it.

Pilous got up to say a few remarks and finished by jokingly saying, "No practice tomorrow!"

The next day, the team gathered for an official team picture with the Stanley Cup and then headed to a Mexican restaurant to celebrate some more. For Pierre, winning the most prized trophy in sport hadn't quite sunk in yet.

"There was no big Stanley Cup parade in those days. It wasn't really until two days later, I went out with Annie to a restaurant with our neighbours, Pat Hart and his wife, and that's when it struck me and I really started celebrating, in my mind. All of a sudden I started feeling great.

"To win the Stanley Cup, Mr. Goalie, Glenn Hall, was sensational, there was no doubt about that, and also a real team effort. Everyone contributed. Everybody played a part of it, the veterans, the youngsters, everyone stepped up. It's a long row."

After three days of celebrating, the players bid each other a triumphant but bittersweet goodbye for another summer. As they left for their individual lives throughout Canada, some stayed in the Chicago area. Pierre returned to Fort Erie with Annie and the kids. He and his teammates were all pleased to have accomplished what every hockey player dreamed of, but few got to boast about—they had won the Stanley Cup.

CHAPTER 13

Easier to Climb the
Mountain Than to Stay on Top

"It's great to be back!" exclaimed Pierre to a crowd of four hundred as he opened the 1961 Fort Erie Trade Fair. "Many people asked me how it felt to win the Stanley Cup. It is obviously a great thrill, but the real thrills come when one is welcomed back to his hometown like this!"

After the cheering subsided, Mayor Herbert T. Guest presented Pierre with a fishing tackle set. The Knights of Columbus of Council #3320 also had a dinner in his honour.

The *Niagara Falls Evening Review* sent reporter Janet Garth to the Pilote home on Aberdeen Court in Fort Erie to do a story on the champion and his young family. A picture accompanying the story showed Pierre and Annie with their three children: one-year-old Renee, four-year-old Pierre Jr., and six-year-old Denise, holding the family dog, Pico.

Annie talked about the challenges and rewards she and her children had in accompanying Pierre to Chicago for the season and to some of the many different events he's invited to during the off-season.

"I and the children enjoy it," explained Annie. "And seeing the different places we visit as well as constantly meeting so many different people is educational for the children. Denise . . . has attended school in Chicago, and since her return she finds there is little difference. I really think that children need their father as much as their mother, so with a little organization, we accomplish both in this family."

Pierre shared his pride in the area, his school days, his interest in baseball, and his late start in hockey. He then boasted that as a young teenager, he had "the largest paper route in all of Fort Erie. Delivering the same paper, the *Niagara Falls Evening Review*, to 94 homes on 23 streets, every evening!"

In early May, it was announced that Doug Harvey had won his sixth Norris Trophy. Detroit's Marcel Pronovost, Toronto's Allan Stanley, and Pilote received votes in that order. It marked Pierre's first time on the ballot.

Besides the usual training camp letter, Tommy Ivan wrote Pierre asking him to be one of the Chicago representatives at the opening of the new Hockey Hall of Fame in Toronto. This joyous event was tempered by sad news the evening of August 14, when he learned that his old Buffalo coach, Frankie Eddolls, had collapsed and died of a massive heart attack while playing golf that afternoon in Ridgeway, Ontario, with Stan Mikita. He was 39.

"It was a shock," recalled Pierre. "Going to the funeral home and looking at him there in the casket, meeting his wife and family. I left with such a deep sense of sadness."

On August 26, Pierre joined Ivan, Bobby Hull, and Glenn Hall along with a slew of other NHLers at the official sod turning for the new Hockey Hall of Fame on Toronto's Canadian National Exhibition grounds near Lake Ontario.

As training camp dawned, Ivan had made good on his pledge to interviewer Ward Cornell of CBC the night of the Stanley Cup win when Cornell asked if he was going to keep his championship team intact for the next season. "Just because you're a champion, that doesn't mean you stand pat," replied Ivan that night. "We're always going to be looking to improve our club if we can."

By the time the team convened, gone were captain Ed Litzenberger, Tod Sloan, Earl Balfour, and Al Arbour. Added to the lineup were Bronco Horvath from Boston and Jerry Melnyk from the Red Wings. Wayne Hillman of Buffalo would see more time with the parent club.

Worried about complacency setting in amongst his championship returnees, Pilous looked over at Pierre as he ate lunch with his teammates after a morning training camp workout.

"Pierre," he asked loudly. "Did you walk all the way from Fort Erie last night?"

"How did you know? Why?" Pierre asked back sarcastically.

"Because, you looked like it this morning!"

As was customary, the defending Stanley Cup champions hosted the NHL All-Stars to begin the season. The 15th annual game, on October 7, at Chicago Stadium began dramatically when Hall received a three-minute standing ovation when he was introduced. With Litzenberger gone, heads turned to Pierre, the 18th captain in Hawks history, as he skated onto the ice wearing the "C."

"There was no discussion about it," recalled Pilote. "Rudy came to me before the season and said I was the captain. He and Tommy had decided. Just like that, the 'C' was on my jersey, no questions asked."

"We originally made Litzenberger captain in the hope the extra responsibility might improve his play," Pilous told the press. "With Pilote it was different. He tries instead of cries. He's the natural leader of the club. He can make the big play. Off ice, he's a good liaison between management and the players."

"Litzenberger was on the way out by then," observed Hull. "And Pierre was more than ready to take over."

Neither the new captain nor the Hall ovation brought any new inspiration to the team's play that night as the defending champions fell 3-1 to the All-Stars. It might have been a harbinger of things to come. After only five games, the Black Hawks were mired in fifth place with just one win.

Things weren't looking any better on October 22, as Pierre and company hosted the hot Canadiens. Appearing in his 370th consecutive regular season game, Pierre's game was going well until he went to check Montreal's Henri Richard.

"The little bugger was coming across at centre. I played the right side," recalled Pierre. "I figured he hadn't seen me, so I stepped in to hit him but at the last moment he saw me and jumped up and his ass hit my shoulder. Boy, it hurt!"

Play continued for a few minutes before being whistled dead. Pierre stoically made his way to the bench, trying to uphold the unwritten rule in hockey—never show your opponent he's hurt you. Trainer Nick Garen immediately came to the aid of the captain.

"Nick, I've hurt my shoulder," were all the words Pierre could muster. Down in the dressing room, Dr. Myron J. Tremaine examined Pierre's arm carefully before muttering: "I think it's broken, Pierre."

"Oh God, no!" the Hawks captain answered in fear.

"I'm only guessing. An X-ray will tell us for sure."

"Dr. Tremaine had this little book with him all the time, all the phone numbers of the specialists he knew," noted Pierre. "He was just a gynecologist, but he'd pull out his little book and we would get the best doctors, the best treatment."

Pierre went to Henrotin Hospital, where X-rays revealed a nasty shoulder separation.

"I've got a separation of about an inch . . . up here," he said, pointing to the top part of his shoulder a few days later to reporter John Kuenster, who visited Pilote in his hospital room. "Oh well. I've been lucky. It's the first time I've missed a game in the NHL in six years."

In their next 11 games without Pierre, Chicago managed only three wins. Their defensive game clearly suffered, as 28 goals were surrendered and they scored only 24 times. By the time Pierre returned to the lineup on November 23 in Toronto, the Hawks were in fifth place. Pilous played him sparingly, as his effectiveness was limited in the 5-2 loss. Another problem for the club was Hull, who only had six goals.

"Bobby had a slow start in the fall of '61," recalled Pierre. "He seemed tired and stressed. Maybe he had worked too hard on the farm that summer, or maybe he had other distractions. He wasn't himself."

Team trainer Walter "Gunzo" Humeniuk took matters into his own hands and gave Hull a new sweater to change his luck. He was now wearing no. 7. It worked. Hull rebounded against the Bruins on the 29th by notching a hat trick against goalie Don Head in a 7-4 win. Things slowly picked up for the tribe as they won six and earned a tie in their next 12 games, scoring 42 goals and allowing 36. Defensively, they were headed in the right direction, but Pierre's effectiveness was compromised by a shoulder injury that was slow to heal.

By Christmas, there were grumblings about the team's record and Pilous's coaching. As the defending champions, they had been expected to be at or near the top of the league from the season's outset, but *Toronto Star* writer Jim Proudfoot put that into perspective.

"The feeling here is that [Chicago] were raised too high at the outset," wrote the noted Canadian hockey scribe. "They stood 17 points out of first place when the regular season ended last March and did not strengthen that lineup significantly. It is more likely they soon will return to third spot, once the effects of injuries to Pierre Pilote, Murray Balfour, and Red Hay wear off and as soon as the New York Rangers come down out of the clouds. And because they're tough and own the best goaltender in hockey, they'll be dangerous again in the spring—with Rudy Pilous as their coach!"

The team's poor performance wasn't totally Pilous's fault, but to add injury to insult, four of his players fell victim to boils. The situation came to a head when Moose Vasko had to be removed from the train and sent to hospital in great distress on December 26, as the team prepared to leave for Toronto. Boils, which resembled very hard and very large pimples, were actually a staphylococcus infection that developed beneath the skin through cuts, scratches, or breaks in the skin, of which hockey players had lots. They were usually on the buttocks and very painful, and it was also not uncommon for more than one person on a team to develop the contagious condition because players dressed, undressed, and showered in close proximity to each other.

Victories did not come easily as they continued to play barely .500 hockey with a 11-13-11 record at the season's halfway point—good enough for fourth place.

Still, the Black Hawks were an exciting young team of attractive stars who played rough and garnered continuous media attention. Dave Anderson wrote a piece for the *Saturday Evening Post* about "Hockey's Gashouse Gang." A large photo accompanying the article showed a menacing group of five Hawks—Pilote, Balfour, Hull, Hay, and Evans, all looking down at the camera wearing Indian headdresses.

"In ice hockey, a certain gangster-like glamour goes along with being a 'bad man'—a player who serves an excessive amount of penalty time for committing illegal violence upon his opponents," started the article. "Such a man is Pierre (Pete) Pilote, the fiery captain of the Chicago Black Hawks. At 5'10" and 178 pounds, Pilote is one of the smaller defencemen in the National Hockey League, but he is one of the best and one of the meanest. Last season, Pilote was banished from the ice more often than any other player in the NHL, drawing a total of 165 penalty minutes. Not long ago he was asked, 'How does it feel to be the league's "bad man," to have led the league in penalty minutes?'

"'I did?' Pilote exclaimed. 'I thought it was one of the other guys on our club.'

"Pilote's assumption was neither unreasonable nor surprising. On the Black Hawks nearly every player is something of a 'bad man.' Four of Pilote's teammates were in the 100-minute bracket last season, and the team as a whole set a new NHL record of 1,072 penalty minutes. The Black Hawks, however, seem to thrive on crime. They are the defending world champions of professional hockey, and a gashouse gang on and off the ice."

Anderson's large piece chronicled the history of Ivan's Hawks rebuild, the toughness of the team, its penchant for fighting, especially Reggie Fleming, Hull's scoring prowess, and Hall's popularity with his consecutive game streak, durability, and the team's success.

On January 17, Hall skated out to start his 500th straight regular season and playoff game to another prolonged standing ovation. During a pre-game ceremony, Hall was presented with a gold-plated goalie stick and a new car to mark the milestone. After a short speech, Hall proceeded to play one of the worst games of his career as the Canadiens thumped the Hawks 7-3.

"I've never fought the puck so hard in my life," Hall admitted afterwards. "That first shot took just one bounce and through my legs it went. I'm glad the first 499 games weren't like this one."

"Glenn Hall's 500th consecutive game was a big thing," recalled Pierre. "Unbelievable! That's a lot of appearances. Glenn would get hurt, get stitched up, and go right back out. He was tough."

Hockey's "Golden Era" produced accounts that were sometimes as entertaining as the games they reported on.

"A crowd of 12,152, which booed the Chicago National Hockey League squad at various intervals in the second period, suddenly switched tunes when Pierre Pilote, Red Hay, and Ken Wharram slammed home goals to hang a seventh loss in a row on the blue-shirted skaters from Manhattan," Ted Damata comically observed of a home game against the Rangers on January 21. "But it wasn't only the Hawks who started on a sour note. Al Melgard was absent from his organ loft because of a death in the family and Lou Frechette, pinch hitter, played the national anthem four tones lower than usual . . . Bernie Izzo, a light baritone was compelled to drop to a deep base. Bernie, except for a couple of gurgles, finally won out—just like the Hawks."

Hull's scoring prowess continued when he racked up four goals against Detroit's Terry Sawchuk on February 1 in a 7-4 win to bring his season goal total up to 30. On Hull's four goals, his captain got three assists.

"Pierre and I clicked together more than any centreman I ever had," boasted Hull. "We had an understanding. I gave him the puck and he gave it back to me, or vice versa. Take a look at who got the assists on my flippin' goals. Pierre must have gotten just as many as my linemates."

Rookie Chico Maki had joined the Hull line in the place of the injured Balfour. "Chico really had speed and fit in well with Bobby Hull when Murray was out," recalled Pierre. "Chico was the real checker on that line, a real team player."

Balfour missed 13 games for an operation to correct his still ailing arm, broken in the previous year's Cup final.

On February 4, the Black Hawks hosted the Leafs. Pierre took inspiration from a nasty first-period shot behind his left shoulder that produced an ugly-looking welt. His answer was to assist on the tying goal and notch the winner himself.

"Pierre Pilote, whose name would fit a New Orleans gambler, took a big chance in the third period last night at the Stadium— and it paid off," wrote the *Chicago American*'s Dan Moulton. "The Leafs had the power play on full throttle in an effort to tie the score . . . the Leafs' crafty Red Kelly was carrying the puck from behind the Toronto net and fed a pass to Billy Harris . . . Pilote, running the risk of getting himself caught out of the play, streaked over the blue line, cut between Kelly and Harris, snared the puck away from Harris's frantically reaching stick, and broke in on Toronto goalie Johnny Bower to score his fifth goal of the year. Pilote's tally saved the Hawks."

"I didn't think it was much of a chance to take because Harris was even with me," Pierre told reporter John Kuentser. "I just stepped in and took the puck. It's something you do naturally."

"He moved in like a cat!" boasted Ivan of Pierre's goal. "Anticipation!"

"That's what's great about this game," Pilous added. "Sure teamwork is important, but there's always a chance for a guy to do a bit of free thinking. Pierre took a risk and provided a tremendous thrill for all of those people.

"This team is just hitting its stride, just as it did last year, at about this time in the season. In fact, we are a few points ahead . . . When you consider the number of injuries we've had . . . you've got to give us a chance, once we get all the players together."

The tribe won their sixth game in a row on February 8 in Boston as Hay and Hull each scored two goals to lead Chicago to a 6-2 pasting of the Bruins. Pierre assisted on both of Red's goals and also got two penalties. It was clear that he was now fully recovered from his shoulder separation. The penalties came naturally with the physical game he played, and he sometimes felt it was part of the reason he was now the Hawks captain.

"The 'A' from previous years and the 'C' in the ensuing years were important because it enabled me to talk to and question the referees," Pierre recalled. "Talking without an 'A' or 'C' would get you in trouble. I could be pretty smart with the refs. You can argue a call, but they're not going to change it. They never do, but perhaps you could influence their next call. The refs were usually reasonable, they knew my tactic, my reasoning, but that was okay—my point was still made."

Things were coming together as Chicago pushed hard to overcome the Leafs for second place.

"There's a definite advantage in finishing second," observed NHL president Clarence Campbell from the Stadium press box during a Hawks win against Boston. "If the Hawks make it to second, then it will be up to Toronto to wear down Montreal in the first round. I think [Chicago] can do it, they're coming back pretty strong."

"We're overdue to win one up there," Pilous said before the club headed to Maple Leaf Gardens. "We'll be playing well and so will they. It ought to be a good hockey game."

It was. Despite the fact that Hull scored his 40th goal to become the all-time Chicago goal-scoring leader, the Leafs shut down the vaunted Hawk attack en route to a 4-2 Toronto win. The loss highlighted the fact that things were not all rosy in Hawkland when an article published that week showed that there was some dissension in the Hawks ranks.

"I was sick of hockey when the season started," Hull revealed in a printed tirade to explain his slow start. "I couldn't wait to take off my uniform after a game. Who could blame me? They worked us to death in training camp. We played 17 exhibitions and had two tough practices a day. My feet were sore and after a while I had no desire to play. There's no question in my mind that I would have had more goals this year if they had been easier on us.

"I'm not going to show up in training camp this September if the same situation exists. Either that or I'll fake an injury and spend most of the time on the rubbing table. I'll be ready to open the season anyway; I'm always in good shape."

Another article by Stan Fischler caught Pierre by surprise when Fischler wrote that an unnamed Hawk player disagreed with Pilote being captain, saying that Pierre was a "management man."

"That Stan Fischler article criticizing my being captain was a jealousy thing from an old clique," explained Pierre. "I was certainly not with management but my philosophy was such that, if you work for and make a company or hockey team successful, then you're going to be successful. What was the best thing for the club? That means trying to straighten out problems, and there were a few problems.

"And there were always a couple of rookies who wanted me to go upstairs, to talk to Tommy or Rudy about playing them more. I would say, 'Look, we have good players here. What are you gonna do, take over Bobby's place? Stan's? Eric's? Wharram's? Chico's? Billy Hay's? I mean, I'm sorry but you're a fourth liner.' The truth hurt and aggravated some people."

Despite a few bumps in the road, the Hawk machine was rolling along and so was Hull. On March 17 in Toronto, no. 7 notched his 47th goal against Don Simmons. Pierre's astute mind was always working. He skated over to Hull, who was just collecting the puck from out of the Toronto net.

"Bobby, can I have that puck?" Pierre asked him. Hull was surprised.

"Gee Pierre, I don't know," Hull answered, unsure amid the celebration. "It's the highest goal I've ever scored. It's near the end of the season. I might not score another one!"

"Are you kidding me?" Pierre answered his teammate with youthful enthusiasm. "Bobby, you're gonna get at least 50!"

Hull thought a moment, then handed him the puck with a gapped-tooth smile.

"Okay, sure. Merry Christmas, Pierre!" Pierre's eyes lit up. He had finally seen Santa.

Chicago won the game 3-1 to inch closer to the second-place Leafs but time was running out. Ensuing losses to Detroit and Montreal shoved the Hawks to third. Their only consolation was that Hull had hit 49 goals. Montreal was yet again their first-round opponents.

With one game remaining and 83 points, Hull was tied for the scoring title with Andy Bathgate of the Rangers, though Hull had 22 more goals. Only Montreal's Rocket Richard and Boom Boom Geoffrion had reached the magical 50-goal milestone. Could Hull, who was scoring goals in bunches, top it? It would be a showdown and Bathgate had home ice advantage on March 26.

From the beginning, both teams assigned their best checkers on the other's scoring leader. New York blinked first. Five minutes into the game, Chicago was pressing and Hull was cutting in towards the right corner of the Rangers net when he received a pass near the goalmouth from Fleming. When Hull flipped a backhand behind Ranger goalie Gump Worsley, the team went crazy as Hull received his "50" puck. He flipped it to the Chicago bench for safekeeping; there was still a lot of game left to play.

"I knew that they were going to check me closely after that because of Bathgate," Hull said later. Time and again, both coaches played their superstars to help them win the scoring title. Hull had the extra incentive of trying to get the elusive 51.

"The game was between Bathgate and Bobby really," recalled Pierre. "We were kind of like bystanders, but we checked Bathgate into the ice. Every time he got on, we either had Fleming or Nesterenko or somebody else on him. We checked, checked, checked!"

Bathgate skated hard and finally scored to draw even in points with Hull. As the game wore on, Hull and Bathgate received over 30 minutes of ice time and roamed about the ice at will, paying almost no heed to positional hockey. With the Rangers leading 4-1, time was winding down as the Hawks tried to feed the puck to their superstar while blanketing Bathgate.

"We didn't want Andy to even touch the puck," remembered Pierre. "We had to stop Bathgate from getting any more points! It was a pretty tough thing to do. He was a great player!"

In his zest to stop Bathgate from beating his scoring buddy, Pierre intercepted a charging Bathgate in his own zone and was penalized for boarding him at the 18:29 mark. The Rangers would be on the power play for a minute and a half. Pilous sent out his Bathgate blanket—Nesterenko. Time ticked away and with 48 seconds remaining, Nesterenko finally drew a holding penalty for tying Bathgate up. The Hawks were two men down now. Pilous sent out Fleming in a last-ditch effort at stopping Bathgate.

At the puck drop, Fleming went right at Bathgate, and kept at him, getting under his stick, pushing him, and staying with him. Finally, the referee had seen enough and called a delayed penalty against Fleming, but the Rangers kept possession of the puck as seconds ticked away. The Rangers threw the puck around in a desperate attempt to set up Bathgate but the Chicago defence tightened up and Hall shut the door until the final buzzer sounded. The Hawks were elated at having won the battle despite losing the war.

"Fleming did his job," a disappointed and frustrated Bathgate said. "He had me completely tied up. Fleming wasn't dirty about it but this Nester [and his elbowing] he's like that all the time! But we made the playoffs. That's the important thing."

It had been an exciting finish, but both men ended the season with the same number of points. Who would get the Art Ross? Two days later, NHL publicist Ken McKenzie announced that Hull got the Art Ross Trophy by virtue of his 22 more goals, but both men would receive a $1,000 cash award. With that out of the way, the Hawks focused on their next assignment—the first-place Canadiens.

At first glance, losing the first two games of the 1962 semifinal series to the Canadiens, 2-1 and 4-3, was a bad omen for Chicago, and the press and bookmakers agreed. Actually, both Montreal wins had been cliff-hangers, especially the second game, where the Hawks were handily winning 3-1 with only nine minutes left in the third when lapses allowed the Habs to tie and win it.

The series shifted to the Windy City on April Fool's Day, and the Hawks were out to prove that they were not jokes.

Game 3 was an unruly affair from the start as Chicago brought the play to the Habs. The game was a full-team effort, but Mikita and Fleming were key performers. Mikita's third-period goal in the eventual 4-1 Chicago win was his third in as many games and Fleming's assist on the Hawks' first goal and his tenacious fore-checking won him accolades.

"Reggie Fleming played an exceptional game and really helped us when the going got rough!" boasted Pilous.

As if there wasn't enough excitement on the Stadium ice, Kenneth Killander, a Montreal fan, attempted to steal the Stanley Cup from its display case in the Stadium lobby. Stopped by 16-year-old usher Roy Cartapassi, who summoned police, the thief said that when the Canadiens were losing 3-1, he thought the only way Montreal would ever get the Cup back was for him to take it.

As the fourth game began on April 3, it appeared that Killander was right as the Hawks opened the scoring in the first period when Montreal's Lou Fontinato and Gilles Tremblay were penalized 47 seconds apart. On the ensuing two-man power play, Hull took a pass from Mikita and Pilote and rammed a 15-foot shot past goalie Jacques Plante at the 1:51 mark. Six minutes later, Plante stopped a Mikita drive only to have Horvath shove the rebound home to make it 2-0 Hawks.

Montreal fought back in the second when Dollard St. Laurent was sent off for holding and Jean Béliveau scored on the ensuing power play to make it 2-1. Four minutes later, Dickie Moore broke free on Hall and tied it up. The period was also rough as Mikita and Fontinato mixed it up after Leapin' Lou had speared the Hawks star. Fleming received a 20-stitch gash on his upper lip after he had his own stick-swinging skirmish with Fontinato. Hull was also cut above his upper lip.

When Fontinato went after Mikita again in the third period and was sent to the penalty box, Hay and Ab McDonald added insurance goals against a lone Hab goal by Tremblay to give Chicago the series-tying 5-3 victory.

Both coaches were fuming after the game.

"It's pretty hard to beat seven men when you only have five!" Blake declared in regards to referee Eddie Powers. "That's three games in a row we had two men out at the same time with penalties. It never happens to the other club!"

"After watching Fontinato go out of his way to spear Mikita, I would say he had been instructed to do so!" countered Pilous. "Mikita has become a going concern tonight—just look at his four assists. I think Fontinato was sent against him as a muscleman. Or maybe he just took it upon himself to go after the little guys."

Powers had handed out 16 penalties in a bid to keep the game from getting out of hand, including the two five-minute majors to Fontinato and Fleming.

"I think Montreal had decided they weren't going to be pushed around anymore," recalled Pierre. "They had a pretty strong team of stars and I guess they realized our roughness had helped us win the year before. We were check, check, checking, and rough and it worked!"

Back in Montreal for Game 5, everyone assumed that the Habs would continue the home team advantage of the series, but it didn't happen as the Hawks beat them 4-3. Chicago smelled blood. Backed by superb goaltending from Mr. Goalie, the Habs were disposed of for the second year in a row, this time with a 2-0 shutout at the Stadium.

Now, it was on to the Stanley Cup finals against Litzenberger and the Maple Leafs, who had disposed of the Rangers in the other semifinal. The Hawks were about to face a team they just couldn't catch or beat during the regular season. In 14 head-on contests, the Hawks had lost seven and tied three.

With the benefit of the last line change, Imlach used Frank Mahovlich constantly, figuring with Nesterenko always on the ice to check him, Hull would be on the bench. It worked, as the Leafs had the definite edge at home and won the first two games by scores of 4-1 and 3-2. Pilous commented that part of the reason his Hawks had lost the two games was that his team "seemed tired." To some, his comment must have harkened back to Bobby Hull's midseason tirade about being worked too hard since the start of training camp.

With the series shifting back to the Stadium for Game 3, it was clear that Chicago needed their fans to get them back into the series, but some supporters were gloomily realistic about their team's chances.

"Toronto in six games!" devoted Hawks supporter Ron Perlove of Lincolnwood told reporter Marvin Weinstein. "Last year's Hawk team was better than this year's. They had more desire, more hustle."

To mute the cynicism, the tribe came out flying with Pilote leading the way. In the second period, Pierre was merely trying to keep the puck in the Toronto end when his weak backhand hit Red Kelly and dropped in front of the Leaf net where Mikita slammed it home. Four minutes later, Pierre took the puck back to the Toronto net. Drawing Bower to one side, he needled a fine pass between two Leaf defenders to McDonald, who scored into the open goal. Later on in the same period, Pierre dove to block an Eddie Shack shot and took another puck in the abdomen, drawing an ovation from the crowd. A third period empty netter in the dying minute sealed a 3-0 Hall shutout. The tribe had life.

"A large share of the credit must go to Pierre Pilote," the press reported. "The Hawk captain started two of the Hawks goals, one with a beautiful fake, and played a spectacular game on defence. But the victory also belonged to every Hawk who showed up."

"They outskated us and they outhustled us!" confessed Toronto coach Punch Imlach.

Again, there was controversy in this series, as NHL president Clarence Campbell reprimanded Stadium announcer Bob Foster for "acting like a cheerleader." When Foster announced Mikita's goal in the second period, he informed the crowd that it was "Mikita's 17th playoff point, which put him three shy of the all-time record." Then when the Hawks were leading Toronto 3-0 with 14 seconds to play, Foster announced, "Mr. Goalie had done it again!" Campbell, who was in attendance, was not amused.

"The public address system is part of the game and the announcer, in effect, is a game official," the NHL boss instructed. "He must act impartially at all times. To act like a cheerleader is completely wrong. Henceforth, the Black Hawks announcer will not (1) refer to Hall as 'Mr. Goalie,' (2) will not refer to Eric Nesterenko as 'Swoop,' (3) will not anticipate details of the game, (4) will not include statistical information during announcement of a goal, and finally (5) will not lead cheers for the home team!"

It was all a sideshow to Game 4 on April 17, as a packed Stadium witnessed a game that was described as "having everything," including five fights on the ice crammed amidst 24 penalties and several fights in the stands. Through all of that, there was a hockey game. Things were even until partway through the opening frame when Bower did the splits in stopping a Hull sizzler and suffered a bad groin tear that forced him from the game and the series.

A minute after his replacement Don Simmons took over, Fleming scored his first goal of the playoffs. When he added another at 7:31 of the final period, the Hawks went on to win handily 4-1 to tie the series at two games apiece. At the final buzzer, euphoria reigned in Hawkland.

For Game 5, Simmons, who'd only played in nine games all year, would have to carry the load. The Leafs also didn't listen to Pilous, who predicted that the Leafs would tighten up and play defensive hockey in front of the young goalie. Toronto instead decided that the best defence was a strong offence and they came at the Hawks hard. It worked and Chicago fell badly to the rampaging Leafs.

"We just simply ran out of gas. When you lose a key playoff game 8-4 it shows that you're tired," said Pilote. "They also had a better third line than we did. We depended too much on our first two lines. They outchecked and outsmarted us."

Back in the friendly confines of Chicago Stadium, the Hawks clearly had their backs to the wall. The Leafs changed tactics and reverted to a defensive game yet still outshot Chicago 27-12 over the scoreless first two periods.

Then at 8:56 in the third period, the Hawks seemed to come to life when Hull put one in, which brought the debris raining down on the ice. The ensuing delay for cleaning took away the momentum, and allowed the Leafs to regroup.

Mahovlich carried the puck into the Chicago end and fed a pass to Bob Nevin, who beat Hall just a minute after the game finally resumed. When Nesterenko took a penalty, the Leafs were circling the wigwam. At the 14:14 mark, Dick Duff fired the go-ahead goal to deaden the Stadium. The Leafs went into checking mode, and the Hawks couldn't mount anything resembling a good scoring chance. At the final buzzer, the Leafs stormed onto the ice to congratulate Simmons. As the two teams lined up to shake hands, the crowd graciously applauded both teams as the organist played "Old Soldiers Never Die."

It was tough for the Hawks to hear the whoops of the Leafs as they received the Cup on Chicago ice, just like the Hawks had done to the Red Wings the year before.

If there was any consolation for Pilote and his teammates, it came in the form of an NHL press release on April 30, announcing that he and Hall had made the Second All-Star Team. Mikita was the First Team centreman.

A few weeks later, it was announced that Pilote had placed second behind Harvey in Norris Trophy voting for the NHL's best defenceman.

But having won the Stanley Cup the year before, all the accolades in the world couldn't help Pierre erase the unsavoury memory of the Toronto celebration on Stadium ice in front of Hawks fans. He hoped to never see such a sight again.

CHAPTER 14

Shakes, Breaks, and Hello, Mr. Norris

Strange winds were blowing in the land of Black Hawk in the fall of 1962. The Chicago brain trust got rid of Bronco Horvath, Dollard St. Laurent, Doug Barkley, and Jerry Melnyk, and picked up Len Lunde and Al McNeil—all minor tinkering.

Then came October 5.

Unable to participate in the All-Star Game unless he came to an agreement with Toronto, Frank Mahovlich signed a new four-year contract with Toronto for $25,000 per year. In a backroom just prior to the game, Hawks owner Jim Norris offered Leafs owner Stafford Smythe a million dollars for the big left-winger. Smythe thought it over and agreed.

The next morning, a buoyant Norris appeared at Smythe's office in Maple Leaf Gardens with a certified cheque in hand. It was the largest sum ever offered for any sporting player, but Smythe backtracked and refused to accept the payment.

When the news of the offer leaked at that night's All-Star Game, it rocked the hockey world. Was it true?

"It certainly was true," marvelled Pierre. "I saw the actual uncashed cheque! The million-dollar deal was no myth! We didn't think anymore of it, and we knew better than to imagine that there was suddenly going to be better salaries for all of us. In time it all blew over."

The Hawks could have used Mahovlich as Stan Mikita missed some early games with a bad ankle sprain and Bobby Hull started the season slowly again.

The Hawks were in second place, losing only three of their first 10 matches, when they went to Boston on November 1.

In the second period, the game was going along uneventfully and Pierre was on the ice with Vasko. The Bruins fired the puck into the Chicago end and Pierre turned to retrieve it. After a mad scramble in the corner, the Bruins managed to wrest the puck from Pierre and fed it back to the left point. There, Boston defenceman Doug Mohns wound up and let fly a slapper that was supposed to be towards the Hawks goal.

"I'm coming back out from the corner and I'm not even in line with or near the net yet!" recalled Pierre with incredulity even after all these years. "Mohns shoots and hits me right in the middle of my left foot. I'm not even near the damn net! Oh it hurt!"

It was a hairline fracture, and Pilote missed two weeks.

The Hawks situation took an even graver turn on November 7 when Glenn Hall, playing in his 502nd consecutive regular season game, finally had to leave it with an aggravated, sore back. He was replaced by newcomer Denis DeJordy and Chicago managed to tie the Bruins 3-3. The injury, a severe ligament strain, forced Hall from the lineup and put an end to his incredible iron-man streak.

Both defensive stalwarts were missed.

"That the absence of captain and All-Star defenceman Pierre Pilote is hurting the team's overall performance was glaringly apparent," wrote Dan Moulton. "Moose Vasko isn't up to handling Pierre's point on the power play and the attack generally misses the tough little veteran's organizational ability."

Despite the fact that they were only two points behind Detroit after 18 games, Rudy Pilous felt that the team needed a shake-up, so he broke up the Million Dollar Line. The move resulted in Hull notching his first multi-goal games in victories over the Red Wings and Rangers with Len Lunde as his new centre.

"We had to do something, anything, to get them moving again," explained Pilous to reporter Jack Griffin. "Sometimes when a line has been playing together a long time, it falls into too much of a pattern."

Prior to their next game, on November 22 against Toronto, Tommy Ivan said that Pierre's imminent return would swing things in his team's favour. Ivan also felt referee John Ashley would have trouble controlling the upcoming game, since there always seemed to be bad blood between the Hawks and Leafs. His prediction was dead on.

A frenzied Thanksgiving Day Stadium crowd of 14,891 cheered as Pilote and Hall returned to the lineup in a game that quickly got out of hand. From the puck drop, Ashley had his hands full and was unable to stop the two teams from going at each other.

With the game still scoreless, Pierre took matters into his own hands as he moved the puck deep into the Toronto zone on a second-period Hawks power play. He fired the puck at the Leafs goal but defender Kent Douglas blocked the shot. Pierre moved in, grabbed the loose rebound, and stuffed it home behind goalie Don Simmons for a 1-0 Chicago lead. With Hall shutting the door, the marker stood up until the final buzzer, with a third period of fights. The Hawks gladly took the two points and a tie for first place with Detroit.

With home-ice advantage, they hosted the Red Wings in a battle for top spot on November 24. In the hard-fought, tight-checking contest, Pierre set up Eric Nesterenko for the Hawks' only goal of the game, which ended in a 1-1 tie. It was clear that Pierre's return had an immediate impact.

With 16 wins, 10 losses, and nine ties for 41 points, the Hawks had their best first-half season in club history.

When the Hawks entered a four-game stretch between January 9 and 13, they beat the Leafs and Rangers, tied the Canadiens, and lost to the Bruins. It was a tough stretch that saw Len Lunde get stitches over his eye, Nesterenko acquire an 11-stitch cut on top of his head, Chico Maki injure his back and wrist, Bob Turner bruise his ankle, Mikita wrench his knee, Kenny Wharram get an infected toe, Pilote and Reggie Fleming struggle through groin tears, and Vasko play with a very sore shoulder. In the last game of that stretch, on January 13 against the visiting Canadiens, Moose had had enough of his injury-plagued shoulder.

"Big Moose was always separating his shoulder," laughed Pierre. "He wore a harness on his forearm with a chain so that his arm couldn't go any higher than his shoulder, because that's how his shoulder popped out. One time he hit the boards in our corner. Wham! He couldn't get back up and he was lying there in agony, his shoulder out again. Poor Elmer! When they wheeled him off the ice the referee shut the door, but I would've liked to see how they got big Moose down those 22 steps! He probably got up and walked down after three steps, otherwise these guys would have died! Moose was heavy! Maybe they slid him down?

"But the best part was a stoppage in play in the third period after three or four minutes. Suddenly the doors opened at the end and Moose skated onto the ice, and the fans went crazy yelling, 'MOOOOOOSE!' Holy shit! He got that in every rink. It was great and Moose loved it! We loved it! He was such a competitor!"

Unfortunately, the injury plague hit Pierre's defence partner again. In their next game, Moose blocked a shot and went off with a sore ankle.

"Moose had a sore ankle after blocking that shot. He could hardly walk, much less play," recalled Pierre. "They took X-rays but nothing showed. Rudy actually asked me if I thought Moose was faking it. I said, 'No. It's really sore.' There was this Japanese doctor in New York who everybody believed in, a Dr. Yakashama, something like that! He operated on more backs. He carried a gun too.

"We're playing in New York and Elmer's playing with this sore ankle. After the game we're about to fly back to Chicago. The bus is waiting to take us to the airport, but first we always had a couple of beers from our suitcase. But this time Elmer says, 'I'm going to see that doctor! He'll fix me up!' After the game he showered quickly, dressed, and was gone! We're finally all on the bus waiting for Elmer."

"Pierre! Pierre! Where's the beer?" Moose said as he finally hobbled aboard.

"What's the matter?" Pierre asked him.

"Oh Pierre, you won't believe it!" Moose sighed.

"What happened?" Pierre asked him, trying not to laugh as Moose guzzled a beer.

"That son-of-a-bitch!" Moose continued. "I'm lying there and this doctor looked at my ankle and he says, 'I'll fix you, Elmer.' I said, 'Great!' So I'm lying there and then suddenly I feel a big needle going into my ankle! He gave me three shots in my ankle and it's killing me! I'll never see that guy again!"

"Elmer didn't like needles," chuckled Pierre. "His ankle felt worse. He's groaning and really hurting. So, Elmer went to another doctor that we used to hang around with, he rented some apartments to some of our players. He ordered another X-ray that showed a hairline fracture. Rudy believed him after that! Poor Elmer, he suffered."

The rest of the players played on, a fact not lost on management as it eyed a first-place finish, something no other Hawks team had done.

"Can we finish first at the end of the season?" wondered Tommy Ivan. "I don't see why we should fade out. We've played pretty steady hockey. If we get the same consistency the rest of the year, I'll be satisfied."

The Hawks dominated the first-half All-Star teams when they were announced on January 18. Publicity Director Johnny Gottselig came down to the dressing room after a morning workout to inform Pilote, Hall, and Mikita that they had been voted to the First All-Star Team, and Vasko the Second.

Montreal goalie Jacques Plante drew headlines when he complained on a train trip to New York on January 26 that the goal nets in New York, Boston, and Chicago were two inches lower, giving the goalies in those cities a 35-home-game advantage. Plante and the Habs were visiting the Windy City the next night. As Plante skated out to his net that night in the Stadium, he found referee Ed Powers measuring the net with a look of concern.

"Don't bother measuring the other one," Plante said. "It's two inches lower as well."

Afterwards, Powers refused to say anything publicly. When reporters contacted the Hawks for comment, Gottselig was fuming.

"That Plante is riding another publicity wave. All this net measurement talk is getting ridiculous!" the PR man said. "I personally measured ours and they are exactly regulation."

They weren't. A few days later, NHL president Clarence Campbell confirmed the goal frames in Chicago were smaller than the regulation size—four feet high by six feet wide. The "error" would be corrected before the next home game vowed Campbell. The same went for the nets in Boston and New York. Jake the Snake got double revenge against the Hawks when the Canadiens won that night, 3-1.

In a *Hockey News* article published around the same time, Pierre is singled out as the leading contender for the Norris Trophy for the best NHL defenceman. Pierre was still not happy with his play. "I always think I should play better," he said. "One season I totalled 37 points and didn't get a sniff of All-Star mention. This season I had only 10 points at mid-season, and look what happened."

Another article noted Pilote had cut his time in the penalty box, with only 28 minutes so far, for a predicted 45 minutes for the entire season—a far cry from his years of 97, 117, 91, 79, and 100. "But don't let this fool any of the opposing forwards into taking liberties in Pilote's defence zone. Pierre is still doing business as usual at the same stand."

At this stage in the season, Hull awoke from his long slump. On January 31 in Boston, "The Golden Boy," as writer Harry Molter labelled him, clearly searching for a suitable moniker, pumped in three goals and assisted on two others as the Hawks shelled the Bruins 9-2. He scored his 20th two nights later in a 3-3 tie at the Forum against the Habs.

Despite the fact that the tribe was at the top of the league, there was growing player dissatisfaction with Pilous's coaching style and his personality.

"There was nothing wrong with Rudy Pilous except we'd outgrown him," recalled Hull. "Rudy had too many 'isms.' He'd say, 'Pierre, where were you when that guy put the puck in the net—up in Nellie's room behind her ass?' or 'Vasko? You were as far away from that guy when he put the puck in our net as a farm boy could throw a big, red apple!' Another was 'Yeah, we're going to O'Hara Field via Manor Heim Row.' Well, it's actually O'Hare Field, via Manheim Road.

"I remember Nesterenko muttering loud enough for everyone to hear, 'You crazy, dumb bastard!' We could all hear him in the dressing room. But all these 'isms' got to us. We just were outgrowing Rudy. The guys were losing respect for him and it came to a head in New York."

Before the February 9 game at Madison Square Garden, the players approached their captain. They wanted to get rid of Pilous.

"I knew we were having trouble. The players were all rebelling against Rudy," related Pierre. "Some were bugging me to get him fired. I thought if a coach needed to be fired, it's up to management. The meeting lasted maybe a half hour. Nesterenko was the leader on this. He didn't like Rudy's coaching, never did. I went around the room and gave everybody a chance to say his piece. Some guys said nothing, but then Jack Evans was the last to speak."

"Look, I've heard all you guys complaining," Evans said. "But I don't think the coach skates in a game. I don't think the coach scores. I don't think he plays goal or defence. I think Rudy is a hell'va guy in a way, a nice guy. It's really us that aren't playing well. It's us. I think if we'd forget about him and just go out and play, we'd be alright."

The players all took a breath, paused, and agreed. Evans's speech bought Pilous some time, an odd situation considering the team was in first place.

"Jack Evans was a good leader that way," Pierre continued. "We had some good characters on the team but some players weren't honest with themselves. They made excuses and blamed the coach, wife, kids, or injuries. The great players never blamed anybody—I can tell you that!"

That night in New York, the Hawks rallied around Hall and held off a last-minute push by the Rangers to preserve a 3-3 tie. In a classic photo of the final Rangers push, you can see all six Hawks on the ice around the goal crease and a Hawks defenceman lying behind Hall making the save in the mad scramble. Ranger coach Emile Francis was so upset when the play was ruled a save that he came storming onto the ice and had to be restrained by his team. Francis felt there should have been a penalty shot. The tribe had pulled together. Then the Hawks beat the same Rangers at home 4-2 on February 10. It was that kind of season.

Pilote's presence, leadership, and play were starting to attract more attention on a team of superstars. John Kuenster tried to capture it for his *Daily News* readers: "Pierre Pilote lifted a beige, papier-mâché hat from the shelf and set it on his head," Kuenster's story started. "The Black Hawks had just finished a workout at the Stadium, and hooted at the outlandish figure of their captain as he strode about the dressing room in the stovepipe.

"'I got this from the boys. They gave it to me after I lost a $25 hat on our last road trip . . . a good $25 hat! Imagine that!'

"The way things are going in the National Hockey League this season, Pilote shouldn't have to think twice about such a trifling loss. He figures to reap a financial windfall by the time the Stanley Cup playoffs are completed." Kuenster wrote that Pilote was the leading candidate to win the Norris Trophy and the associated $2,000 bonus.

Vasko raved about Pierre being light on his feet. "That's why he's so shifty. He's a good offensive player . . . he's got a hard shot on the net and he usually gets his shot through when there are a lot of legs and bodies in front of him."

"I always said that it takes about five years for a defenceman to develop in this league. It takes that long for his mind to catch up with his legs," Pierre told Kuenster. "I'm a strong believer in the saying 'possession is nine-tenths of the law.' If you've got the puck, the other guys can't score . . . they've got to take it away from you."

After losing to the Canadiens on February 16, the Hawks beat the Bruins 3-1 at home, with Hull notching all three Hawks goals for the hat trick against Bruins goalie Eddie Johnston. The morning after, a hockey legend was made—off the ice. Bobby Hull entered the Chicago Stadium through Gate 3½ and turned right to head to the office.

"Don Murphy had just come out of the office," recalled Hull. "Murphy was Mr. Arthur Wirtz's front man on the Ice Capades. Murphy always smelled, always stunk! We called him and Chip Magnus, who was with the *Chicago American* newspaper, 'Linus and Pigpen.' They always had the same clothes on and stunk like sheep herders.

"So when I got about halfway to the office, Don Murphy and I met and he said: 'Holy Christ, Bobby! You were really flying last night! You were just like a jet out there!' Then he just stopped and when I turned around, he got this expression on his face and he started yelling, 'Yeah! Yeah! The Golden Jet! Yeah!' And that's how 'The Golden Jet' all started."

In Detroit for a game on February 21, some players were having a morning coffee in the hotel coffee shop when *Sun-Times* reporter Jack Griffin asked them to explain their first-place standings.

"There's prestige in winning the championship. You can feel it," Pierre answered. "This is a game where everybody depends on everybody else. Everybody's got to work. One guy can upset the whole cart. We take Glenn Hall for granted. Oh, so many games he's kept us alive through the first two periods until we could get going."

Against the Wings, Pilote went to hit Larry Jeffrey, but the Wing sidestepped and Pierre crashed heavily into the boards, twisting his healed left foot. Pain shot immediately through his foot as he gingerly made his way back to the bench. He tried playing later but it was too painful.

The next day X-rays revealed the return of the same hairline fracture. Ordered to use crutches, the injury was timely, though, because Pierre was around when Annie gave birth to David, in February 1963.

Hull was next on the disabled list, with a strained ligament in his left knee.

Pierre and Bobby were back in the lineup as the Hawks travelled into New York on March 6. An article in the *Tribune* let it be known whose absence had been instrumental in the recent Hawks slide.

"Ready to take his regular defence role over after five games' absence with a hairline fracture in his left foot will be captain Pierre Pilote, who has been sorely missed during the last three matches, in which the Hawks picked up only a single point by tying one and losing the other two."

Their return didn't matter, as the Hawks lost the game 5-2 to the Rangers and then Toronto moved into a first-place tie with the idle tribe three nights later when they beat the Wings. The pressure was on for a head-to-head contest in Chicago on March 10. The Hawks had a chance to pull ahead in the standings and had a 1-0 lead, but with five minutes left in the game, Bob Turner lost the puck to Toronto's Bob Pulford. His pass to Red Kelly ended up behind Hall. The game ended 1-1.

In the March 16 edition of the *Hockey News*, Toronto sports reporter Milt Dunnell did a column on Pierre.

"Monsieur Pierre Pilote is a piece and a part of all the best blue-liners you have seen, over the last dozen seasons on the big ponds," Dunnell began. "He blocks a shot and you remember Doug Harvey . . . Pierre wheels from his own zone and you think . . . Carl Brewer . . . None of this is coincidental. Monsieur Pilote is a composite of do-it-yourself defencemen who have earned his envy and admiration. There is even a chunk of Pierre Pilote in the composition."

"I began watching and learning from other stars," Pierre told

Dunnell. "Don't think I'm boasting but I studied Harvey until I was able to anticipate many of the things he was going to do. I'd bet I have intercepted more of his passes than almost anybody else in the league. Ask him some time."

That night in Toronto, the Stanley Cup seemed far away and so did first place when the Leafs easily disposed of the listless Hawks 3-0 at the Gardens to grab sole possession of it. The Hawks hadn't been anywhere else except first since December 2.

"Imagine, coming up with a display like that at this stage of the season!" lamented an angry Pilous to the press. "The team performed like a last-place club. But this pennant race is sure not over yet. There are still four games to go and we can win it!"

At the other end of the spectrum, Leafs boss Punch Imlach was all smiles.

"It took us a long time, but we are first now and I know we can stay there," Imlach said. "I don't think our boys will let down. They realize every game is important and are hitting a peak for the playoffs."

The slide continued for the Hawks when they lost their next two games, both to Detroit. Their closing stretch collapse had Pilous scrambling to come up with a solution.

"It might be that I'll have to break up our line combinations," lamented Pilous to Kuenster while sipping a Scotch and soda during a Chicago Black Hawks Standbys fan club dinner on March 20, at which all the players were present. "We've gotten too set in our patterns and the other teams have caught on to us."

The bench boss admitted that a few injuries had not helped the cause, but he seemed at a loss to explain or solve their skid. Pilous left the party early, but Kuenster stayed to watch the Hawks drinking and socializing with their fans. He felt their behaviour was detrimental. "All the Hawks . . . had a carefree time despite the fact they have little reason to rejoice about anything," Kuenster wrote. "They have lost their last three games and have managed only one victory in their last nine starts. Yet, there they were Wednesday night, accepting fawning praise from their delighted followers, signing autographs, and partying past midnight. . . . No one seemed in a rush to get home Wednesday night. It was just one more instance of how a team can be lionized at social affairs to their own detriment. And, maybe the Hawks have been doing too much socializing lately."

First place was a little farther away for the boys by the end of that night as the Leafs tied the Canadiens 3-3 to stretch their lead to four points. With only two games remaining in the schedule, it was the tightest race to the wire the NHL had seen in a long time with the Leafs in first with 82 points, the Hawks and Canadiens tied for second with 78 points. The Hawks knew they had to pick it up and win both games and hope the Leafs would lose their two.

Going into the unfriendly confines of the Montreal Forum on March 23 to face the injury-plagued Canadiens, the Hawks and Pilote had something else on their minds—Hall's chance at a Vezina Trophy. Hall's closest competition in goals-against was Plante, who had one more, and Toronto's Johnny Bower with six more.

Pierre addressed the team. "Hey gang, let's not forget that Plante won the thing a half dozen times!" he yelled in the dressing room. They didn't have to be told the "thing" was the Vezina Trophy. "Three years ago, Glenn lost out on the final night because we allowed five goals. We don't want that to happen again!"

The team got their captain's point and charged out onto the ice, knowing they had to score on Plante and stop the Canadiens, plain and simple. The defensive struggle had only 12 shots in the first period. Pierre picked up an assist on Murphy's goal to answer the Canadiens goal by Hicke.

The Hawks tightened up the defence and allowed the Canadiens only four shots on net in the second while they threw 13 at Plante in a desperate bid to pull away. But it was the Canadiens that scored three times, until the halfway point of the third. There is no explaining what happened next as the Hawks were desperately trying to force the play into the Montreal end but the Canadiens were throwing up a wall around Plante. Chicago couldn't get a shot until Wharram scored from Murphy and Mikita, and three minutes later Pierre set up Fleming for another. Plante and Hall were now tied for the Vezina. With three minutes remaining, the teams were checking frantically.

With a determined look on his face, Pierre took matters into his own hands. Getting hold of the puck, he took off, zigzagged out of his own end, crossed the Montreal blue line, faked a pass, then dropped the puck to Murphy, who shot. Plante stopped it but Pierre stuffed home the rebound to tie it up and notch his third point of the night. Amazingly, the Hawks had managed only four shots on the Montreal net in the third period but three of them went in, and the game ended 4-all.

Montreal's 23rd tie of the season set an NHL regular season record for draws. By getting only one of two points with one game remaining, the Hawks gave first place to the Leafs. The Leafs lost that night to the surging Red Wings 2-1.

Though Mr. Goalie stopped the nine of 10 shots directed at him in the third, the four goals didn't help his bid to win his first Vezina. He was still only one goal ahead of Plante and his lead over Bower was now down to three. It was Vezina nail-biting time.

Pierre's game against the Habs earned him rave reviews in the next day's Québec papers.

"Pilote contributed his finest game of the season," lauded *Montreal Star* columnist Red Fisher. Indeed he had. He wanted that Vezina for Hall.

For their last game of the regular season the Hawks travelled to Boston, and though the last-place Bruins were 34 points behind them, anything could happen. Montreal was headed to New York.

Pierre again concentrated on defence and stayed at home in front of Hall. He didn't get any penalties and didn't figure in any scoring for the Hawks, but he was on the ice in the dying seconds as the Hawks held a 4-3 lead with the Bruins buzzing around Hall. Near the end, Pierre blocked a Leo Boivin shot—with his head. The puck produced a two-inch gash into his skull, but more importantly to the Hawks captain, it stayed out of the Chicago net and the score stayed the same until the final buzzer. By virtue of the Canadiens losing 5-0 to New York and the Leafs losing again to the Wings, this time 3-2, Mr. Goalie had his first Vezina.

After the game, Pierre happily received a dozen stitches to close the huge cut.

"I'll never forget that one," Pierre later said. "Those 12 stitches hurt more than anything I've ever known . . . like somebody was pressing a hot poker into my head. It throbbed so much; I couldn't sleep for a few days afterwards."

Three days later, the wound reopened and when Dr. Tremaine suggested that it might require another 13 stitches to close it again, Pierre shook his head.

"No you don't, Doc," said the ever-superstitious captain. "Not 13! Find room there for one more."

As the Hawks headed into the playoffs against the fourth-place Red Wings, they were 2-to-1 favourites, but Detroit was hot, having finished their season on a high note by beating Toronto twice. Still, Chicago had home-ice advantage. They unleashed Hull in the first period of the first game and he notched two goals en route to a close 5-4 victory.

Things got heated in Game 2 and the physical play cost the Wings as they took penalty after penalty in a bid to slow down the Hawks. The turning point in the series occurred in the third period when Hull was sent out on another power play.

"Pierre and I played the point on the power play. Our play was the left-winger would come down and turn in along the blue line," recalled Bobby Hull. "Then I would grab the biscuit and go around the left-winger. But on this one power play in Game 2, Bruce MacGregor was backchecking. Kenny Wharram was on the other side and I'll never forget it . . . I went to give Kenny the puck and instead of MacGregor turning and chasing me, he swung around the other way as I was dropping my shoulder to cut in. MacGregor's stick came up and the heel of his stick hit me right on the nose! Wham!"

"Bobby was lying there in the room and of course Dr. Tremaine pulled out his little book," related Pierre. "He got the best specialist, who was about to fly to Florida or somewhere, and they got him off the plane."

On the extended power play the Hawks scored twice more to cinch a decisive 5-2 victory. But it had come at a price—the Golden Jet was grounded.

"MacGregor's stick broke both my orbital bones," recalled Hull. "I had two 2-½-inch cuts up to my sinuses and my eyes were swollen shut! And the doctor who looked after me, his name was Dr. Slaughter! No kidding!"

Hull, looking like a badly beat-up boxer, stayed back in Chicago as the team travelled to Detroit for Game 3. Mikita picked up the slack in Hull's absence and scored twice, but the Hawks should have stayed home too—they played tired. The Wings outskated and outshot them 44-19 in a 4-2 victory.

Back in the lineup for Game 4 with a heavily bandaged nose, Hull scored in the second period to tie the game at 1. His effectiveness was compromised, and Detroit outskated and outshot the Hawks again for a 4-1 win.

In Game 5 at Chicago Stadium, Hull showed grit by scoring in the first period to tie the game. Both teams checked fiercely as play seesawed back and forth until Detroit's Parker MacDonald took a golf swing at a wildly bouncing puck that ended up behind a surprised Hall. The goal stunned the home crowd into silence, fired up the Wings, and deflated the Hawks who never recovered. Detroit won 4-2 to take a stranglehold on the series.

With a two-day break, instead of giving his battered and weary troops a rest, Pilous worked them to the bone. His caveat for a loss was always the same—punishment and hard practising.

"The day before the next game, Sid Abel sent his Detroit players to the racetrack to relax and we were out on the ice practising!" complained Hull. "They had the day off and they came back fresh and we weren't! We were worn out! The guys need their rest, but no, not Rudy Pilous."

A raucous Olympia crowd greeted the two teams as they took to the ice on April 7. The Wings smelled blood and Hall literally tasted it when a shot ripped his lip in the first period and he had to leave to get stitched up. Hull, sporting a swollen black-and-blue face, showed the stuff he was made of by scoring a hat trick to go along with Nesterenko's single, but the Hawks were bounced from the playoffs with a 7-4 trouncing.

In the losing cause, Pierre had garnered eight assists, which put him second in team playoff points behind Hull's eight goals and two assists.

"That 7-4 loss, we weren't in the game," recalled Pierre. "And Rudy was not a tactician, not a line-matching person, he was not sophisticated. He was a rah-rah type, and after a while, players grow tired of it."

A dejected and tired Hawks team boarded the plane for home while the Wings went on to face the Leafs. Toronto took its second straight Stanley Cup.

During the Stanley Cup finals, Pierre and Bobby were interviewed on live TV in Detroit. When Hull was asked what he thought had caused the powerful Hawks to lose to the fourth-place Red Wings, the Golden Jet didn't hesitate.

"Bobby just turned and pointed out at Detroit coach Sid Abel," related Pierre. "Then the announcer asked, 'Well what do you mean?' and Bobby answered, 'We just got outcoached.'"

Mikita had similar feelings. "The Red Wings wanted to play for their coach," he stated. "Unlike our coach, Sid Abel sometimes pats his players on the back."

To Jim Norris, a man who flew in from his Florida home every Sunday to watch his beloved Black Hawks, defeat did not rest easily. Having been an NHL governor or alternate governor for over 30 years, the multimillionaire had been around hockey for over 40 years since the time his family had operated the old Chicago Shamrocks.

"I live and die with the Black Hawks," Norris had told Bill Gleason of the *Chicago American* earlier in the year. "I've been in horse racing for a number of years and it's nice, but horses aren't hockey. I'd much rather win the Stanley Cup than the Kentucky Derby."

In mid-April, the 57-year-old Norris sat in the plush chair of his Chicago office to tell Joe Mooshil of the Associated Press that he was still upset over the loss to Detroit.

"Let's face it; I'm not getting any younger. There might not be many more chances. We were in first place for three months. Then we failed to win the title, then we get knocked out by Detroit, a club which finished behind us. If it weren't for hockey, this stadium would probably be a garage now. We used to have rodeos, the circus, bike races, and boxing. But those days are gone. Hockey keeps this building going."

Having poured more than two million dollars into the Chicago hockey franchise along with partner Arthur Wirtz, Norris explained that he was prepared to do more, hence the failed Mahovlich bid.

"I was sincere," Norris snorted. "It wasn't a smart move financially but the deal I agreed to would have been made. I would have built a competitor out of the team. It would demoralize the other teams. Since they finished one game ahead of us, we probably would have won the championship. That alone would be worth one million dollars."

But clearly change was in the wind, and on May 6, Pilote was finally recognized for his impact with the Norris Trophy as the top NHL defenceman.

"Winning the Norris didn't really sink in at the time. It took awhile," recalled Pierre. "Afterwards, to be recognized in the same class as Doug Harvey was pretty special."

He picked up $2,000 with the award, which included $1,000 for winning the overall voting and $500 for leading in the balloting in each part of the season. Articles pointed out that his ankle injuries in November and March forced him to stay back more as he garnered only 8 goals and 18 assists, fifth among defencemen, but credited his award to the fact that he drew a minuscule 57 minutes in penalties, the lowest of his career, and little more than a third of his 165 minutes in 1960–61.

On the same day, Mikita, Hall, and Pierre were selected to the First All-Star Team. Moose and Hull were selected to the Second Team. Pierre garnered a further $2,000 for making the First Team, $500 for both halves of the season, and $1,000 for ending on it.

Kudos also came from two separate telegraphs from Frank J. Selke of the Canadiens to Pierre's Fort Erie home. It must have been a pleasant surprise for Pierre coming from a man who had watched the great Doug Harvey all of those years.

Where Selke had helped shape Harvey, it was Rudy Pilous who believed in Pierre Pilote. From his days saving Pierre from an Art Jackson cut as a Junior Teepee to promoting him as Hawks captain, Pilous had always been there.

What came next was painful.

On May 22, the Hawks announced that Pilous's contract would not be renewed. "Owing to the absence of Jim Norris, chairman of the board, who is in Europe, no decision on a new coach will be made until after the NHL draft meeting in June," read the short communiqué from Tommy Ivan. PR man Johnny Gotseling had been let go earlier.

From his home in St. Catharines, Pilous took the high road. "I have the warmest feelings towards Mr. Norris, Mr. Ivan, and the players," he said. "I wish them every success."

In Fort Erie, Pierre had a feeling that Rudy's dismissal was coming and felt helpless to help his old friend.

"I sometimes wondered if I could have helped him, defended him, but the game was changing," said Pierre. "Rudy was not a tactician, not a line-matching person. The writing had been on the wall."

For Pierre, torn between loyalty and pragmatism, it didn't mean he had to like it. He didn't.

And what would life be like with the rumoured new coach Billy Reay?

"He's just like the Rocket!"

For Pierre, the summer of 1963 entailed operating the laundro-mats in St. Catharines and Welland and helping Annie with their growing family. Though his career was in full gear, he knew that as his 32nd birthday approached, hockey wasn't forever. Thinking ahead, he enrolled in a business administration correspondence course at a Chicago school.

"I like a challenge," he told the press. "I think I have a feel for business. If I don't stay in hockey when my playing career is over, I may go into business all the way."

A bigger change was about to come into his hockey life with the appointment of William Tulip "Billy" Reay as Chicago head coach.

Born August 21, 1918, in Winnipeg, Manitoba, the 5'7" 155-pound Reay had been a tough, two-way player who won a Memorial Cup in 1937–38 with the St. Boniface Seals and an Allan Cup with the Québec Aces in 1944. After joining the Montreal Canadiens in 1945 they won the Stanley Cup in his first season and again in 1953.

In a 10-year playing career Reay scored 105 times, accumulating 267 points in 479 games while garnering 13 goals and 29 points in 63 playoff games. He is credited as being the first player to raise his arms after scoring a goal, a habit that quickly spread.

After retiring, he coached teams in Seattle and Rochester before ascending to bench boss of the Toronto Maple Leafs in 1957, a tenure that lasted only a season and a half. He ended up guiding the Buffalo Bisons to the 1963 Calder Cup championship and now, with Rudy Pilous gone, he was the logical choice.

"Billy Reay was an ex-player who had won a lot of great championships," recalled Pierre. "You immediately respected his hockey experience and knowledge."

That June, major change was in the NHL air when Tommy Ivan and Reay attended the initial NHL amateur draft. For the first time, all teams got a fair chance to pick the best amateur stars. Gone were the dreaded "C" form and farm system by which teams had owned a player for life. Each team got four picks, but the talent pool was meagre. The Hawks only used three of their picks, selecting Bill Carson, Art Hampson, and Wayne Davison. They also sent Ron Ingram and goaltending prospect Roger Crozier to the Red Wings for bad boy Howie Young, who was known around the league as a talented but temperamental defenceman who took stupid penalties and argued with officials.

At the meeting, Reay ran into the always affable Pilous, who wished him well. Pilous was scouting for the Leafs.

"Got any advice for me?" Reay asked him.

"Yeah! Finish first!" Pilous told him with a smirk.

If Ivan thought he might have a relatively quiet summer, he was mistaken. His new acquisition, Young, was arrested for drunk and disorderly conduct at a Detroit restaurant, where he fought the arresting police officers. Young was fined and sentenced to 90 days in jail prior to camp.

As camp started, tough guy Reg Fleming started swinging at goalie Glenn Hall, who he claimed had tripped him. Young stepped in to separate the two men. The move raised eyebrows.

"We teased Reggie, because he came from Montreal," Pierre remembered. "We'd call him 'CH.' He didn't know what CH meant, that it was on the Habs sweaters. I think Billy Hay gave him that handle."

"Reggie Fleming had a heart of gold and great parents too!"

recalled Hull. "When we'd go to Montreal and his parents' place, we'd send the rookies in first because the first two guys through the front door would be hugged by Reggie's old man, a big former football player with the Alouettes. He'd just grab them with his big, gnarled old hands and whack 'em on the back. Those poor rookies! Ah shit, we laughed!"

For Pierre, the autumn ritual separated the men from the boys. In an exhibition game in Baltimore, an opposition rookie, Dave Richardson, roughed Pilote in front of the Hawks net. Before the youngster knew it, a pair of Norris-winning arms flung him to the ice in a heap. Pierre stood over the young man, awaiting a reprisal, but none came. As Pierre skated away triumphantly, a local reporter turned to another and said enviously: "That guy is a dirty, filthy hockey player . . . but brother, I wish he was on our team!"

Mikita, involved in stalled contract negotiations with Ivan, missed the All-Star Game in Toronto. Hull (now wearing no. 9) and Pilote participated, as they had inked new deals. For his part, Pierre's Norris and First All-Star team nods helped him enormously; a raise was without question, to Ivan's chagrin.

"I did very well," Pierre smiled. "When you've got those aces up your sleeve, you've got a heck of a bargaining chip. Tommy was always one to grudgingly recognize success."

The Hawks opened the season at home against New York on October 9, with the masked marvel, Jacques Plante, now in the Rangers net. The tribe took no pity on Plante and handed him a 3-1 loss.

On October 20, the Hawks hosted the Canadiens. The weakened Habs had been picked to place fourth or even fifth this season, but they showed amazing tenacity and one of the reasons was a new player in their lineup—John Ferguson. Brought in as an enforcer, Ferguson had shown his mettle by easily disposing of tough guy Ted Green in a fight in his very first game in Boston Garden.

Ferguson was taught a life lesson from the veteran Hawks captain.

"I read about this Ferguson kid, how tough he was," recalled Pierre. "In our first meeting, he was coming out of his zone and I cut across to intercept him, right in front of the Montreal bench. Fergie had his head down. I coulda killed him but I just banged my stick on the ice. He suddenly looked up and passed the puck just as I missed him. Imagine me corking him in one of his very first games. I would've looked like an asshole and he would have been after me for life! His bench must have told him, 'Look, Pierre gave you a pass! Don't put your head down like that, you'll get killed!'

"He must have remembered that because, as tough as he was, he never bothered me. He would battle Bobby and Nesterenko, beat them to a pulp. He did a lot of guys in. We would certainly clash, pushing and shoving in front of the net, but he left me alone, really. I don't think he wanted to fight me, and he had lots of opportunities to. I saved him from a one-way ticket to the first aid room or the minors and maybe he remembered that? Who knows? I know he seemed to respect me from day one."

Respect was not something that the mouthy Young had for referee Vern Buffy.

"Vern Buffy had his work cut out with Howie Young," observed Pierre. "It was natural to concentrate on the guy who created the most trouble, and Howie made trouble. He was such a fast skater that when he went at players it looked like charging. The sticks would come up, so really, he was in that soup all the time. The referees were always watching him. He deserved a lot of his penalties, but they missed a lot too."

The Hawks stayed hot to remain in first place and the impact of the new coach was evident, but for Pierre Reay's attitude was unorthodox and at times comical.

Reay was always mindful of the boys drinking and being hungover, and he soon developed a habit of skating the team hard and then summoning players over to talk so he could smell their breath. Pierre was on to him.

"You'd see his nose twitching, to smell us," Pierre recalled. "This one time, I hadn't anything to drink the night before, and he called me over. I went right up to him, his nose is twitching, and I get close, real close, purposely breathing right on him."

"Billy, do you have a cold?" Pierre asked Reay as his nose worked.

"No, I don't have a cold," Reay answered. His captain moved in even closer.

"Billy, is everything okay?"

"Yeah, yeah, everything's okay," the coach answered, backing up. Suddenly a smile crossed his face. He realized his captain was on to him; maybe all the others too. Pierre skated away smiling to himself.

"Billy was a smarter inside hockey coach than Rudy," noted Pierre. "He never bothered to change my game, or Bobby or Stan's. He left us be."

In Toronto on November 2, Hall shut out the defending Stanley Cup champion Leafs 2-0 to extend their streak to eight games without a loss. At home three nights later against the Rangers, the game was tied at 2 apiece when Pierre broke free in the final minute of play.

"The Rangers obviously were content to settle for a tie with the hottest team in all of hockey, but captain Pierre was having no half-loaves last evening," wrote the *Tribune*'s Charles Bartlett. "Pete knocked down the puck at mid-ice on the Madison Street side of the rink, eluded one Ranger check, and dashed into New York ice. Twice he was detained by the Rangers defence pair of Al Langlois and Doug Harvey but he kept on skating toward the New York goal." Pierre passed it to Red Hay, who got it to Hull for a goal. "Certainly no single goal in the Hawks spectacular record of only one defeat in their first 11 matches merited a more deserved assist than the Hawks' own leader, Captain Pierre Pilote, earned as the red light flared at 19:40."

"This is one of Pierre's biggest attributes," Reay said after the game. "When he knows the club really needs a goal he's just like the Rocket [Maurice Richard]—he's a fanatic. I was glad to see Bobby get that goal. He played so hard and well, Pilote too."

The accolades continued for Pierre, including a story in the

Chicago American. "If Pierre Pilote were anything less than one of the most determined men in the NHL . . . history indicates that what he wants, he gets, mainly because he's utterly contemptuous of any obstacles which might stand between him and his goal," began the article, which also quoted GM Ivan praising Pilote's loyalty. "The loyalty was displayed last year when many of the Hawks stars were in almost open revolt against Pilous. Several even made comments on their opinions of Rudy's coaching ability within earshot of reporters. But if Pilote had an opinion, he never voiced it. He simply went about his job, and if the rest of the crew had come close to matching his effort, there would have been no late collapse, no playoff drop."

"You just have to keep hustling, hustling and sacrificing," Pierre was quoted. "You have to deny yourself certain pleasures and you have to be willing to punish your body. The trouble with a lot of the kids playing now is that they think just because they have some talent, they need nothing else. Talent just carries you so far. There are a lot of very talented guys playing in beer leagues around Canada because they were willing to try to get along on their ability alone."

When they finally lost in Boston 4-2 on November 10, the tribe set out on another unbeaten streak. On November 17 they chewed up the Leafs in a 6-0 romp that saw Pierre assist on two of Hull's three goals. Numerous fights erupted in the stands when tormenter Eddie Shack was levelled by a Fleming elbow in the third period that left Shack's nose a bloody pulp.

"I just put Reg in against Shack to see what Shack could do," said Reay after the game. "Now we know."

"Eddie was coming around one of his defencemen, looking down at the puck, and Reggie nailed him," recalled Pierre. "Shack's on the ice and the fans are just jumping up and down, screaming, and there's blood all over the ice. Reggie's got one hand on his hip, being very proud. All of a sudden, Howie Young jumps on the ice, puts Reggie on his shoulders, and parades him around the rink. People just went crazy."

In a November 20 game against the Wings, the tribe was cruising along in the third period towards their ninth straight win at home when Pierre dropped to his knees to block a Norm Ullman shot.

"Ten feet in front of the net, I went down too fast and Norm's shot went right into my nose! Oh boy! I got up bleeding and went downstairs, and Dr. Tremaine was waiting and he said, 'Well, we'll have to put a tape on there and tomorrow we'll take an X-ray and see what we're gonna do with it.' I said, 'Oh no, doc, let's deal with it right now!' So I lay down and he grabbed my nose and went crunch, crunch.

"He said, 'Pierre, it looks pretty good.' I said, 'Oh no! Let me have a look at it first.' I got up, looked into a mirror and, no, it wasn't quite straight yet. He crunched it again and I looked again and I said, 'Yeah, okay, that's good.' So he taped it and that was that."

After the game, Ron Murphy entered the Hawks dressing room, looked at Pierre's swollen and grotesque nose, and said, "Hey, you remind me of Eddie Shack!"

"Ha!" Pierre snorted. "I should look so bad!"

X-rays the next day revealed no major damage and Pierre suited up for the team's next game against Montreal, which they won 7-3.

A sad day in hockey occurred on November 26, when the Rangers unconditionally released 38-year-old defenceman Doug Harvey. Dink Carroll of the *Montreal Gazette* penned a tribute to the legendary defencemen who had won seven straight Norris Trophies.

"During his peak years, Harvey was incomparable," wrote Carroll. "There were other great rearguards before him . . . Eddie Shore, Sprague Cleghorn, Eddie Gerard, George Boucher, and King Clancy to mention a few—but none could do so many things as well as he could. There are a number of defencemen in the NHL today who modelled themselves after Doug Harvey, including Chicago's Pierre Pilote."

"I learned a lot by watching him" Pilote admitted to Carroll. "You learn from the best, and as far as I'm concerned, he was the best."

In Toronto on December 7, Shack ambled up to Pierre during a break in the action for some lighthearted kibitzing.

"Word got around the league about my broken nose," Pierre recalled. "Eddie Shack comes up to me on the ice, smiling, puts his glove up into my face, and rubs his glove right over my nose saying, 'Hey Pierre, how's it going?' Did that hurt! I could have killed him! He laughed. I didn't."

With the Leafs ahead 3-0 and less than four minutes left in the game, Chicago's second tremendous undefeated streak was about to come to an end and tempers were high. Fleming finally had enough of Shack's antics, and he high-sticked the Clown of Carlton Street in the Leafs end behind the play. Shack collapsed onto his knees, blood spewing from his mouth.

Then all hell broke loose.

Both benches cleared and players were paired off with at least nine fights going on simultaneously. It took 20 minutes for order to be restored, and when the smoke cleared referee Frank Udvari handed out seven majors, six misconducts, and three game misconducts, but harsher penalties than the $825 in automatic fines were yet to come.

After league president Clarence Campbell reviewed tapes of the incident and received reports from officials, he announced a record total of $4,925 in fines, including $1,000 each to coaches Reay and Imlach.

In helping Chicago win two of their next three games after the Toronto debacle, Pierre made his mark on December 15 against the Wings when he tallied a goal and an assist to notch 27 points in 29 games—almost a point a game. He was hailed as the most offensive defenceman of his era, but it all didn't matter as his team suddenly stalled.

Arriving in Montreal the night before a tilt on December 21, the players were all doing their own thing. Pierre headed alone to the Monterrey Club, a country bar on the corner of St. Catharines and Peel, to unwind and have his favourite nightcap—a crème de menthe with 7UP.

Sitting quietly at the back, Pierre hadn't been there long when a very intoxicated Young staggered in. Young made his way to the stage and wanted to sing with the band. Bouncers tried to get him off the stage, but he was not cooperating. Finally, Pierre had seen enough; he headed to the stage and grabbed Young, who went to punch but stopped when he saw his captain.

"Pierre, they won't let me sing."

"I know, Howie. Come on, let's go. Let's get back to the hotel. It's curfew time."

"But Pierre, I wanna . . ."

"Not tonight," Pierre answered as he slung Young over his shoulder and carried him the few blocks to the hotel. He deposited Young on his bed and then closed the door. Pierre felt good that he had done his duty and saved Young from trouble. Or so he thought. Dressing beside Billy Hay for the next morning's skate, Pierre retold his Young adventure.

"Yeah, I heard you, Pete," Hay said. "But that wasn't the end of the story."

"No?" Pierre turned in wonderment.

"Nope," answered Hay. "Your door had no sooner closed, when Howie was out like a shot, and never came back till five this morning." Pierre could only shake his head in disgust.

"That was Howie," recalled Pierre of that night. "He was a sick alcoholic. It was too bad because he had a lot of ability. He was a big guy, a really good, fast skater, who never helped himself."

At the end of December, the Hawks regrouped and won three of four games and sported a 20-8-7 record and a five-point lead over the second-place Habs at the season's halfway point. The *Hockey News* predicted that with the Hawks playing so well, they may comprise the whole First All-Star Team.

The Black Hawks did place Hall, Hull, Pierre, and Wharram on the mid-season First All-Star squad, with Mikita and Vasko on the Second.

Hockey writer Stan Fischler wrote an extensive article on Pierre in *SPORT* magazine. "For years Pilote's fighting overshadowed his overall hockey skills. Now, though he's still brawling, he's known as the best defenceman in the NHL."

"There's no question about it," Punch Imlach said. "Pilote is heads above anybody in the league."

While the story concentrated on Pierre's rough play, he resented the image of himself as a brute and insisted that he preferred a clean game even if it meant losing. "We're not a bunch of animals who go around eating each other up!"

"His All-Star credentials are impressive," Fischler writes. "Going into the present season, he's played 488 games, scored 47 goals and 193 assists, unusually high for a defenceman. . . . As for penalties, he's collected 740 minutes for an average of 1.5 minutes per game. Significantly, the total has declined since he led the league with 165 minutes in 1960–61."

The Hawks must have had swelled heads from reading the headlines about their All-Star greatness because they went into an extended slump, winning only two of their next six games. On January 16, after a 1-0 loss in the Forum, Reay defended his team.

"Sure, we went into a bit of a slump," Reay admitted. "I think that big 12-point lead we had at one time had something to do with it. Everybody was writing about the team—how great they were—and I think maybe the players began to believe their press clippings. They thought they could ease up a little and still win, but you can't do that in this league."

The Hawks were on the verge of being nudged out of first place by Montreal and Toronto when they hosted the Leafs on January 19. Pierre remembered the game well, but not because the Hawks lost yet again, 2-0.

"It was payback time for Eddie Shack against Reggie," Pierre recalled. "This was now a month or two later. Reggie's speciality was penalty-killing, and he was out covering the point on the penalty kill. Shack was not an offensive threat but Punch had put him in there, on a power play. The puck was in the corner and Reggie was just standing on the point looking into the corner when Shack high-sticked him in the back of the head, right in front of our bench.

"Reggie's down on the ice, blood everywhere, but you know what? The referee didn't see it and we didn't holler too much about a penalty because we all knew it was coming. Shack had been waiting for a long time to get Reggie back. After, Eddie danced around like a peacock, he was so proud. When he went to the bench, he was all smiles, but the fans were screaming. Poor Reggie. He asked, 'Who hit me?' He didn't even know."

Fleming required 21 stitches to close the gaping wound and was so incoherent that Dr. Tremaine had him sent to hospital for observation.

Columnist Dick Hackenberg of the *Sun-Times* noted that it was no coincidence that the Hawks skid coincided with Pierre playing more defensive hockey.

"Including Saturday afternoon's 5-3 loss to Detroit, the Hawks had crossed the 46-game mark fighting for their lives, and Pilote had been able to add no goals and only four assists in 17 contests . . . while it can be argued that a good offence is the best defence, or vice versa, the fact remains that when Pierre flashes into the opponents' end of the rink, he just might score and they can't as long as Pierre controls the puck. Pierre's style of play, with his clever stick-handling, arouses mixed emotions in the crowd. When he's good, he's very, very good—the fans take that for granted. When he's bad, he's very, very bad and the fans jeer."

Reay talked about his captain. "His biggest trouble is being too intelligent," Reay said. "Sometimes he tries to out-think the other guy, but if the guy doesn't do the orthodox, Pierre is left standing there like a rank amateur."

On January 30, the Hawks had grown tired of the Howie Young saga and placed him on waivers, meaning other clubs could purchase him for the rock-bottom price of $20,000. Young was purchased by the Western Hockey League's Los Angeles Blades.

"Hooray! A big relief," recalled Pierre of the team's reaction. "We didn't have to worry about him anymore. We never knew what he was going to do—on or off the ice!"

With the distracting Young gone, the Hawks lost only once in seven games during the first two weeks of February.

Against the Bruins on February 16, a normally calm Vasko got into a scrap with Boston's aggressive rookie centre, Orland Kurtenbach. Moose traded punches with the tough Kurtenbach, while Mikita went toe to toe with defenceman Tom Johnson and two more defenders. Chicago rookie Aut Erickson tangled with Ted Green. Referee Frank Udvari dished out 96 minutes in penalties, but the battling Hawks won the game 5-3 to maintain their share of first place.

"Moose's fight with Kurtenbach was right at centre ice," remembered Pierre. "The two of them were tall, but Orland had long arms that he wielded like a boxer. Elmer was strong but he was not quick. Orland was really quick. The Moose took about six punches over his eyes and nose in about two seconds! Poor Elmer, he was not a fighter, he was a lover. But after that, I realized that I've got to stay friends with that Kurtenbach guy! He could swing! Elmer taught me that lesson—the hard way!"

For Pierre, another lesson was emerging with Coach Reay. "At the end of each practice, Billy would let the others go, Glenn, Stan, but he would always make me, Elmer, and Bobby stay an extra half hour on the ice," recalled Pierre. "A half hour extra—every time! Whether he thought it was the way to keep us in shape, I don't know. We were always the last guys to leave the ice. Always! He would work us hard. We didn't resent it, but we didn't like it. I know Bobby didn't like it. I never understood it."

Chicago fans had always been finicky. They loved you one minute, hated you the next and always expected the best from their players. Everyone was subjected to booing at one time or another—even Mr. Goalie faced the wrath of the Madison gallery gods after a soft goal. In a home game against the Red Wings on February 27, the boo-birds were out in full force, their sights set on Pierre.

"Coach Billy Reay was discussing the fans' misplaced wrath Thursday night after Pilote had scored one of the goals in the Hawks 4-2 victory over the Red Wings, a triumph which pulled them back into a first-place tie with Montreal," wrote a perplexed Dan Moulton. "'Look at the figures,' said Reay as he leafed through the game statistics. 'Pierre was on the ice for three of our goals and he wasn't on the ice when the Wings scored either of theirs. Yet, the fans were giving him trouble all night. They don't appreciate the guy at all and he's just the best around right now.'

"Part of Pierre's problem . . . he does handle the puck more often than most defencemen, which increases his chances for error. 'Sure, everything can't work out right,' continued Reay. 'But Pierre makes more good plays than he does bad.'"

"I hear them yelling at me," Pierre told the scribe. "But I don't worry about it. I figure I have more on my side than there are against me. I just have to go along and play my game. Sure, there are times when I out-think myself and wind up looking bad. It happened in this game as a matter of fact. I thought I saw an opening for a pass but it closed just as I made a play that was risky under any conditions."

The March issue of *Hockey Pictorial* had Pierre on the cover, calling him hockey's number one defenceman. For the first time, an article concentrated on Pierre the man as much as the hockey player. Harry Molter's story began by describing a recent speech Pierre gave to Chicago businessmen at the Illinois Athletic Club, one of a dozen he delivered during the season. "He's doing it for two reasons: to help promote sales of Black Hawks tickets and . . . his own personal future."

"It's possible I may settle down in Chicago with my family after my playing days are over," Pierre told Molter. "These speeches give me good exposure to businessmen in the area. And it's good experience for whatever I do eventually, to talk in front of a group. Most players don't like to do it and I was pretty nervous when I started, but like playing hockey, you gain confidence with experience.

"I read a lot, educational articles, books about business,

advertising and selling . . . I read a lot on the road, the financial pages of the newspapers. I don't have a particular goal. I would like to stay in hockey in some capacity, but travel and time away from my family is a big factor . . . I have a wife and four kids and the shifting around of schools is difficult on them. It's not only two school systems but two countries. I help the kids with their homework. They have a lot to catch up after going the first two months in Fort Erie. I do the twist with the kids too. I'm forced to.

"We had our troubles during the middle of this season and some nights I felt I was carrying the Chicago Stadium on my back. When you're winning though everything goes right and you can't wait for the next game. One individual on a hot streak can pick up a whole team."

The battle for first was fierce. On March 5 they tied the Bruins and three nights later defeated the Leafs 4-3. The Hawks were in first place, two points ahead of the mighty Canadiens, who they faced next. Their records were almost identical.

The Habs edged them in the Forum 4-3 to pull even for first place—again. Montreal was now one goal ahead of Hall in the Vezina race—again.

The tribe didn't help their cause when they lost their next match against the Wings, 5-3. When they hosted the Rangers on March 17 in the penultimate game of the season, they pulled it together defensively and notched a 4-0 Hall shutout. That really helped Mr. Goalie's Vezina cause versus Montreal's Charlie Hodge.

Heading into the last game, everything was on the line. The Canadiens were ahead by one point and the two teams were tied in goals-against.

The Hawks defeated the Bruins 4-3 in Boston, but their hopes were dashed when the Canadiens won their game by a meager 2-1 score to clinch first place by a measly point. Hodge nudged Hall by a two-goal margin, for the Vezina, 167 to 169. To add insult to injury, Montreal coach Hector "Toe" Blake was voted Coach of the Year, nudging out Reay just as the playoffs were set to begin.

It was a bad omen as they prepared to face the fourth-place Red Wings.

A pre-playoff article on Pierre at his Stickney home, where he and his family stayed for the past three seasons, gave readers a glimpse into his life.

"It's somewhat like a little island of relief away from the tumult of the hockey club," said Pierre. "It's nice and quiet, close to school and church, and these are very important factors in helping us choose a place to live. We hope that next season when we settle here, we find as fine a place, but there are things we have to attend to in Ontario this summer, which keeps us from settling here permanently."

It was clear Chicago's interest in hockey was growing when it was announced that the Ritz Theatre and four other venues would air closed-circuit telecasts of the first Hawks home games. Ticket prices for the theatres were $3.50 and the viewing screens were 20-feet wide and 15-feet tall, slightly smaller than regular movie theatre screens.

"The fans in Chicago were great and the fan club, the Standby Club, used to really support us," recalled Pierre. "We made some good friends there. Benny Cline, Richard Heisenheart, and Helen Urich stand out. Fred Marsella was our butcher. He always sat in the organ loft with Al Melgard, the organist. If I had an extra ticket, Fred's wife, Joyce, would accompany Annie to the game. Joyce once told me that when they went to the ladies room, Annie would always, always, use the same stall no matter how long the lineup. It apparently had good luck."

As Pierre and company focused on disposing of the Detroiters in their quest for another Stanley Cup, they should have been wary of the fact that the Wings and the Leafs were the two hottest teams down the stretch, each winning six of their last nine games.

In the first game of the 1964 semifinals played at the Stadium, Hull and Howe were kept off the scoresheet by the other team's best checkers, but the Scooter Line came through to help secure a 4-1 victory. Despite having played a key part in the victory, Hall was not totally pleased with the night's outcome.

"I think hockey is a wonderful game, I really do—to watch, but I hate every minute I play!" snapped Mr. Goalie to a surprised reporter who had suggested that Hall might have had an easy night of it. "I'm sick to my stomach before the game, between periods, and from the start of the season to the end. There's no such thing as an easy night for a goalie; not even if he never gets a shot to stop during the whole game!"

Detroit came to play in Game 2 despite goalie Terry Sawchuk jarring his shoulder yet again and being forced to leave the game mere minutes into it. After a 16-minute delay, replacement Bob Champoux came in and the Red Wings tightened up, eking out a 5-4 win to stun the home team and its supporters and tie the series.

Hawks fans became so unruly after the game that Gordie Howe punched one—Robert Rosenthal—in the mouth. In court, the case was dismissed as Rosenthal admitted he provoked Howe.

For Game 3 in Detroit, Sawchuk provided a little Stanley Cup drama of his own when he left his hospital bed, where his arm had been placed in traction for a pinched nerve, to face the Hawks. Chicago threw 26 shots at him as he played through pain that forced him to drop his stick twice during action. Sawchuk managed to whitewash the tribe 3-0. The Wings were up two games to one and hadn't lost to the Hawks on home ice in 13 games.

The Olympia was packed to see Sawchuk start Game 4, but the pain in his shoulder grew worse as the game went on and after a minute into the second period he couldn't continue. After a 22-minute delay allowed Roger Crozier to dress, the stoppage seemed to cool off the Hawks and the Wings closed ranks in front of the little Bracebridge, Ontario, native. Detroit was ahead 2-1 at the 9:24 mark of the second when Pierre pushed the play into the Detroit end and scored to tie the game, where it stayed until the end of regulation time.

Play see-sawed back and forth until 8:21 of the sudden-death overtime, when Murray Balfour tipped the winning goal past Crozier to tie the series. Amidst the Hawks celebration was the forgotten fact that Pierre's second goal of the series, when added to his five assists, gave him seven points, making him the point leader thus far.

Coach Reay was fuming about the long delays as a result of Detroit's goaltending changes due to Sawchuk's injuries. Reay called the waits "the greatest stall in Stanley Cup history."

On April 5, the Hawks hosted the Red Wings in the Madhouse on Madison. From the beginning of "The Star-Spangled Banner" through the three periods of play, the fans yelled themselves hoarse. Crozier, in net for the Wings, played a strong game, but referee Udvari provided the drama when he disallowed a Wharram goal. A few minutes later he reversed his call and allowed the goal to stand. The roof practically lifted off the old building when Mikita notched the go-ahead and winning goal to pull out a 3-2 Hawks win.

After the game, emotions were running high as Detroit coach Abel was livid at Udvari's changed call on Wharram's tying goal. He called the referee's decision "gutless" and his reversal the "worst call I've seen in my 30 years in hockey!" NHL president Clarence Campbell was not amused and fined Abel $500.

The fine was a rallying point for his troops before Game 6. It worked, as the Wings embarrassed the Hawks by a 7-2 score that saw goalie Hall replaced by DeJordy in the third period with Detroit up 5-2.

Prior to Game 7 in Chicago, Campbell wasn't finished giving his elevated opinion on matters that affected his game. He had heard Ivan's complaining of injuries to Sawchuk and the game delays they brought about.

"These delays are certainly not looked upon with favour by the spectators and also cause considerable problems in telecasting and broadcasting the games," the NHL president warned. He said one possibility to prevent delays was for each team to dress two goaltenders and that such action may come into effect as early as next season.

"Delays cooled you off," recalled Pierre. "If you had a team on the run and the goalie gets hurt then he's taken away and we gotta wait. In earlier years, Gunzo was our spare goaltender. I mean, he was our skate sharpener for goodness' sake! He practised with us, but he was not a goaltender. That was another reason why Glenn Hall played so many games. It happened against us with other teams. Hockey had to come out of the dark ages when it came to back-up goalies being ready to go in. Baseball had relief pitchers ready. Thank goodness Gunzo never got into a game!"

In Game 7, Hall returned to the net and was hit for two goals in the first period by Howe and Floyd Smith. Though the Hawks notched two in response, the Wings struck twice more and tightened up the defence. The tribe just couldn't catch them, resulting in a disappointing 4-2 loss and another elimination in the first round of the playoffs.

As if the playoffs hadn't gone bad enough for the Hawks, catastrophe almost befell the team off the ice weeks later when Hull was involved in a car accident that could have easily taken his life: his car skidded on wet pavement in suburban Allan Park and slid under a semi-trailer truck.

"I went under the windshield, and the car went under the trailer between the wheels," recalled Hull. "It made a convertible out of my station wagon. I was lucky! My brother Dennis and Dr. Montgomery were in the car with me. As I lost control I yelled to them, 'Duck guys, I'm gonna hit him.'"

Hull was admitted to Henry Ford Hospital and was held overnight, but a spokesman said his only apparent injuries were minor ones to his hands.

For Pierre, if there was a balm to soothe the sting of the playoff loss, it came in the form of a second straight Norris Trophy. The accomplishment was overshadowed in Hawkland by the earlier headlines of Mikita winning the Art Ross Trophy for the league scoring championship and Kenny Wharram winning the Lady Byng for sportsmanship and the Hawks filling five of six positions on the First All-Star Team: Hall, Pilote, Wharram, Hull, and Mikita. Vasko made the Second Team.

"Elmer had such a great season that year, they should have given us the whole First All-Star Team," complained Hull.

"Individual honours and general embarrassment continue to mount up for the Black Hawks," wrote Dan Moulton. "How can a team with so many stars fold up as completely as the Hawks have for the last two years?"

Perhaps the answer lay in the pages of George Vass's Questions & Answer column when Hawks fan Gene Gasiorowski wrote: "Dear George, now that the hockey season is over, I hope somebody does something about the awful Hawks defence. . . . The team has one good defenceman, Pierre Pilote. Billy Reay should emphasize defence. . . . It wasn't the offence that lost the Stanley Cup for the Hawks, it was the defence, just as defence won the Cup for the Maple Leafs."

"Dear Gene," began Vass's response. "You're right, it wasn't the offence that lost the Cup for the Hawks, it was the defence. Goalie Glenn Hall was so shell-shocked that he applied for the Purple Heart—but what he needed was Blue Cross."

It was easy to kick a team when it was down, and the Hawks were kicked good and hard. Still it was a reasonable question on every Hawks fan's mind—why did the big vaunted, star-filled Hawk machine shut down in the playoffs again? It was one of the biggest hockey mysteries from the 1960s. Nobody had an answer.

CHAPTER 16

A Swingin' Record Setter and DSMO

As he surveyed yet another early playoff exit, Tommy Ivan faced the challenge of changing his lineup but not weakening his team. He elected to ship Ab McDonald, Murray Balfour, and Reg Fleming to Boston in exchange for 31-year-old Doug Mohns.

"In trading for Mohns, the Hawks got a player similar to their captain, Pierre Pilote," the press wrote the next day. "Mohns is also a fine offensive defenceman—and a good defensive forward when moved to that position."

If Ivan was thinking he'd acquired another Pilote, who combined solid defence with strong offensive abilities, it didn't show in his first public comment about the trade.

"He'll add punch to the Hawk scoring attack," was all the GM said.

"Murray Balfour was a good player. A real hard-nosed kid, built like a brick shithouse who could skate," Pierre recalled. "He played well with Bobby. I was saddened to see Murray go. I didn't know why they traded him."

The Mohns trade was a window into Ivan's thinking and perhaps therein lies the reason the Hawks were having trouble in the playoffs: Ivan's emphasis on offence. Scoring prowess was the Hawks' bread and butter in the regular season, so why change for the playoffs?

Aware of his growing notoriety and many appearances as captain of the Hawks, Pierre started to see himself as a marketing commodity. He also saw the Golden Jet and Mr. Goalie as two other very marketable athletes.

"I had been contacted by two fellows who had a public relations company in Hamilton," Pierre recalled. "At that stage of our careers, I was equal to Bobby, you know what I mean. Glenn Hall was doing very well. Through these guys the three of us did a few public appearances, which went very well. All of a sudden, they realized we should formalize things, so in the summer of 1964, we formed H-P-H Limited—Hull-Pilote-Hall."

Also that summer Pierre joined the staff at a hockey camp in Fenelon Falls, near Peterborough, Ontario. The Byrnell Manor Boys Camp, a 240-acre camp on the shores of Cameron Lake, was originally a farm converted into a Christian summer camp. Owners Frank and Anna Stukus had the novel idea of combining a hockey school with a summer camp. Other staff members included Allan Stanley, Milt Schmidt, and Ed Chadwick. Punch Imlach and Muzz Patrick sent their boys there.

The Pilote family took full advantage of the summer employment scenario. Annie and the kids stayed at a large cabin on the lake while Annie's two Pierres were off to hockey school each day, the elder as an instructor, the younger as a student.

"We stayed at this cottage on Cameron Lake and it was great," Annie reminisced. "The kids really enjoyed it. We had lots of fun and lots of company throughout that summer."

The six-week hockey camp was also a good way for Pierre to get in some skating and light conditioning; a big part of being in shape was weight control and he had a theory in its relation to hockey.

"In those days, 30 was old, but I couldn't figure out why players weren't playing longer, but then I did. A lot of guys would break into the league young, fit, and weighing 165 pounds or so, not big but tough and fast. During the summer off, they would put on 10 pounds. It was easy to do if you didn't watch yourself. Then, at training camp they'd lose eight pounds and keep two. After 10 years, you're 30 with an extra 20 pounds. It doesn't really show but it's harder on your body, slows you down, and all of a sudden, in your thirties, you're down in the minors.

"The guys who stayed longer, Lindsay, Mikita, Howe, and Richard, all kept their playing weight the same. Guys with the extra weight were gone. Of course injuries didn't help, but weight made a big difference. And on our team, big Moose, Elmer, our all-time heavyweight, always had trouble with his weight, especially this one year."

September 1964 came and it was weigh-in day at the Hawks training camp. It was obvious that Vasko, who'd had a particularly enjoyable summer, had packed on a little more beef than usual. He was surely over his playing weight of 222, but that was okay because trainer Nick Garen weighed everyone, wrote down the figures, and they'd all get on with camp. Moose would lose his weight like he'd done in the past. It might take him half the season but that was alright, usually.

The players were taking their street clothes off as the old reliable bean scale was brought out from the back room for the annual ritual. All was normal until Billy Reay walked into the room with a clipboard and pen in hand.

"Okay boys, step right up! Let's see how bad you've been this summer!"

Elmer's head shot up. Where was Nick? Nick had always done weigh-in. He and Moose got along real well, had an understanding, always kibitzed about his weight and then got on with camp. Reay was standing by the scale!

One by one, the players stepped on the scale. Reay watched carefully and made the odd adjustment himself to ensure accuracy to the nearest half ounce. Moose hung back. A few players got dirty looks from Reay and a snide comment about their weight, but Reay knew that camp would trim waistlines, especially his camp; he'd work their butts off.

Moose was sweating, scared. He continued to hang back, hoping Nick would show up and finish the weigh-in but it wasn't happening. The players were trying not to snicker because they knew Moose was about to fail his test.

"Elmer's approach to early weigh-in was to *pray* he was close to his playing weight," recalled Pierre, laughing at the memory. "That day, Moose was in panic mode. We're all watching, trying not to laugh. You could hear a pin drop."

Finally, his moment of truth arrived. He couldn't delay it any longer. He was the last guy.

"Okay, Elmer, let's go!" Reay intoned. "Your turn!"

Moose gulped and stepped forward. He placed the measuring weight at his starting point of 210. The balancing arm didn't budge. Elmer laughed nervously. Reay didn't. He wasn't blind either. Moose moved the weight to 220, a touch below his usual playing weight. The scale didn't budge. Not a hint of movement. Around the room, everyone was watching. Light snickers could be heard. Moose gulped. Reay was staring right at him. Moose gulped again.

Up a pound; nothing happened. Moose prayed, but the arm didn't budge until 230, when it moved—slightly—but settled back down. Reay stared at Moose.

Elmer broke in to a full-scale sweat. At 231, the balancing arm moved precariously near the middle of centre—then settled on the bottom again. Moose laughed nervously and sheepishly put it up another pound to 232, and finally the arm settled in the middle, balanced. Moose was relieved. Reay was not.

"Moose! Are you kidding me? Coming to my camp like this?" Reay exploded. "Hope you enjoyed your summer, Moose! Now enjoy this—I'm fining you a $100 for every pound you're over 222! Hear me? You have two weeks to lose it! Lose 10 and it won't cost you a dime! Anything over 222 and it's a $100 per pound! Got it?"

Moose could only nod as he stepped off the scale under Reay's glare. There were guffaws and laughter around the room. Reay turned, seething.

"Let this be a lesson to all of you!" Reay yelled, storming out. Moose faced light-hearted kibitzing from the other players, especially from Pierre, whom he sat beside.

The exhibition schedule was not kind to the Hawks. Pierre pulled a groin muscle against the Bruins, Hull was still nursing a sore hand from the car crash, and Kenny Wharram was struck in the forehead by a puck and required surgery to repair a fractured skull.

After 10 days, Ivan was also sending players to the minors, and Moose was a candidate.

"Elmer wore a big sweat jacket when he practised, as if he ever needed a sweat jacket!" recalled Pierre. "He worked and worked, avoided his beers. Poor Elmer. Then Billy Reay came in after two weeks and got out the bean scale."

Elmer approached the scale knowing that his weight was down, but every pound counted. His teammates were all rooting for him. The scale settled in at 224 pounds, just two pounds over his goal. Elmer let out a nervous laugh and sighed.

"Good work, Vasko, but you're still two pounds over," Reay boomed. "It'll still cost you 200 big ones. And Elmer—keep it there or even lower. I'll be watching!"

"It was a memorable moment with Moose," said Pierre. "Oh, we laughed and teased him about it for years afterwards!"

As the Chicagoans prepared to open the season, Ivan added three rookies in an attempt to bolster the lineup: Fred Stanfield, a classy, young centre; Doug Jarrett, a hard-checking defenceman; and Dennis Hull, a left-winger like his older brother Bobby.

NHL president Clarence Campbell was on hand at the Hawks home and season opener, on October 14, to present Stan Mikita with the Art Ross Trophy; Wharram, the Lady Byng; and Pilote, the Norris Trophy.

"When I got that second Norris, they were giving small plaques as a keeper," recalled Pierre. "I didn't want another plaque, so I paid $50 out of my own pocket to get a miniature Norris Trophy made. The league had started to do that. I got one made for the year before too. It became the norm for winners after that but you had to pay for it."

The awards and ensuing ovation boosted the team to a 3-0 shutout against Boston. The boost didn't last long because after two weeks, the new-look Black Hawks were stuck in fourth place. What was wrong?

On October 27, Gordie Howe told the *Montreal Gazette* that the Hawks' power play was the key to the team's success. "Chicago Black Hawks had the best power play in the NHL last season. When you have Stan Mikita, a fine puck carrier, and Bobby Hull one of the better puck carriers, and Pierre Pilote, who can move the puck very well, you automatically have an edge. So you've got a combination of good puck carrying, good hard shooting, and fellows who can make the plays."

On November 1 in Boston, the three ex-Hawks handed their former teammates a 5-2 loss, Boston's first win of the young season.

"I got into a battle with Reggie Fleming, who was playing for Boston; I was fighting a friend of mine!" recalled Pierre. "On the way to the penalty box I said, 'Reggie, I thought we're friends, we'd leave each other alone?' Reggie looked at me, winked, and said: 'Pierre, you know I lie sometimes!'"

Pierre had a slow start, and in another November game against Toronto, the press blamed him for allowing an important goal, leading Hawks fans to boo him. Before a rematch against the Maple Leafs on November 21, it was noted that "another pleasure for Reay to watch has been the progress of the veteran defenceman Pierre Pilote, who came on slowly the first 10 games but lately has been the hottest blueliner in the league!"

The tribe lost to the Leafs that night 1-0, which didn't help, but they rebounded to shellac the visiting Canadiens 6-2 on November 22, with Pierre leading the way.

"Too many Black Hawk fans will refuse to believe this but . . . Pierre Pilote finally has regained his place as the National Hockey

League's outstanding defenceman," wrote Dan Moulton. "Pilote's performance gained only scant recognition from a large, vocal body of fans who apparently refuse to believe the evidence their own eyes produce. . . . The tough little man topped off a comeback from a slow start."

"Pete's been playing that way the last couple of weeks," noted coach Billy Reay. "I'm just glad that his work is starting to pay off!"

"I look better because the team looks better," Pierre humbly told reporter Ray Sons after his three-point night. "Hockey is a team game, and you look good if the guy next to you does."

The win pushed the Hawks into a third-place tie with the Canadiens and, oddly enough, was Hall's first victory in weeks as DeJordy had been sharing the net equally and had six victories in a row.

At the team's annual Christmas party on November 25, there was a penalty box full of gifts handed out by Santa himself. At the event, organized by Pierre, it was noted that Bobby Hull Jr., dubbed the "White Tornado," was a going concern on the ice, while at one of the nets eight-year-old Pat Hall, son of Glenn, was trying to score on Pierre Pilote Jr.

"I want to be a forward," said young Hall wearing no. 9. "It's not so dangerous as playing goal."

"I want to be a left-winger!" answered Pierre Jr., also eight. "That's where Bobby Hull plays!" Pierre and Glenn, standing nearby, could only smile.

"What I remember most about skating on Stadium ice was the Hawk logo, the Indian head at centre ice. It was beautiful," said Denise Pilote. "The colours were so vivid and strong. I used to trace it with my skates."

The Hawks went winless in their next five games. Clearly frustrated, tired, and openly miserable, Hall requested a three-game respite—highly unusual coming from the iron man of goaltenders. Management recalled DeJordy from Buffalo, but if Hall was frustrated, so was the team's owner.

"This situation is no longer funny," Jim Norris sounded off before his team headed to New York. "We're going to make some moves if things don't improve!"

He singled out the poor play of Wharram, John McKenzie, Mikita, and the Hawks defence, as the team had been outscored 20-12 in their last five games. Norris found no fault with the NHL's scoring leader, his Golden Jet, who had scored in four of the last five games, no doubt aided by Pierre, who garnered 10 points, all assists, in 16 games thus far—good enough for 20th place in the NHL scoring race.

Norris's criticism took hold as the tribe turned things around by trouncing the Rangers 6-1 on December 9 and Doug Mohns picked up his first goal as a Hawk. Chicago won their next seven games before Christmas, healthily outscoring their opponents 35 to 14. They were on a roll.

If hockey was important for Pierre, so was family. He flew out of Boston on December 21 to be home on time to take Pierre Jr. to his hockey squirt game at the Common the next day. When Pierre Jr. scored a goal, with help from teammate Kenny Wharram Jr., the youngster skated by his father and held up two fingers: "That's two so far, Dad!" Pierre Sr. smiled but shook his head.

"You guys should have passed the puck around more on that play," Pierre cautioned his son. Reporter Bill Gleason, who had arranged an interview with Pierre at the little league game in Oak Park, watched the exchange between father and son. Talk soon turned to the Hawks.

"What we have in mind now is to outcheck the other team, not outscore them," Pierre explained. "It's always been said in hockey that if you're in the right place defensively, you'll be in the right place offensively, and it's been working out that way for us."

After tying the Maple Leafs on Christmas Day, the Chicagoans won their next five and tied one, which stretched their undefeated string to 13 games.

With two assists in a January 9 7-2 victory over Detroit, Pierre got two goals the next day in a 3-2 win over the same team. The points propelled Pilote into fourth place in NHL scoring, tied with Phil Esposito and Howe at 34 points each, 23 behind league leader Hull. The wins pushed Chicago into first place.

In his memoirs referee Vern Buffy shared a funny incident involving Pierre during a game in Montreal. Buffy, always one to have impeccable hair, was using a new product—hairspray. As he skated out on the ice, Pierre came over to him smiling.

"Hey Buffy, you look good, but I've always wanted to ask you about your hair."

"My hair?"

"Well, you never have a godamned hair out of place. Is that a wig? I'll bet you've got a rug on there."

"Hell no!" Buffy answered back. "I don't have a bloody wig. This is all my own hair!"

"Really?" Pierre answered with a disbelieving laugh.

"Yeah really. If you think this is a rug, try pulling on it!"

Pierre didn't hesitate and started pulling Buffy's hair.

"What the hell?" Buffy yelled, shocked that the Hawks captain had actually taken up the challenge.

"Yeah, I guess it's real, alright!" Pierre said with a big smile before skating away.

An article in the *Toronto Star Weekly* magazine had Canadian hockey fans taking notice of "The Swinging Team from a Swinging Town." The cover picture showed Mikita, Pilote, and Bobby Hull stopping abruptly before the camera, snow flying high from their skates.

"No team reflects its city more than the Chicago Black Hawks," wrote celebrated Canadian journalist Peter Gzowski. "Chicago seems to have everything . . . it is a man's town and a young man at that! It has great steaks, good jazz . . . *Playboy* and *Esquire* . . . with the best new architecture to go with the best old . . . it exudes vitality, it swings!

"All of these characteristics; lusty, youthful vitality, good looks, and the air of being . . . *with it,* are shared by the player who sets the style for the Hawks: Bobby Hull. Behind Hull, the Hawks have a galaxy of remarkably talented players. At least one of them . . . is the brawler, the tough guy, Stan Mikita . . . one of the most effective hockey players in the NHL.

"With Mikita and Hull, and at least two others—Pierre Pilote, their scar-faced captain who has been named the league's outstanding defenceman for the past two seasons, and Glenn Hall, their enduring, superb goalie—the Black Hawks have the finest collection of superstars in the game. . . . On and off the ice they have something of a swagger. . . . Their best years are probably ahead of them, as befits a team from a young man's town."

Ivan voiced frustration about the close checking Bobby Hull had been receiving from opponents, and the lack of penalties called over the infractions. The GM's mood soured even more when the Golden Jet was sidelined with torn right knee ligaments after a knee-on-knee collision with Toronto defenceman Bobby Baun during a 6-3 Hawks win on February 6. The next night, with a cast on his leg, Hull watched his teammates lose 2-1 to the Leafs.

His captain wasn't surprised by Hull's injury. "A lot of guys went at him and I would wonder how he got by them," recalled Pierre. "This one time I'm scrimmaging against him in practice. He came at me with the puck and, as I went to take him out, he's suddenly stepping around me, with his knee. He was able to give you that one knee but then be transferring his weight to the other knee in one motion and be going around you. It was amazing! I saw for myself how he got around people, but his daring move was constantly putting his knees in close proximity to his opponent and sometimes he paid for that."

A few weeks later Hull returned in a game against the Canadiens.

"The night's drama was supposed to be 'Bobby Hull Returns' but it turned into something like 'The Perils of Pierre,'" went the February 15 story in the Chicago papers. "The sensational Hull was back on the ice in Chicago Stadium but Pierre Pilote kept hogging the spotlight!

"The swift-skating Canadiens rocked the Hawks back on their heels in the first period, shelling goalie Glenn Hall with 14 shots. Claude Larose stuffed the puck past Hall for the period's only score. Then Pierre took over in the second period . . ."

With Montreal shorthanded Pierre let go a long zinger that Esposito deflected past Charlie Hodge. When Dave Balon put the Canadiens ahead a few minutes later, an ensuing scuffle in front of the Hawks goal between Pierre and Balon left the Canadien prostrate on the ice and done for the night.

"It was an accident," Pierre explained. "I backed up and fell over Glenn Hall's legs and my stick came up and hit Balon."

A few minutes later, a Pilote slapshot found its way through Hodge for his eighth goal of the season, tying his previous season high. The last period had barely started when Pierre was whistled to the penalty box for his reaction to an offside call. Asked by reporters after the 2-2 tie what prompted the misconduct, Pierre answered: "I told the linesman to take an eye test!"

With Hull out of commission with a second knee injury, Mikita moved ahead in the NHL scoring race, but Pierre's exploits were also gaining notoriety when *Hockey Illustrated* did a story on him, showing a series of action pictures of Pierre attempting to score on Rangers goalie Gilles Villemure and defenceman Jim Neilson, a fellow aboriginal player. The pictorial was well timed, as H-P-H was formally being presented to the press.

"Bobby Hull announced recently that he, Pierre Pilote, and Glenn Hall have formed their own public relations company, H-P-H, which books speaking engagements for hockey players," stated the story. "A limited operation, there are many more sources of income to be exploited if the NHL expands to include cities on the west coast."

On February 25, it was noted that the Hawks' magic number to clinch the NHL regular season title was nine. Through the next couple of weeks, the Hawks played .500 hockey but turned it up a notch when they hosted the Canadiens at the Stadium on March 7 and handed the Habs a 7-0 shellacking.

The giddy win was overshadowed by a moment of sheer terror in the last minute of the game when Montreal goalie Gump Worsley was levelled by a blistering Hull slapshot.

"The puck hit Worsley on the right side of the head and the colourful, roly-poly veteran slumped on the ice, unconscious," went the report of the scary incident. "Seldom in the rowdy history of Chicago Stadium had there been such a hush; players moved in around Worsley. Hull knelt at the side of the goalie. Dr. Myron Tremaine was quickly summoned to the net. But the plucky Worsley not only got up but finished the final 28 seconds of play while receiving a rousing ovation from the Chicago fans. Worsley spent the night at Henrotin Hospital for observation and X-rays."

Pierre's boo-birds were quieter now, as indicated by a fan letter sent to a Chicago columnist on March 16.

"On the bright side of the Black Hawks is the hot stick of defenceman Pierre Pilote," wrote Gene Gasiorowski from Chicago. "Up among the league's leading scorers, Pierre is making like another Bobby Hull. I don't know what he eats for breakfast, but the rest of them should eat the same!"

"Dear Voices," answered the columnist named Harry. "Pierre (bright side) Pilote needs only two more points to break Babe Pratt's National Hockey League record of 57 points scored by a defenceman."

After getting an assist in a 2-1 loss in Boston, appropriately on St. Patrick's Day, March 17, Pierre and the Hawks went into Montreal for a game on March 20. Despite the 3-2 loss to the Habs, Pierre made history by notching two assists to break Pratt's 21-year-old record.

"It wasn't a big deal," recalled Pierre. "The players made sure that those two pucks made it to the bench. I got them after the game. It was a record I was certainly proud of. But there was no time for dancing; we were trying to win hockey games."

After their team lost 5-1 in Detroit, Hawks management announced the best playoff seats would cost $9—almost three dollars higher than anywhere else in the league, and that away playoff games would be carried on closed-circuit television at the Stadium for $4, $3, and $2 respectively.

Chicago fans were in a foul mood and before the March 23 game pamphlets were circulated at the Stadium, urging a boycott of the telecasts. With a gimpy-legged Bobby Hull back in the lineup and the Hawks losing 3-2 in the final period, the spectators booed Hawks players and jeered the public address announcer at every turn. "Norris is a fink! Norris is a fink!" the crowd screamed.

Garbage littered the ice when referee John Ashley gave Red Hay a slashing penalty followed by a 10-minute misconduct for arguing the call. After order was restored, the Hawks lost the game and ended the season on an ugly five-game losing streak. Their 34-28-8 record put them in third place and their first-round opponents would be the league-leading Red Wings. The silver lining was Mikita winning the league scoring championship with 87 points. Pierre was pleased with his season, setting a single-season record for points by a defenceman at 59, in 68 games.

As the underdog Hawks prepared to face the hot Wings, completely forgotten was the fact that Chicago had taken 18 out of 28 points against the Detroiters during the 14 regular season games. But heading into the Detroit series, Pierre became aware of a definite lack of enthusiasm in the city, perhaps due to the negativity associated with the ticket prices and the closed circuit broadcasts.

"There was no excitement like other series we had. Chicago fans loved Gordie Howe, Delvecchio, guys like that," he said. "We players didn't have a big hate on for them, that edge that gets you up for a series. We could have used that."

The Wings won the first two games in Detroit, 4-3 and 6-3.

In the second game, the Wings netted four power play goals. It was a rough game, with Larry Jeffrey of the Wings carried off on a stretcher after a collision with Bobby Hull and sent to hospital for a suspected back injury. He returned later to play a key role in Pierre's playoffs adventures.

The Hawks rebounded at home and captured the next two. The teams split Games 5 and 6 before returning to Detroit for Game 7, where the Hawks showed grit and determination by stunning the Wings 4-2 to eliminate them. A collision between Pierre and Jeffrey put Pilote's future participation in doubt as the Hawks prepared to face the Canadiens in the 1965 Stanley Cup final.

"I went into the corner with Jeffrey and we collided, a freak collision," recalled Pierre. "After the hit, my shoulder hurt a bit but I finished the game. The next day though was a different story."

"Except for the loss of Jacques Laperierre, the Canadiens should be in excellent condition," stated the *Palm Beach Post*. "Such is not the case with the Hawks captain Pierre Pilote, who injured his left shoulder in Detroit, in addition to back miseries, which [coach] Reay says would have sidelined many players of lesser ability."

Pierre, diagnosed with a mild separated shoulder, and Wharram, suffering from a bruised knee, missed the first two games in Montreal. Their absence was felt as the Canadiens eked out 3-2 and 2-0 wins on the basis of tight checking on Hull and Mikita that rendered them ineffective.

The Hawks, down two games to none, were almost in panic mode, and missing No. 3. They needed him back badly so team physician, Dr. Myron Tremaine, sent Pierre to hospital for a new, controversial treatment in a bid to get him on the ice.

Pierre's overnight treatment consisted of having a red salve dabbed on his shoulder every hour in an effort to heal it and dampen the pain. The salve was actually a solvent known as DSMO, or Dimethyl sulfoxide. DSMO was supposed to eliminate pain, reduce swelling, relieve inflammation, and tranquilize. After being painted or dabbed on the injured area, it was allowed to penetrate

Bobby Hull and Pierre's daughter Denise checking out Pierre's shiner, one of many he would have over the course of his career.

Pierre: "Here I am skating away from my old nemesis Henri Richard,
'The Pocket Rocket,' in one of my favourite pictures of all time. He was
a great skater and goal scorer." FRANK PRAZAK / HOCKEY HALL OF FAME

Pierre's first posed photograph after being named captain of the Hawks. Not knowing any better, the team's equipment manager, Walter "Gunzo" Humeniuk, actually sewed the "C" on the wrong side of the uniform.

MACDONALD-STEWART / HOCKEY HALL OF FAME

Pierre proudly sporting Gunzo's right-sided "C" in the fall of 1961. Despite being on a team of superstars, he would be captain for seven seasons, the longest-serving captain in Chicago history. © LIBRARY AND ARCHIVES CANADA. REPRODUCED WITH THE PERMISSION OF LIBRARY AND ARCHIVES CANADA

A familiar scene throughout the 1960s: Pierre is about to make a breakout pass from behind his net. His offensive and defensive skills compared to Montreal's great Doug Harvey, Pierre was often recognized as the catalyst of the powerful Chicago attack.

On April 16, 1961, the Hawks excitedly gather around the Stanley Cup they had just won on Detroit Olympia ice after beating the Red Wings 5-1 in the sixth game of a tough, hard-fought series. It was and always will be the greatest thrill for every NHL player to win the elusive trophy.

Hawk wives with the Stanley Cup, in a photo taken at the official celebration dinner at the Bismarck Hotel in Chicago on April 17, 1961— the day after their husbands had won the Cup in Detroit. (Annie is second from the right.) LE STUDIO DU HOCKEY / HOCKEY HALL OF FAME

This family shot was taken at their summer campsite near Lindsay, Ontario. Pierre taught at the nearby Byrnell Manor Boys' Camp summer hockey school on nearby Cameron Lake, owned by Frank and Anna Stukus throughout the early 1970s.

PILOTE FAMILY COLLECTION

On October 14, 1964, at the Hawks home and season opener at the Chicago Stadium, NHL President Clarence Campbell was on hand to present Pierre with the 1964 Norris Trophy, his second consecutive as the NHL's best defenceman. LE STUDIO DU HOCKEY / HOCKEY HALL OF FAME

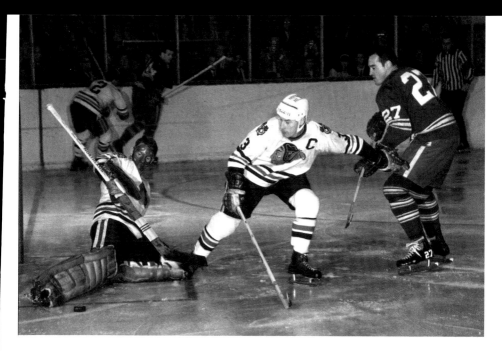

In February of 1968, Pierre started wearing a helmet following the shocking death of Minnesota player Bill Masterton, after the North Star forward had been checked and struck his head on the ice, an event that Pierre called an eye-opener.

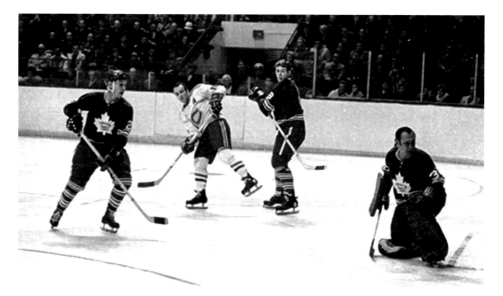

Here is Pierre as a Leaf, wearing the unfamiliar no. 2 during the 1968–69 season. The Toronto season was his last.

Pierre's first post-retirement business venture was making luggage and tote bags. Here he is at his Toronto plant with some of the staff of his International Travelware company. JOE RIZZUTO

In the mid-1970s, old hockey stars and beer seemed to go hand in hand, as seen in this Miller Lite commercial. Pierre's hockey buddies are Bill White (seated left), Eddie Shack (seated centre), Billy Harris (standing far left), Bob Nevin (farthest back row, left of centre), Bobby Baun (standing far right), and Bruce Hood (standing directly behind Eddie Shack and Pierre). PILOTE FAMILY COLLECTION

Pierre and Annie aboard the HMS *Tecumseh*, an 1812-era warship that was stationed at the British establishment in Penetanguishene in the late 1990s. The replica sailed out of Discovery Harbour, a historic site situated on Penetanguishene Bay. PILOTE FAMILY COLLECTION

Pierre and Annie were front and centre with Lord Stanley's Cup in Chicago's United Center as they helped the Hawks celebrate their recent Stanley Cup victory in 2011. CRAIG CAMPBELL / HOCKEY HALL OF FAME

The current Blackhawks honoured the heroes of the 1961 Cup win with a special 50th anniversary night at the United Center in 2011. From left to right: Bill Hay, Stan Mikita, Glenn Hall, current Hawks Chairman Rocky Wirtz, current Hawks President John McDonough, Bobby Hull, Ab McDonald, and Pierre.

Pierre with his two brothers, Gilles and Florent, in the summer of 2012.
PILOTE FAMILY COLLECTION

The Pilote clan gathered in Penetanguishene in May 2012 when Pierre was made an "Honorary Ambassador" of the Penetanguishene Sports Hall of Fame. PILOTE FAMILY COLLECTION

Pierre standing in front of the large mural of himself that graces one of the walls of the United Center in Chicago. PILOTE FAMILY COLLECTION

for 30 minutes and then wiped off. A derivative of wood pulp waste, it was also used in dissolving synthetic clothing. Its use and safety was questioned by the U.S. Food and Drug Administration and would eventually be banned outright. But not yet.

"It burned like heck, stunk, but it took the pain away," Pierre recalled. "After three minutes you could feel it burning deep down inside the muscle. Then you smelled like you'd been dipped into a bucket of oysters and then you got the garlic taste in your mouth. It took the pain away, there was no doubt about that."

Pierre checked out of hospital and headed to the Stadium where trainer Garen continued the once-an-hour treatment to Pierre's shoulder until game time.

"Pilote's absence was most noticeable, especially on the power play," went the story in that morning's paper. "Wharram, who seems to go particularly well against Montreal, is nursing a twisted knee. Chicago coach Billy Reay said Wharram may start tonight but Pilote's status is doubtful. Pilote's injury has dumped a heavy burden on 26-year-old rookie Matt Ravlich, who has to fill in for Pilote on the power play and kill off penalties as well."

The Canadiens rode the train into Chicago while the Hawks came out of their retreat at Rockton, 90 miles outside of Chicago, to do battle. Wharram and Pilote both played starring roles in the 3-1 victory.

As the game ended, fighting broke out on all fronts, with Chicago's Ravlich and Montreal's Ted Harris sparring and some Canadiens on their bench swinging their sticks at the unruly fans behind them. Goalie Worsley had a verbal battle with fans behind his net, and banged his stick against the glass.

"We had a lot of chances and we missed them, that's all there was to it," was the only thing Montreal coach Toe Blake had to say afterwards.

Worsley was not so quiet, chiming to reporters that Esposito had kicked the puck into the net from the corner of the crease on a Chicago goal and also that fans behind him became unruly due to the effects of alcoholic beverages with seconds left in the game. "That's when I blew!" he exclaimed.

"Our fans used to throw stuff at Gump, trying to get him off his game," remembered Pierre. "He'd get mad, throw his stick, bang the glass. Oh, Gump was a character!"

Pierre was asked after the game whether his shoulder had stood up to the test.

"Sure, it hurt every time I got hit, but I think I'll be alright now," he answered.

The fourth game was another unruly affair, and the rowdy Chicago crowd had an effect on Montreal as the Canadiens were assessed 14 penalties from referee Vern Buffy as the Hawks coasted to an easy 5-1 win. After the game, Blake had to be restrained from going after Buffy on the ice. As he got to his dressing room, the coach was furious.

"I want to see how much guts you guys got," Blake shouted at reporters. "Go ahead and write the game the way you saw it. I'll buy the paper to see it!"

As he slammed the door behind him, the tied series shifted back to Montreal. The Canadiens had the last laugh in Montreal as they shellacked the visiting tribe 6-0 to take a 3-2 series lead. The game's tempo was set when tough guy John Ferguson effectively battled Nesterenko.

Chicago was "psychologically high when the fifth game began and we were a bit back on our heels," wrote Ferguson years later. "I went after Nesterenko less than five minutes into the fifth game, threw three punches, and gave him six stitches over the eye."

"Fergie got Eric right along the boards, between our bench and the end boards," recalled Pierre of the incident. "Eric was not a dirty player but I guess he got into their faces. He was big, strong but lanky. It didn't take long though; Fergie could really fight. Eric was not a fighter."

In Chicago, the Hawks had their backs against the wall, and

treatments of DSMO continued for Pierre, but he questioned its after-effects.

"After a while, that stuff really started to affect my mental state, like sniffing glue I guess. I couldn't believe it! I started thinking afterwards that I should never have gone for that treatment. Nick Garen didn't know anything about it either. Nobody did! But you do what you have to for the team."

The salve seemed to work though as the Hawks won Game 6 in Chicago 2-1 on April 29. You just knew it had to be Chicago's night when Moose scored his first playoff goal since winning the Cup four years earlier.

"The shot bounced from post to post," Vasko said afterwards. "I was waiting for it to stop bouncing before I finally took a crack at it."

The Hawks GM was asked if his team would be up for the seventh game in Montreal.

"A team should be up for any game," snorted Ivan. "Not only the seventh game of a Stanley Cup final! It's just another hockey game."

In the end, it was, for Montreal. The "homer series" prevailed as the Habs raced to a 4-0 first period lead and that's the way it stayed as Montreal coasted to a Worsley shutout. It was "just another Cup" for Montreal.

Pierre was selected to the First All-Star Team for the third straight time and was awarded his third straight Norris Trophy as the NHL's best defenceman. Besides the honours for Pilote, Hull picked up the Hart Trophy as the league's MVP, and the Lady Byng Trophy for sportsmanship along with a First Team All-Star berth; Mikita made the Second Team.

Not able to rest long, Pierre, Bobby, and Glenn were appointed to the new Simpsons-Sears Sports Advisory Council, engineered through their company H-P-H. They consulted on a line of hockey equipment sold by the store, giving them their seals of approval.

Though the contracts weren't yet signed, Pierre was informed he would be travelling for Simpsons-Sears in the summer, something he would have to coordinate around his six-week stint at the hockey camp in Fenelon Falls.

He wasn't sure what the Simpsons-Sears gig entailed, but he knew that he was scheduled for an eastern Canada promotional tour in May that would further enhance the fortunes and aware-ness of H-P-H, his other challenge outside of hockey.

And Pierre always liked a challenge.

CHAPTER 17

Absence Makes the Hawks Grow Fonder

It was an eventful spring of 1965 for Pierre. In May, he visited St. John's, Newfoundland, as part of the Simpson-Sears Sports Advisory Council. His visit made headlines and caused quite a stir as he attended the Prince of Wales Sportsman's Show and signed autographs for crowds of hockey-starved fans at the store. But there was more to it than that.

"From the beginning, we were involved in choosing hockey equipment, looking at it, making suggestions, improvements before we would endorse it," recalled Pierre. "Simpsons-Sears catalogues would then appear with our picture on certain pages endorsing their hockey products, games, sticks, equipment, that kind of thing.

"We used to get a type of commission. We would get, say, 25 cents on every pair of skates, sticks, games—that's how we got our money. Then it would go to H-P-H, run by our two agents, and they would communicate to us when we had to appear. They took their share and we had our share. That's how it started in the early years. That was the year that Bobby really took off, which really helped Sears and really helped us at H-P-H. We would travel, meet buyers, customers, appear at shows, one week out east, one week out west."

In spring 1965 sad news out of Saskatchewan informed the

hockey world that Murray Balfour had succumbed to lung cancer in a Regina hospital. He was only 28 years old.

"He wasn't in Boston very long when he wasn't feeling well," said Pierre. "By Christmas he was in the minors and then they discovered how sick he was. It was too bad. He was far too young."

A few months later, the Golden Jet shook up the hockey world. In Honolulu, Hawaii, for a sports dinner preceding the Hawaiian Open Golf Tournament, Bobby Hull told a sportswriter that he deserved a big raise.

"I am not being conceited when I say I am worth $100,000 to the Black Hawks," the reporter quoted Hull. "I am the big draw for the club and I feel I am to hockey what Mickey Mantle and Willie Mays are to baseball. The Hawks have been making big money ever since I have been with them and I think I can convince them that I deserve much more than I am getting." According to the story, Hull and Gordie Howe were the NHL's top-paid players at $35,000 to $40,000.

"When I got back, the phone was ringing off the wall!" Hull recalled with a smile. "I remember Gordie Howe being quoted as saying, 'Who's this brazen upstart wanting $100,000?' But there was the damn guy who should have been raising all of our contract levels—he and Béliveau and the Rocket. So I was the first guy to ever make waves, talk that kinda money."

A few days later, Hull backtracked, saying he regretted going public with his demands before talking with the Hawks.

That summer the Pilote family was about to grow.

"In Chicago, I did my banking at a strip mall in Oak Park and I got to know the janitor there," related Pierre. "One day, he said he knew someone who had just had a batch of puppies, nice dogs. Next thing I know, I'm having drinks with this tall, Lebanese fellow named Jim Thomas at his home and we're looking at these puppies with Annie. You know how puppies quickly grow on you.

"I bought this puppy for $250, a German short-haired pointer, a field dog. Then I met this professional dog trainer named Pete

Kainz, who said to me one day, 'Hey Pierre, your dog is not going to do well in Chicago. The salt in the city is going to ruin his pads, his feet. You have a great dog there! I'm going to Florida for the winter. I'll take him with me and for $100 a month I'll take care of him and train him.' I said sure. A month after he had my puppy in Florida, he sent me a letter saying he had entered my puppy in a couple of field trials down there and had won!

"I took the dog that summer with us to Cameron Lake and we would go for walks in the bush. I hadn't named him yet. He was quite the dog. I had to give him a name. So one night were sitting with friends, having a few drinks and trying to come up with a suitable name for my dog. Finally my friend says, 'Trophy,' after my recent Norris Trophy wins. That's how Trophy got his name and it was very suitable because he would win many awards before we were done together. He was special."

Training camp in the fall of 1965 was in Chicago instead of St. Catharines for the first time in nine years.

Hull walked out of camp one day when coach Billy Reay barred Hull's two sons, Blake, aged 5, and Bobby Jr., 4, from the Stadium dressing room. "There's nothing I can do," said general manager Tommy Ivan. "I must back my coach."

"His two kids used to run around the dressing room all the time, especially young Bobby, he was a big kid. We'd be having a meeting and he'd come and sit down beside us. Billy Reay didn't like that," recalled Pierre. "Young Bobby was really a going concern, a handful. He would walk all over in the dressing room, picking up sticks, shooting pucks.

"A lot of the kids came in and went out for a skate before our practices. My Denise and Pierre Jr. would come, Glenn Hall and his kids, a lot of kids. One time though, after a team meeting, we climbed up the 22 steps, looking to see what the kids were doing, and young Bobby was pissing right at centre ice!"

"As the oldest, I had to get on the ice and kind of patrol the other little ones, push them around the ice as they held onto chairs," remembered Pierre's oldest, Denise. "But those Hull boys were busy, a going concern! We would then watch practice from up in the stands and naturally get running around and playing. Sometimes I wonder how we never got killed, but we usually tried to keep it down, because if we ever got a dirty look from our dads on the ice, it was game over."

"I remember Glenn Hall used to let me score on him," added Pierre Pilote Jr. "During practice we would tear around the Stadium, the organ loft, the Zamboni room, balconies, the dressing room, everywhere. And after practice we would go back out on the ice and if the Stadium crew was covering the ice with big sheets of wood, to change it like for a concert or a basketball game, I would skate on the last patch of eight-foot-by-eight-foot ice until they put down the last piece."

Hull took his family to a nearby farm to stay out of the spotlight. It was a testy time for sure. Even owner Jim Norris, a full-fledged Hull fan, said that the league's economy prohibited Hull's astronomical salary demand. Norris called Hull's actions "childish" and threatened to fine him $1,000 a day if he didn't return within a few days. Hull shot back that if the Hawks didn't want him they should trade him.

"I'm sure everything will work out," commented Ivan calmly, hopefully.

"There was a misunderstanding which has been patched up," said Hull diplomatically after four days when he finally emerged from a meeting with Ivan. "I understand now why management wants to keep the dressing room strictly for players during training. We have a lot of young players trying to make the team and they shouldn't be distracted."

One of those young players who made the team was a goalie named Dave Dryden, who dislodged Denis DeJordy for the backup spot. The previous year, Dryden had been a Toronto schoolteacher.

"DeJordy had become something of a problem," Reay told Dink Carroll of the *Hockey News*. "Last season he thought he should play

70 games and he kept arguing about it . . . with Glenn Hall ahead of him? The whole thing got tiresome. Dryden had a very good training camp and we decided to make the change."

One of eight players assigned to the St. Louis Braves of the Central League was a young defenceman named Pat Stapleton. A rookie who did make the team was Ken Hodge, a 6'1" right-winger who had amassed an impressive 123 points with the St. Catharines Teepees.

"Hodge was big, like Dennis Hull," recalled Pierre. "When they played junior hockey they could bully the smaller players around, and score their goals, do what they wanted, but they didn't have all the moves, they weren't quite fully developed for the big leagues. I remember at practice Billy Reay used to put a bunch of old tires spaced about six to eight feet apart and get Hodge to stickhandle around them. He had great promise but he needed some refining."

"Ken Hodge's initiation to the team did not go smoothly," Pierre related. "We were still travelling by train sometimes and on one of our first road trips we went to grab him but he ran and locked himself in the bathroom. We smoked him out, but in the process there was $500 in damages to that railcar that the team had to pay for. Tommy Ivan reminded us. We got Hodge out though."

Pierre made a quick impact in an exhibition win against Montreal on October 17, when he raced towards the Montreal net at the opening faceoff and tipped in a Bobby Hull slapshot just 14 seconds into the game.

As the season approached, NHL owners realized that not having some of their stars play in the All-Star Game due to contract holdouts was hurting the game, so they decided to allow unsigned players to play. The morning of the game, a rash of signings took place with the Leafs inking holdout Bobby Baun, while the Hawks signed Hull to a "substantial increase" over his previous salary, reportedly in the "$50,000 range."

Prior to their opener, the Hawks signed two-time league scoring champion Stan Mikita to $35,000 per season, though salaries were still not being officially disclosed.

When Dan Moulton predicted in *the American* that a league title was there for the Hawks to claim, he was looking pretty smart when the Chicagoans won their four first games, all on the road against Toronto, Boston, Detroit, and Montreal. After their first seven games the Hawks had six wins and a tie.

H-P-H also had a great start. On October 29, a press photo showed Pierre signing a contract with Simpsons-Sears as a member of their newly formed Sports Advisory Council while Hall and Hull waited their turn to sign. Simpsons-Sears president James Button looked on and said that that the Council was "set up to develop safer, more practical sports equipment for amateurs' use."

The Hawks didn't like missing out on the trio's growing public image, and when Hull went to endorse a breakfast cereal, the club stepped in. Using the rest of his teammates as leverage, the Hawks suggested a three-way split between them, Hull, and the rest of the players. Hull balked and killed the deal.

"When we started doing promotions, we had to ask the Hawks if we could do them," recalled the Golden Jet. "If they refused me, I went ahead and did them anyways. But there weren't a helluva lot of endorsement deals back then. In the mid-'60s, before CCM and Bauer came along, Pierre, Glenn, and I did sign with Simpsons-Sears. It got us started."

The Hawks point streak and first place were on the line when they hosted the Habs on November 13. Bobby Rousseau and Jean Béliveau were right behind Hull in the scoring race.

It was a rough affair from the puck drop as captain Pierre led the way, getting into a first-period fight with Red Berenson. When the Canadiens went ahead 4-2 a few minutes into the third period, things turned nasty and again Pierre was front and centre as he and Claude Provost started shoving and swinging at each other. In the melee of players and mayhem, referee Frank Udvari tossed Pierre from the game. The controversial loss was Chicago's first and the Canadiens moved into first place.

In mid-November, Bobby Hull went down with another knee

injury, but his teammates picked up the slack. For the rest of the month and well into December, the tribe had 13 wins and two ties in their first 20 games. Pierre had 12 assists and was playing great hockey, but an injury forced him out of a weekend set against the Canadiens. When the Hawks lost both games, the Chicago hockey scribes took notice, and it was headline news for his return on December 15 as the tribe smashed the Bruins 8-4.

Norris was always generous at Christmas with his players. "That year, Mr. Norris gave us all a little TV; it had a small eight-inch screen," recalled Pierre. "It was portable and you could put in your car. It had rabbit ears that you put outside the side window. It worked great! The kids thought it was the cat's meow. One year he gave us big tri-oceanic radios. It was his way of saying he appreciated us. Mr. Norris gave us some very nice Christmas gifts."

As the New Year began famed Canadian writer Jim Hunt did a feature on Pierre in the January 1 *Toronto Star Weekly*. It featured photographs of Pierre by the famed hockey photographer Harold Barkley.

While the article did talk of his prowess and skill as the NHL's best defenceman, Hunt seemed to want to spotlight Pierre's years as a tough guy, carefully listing the fights and battles Pierre had had over the years in Buffalo and Chicago.

"Sure, I spear occasionally, but I'm not the only one," Pierre admitted. "You should see the black-and-blue marks on my chest. You don't hear me crying. The guys that do should get out of hockey into another job."

When Hunt continued to press about his rough play over the years, Pierre grew testy. "Can't you forget about all that fighting stuff?" he implored Hunt. "All that took place when I was younger and didn't know any better. Sure, I will still hit back when someone plays a dirty trick on me—after all, you can't let them push you around in this game, or they soon lose respect for you—but I don't go looking for trouble!"

Hunt drew comparison between Pilote and Doug Harvey. "He

learned so well that Pilote is now the closest thing to Harvey in the
NHL. He runs the Black Hawks on the ice in the same cool way
Harvey used to operate the Canadiens. It is Pilote who usually orga-
nizes the attack, gets the puck out of his own zone onto the sticks of
the forwards such as Bobby Hull or Stan Mikita," wrote Hunt. "The
Black Hawks management recognizes Pilote's value to the team by
paying him a salary of $18,000, one of the club's highest."

"He's the best offensive defenceman in the league!" exhorted
Reay.

"He's one of the most natural players I've ever seen," added
Ivan. "He anticipates the play almost before the opposition know
what they are going to do."

"I can't blame Pierre Pilote for trying to get himself a new image,
but I doubt he'll succeed," Hunt summarized. "The old Pierre
Pilote was too tough a competitor to be forgotten that quickly by
hockey fans, many of whom would much rather talk about a good
brawl than about a picture goal."

Another accolade came to Pierre and three of his teammates
when *Hockey Illustrated* published its All-Time All-Star Teams.
Chicago columnist Dick Hackenberg wrote that he felt the Hawks
were currently very blessed.

"Unfortunately all-time All-Stars are names requisitioned from
memory's storehouse or plaques or pictures on a wall. They're
even harder to come by as members, still, of the teams with which
they established their remarkable reputations," he wrote. "That is
why the current *Hockey Illustrated* . . . had such an impact on me.
No fewer than four men of the moment are listed for the Black
Hawks—Bobby Hull and Pierre Pilote on the First Team, Glenn
Hall and Stan Mikita on the second. Hull and Pilote cavort in the
misty company of Chuck Gardiner, Earl Siebert, Max Bentley, and
Bill Mosienko. Hall and Mikita skate the ethereal ice with Lionel
Conacher, Bill Gadsby, Doug Bentley, and Mush March. These
four have become, you see, a legend in their own time, and no
other city in the National Hockey League has been so blessed."

The Pilote kids also felt fortunate. "I would be dressed in a suit and tie, little trench coat and fedora, and we kids sat between the two players benches," recalled Pierre Pilote Jr. "The atmosphere was electric and loud. When the referees came onto the ice, the organist would play 'Three Blind Mice.' I got to watch not only my dad and Bobby Hull but the likes of Frank Mahovlich, Jean Béliveau, and Gordie Howe up close! Wow!"

The Hawks, in the midst of a New Year's winning streak, headed into Montreal. As captain of the club, Pierre had to deal with players' complaints and idiosyncrasies. Their new goalie had a dandy trait that Pierre had to deal with.

"Dave Dryden was a notorious tightwad," related Pierre. "When the team was out of town and we went out for a few beers and bite to eat, the whole team split the bill whether you drank one beer or 10. No questions asked. I and the guys noticed that Dave Dryden would have one beer, order a burger or sandwich, quickly call the waiter, pay for his small bill, and leave. He did this time after time and I thought, 'Okay, we're going to teach you a lesson, Mr. Dryden.'

"So I set up this scenario with the guys. We're in Montreal and we go to this very ritzy joint, on purpose, and we're all ordering lobster, shrimp, steak—the best—and we're having our fair share of beers too. We order the best! Of course Dave orders a little sandwich and one beer. I'm watching him!

"Just as he's about to call the waitress over, I yell out to everyone, 'Okay, I'm calling a team meeting! This is a team meeting! Right here and now! A team meeting—nobody leaves!' The unwritten rule was you couldn't leave a team meeting, you had to stay for its duration, no questions asked. So Dave sits back down and the guys play it up, talking about the team, games, issues, and we keep ordering food and beer. Dave is there nodding his head, but we keep going, going, going, talking, eating, drinking. Nobody can leave!

"So all of a sudden, I call for the bill; it's ready instantly. 'We're all going to share,' I say. 'Everybody, and you too, Dave, your share is $35!' He nearly fainted. He'd only had a sandwich and one beer. I taught him a lesson. He knew we were on to him!"

The January 9 bout in Toronto was another rowdy affair. Pierre picked up his 22nd assist when he helped on the Golden Jet's 32nd goal of the season, but the most notable statistic of the night occurred in the second period with the Hawks ahead 4-2. Pierre and Kent Douglas squared off after Douglas flipped him over his shoulder at the blue line and both began swinging.

"That son of a bitch Douglas," Pierre recalled. "I went to swing at his jaw but the bugger put his head down. I hit him on the forehead! Oh did that ever hurt! It must have been a trick that Eddie Shore had taught him! We went to the penalty box and we're growling at each other but as I'm sitting there in the box my hand really hurt. I went to put my glove on but there was just no way!"

At the next stoppage in play, he called over the Golden Jet. "Hey Bobby, I think this thing is broken," Pierre told him. "We'd better put someone else in here." Pilote was replaced as he headed off to the dressing room.

"Pierre, I think it's broken. We'll send you for X-rays to be sure," the team doctor said after examining him.

As Chicago vanquished the Leafs 5-3, Pierre went to the hospital. Despite the win, the mood in the Hawks dressing room was unusually quiet. Dr. Myron Tremaine, Reay, and Ivan waited for a telephone call from Henrotin Hospital. When the phone rang, there was no need to ask for quiet as Tremaine listened for the verbal report on Pierre. He nodded, hung up, and turned to the others.

"Pilote has a fracture of the base of his right thumb. He'll be out for five or six weeks, at least I would anticipate it'll take that long." His statement took the air out of the room. Reay emerged from the dressing room with a stoic look to tell the waiting press: "Tough break, but some of the other guys will have to rise to the occasion," Reay said. "These things happen all the time in sports and you just have to get along."

It was already clear to the press from his third-period absence that the Hawks were going to miss their captain. "The extent to which the Hawks figure to miss their doughty, little captain became apparent during the final 20 minutes," wrote Moulton. "The Hawks had built up a 4-2 lead in the first two periods and seemed to have the situation well in hand. But without Pierre's organizational ability and general steadying influence, the Hawks defence scrambled much of the way in the third frame."

A picture in the January 12 edition of the *Tribune* showed Pierre at his Oak Park home, his right hand in a cast, surrounded by his children, as Annie overlooked the scene.

"Thumb fun! Well, Daddy's not so sure," read the caption.

"We were always so important to Dad," recalled Denise. "He would always walk in the door from a road trip to Canada with a big smile and a blue and yellow box of Cherry Blossoms! And I remember my dad always kissing my mom. And Mom always made sure we behaved when the press was around our home."

An article in the *Lewiston Evening Journal* was blunt about the situation: "The loss of the rugged Pilote is expected to cripple the championship chances of the Hawks, now leading the NHL by three points."

Though the Hawks tied the Bruins in their next match without Pierre, they proceeded with a three-game losing streak. It was a tough injury for Pierre to weather and even harder for him to watch the team struggle. Three of the Hawks, though, were named to the first half First All-Star Team: Hull, Hall, and Pilote. All received a $500 bonus for the selection.

Pierre's All-Star berth coincided with a Chicago 4-0 shellacking in Maple Leaf Gardens. After a lifeless tie against the Canadiens at home on January 23, the Hawks were now winless in six games, all missed by Pierre. By Monday morning, the quarterbacks throughout the league were in full swing in declaring the woeful Chicago play a direct result of the tribe missing Pilote's presence on the blue line.

"It became evident in Toronto on Saturday night, that the

real key-man of the high scoring Chicago Black Hawks is Pierre Pilote," wrote Jim Coleman in the *Hamilton Spectator*. "Hull and Mikita receive most of the publicity ink. However, the mounting evidence indicates that Pilote is—and has long been—the heart of the team. . . . However, you don't really appreciate Pilote's great ability as a defensive player until you watch the Black Hawks when he is absent from a game. I would like to submit the name of Pierre Pilote as a candidate for the Hart Trophy. He is the most valuable member of the Chicago Black Hawks. "

A week after he had been injured, Ivan sent Pierre to scout their minor league team in St. Louis.

"Dennis Hull had been sent there around Christmas and Babe Pratt's son was there," recalled Pilote, who visited Hull's home for dinner. "Gus Kyle was the coach. I saw a few games, made a few notes. I thought Dennis would be back up, but Pratt couldn't handle the puck."

Back in Chicago, Ivan asked Pilote his thoughts on Kyle. Pierre was perplexed. "I thought you wanted me to check on the players. You never told me to keep an eye on the coach," Pilote answered. "Dennis played well, but I don't know about that Pratt kid. But the coach—I don't know."

"That's how I left it. Gus was a great guy. He had invited me to his house. I couldn't believe that Ivan had wanted me to report or spy on Gus. I'm a player. What the hell was going on? I smelled a trap and I wasn't about to be a part of it."

Pat Stapleton had been called up from St. Louis when Pierre went down with his injury. In Stapleton, the Hawks had a defenceman in the mould of Pilote. He was making an impression. In a comedy of errors in a game against Detroit, Howe got credited for a goal that Stapleton accidentally shot into his own net.

"Did you shoot that puck into our own net?" Stapleton was asked angrily by Reay as he came to the bench.

"I'm afraid so," replied Stapleton with a straight face. "But you know, coach, when I'm in that close, I'm really deadly!" Reay didn't have a comeback.

On February 15, Pierre had his cast removed. Though there had been high expectations for him to play the next day in New York, it just couldn't happen that fast.

When he stepped back onto the ice the next night he had missed 17 games, but the gritty Hawks had climbed back into first place.

Pierre got onto the scoresheet early with a first-period assist on a Chico Maki goal in an eventual 5-1 victory over Boston that saw the Golden Jet net his 47th goal. Pierre felt good to be back but the long layoff had taken its toll. "When I came back, it took a good four or five games to get back into it and the thumb was still a little tender."

Paired with Stapleton, Pierre knew the kid needed some tutoring. "Whitey, when the guy shoots the puck in on my side, you're just standing up at the blue line. You can't do that," Pierre instructed. "If I'm standing up at our blue line and they shoot it behind me, you have to go and get that puck. And don't wait until they shoot it in, you have to start moving beforehand, then you've got three or four steps on everybody." Stapleton's play improved.

On February 25, the Black Hawks family was rocked by the death of co-owner Jim Norris. Hospitalized for 10 days, the 59-year-old's heart had been weakened by two previous heart attacks.

"He had always had trouble with his heart. Billy Reay, Bobby, Billy Hay, and I, and I think Glenn and Stan, went to represent the team at his funeral. We took a plane from Chicago to New York, and got a big limousine to the wake at the other end of Long Island. It was a long ride from the airport. Mr. Norris had a big, beautiful home there," said Pilote. "We spent some time with Mrs. Norris, a beautiful, tall woman, very nice. After we went to the funeral home, we flew back to Chicago."

Though the tribe played only .500 hockey through the rest of February and into March, they were first-hand accomplices to history when the Golden Jet scored his record-setting 51st goal in a game against the Rangers on March 12. Hull skated over to the glass and blew a kiss to his wife, Joanne. He then reached down, grabbed a hat, and shoved it on his head, triggering another roar from the crowd of 22,000. The ovation lasted 10 minutes.

Post-game, asked to kiss his wife again by photographers, he happily obliged, but not before slipping his dentures into place. "You guys are always trying to catch me without my teeth in," he laughed. "But not this time."

Hull's stick stayed hot but the Hawks won only four of their final nine games and the Canadiens took the lead. On April 2, Montreal crushed Chicago 8-3 at the Forum, a game in which Hull scored his 54th goal. In the last game of the season Hull picked up an assist for his 97th point—a new season point record.

If it seemed as if the Hawks were limping towards the post-season, a good omen was the fact that they had defeated the Red Wings 11 times in 14 regular season games and, after beating them 2-1 in the first game of their 1966 semifinal series, it seemed that the trend would continue. They got a rude awakening at the Stadium in the second game when the Red Wings crushed the Hawks 7-0 on a Roger Crozier shutout. The game was an embarrassment.

"We couldn't do anything right," said Pierre of a night he would have rather soon forget. "We were just flat, plain and simple. We weren't sharp. I don't know what it was but we weren't ready."

As the series shifted to the Olympia for the third game in the series, the Hawks showed some life by bouncing the Red Wings 2-1 but it was all the life they had. Bryan Watson effectively neutralized Hull while nobody tied up Howe, and the Wings won the next three games.

"We were not a playoff team," admitted Pierre. "We played offensive hockey. We were not a defensive club. And when we got eliminated on a Tuesday well, we never played well on Tuesdays. It's just amazing,"

Almost embarrassingly, the Hawks placed four members on the NHL First All-Star Team: Bobby Hull, Hall, Pierre, and Mikita.

Detroit's Howe and Montreal defenceman Jacques Laperriere also made it. The 24-year-old Laperriere also won the Norris Trophy, ending Pilote's three-win streak. The Hab garnered 89 points to Pierre's 54 in the voting. Without hesitation Pierre would have voted for him too.

"Jacques had a very good year," Pierre recalled. "He had played very well. I'm not making excuses but to win a Norris, you can't miss 17 games in a season. Laperriere was very deserving, a great defenceman. And I was not as effective after I had come back with the thumb. It was sore. It was a season and playoffs that I wanted to forget."

He and Annie packed up their belongings to move back to Fort Erie for the summer. An upcoming fly-in fishing trip would help him forget too. If that didn't get his mind away from a disappointing hockey season, nothing would.

CHAPTER 18

Hey Muldoon, Get Out of Here!

With the season of disappointment behind him, Pierre got away from it all when he first flew to Vancouver for Simpsons-Sears and then to the Canadian Maritimes on a swing that included a Simpsons-Sears–sponsored fishing trip in early April.

"I first went to New Brunswick to the Miramichi River where we were testing fishing equipment," he recalled. "I fished with the great baseball player Ted Williams. He had a fishing camp there. He was a sports advisor for Sears USA, so that's how we met. We had a great time."

Next up was a flight to St. John's, Newfoundland, for the opening ceremonies of the Second Annual Sportsman Show on May 17. "I know you're sorry Bobby Hull couldn't get down here this year but that couldn't be helped," Pierre told the large crowd. "The reason Bobby couldn't attend was due to the fact that . . . Brian Watson couldn't attend either!" The crowd roared with laughter in reference to the effective checking Watson had thrown on Hull during the semifinal. At the Simpsons-Sears booth, Pierre signed autographs and answered questions. He visited also Bishops College, Brother Rice Junior High School, United Collegiate, and Booth Memorial high schools before signing more autographs at the large Simpsons-Sears store on Water Street.

The NHL's 1966–67 season was momentous, as it marked its

50th year of existence and was the last for the six-team league, with expansion slated to double the franchises the next year. For the Black Hawks, things were a little uneasy as training camp opened without Glenn Hall, who insisted from his farm in Stony Plain, Alberta, that he was retiring. He had been late for camp before, but this time he seemed to mean it.

"As far as I was concerned, Glenn never got paid enough," Pierre said. "He should have been the highest-paid player on the club. He saved us so many times. He was his own man and had come to camp late before saying he was always 'painting the barn.' So his lateness was not something new. Maybe he was holding out for more money, I don't know, but he deserved it if he was."

As training camp ran its course, Moose Vasko, whose play had slipped the past couple of years, left camp. The Hawks didn't try to change his mind.

"Moose showed up to camp overweight, really overweight, more than last season," Pierre explained. "I don't think they offered him a lot of money and he had a job at a liquor store, so he walked out. It was getting harder for him to get into shape. With each passing year, he had to work harder in training camp, so he decided he'd had enough."

As camp broke and still no sign of Hall, Tommy Ivan realized that it might just take a little something extra to get him back. Ivan offered Mr. Goalie a big raise—to $40,000. It made him the highest-paid goalie in the league. Surprisingly, Hall merely told him he'd think about it.

With Denis DeJordy in their net, the tribe opened the season strong, winning their first four games and outscoring the opposition 22-11.

A newcomer improved the team. "Ed Van Impe's arrival on defence really helped us," recalled Pierre. "He was a very solid, stay-at-home defenceman who could hit. He was really tough in front of the net, could take guys out and was excellent with the puck and rarely lost it."

Ten days into the season, Hall accepted Ivan's offer. The reality was that Hall just couldn't turn down that much money. Despite the news, the word on the street was that the defence had to improve.

"So even though the spotlight is now on the Hawk forward lines, it's their defence that will either boost them to their first league championship or drop them into the also-ran category—again," wrote Chip Magnus of the *Sun-Times*. "With the return of Glenn Hall [and with DeJordy], the Chicagoans are solid in goal. Then, of course, there's Old Reliable, Pierre Pilote, who [last year] was slowed by injuries. . . . He's looking like the plucky Pierre of old!"

With Hall not quite ready, DeJordy and the Hawks hosted the Bruins and their shiny, new defenceman with a brush-cut, some kid named Orr. The rookie showed his stuff throughout the game as he and his teammates handed the Hawks their first loss in five games, 3-2, on November 1. The Hawks took notice—Bobby Orr had arrived.

Five days later, Hall finally started for the tribe and avenged the previous loss by beating the Bruins 4-2 in Boston Garden.

Though the Black Hawks had only lost three games all through December, it was New York that was leading the league. The surprising Rangers had won eight of their last nine games as the tribe headed into Madison Square Garden two days after Christmas. Goalie Eddie Giacomin had blanked them two games in a row and the streak looked safe when he stopped a Chico Maki drive just 47 seconds into the game. The Rangers took the rebound to the other end of the ice and scored on Hall. It stayed that way until Pierre set up Mikita in the second to even it up. Giacomin kept the game tied despite the Rangers being outshot 21-14 over the first two periods.

The third period started ominously as referee Vern Buffy gave Maki a hooking penalty just 24 seconds in. Pierre became irate and argued so vehemently that Buffy slapped him with a 10-minute misconduct. The Rangers scored the go-ahead goal on the ensuing power play, but the Hawks fought back and Mikita tied it up a minute later for his second of the night.

As the period wore on, tempers flared, especially after Pierre received an elbow to the jaw from tough guy Vic Hadfield, and no penalty was called. Hadfield had been hitting Hawks all night and getting away with it. Pierre wouldn't forget the infraction. There would be time for payback.

When Bobby Hull scored with less than four minutes remaining, the game became even more intense. The Rangers pulled Giacomin in the last minute in a desperate attempt to tie it up. The Rangers swarmed around the Hawks cage as Hall and company held them off until the final buzzer. Pierre saw his chance, grabbed Hadfield and nailed him with a right hand. It was a mistake.

"I should have never done that," Pierre recalled. "He was tough. That son of a bitch would be after my ass for the next two years! We would be into a two-year battle. He had played with us, had been a friend of mine, but after I corked him, he turned mean. Sometimes you make mistakes and that was definitely a mistake!"

The Pilote-Hadfield bout soon gave way to a Ken Hodge–Reggie Fleming bout. Both benches cleared as Buffy tried desperately to restore order. After the dust had settled, the win brought the tribe to within two points of the Broadway Blues. When the Hawks next beat the Bruins and the Rangers lost to the Leafs, the Hawks and Rangers were tied for first place, but Chicago had four games in hand.

Reporter Jack Griffin, looking for a story, entered the Hawks dressing room after a Boston game on New Year's Day, but, thanks to "Professional Poise," found no one who wanted to talk—except for Pierre.

"Pierre Pilote will talk about anything, mostly his hunting dog. Pete will talk about his dog even if you don't ask him," wrote Griffin. "'Winning everything in sight,' he said. 'You ought to see the chest on him.'"

Trophy was Pierre's pride and joy. They often went hunting together in nearby Wisconsin, where Trophy's winter kennel was. Sometimes they were joined by the Hull brothers.

"Pierre's dog, Trophy, wow!" recalled the Golden Jet. "He was a real trophy dog, let me tell you! He was great, amazing! We had such good times on those hunting trips!"

Griffin took note of the fact that Hall, the hero of the win, had already showered and was gone. "Maybe this is the Hawks' year although a guy who has lived with them for 14 years gets a little wary for predictions. If it is, it will be because a quiet, moon-faced veteran finished painting his barn and came down to play catch with an ambitious youngster."

The writer's wariness was correct as the Hawks slipped into their first real slump, winning only one of their next five games to finish out the first half of the season. But help was on the way with the arrival of Bill "Red" Hay out of self-imposed retirement on January 11 to help the Hawks beat the Red Wings 6-1.

"Red's arrival sure didn't hurt. He had been too young to retire," observed Pierre.

"That was the year Chicago had everything," Rangers coach and GM Emile Francis said in the Stephen Cole book *The Last Hurrah*. "Pilote was a beauty back there on the blue line. He reminded me of Harvey on a power play. He saw the whole ice and could make the perfect pass . . . they seemed to have the best of everything . . . goaltending, defence, goal scorers, checkers . . . "

On January 15, the Hawks shut out the visiting Leafs 4-0 before the first-ever mid-season All-Star break. They were still tied for first with the Rangers.

The NHL's 20th All-Star Game, played in Montreal on January 16, was an oddity, since the players were chosen from the season before. Hall called the game "stupid," stating the All-Star selections should have been from this season's first-half standouts, not last year's. Some players felt embarrassed about participating.

"They're not even going to let us use the kid," noted Hull about Orr.

Pierre participated in his seventh straight All-Star Game, a dull affair won easily by the Canadiens 3-0. The only notable excitement occurred when Montreal's John Ferguson knocked out Detroit's Norm Ullman. When criticized for punching in a game that was supposed to be friendly, Ferguson was unapologetic. "Whenever I put on a Canadiens uniform, I want to win. Doesn't matter who we're playing, Toronto or the All-Stars . . . they're the enemy and I want to beat 'em!"

"All-Star games were always odd. You're sitting beside these opponents, enemies you've battled, with the old animosities," recalled Pierre. "The one good thing, the troublemakers, the enforcers, usually never made the All-Star Teams."

As the schedule resumed, the Hawks took off. Heading into a January 22 match against the visiting Canadiens, the Hawks were four games without a loss.

Some of the press started to openly worry whether the tribe's great play wasn't peaking too soon in the season. You couldn't blame them. Used to their late-season near-misses or collapses, there was apprehension.

"The question must surely be whether the Hawks can survive a full National Hockey League season and still be the masters at the end," wrote Jack Griffin on January 25, with still 30 games to go. Billy Reay was even more cautious when he requested of the *Sun-Times* writer: "Please, don't try to win us a pennant on paper until the season is over."

When Chicago closed out January with easy 5-2 and 5-1 wins over the Leafs, they opened a nine-point spread over the fading Rangers. Their power was on full display in the opening seconds of the second win, when Pierre set up Mikita's backhand goal past Johnny Bower just 23 seconds into the game.

Chip Magnus asked Pierre if the play had been planned. "No, but Stan likes to pass back to the point, and he knew I'd try to shoot on the net."

The last win was costly though, as Hall needed 45 stitches to close a second-period cut over his left knee that kept him out of action for most of February.

With the Rangers in a downward spiral, Ivan attempted to keep the team focused. "Nobody's overconfident around here!" he said, almost as a warning.

When DeJordy got back-to-back 5-0 shutouts against the Bruins and the Canadiens, it was hard not to get giddy. So desperate was Montreal coach Toe Blake in the second game to stop the Hawks juggernaut that he switched goalies after each of the three Chicago first-period goals. Pierre picked up a couple of assists on the night.

On February 11, the Hawks went into Toronto full of confidence, but the Leafs had a game plan. After the Hawks had jumped out to a quick 2-0 lead, the Leafs started hitting. At one point when big Peter Stemkowski nailed Pierre with a second-period hit, Pierre snarled at him, "I'll get you!" as he picked himself off the ice. On the next shift, the big Ukrainian smashed Pierre into the boards again and commented: "Want me? Here I am!" Pierre obliged and it was a rough night for both teams, ending 4-4.

As if the evening hadn't been tough enough, the heater in the Hawks' railcar broke, ensuring a frigid overnight ride home, their only source of warmth being hot coffee and warm toast. After a cold, miserable night, the team arrived at 11:30 a.m. and went straight to the Stadium, shrugging off a slow start to beat the Wings 3-2.

The team's 15-game unbeaten streak couldn't last and came to an abrupt end after two losses against the second-place Rangers.

Though Chicago still held a 12-point lead over them, nobody wanted to talk when reporter Chip Magnus entered the Hawks dressing room. So he went to Pilote, "the team leader, the wise veteran who will probably become a National Hockey League coach someday. The losses hurt him too but he can speak the team's feelings and keep the loss in perspective."

"I'm not letting out any secrets by saying the Rangers are a good team," Pierre admitted to Magnus. "They're big and durable. It wasn't like our earlier games with other teams. We couldn't wear them out. Sure they had a really bad slump but you can't count on that sort of thing going on all year."

New York's coach was analytical and defiant. "Chicago isn't 12 points better than the rest of the league!" Francis told columnist George Langford. "The league is too well balanced. And believe me, this race is anything but over. We won two games . . . by checking, skating, and playing our positions.

"Part of the secret of stopping the Hawks is stopping Pierre Pilote. He is the most dangerous defenceman in the league and it's amazing how many scoring manouevres he starts. He can wheel around you and get a charge started before you know what happens unless you stay right on top of him all the time."

With their team looking a little worn from the pressures of their amazing first-place run, a six-day pause in their schedule allowed the team a three-day holiday in the Florida sun. When they returned, practices were optional for a few days. In their next game, a well-rested Hawks team thumped the visiting Bruins 6-3 on February 25, tied the Canadiens, then beat the Rangers and Bruins before heading into Toronto on March 4 for a date with a legend.

Toronto goaltender Terry Sawchuk had racked up 99 regular season shutouts in a 17-year career laced with controversy, injury, and glory. Having just come back from an extended layoff with back troubles, his body was constantly reminding him that it had a lot of hard miles on it. His return had vaulted the Leafs to a 10-game run that enabled Toronto to challenge the Rangers for second place.

On this night, with the collegial King Clancy behind the Leafs bench in place of the exhausted and hospitalized Punch Imlach, the Leafs responded by outhitting and outshooting the Hawks 31-14 over the first two periods. In the third period, the Leafs realized history was in the making and kept the puck away from the Chicagoans. When the final buzzer sounded, Sawchuk had his hundredth career shutout in a 3-0 win.

"The first hundred are the hardest," Sawchuk quipped.

The tribe enacted revenge the next afternoon in Chicago by beating the Leafs with Johnny Bower in net by a 5-2 score. After beating the Bruins 3-1 on March 8, clinching first place was in sight.

"What do you mean we have it all wrapped up?" snapped Pierre to reporter Dan Moulton when asked about sealing the league crown. "Sure, New York is in trouble now, but what about Toronto? The Leafs have 12 games to play against our 11 and we have 19 points on them. That means we still have to pick up five points on them some way!"

Led by Mikita's league-leading 84 points, the Hawks had six of the top 10 NHL scoring leaders: Bobby Hull, Kenny Wharram, Phil Esposito, Doug Mohns, and Pilote.

As the Hawks closed in on the title-clinching game, it was clear the other teams weren't simply going to roll over and give it to them.

After being down 3-0 in the first period in Montreal on March 11, the Hawks fought back for a 3-3 draw that gave the team a real lift. When the Rangers tied the Leafs the same night, the Hawks needed only one more win to clinch their first title and the Leafs were coming in the next day. To beat Toronto, they had to conquer The Curse of Pete Muldoon.

Peter Muldoon had been appointed the first Chicago coach in 1926. The team made the playoffs in the 1926–27 season but Muldoon was always hindered by the team's meddlesome owner, Major Fred McLaughlin. When they finished third, the owner did not hesitate to tell his coach that they should have been first. After losing to the Boston Bruins in the semifinal, they argued again and Muldoon was fired.

Sixteen years later in 1943, after the Hawks had finished out of the playoffs again, *Globe and Mail* columnist Jim Coleman was having a slow news day. He creatively wrote of Muldoon's firing, and would later admit fabricating Muldoon's threat: "Fire me Major and you'll never finish first. I'll put a curse on this team that will hoodoo it until the end of time!"

True or not, the story surfaced with each year that the Hawks missed winning the league pennant, and the "Curse of Muldoon" was invoked to explain the shortcomings.

The sold-out game against Toronto was a battle from the

opening faceoff as Pierre got a penalty for hauling down Bob Pulford on a breakaway. Toronto argued for a penalty shot but referee Buffy disagreed. Then Matt Ravlich beat Sawchuk on a breakaway, but the crowd went crazy when the goal was disallowed by a delayed penalty call against Eric Nesterenko. Hall and his defence kept the game scoreless until goals by Hodge and Bobby Hull put the tribe ahead for good. Play see-sawed back and forth as the tribe skated and checked feverishly until the final minutes wound down of a well-deserved 2-0 shutout.

"There was an explosion," wrote Chip Magnus. "More than 18,000 hysterical fans rocked the Stadium, throwing anything handy and screaming, laughing and weeping for their favourite team in the whole universe." Forty years of waiting were over.

Pierre was carried off the ice by Hodge and champagne sprayed in the celebratory Hawks dressing room.

"The Curse of Muldoon is dead! We buried Muldoon!" exclaimed Reay.

Pierre blew a kiss to Bobby Hull while Esposito danced a jig. In the mayhem, players, trainers, and reporters were either drenched in champagne or thrown into the showers. Or both.

"The monkey's gone!" Pierre shouted above the din. "There's no more monkey on my back, on anybody's back!"

"It was a long time coming," Pilote told Jack Griffin. "A long time . . . I thought it would never get here. I never was so nervous in my life. Before the game I mean. It just built up. It had to be here!"

"My knees were shaking out there," he then told reporter Robert Markus. "You can't believe the pressure. You fellows said we had it all wrapped up, but we didn't think so."

Bobby Hull sat next to Pierre with a bucket of iced champagne at his feet and was happily uncorking bottles, sending the cork projectiles bouncing overhead. Hull poured some of the bubbly over Pierre's head.

"Ouch! That burns my eyes!" Pierre screamed happily.

Hall, the man most responsible for the 39-save shutout, showered and was quickly dressed. As he strolled out, Bobby Hull shoved a bottle of champagne towards him, but Mr. Goalie shook his head and headed for the door.

"I'm going out to celebrate quietly with friends. We have nine more games left," he warned his teammates.

"I'm happiest for the players and Billy Reay," explained Ivan. "They deserved to win this for they worked hard and they played as a team—that was the big thing! I'm naturally disappointed because Jim Norris isn't here. I think he would have gotten a lot of satisfaction out of this. "

Like Hall, Reay cautioned that there were still nine games to go, and suggested that his team would give an honest effort in their remaining games and not coast. In the losing dressing room, Imlach, back behind the bench, was blasting his troops. It was left to assistant coach Clancy to talk to interested scribes.

"I'd say the Hawks are the best hockey team I've seen in this league in years," King told Doug Gilbert. "They've got good young defencemen, and terrific power up front. . . . I know how to beat them but I'm not going to tell. I won't say that we will beat the Hawks if we meet in the playoffs, but we'll make it a hell of a series, and there won't be any 5-0 games either."

The tribe next beat the Rangers 3-1 in New York but were crushed by the Leafs in Toronto 9-5 on March 18. Perhaps the shellacking was Clancy's game plan or perhaps the Hawks were distracted by the official Chicago celebrations that were to take place the next day after hosting the Canadiens.

On March 19, the Prince of Wales Trophy was in the building for the beginning of the Canadiens game. Captain Pilote and owner Arthur Wirtz were called to centre ice to accept its presentation from D. Robey, the British consul-general, during a pre-game ceremony. Horns blared, the Barton organ sounded, and the crowd went crazy.

The Canadiens, the previous winners, didn't take too kindly to the whole affair and came out flying at the Hawks, especially Henri "Pocket Rocket" Richard. The Hawks pushed back immediately as Richard was checked heavily by Pierre, a neat, low hit that sent Richard's legs up over his head in a somersault that excited the crowd. The Hawks were clearly after Richard when Doug Jarrett was called for boarding him. It was fight day in Chicago, and referee John Ashley called 17 penalties—11 of them for fighting. Despite the focus on him, Richard shone by notching a hat trick and assist in the 4-4 tie, the seventh tie between the clubs.

"Seven ties is kind of astonishing," remarked Reay. "But I guess it just means we're two pretty well-matched teams."

With the other teams battling for second place and home-ice advantage, any thoughts Chicago had of coasting through the rest of the schedule were out the window. But first, they were having a party. After the team had dressed, they headed for a celebration and dance in the Green Room at the Bismarck Hotel, where the first-place trophy was the centrepiece of the occasion.

"It looks a little lonely right now, doesn't it?" remarked Wirtz to those around him as he gazed at the hardware. "Hope it gets some company before the season runs out."

Over 200 guests packed the ballroom, drank champagne, ate, and danced, led by the players and their wives. At one point, Bobby Hull grabbed the band's microphone to tell a story.

"Once, Stan and [Henri] Richard were in the penalty box," the Golden Jet began, mimicking Richard's heavy French accent, "and Richard said, 'Meekeeta, you . . . foreigner, you not even know how to talk the English?'" Amid the laughter, he said, "Wait a minute, I think I'm telling it wrong."

"You're too late!" Mikita yelled at him. "You already blew the punch line!"

More laughter and clowning ensued before dancing rounded out the evening. As skipper Reay looked on, he knew the boys deserved this. It had all been a long grind.

The public celebration continued the next day in a slight drizzle as the players and wives met at the corner of Wacker Drive and State Street and boarded a large, colourful parade gondola. Led by the 88-piece Chicago Fire Department championship band, its bandmaster Louis Lason, a colour guard, and St. Bernard mascot, the parade headed south down State Street, west on Madison Street, before turning north on LaSalle to City Hall, where city officials received them in a packed council chambers.

"This is a really exciting and thrilling day in Chicago!" exclaimed Mayor Richard Daley. "The great Black Hawk hockey team, representing the name of Chicago, has performed in an excellent way! And we'll take the next one too!" he said, which brought another roar from everyone. He then presented Pilote and Wirtz with the five-foot-tall Mayor Richard J. Daley Trophy to loud applause.

"And you and I will be doing this again next season!" he said to the Hawks captain to more cheering.

"Well, with expansion coming up and the election coming up, all you and I can do is wish and hope!" Pierre answered him to roars of laughter again.

"I think he would make a great mayor if he ever decided to run!" Daley said, motioning to Pierre to laughter and applause. Wirtz thanked the mayor and the people of Chicago for their continued support before Pierre called the players up one at a time to receive certificates from the city. Then it was back to hockey. The regular season wasn't done, but neither was the celebrating.

After a 3-3 tie against the Rangers at home on March 22, the Black Hawks Standbys fan club hosted a dinner and dance for the team at the Farm Club on Cicero Avenue. Pierre went up to address the crowd.

"With all this free champagne, men, we should have brought a bathtub and saved Billy [Reay] some money!" he said. When someone in the back of the room heckled him, Pierre looked up and smiled.

"Hey Muldoon! Why don't you get out of here!" he yelled to howls and applause.

"This is the greatest sports team that has ever represented Chicago," Reay added in his short remarks to the gathering. All the players received some type of award. Mikita received the Most Valuable Player Trophy, voted on by the players, and the Czech was touched. "A trophy that is voted by all the players belongs to all the players," he said.

When Bobby Hull received his trophy, he was thinking of another trophy. "If we don't start playing better defensive hockey and make sure that the Vezina Trophy goes to Glenn Hall and Denis DeJordy, we should all be shot!" he warned seriously.

A good omen for two of the Hawks occurred on February 25 at Ridgeland Common Arena when Doug Mohns Jr. and Pierre Pilote Jr. helped their Oak Park squirt hockey team capture the Illinois State Hockey Championship with a 3-2 thrilling double-overtime victory over Wilmette.

Their fathers would need it, as the Hawks soon realized that the other teams were gunning for them. On March 26, at the Olympia, the Red Wings, out of a playoff spot, played an especially physical game in beating Chicago 4-2. Bryan Watson was let loose on Bobby Hull again and bad boy Howie Young joined the party.

"It was a gory spectacle, worthy of Nero, staged for Olympia vampires who wanted to see Bobby taken apart in the final Hawks appearance," wrote Magnus. "Gordie Howe slammed his stick into Stan Mikita's mouth to show Stash what Detroit thought of him, and some Wings fans began to rough up Hawks players on the bench.

"Now nobody wants to advocate violence . . . but the Hawk fans wouldn't object Tuesday night if board chairmen Doug Jarrett and Pierre Pilote and Kenny Hodge were to show the Wings what they're going to get if they continue with their Kamikaze attacks."

For the rematch back at the Stadium on March 28, the fifth-place Red Wings had one thing in mind: inflict injury. And they did. Detroit's Bert Marshall hauled Ravlich down from behind and threw him into the boards, breaking Ravlich's left ankle. There was no penalty on the play. It was not pretty when Bob Falkenberg threw his knee into Hull's knee and the Golden Jet limped from the ice as Detroit coach Sid Abel laughed heartily. Hull was done for the game and maybe more.

The Hawks bounced Detroit 7-2 and threw 48 shots at goalies Roger Crozier and George Gardner. A gleeful Abel barred the media from their dressing room after the game. When doctors examined Hull's strained left knee ligaments, they remarked that the damage wasn't as bad as they had first thought, but still, they recommended that he sit out the last three games of the season. The win could have been very costly.

"We go along with what the doctor orders," Ivan said without hesitation. Better to rest him for the upcoming playoffs. That was more important than three meaningless games, except that Hull, at 52 goals, would be unable to surpass his record of 54.

Going into New York for the final game of the season, the Hawks were a bruised but proud lot who added two more trophies to their mantle—the Art Ross scoring title for Mikita, and the Vezina Trophy for goalies Hall and DeJordy, whose 11-goal lead over Giacomin of the Rangers was safe.

In the second period with his team up 4-0, Pierre levelled Fleming with a hit that his former teammate didn't particularly enjoy. Halfway through the second period, DeJordy was racing to the Hawks bench on a delayed penalty when Fleming nailed him as he and Pierre were racing for the puck. With DeJordy sprawled on the ice, a bench-clearing brawl ensued before the goalie slowly got up, shook but unhurt.

While DeJordy registered his fourth shutout of the season, the night belonged to Pierre and Stan Mikita. Pierre's assist on Hodge's third-period goal tied his own season assist record for defencemen at 46, while Mikita's third assist of the night on the same play tied Hull's season point record at 97. In a bid to help both men break records, Reay kept them out for the duration of the game as their teammates tried desperately to help both men with their records, but to no avail. Time ran out.

As Pierre boarded the flight home that night he was satisfied with another record season. He had played well, stayed healthy, and was the captain of a great first-place team. And in the process, his tribe had established eight new NHL records: most goals by a team (264), most assists by a player (Mikita's 62), most points by a centre (Mikita's 97), most team victories (41), most team points (94), least number of losses (17), and the least number of goals against (170). Pierre and Mikita had tied their two marks. They also basked in the triumph of the Vezina win, a standard of good defensive hockey. Good defensive hockey won Stanley Cups they knew. That in and of itself was another good sign. Maybe this would be the perfect season—first place and a Stanley Cup?

Their first-round opponents would be the aging, third-place Toronto Maple Leafs, who had been squeezed out of second place by the mighty Canadiens. The Hawks had had Toronto's number all year, with a record of eight wins, four losses, and two ties and had outscored them 55-37. It should be more of the same, despite their last meeting. It didn't matter. They had handled the Leafs with ease all season.

As the plane lifted off the New York tarmac and headed for home that night, it had been a long, tough season. Was anybody remembering King Clancy's prediction against the Hawks from a few games back—*I know how to beat them . . .*

Surely not. Not on this triumphant night.

Final Assault on the Bridge

Preparing for the playoff battles ahead, the Hawks were clearly relaxed. Prior to their first practice at Rainbo Arena, Glenn Hall shot some pool against Kenny Hodge, who wore flowery shorts. Billy Hay was glad to have rejoined the team partway through the season. "Better late than never! What a team!" he quipped to reporter Ted Damata.

"Billy made this team jell . . . used the players right, the bench . . . he read them good," Eric Nesterenko said, praising coach Reay, while Phil Esposito hammed it up for the press when he talked of the upcoming All-Star votes. "All I want is just one vote, just one and I don't care if it's for the Fifth team!"

When asked to make a statement, Pierre turned to his young son, David.

"Davey, say something for the press," Pierre coaxed, but little David, unsure, continued to silently eat his popcorn. If the air was light, so was Reay's approach to this playoff series.

"We're just going to skate," Reay said. "We'll be on the ice again Wednesday and again Friday."

"Billy Reay's approach to that playoff series was pretty relaxed," recalled Pierre. "He didn't try to change our style, didn't really have a game plan, to play defensive hockey. The reason we won the Vezina, besides the great goaltending, of course, was the fact that if you have the puck, the other team doesn't. A good offence can be a great defence! That season, we had the puck a lot. We had no plans to change our style. Why change? We had such a great team and such a great year. We were relaxed, waiting for Toronto to come to us."

Toronto coach Punch Imlach wasn't relaxed. It was one thing to drill a team hard in training camp to whip them into shape, but to continue it at season's end, when a team could be tired before the playoffs, seemed sheer lunacy.

"Punch was a pusher," recalled defenceman Red Kelly. "He liked to practise, practise, practise. In this respect, he had a real problem with some of the younger players on the team who rebelled against him. We veterans understood what he was doing but the youngsters didn't appreciate his drill-sergeant mentality."

Imlach flew his Leafs to Trenton, Ontario, and then bused them north to Peterborough, where they usually held their training camp. They spent three days focused on hockey with two practices a day and game movies at night. He planned to fly them to Chicago for Game 1, fly them back to Toronto to practise, and then fly them back to the Windy City for Game 2. Imlach bristled when reporters wondered why they just wouldn't stay in Chicago to rest between games.

"Don't tell me how to coach my hockey club! If I want to fly 'em across the continent, I'll fly 'em," Imlach boomed. "I don't want 'em lying around in a hotel in Chicago."

In Peterborough, Imlach's plan backfired. On the first day of practices, Sawchuk was hit hard in the left shoulder, bruising it badly. The next day, the crazy Eddie "The Entertainer" Shack showed up and acted like a loose cannon, first getting into a fight with Bob Pulford, and then levelling Sawchuk with a slapshot to his already bruised left shoulder. Shack laughed about it afterwards but Imlach didn't. "Thank God it wasn't Bower," Punch mused to himself as he had planned to start the China Wall in the series. The next day, his nightmare materialized when Bower, not holding his stick properly, broke a knuckle stopping a Pete Stemkowski shot.

Frustrated at the turn of events, Imlach ordered his team off the ice early at their last practice. Meanwhile, the Hawks practised quietly at home and waited confidently.

The Chicago press was unsure how to assess the upcoming series.

"There is opinion in some ill-informed quarters that the Black Hawks will have an easy time of it in the Stanley Cup playoffs," wrote John Kuenster in the *Daily News*. "Pete Pilote, captain and veteran defenceman of the club, raises a dissenting voice. 'Like hell,' says Pete, who makes his home in Broadview, with his attractive wife, Anne, and four children. 'Those three other clubs [Toronto Maple Leafs, New York Rangers, Montreal Canadiens] are pretty tough. We'll be "up" for the playoffs, but anything can happen in a seven-game series.'

"So as the hockey world awaits the Stanley Cup series, we'll go along with Pilote and agree that there are rough times ahead for the Hawks, especially with Ravlich out and Hull suffering from a recurrence of a knee injury . . . But, just to make this a sporting proposition, and show you how whimsical sports writers can be sometimes, we still think the Hawks will win the Cup . . . in about 12 games."

As the two teams took to the ice on April 6, there couldn't have been more of a contrast between two teams. Baby-faced Denis DeJordy was in the Hawks net, full of confidence, fresh off his Vezina win with Hall. His teammates, full of zeal and firepower, whizzed about the ice in the pre-game warm-up. The Leafs skated onto the Chicago ice slowly, methodical and determined. They had the ancient Sawchuk in goal, there by virtue of Bower's injury. He was slow and smooth, almost like he was conserving his energy. His teammates were a mix of young stalwarts and tough, grizzled veterans who had a game plan—slow down the Hawks.

When referee John Ashley dropped the first puck, it was clear from the outset that the strategy for the Leafs was to hit.

Just past the five-minute mark of the first period, Pat Stapleton's point shot was stopped by Sawchuk, but Ken Wharram popped in the 15-foot rebound to put the tribe up 1-0. The Leafs responded when Frank Mahovlich tied it two minutes later by banging in a short Dave Keon pass behind DeJordy. The goal had broken a Hawks cardinal rule.

"Against Toronto, the key was to stop Frank from scoring in the first period," recalled Pierre. "If he got one, it lit him on fire. He was the big gun. We had to keep hitting him. He played on my side of the ice so I'd go after him. When he'd jump out of the way from a hit—I knew I had him that night. And Eric Nesterenko was on him, to stop the Big M."

With Stapleton and Pulford in the penalty box, the ensuing four on four was to Chicago's advantage and they quickly moved the puck into the Leafs end. Jarrett passed to Pierre. His 35-foot shot found the back of the Leafs net as Bobby Hull sat in the crease distracting Sawchuk; 2-1 Chicago.

When Bobby Baun went off for slashing Mikita just as the second period started, Imlach was furious. He'd warned his team against taking stupid penalties. The Hawks pounced on the power play, with Hull taking a pass from Pierre and banging it into the Toronto net. The delirium in the Stadium continued unabated when Mikita made it 4-1 12 minutes later, crashing the net as Sawchuk was trying to smother the puck. Sawchuk and the puck ended up in the net.

Chicago's Lou Angotti made the score 5-1. With 11 minutes to go in the third, Doug Mohns was penalized and Imlach pulled Sawchuk. But just 11 seconds into the five on three, Pulford took a penalty to nullify the two-man power play. Imlach was livid as he was forced to send Sawchuk back into the net. "Goddamn penalties," he fumed to his players. Ashley called 20 penalties in the rough game, 11 of them against the Hawks.

"Thursday night, 18,000 Chicago Stadium fans were served a delicious Hawk speciality," wrote Magnus with a culinary angle on the game. "The big tough hunks of beef from Toronto were par broiled by a 5-2 score. Not that it was easy work putting Punch

Imlach's rowdies into the oven. . . . Denis [DeJordy] was the master chef. He was spattered with 44 Leaf shots, and let only two get away. . . . Otherwise he was guarding his net as a cook guards his kitchen. . . . But everyone agreed that Denis's Maple Leaf Hash was a tasty dish to set before King Clancy."

"We just couldn't handle their power play and we couldn't handle them on the four on fours either," Punch told the press, while Reay thought that DeJordy outshone Sawchuk. All agreed that Sawchuk looked tired and played that way.

The final score had been comfortable, but as the Hawks left the ice that night, relieved, they were also bruised, as epitomized by Hull, who confided that he was so banged up that he felt like an 80-year-old man. The Leafs immediately flew back to Toronto for two full practices before the next game in Chicago, while Reay gave the Hawks two days off due to the Ice Capades being in the Stadium until their Sunday rematch.

In keeping with the food theme, the *Sun-Times* decided to run stories that week on the home cooking for the three prominent Hawks: Pierre, Bobby Hull, and Mikita. In the "Good Food" section of the paper the day after Game 1, reporter Becky Blum wrote of her visit to the Pilote household in Broadview a few days previous.

"I thought you'd want an authentic look to your story, so I wore exactly what I cook in," laughed Annie as she let Blum in the front door and into the kitchen, where she made one of her family's favourite dishes. "We are all very fond of Chinese food and it really helps Pierre, as he must keep his weight down during the hockey season. I make a lot of Ukrainian dishes too; however Pierre finds the Chinese food better for him while he's in training."

"I love children and I try to engage in a lot of activities with mine," Annie continued, mentioning horseback riding. She also talked of all the moves over the years to seven different houses. The reporter wrote that the shrimp fried rice was "delicious."

Prior to Game 2, Imlach absolved Sawchuk of any blame in the first loss. "I'm not going to criticize a goalkeeper who has 100 shutouts. It says in the book how good Sawchuk is and I feel like the book says. He's been awful good a lot of the times."

Magnus interviewed Pierre about the Leafs' tactics in Game 1. "One of their best manoeuvres is the stick grab," Pierre told him. "They love to do that! They grab your stick and won't let go and if you try too hard to get it away from them, you wind up with a penalty." Pierre was asked if he would ever grab another player's stick.

"Me? I should say not!" he answered, trying to keep a straight face.

When the two teams took to the ice at the Stadium on April 9, the playing surface was heavily rutted and mud-splattered due to the Ice Capades.

From the puck drop it seemed like the teams had switched uniforms. The young Hawks seemed sluggish while the old Leafs had a spring in their step. Sawchuk also informed the Hawks early that his shaky Game 1 performance was behind him when he stopped a Hull blast so thoroughly that his suspenders came unclipped. Then the Leafs pushed the Hawks back into their own end and tireless checking forced a turnover before Stemkowski banged a 10-footer into the Hawks goal behind DeJordy. Toronto 1-0.

The goal shook the Hawks out of their lethargy and they came at Sawchuk full throttle. Pierre fed Nesterenko alone in front of the Toronto net but Sawchuk stayed with his dekes and stopped the shot with his stick. When Horton received a penalty at the 14:54 mark, the Hawks power play set up. This was their chance to get back into the game. After Sawchuk stopped Hull twice and Mikita in all alone, the goalie was allowed to go to the Leafs bench for a leg strap adjustment by referee Vern Buffy. The old delaying tactic helped his tired penalty-killers, Keon and Armstrong, catch their breath. The Leafs got their second wind and, while still short-handed, Armstrong fed the puck ahead to a flying Keon, who broke in alone on DeJordy and whistled a shot by the youngster's glove hand into the net to make it 2-0 Toronto. The short-handed goal was a dagger to the Hawks' heart and the organ and the crowd was silent.

As the second period was set to begin, "the Stadium ice looked like a frozen sewer," the *Tribune* described in the next day's paper. "There was enough mud to satisfy the most finicky hippopotamus!" The ice conditions were nullifying a strong Chicago advantage— their speed.

The game continued to be rough when Larry Hillman cracked Mohns over his already sore back and a collision between Bobby Hull and Armstrong sent the Toronto captain to the dressing room for the rest of the night. Jarrett threw a football clip on Mahovlich in an attempt to slow down the Big M, but when the Leafs went up 3-0 on a power play goal at the 8:24 mark of the second, the hole the Chicagoans were digging deepened.

Moments later, Mikita brought the tribe some hope when his 30-foot wrist shot from a bad angle eluded Sawchuk, to make the score 3-1. The Hawks sensed their moment had arrived and the crowd came to life. Minutes later, Esposito broke in all alone and tried to deke the Uke, but Sawchuk stayed with him and made the stop. The crowd was beside itself in frustration. Sawchuk then stopped bullets from Bobby Hull, his brother Dennis, and Jarrett, but did not bend.

Sensing victory and a need to protect Sawchuk, the Leafs switched gears and played exclusively defensive hockey, clogging the centre ice area with a tight-checking blanket across their own blue line that forced the Hawks to play dump and chase—not their style. It didn't work.

After the loss, Reay was asked the secret to getting through Toronto's wall of defence. "There's no magic formula for getting past that Leaf setup," said Reay. "We've just got to do what we've been doing—but do it better. They wanted that one victory here and got it! Now of course, we'll have to win one at Toronto."

In front of the Leafs dressing room, a gleeful Imlach plopped himself into a red chair before waiting reporters. With his fedora tilted sideways, he crossed his arms and yelled, "Okay, let's go!"

When a Chicago reporter asked him if the win was a surprise, he bristled. "From all I read, Chicago is the best team . . . they've got 10 All-Stars, count 'em if you want . . . all we got is a bunch of pluggers . . . we won by check, check, checking!"

Asked if the ice conditions were a factor, he snarled. "We both used the same ice!"

In the days after Game 2, the Chicago press pounced on the game's ice conditions and how it hurt their speedy team.

"Chicago Stadium management booked the Ice Capades into the building at a time they knew the Hawks would need the ice for the playoffs," questioned the *Tribune*. "The family Wirtz, which owns the Stadium, also owns the Black Hawks. Didn't they think the Hawks would make the playoffs . . . or didn't they care?"

In a bid to shake things up for Game 3, April 11 in Toronto, Reay started Hall in net, a move that he hoped would spark a more open, free-wheeling Hawks style. The always good and fast Gardens ice would help too. It worked—for the first 10 minutes.

The Hawks came at Sawchuk with everything they had. Hull blasted one at him from 20 feet out that the Uke deflected wide with his pad. Angotti then broke in alone but Sawchuk made a great glove save. Then at the eight-minute mark, Hull again blasted one at the Toronto net that the goaltender stopped with the inside of his arm. The Leafs, on their heels, regrouped. At the 11:10 mark, Pierre got caught up ice and the Leafs counterattacked on a two on one against Jarrett. Using Red Kelly as a decoy, from the faceoff circle Ron Ellis fired a quick shot that squeezed through the short side on Hall to put the Leafs up by one. The goal deflated the Hawks while Toronto came on so strongly they eventually outshot the Hawks 18-16 in the first period. Both goalies were playing at the top of their game.

When Mahovlich scored for the Leafs halfway into the second period, the wind came out of Chicago's sails and the Leafs gained resolve by resorting to their tight-checking game. The Hawks got fewer shots than in the first, and when Jim Pappin beat Hall with just 45 seconds left to play in the second to make it 3-0, the writing was on the wigwam.

Toronto threw up a third period defensive blanket at their blue line and the checking both ways had the teams exchanging even fewer shots. When Hull broke Sawchuk's shutout on a Chicago power play with just three minutes remaining in the game, the Hawk celebration was muted. That was it for the scoring. The headline the next day said it all: "Sawchuk sparkles in nets."

Both teams were banged up. Toronto had Keon and Pappin playing hurt and Armstrong was missing in action, while the Hawks had a gimpy Hull, Mikita, and Mohns.

As they regrouped, the Hawks were hoping that their youth was going to start to be a factor in the series. The next game, the third in five nights, was harder on ageing Leafs like Marcel Pronovost, Armstrong, Allan Stanley, Kelly, and Sawchuk than any of the younger tribal warriors.

For Reay, this series was personal. He hated losing, especially to Imlach, the man who had once fired him. Prior to Game 4, he blasted his troops, saying their efforts weren't up to par. They needed to skate harder, check harder, break out of their own end faster, and most of all, get that all-important first goal.

From the puck drop, Mikita shot the puck up the boards to a breaking Mohns, who beat Horton to the puck. Mohns fed a cross-ice pass to Wharram, whose wrist shot sailed past a startled Sawchuk and into the Toronto net with just nine seconds gone in the game, tying a Stanley Cup record. Reay breathed a sigh of relief.

Three minutes later, Keon took a Mahovlich pass and rifled it through a sliding Ed Van Impe and Hall to tie the game.

"Dave Keon was on fire in that series," recalled Pierre. "My play was to go around the net and take off. I would have five feet on him. There weren't too many guys who could catch me, but you know, by the time I hit the blue line, he was tapping me on the ass, and he had me before the red line!"

Pierre took matters into his own hands when he took the puck, circled the Leafs net, and fired a backhander past Sawchuk to put the tribe up by one again at the 8:32 mark. A minute and a half later, during four-on-four play, Horton tied it up. In a bid to keep hitting them, the Leafs took three penalties in the last 10 minutes to try to slow down Hull and company. At the end of round one, the Hawks went to their dressing room having only outpunched the Leafs by one shot, 13-12.

Chicago's firepower came out in the second and Sawchuk's stamina was severely tested. Having not played more than two games in one week all season, he was now into his fourth.

The Leafs stood up at their blue line and the Hawks had to start dumping the puck in. As Toronto's aged defence scrambled back for the puck time after time, the Hawks slowly wore them down. Mikita and Hay were stopped on breakaways and then Sawchuk made a nifty kick save on a Jarrett wrist shot that had the Gardens crowd cheering. Sawchuk took two Hull blasts to his upper body that hurt.

A few minutes into the last frame, Nesterenko took a shot at the Leafs net that Sawchuk couldn't control. Nesterenko pushed through Stanley and banged away repeatedly at the rebound until he had pushed both Sawchuk and the puck into the net for the Hawks' third goal. Six minutes later, Pierre fed a pass to Hull, who wound up and blasted a zinger along the ice past a flinching Sawchuk for a 4-2 lead. It was Pierre's third point of the game.

The Leafs and Sawchuk tired visibly and with the Hawks seemingly in control, the rough stuff started. Bobby Hull was decked a few times and Maki body-slammed Ellis. Pulford flattened Pierre. Pierre flattened Keon. In a three-man collision with Stanley and Dennis Hull, Hull's stick was pushed up into Horton's face and his nose cut badly, leaving a trail of blood. Mohns, his sore back bolstered by pain-killing injections, was crumpled on more than on a few occasions. Hall suffered the most damage of all when his face caught a rising Pappin slapshot that forced him from the game with a 25-stitch gash to his mouth and the loss of two teeth.

With three and a half minutes remaining, the Leafs weren't giving up. Imlach pulled Sawchuk and Toronto scored on DeJordy, making the score 4-3. With 90 seconds to go, Sawchuk was pulled from the net and the Leafs continued to push. They controlled the puck in the Hawks end and DeJordy had to make excellent stops on Keon and Mahovlich before the siren sounded to end the game, preserve the win, and tie the series for Chicago.

"It was murder, absolute carnage from beginning to end!" exclaimed Magnus in the *Sun-Times*. "The Black Hawks and Maple Leafs tore into each other for 60 minutes . . . the 15,854 fans who jammed Maple Leaf Gardens were wrung to exhaustion, the Hawks were bruised and limping, and the Leafs nearly had to be carried out in baskets. It was fought brutally."

Punch held court for reporters and was fuming. "Ask me a million questions, but don't ask me about the refereeing. I don't want to talk about the fucking referees! It's a fucking disgrace! On Nesterenko's goal, my guy [Sawchuk] had control of the puck twice. Then Nesterenko started banging away. He shoulda got a goddamn penalty, not a goal!"

"Holy mackerel!" Reay exclaimed to reporters afterwards. "They raised the ticket prices for these games, but the fans sure got their money's worth. This was the game we had to win, but I'm afraid we won't be able to use Glenn on Saturday. He took a real beating and DeJordy is our likely goalie."

When Punch was asked which goalie he was starting the next game, he laughed. "You guess which one and I'll start the other guy."

"With only 38 hours rest—the two teams will knock heads there [Chicago] at 12:30 p.m. Saturday," Magnus predicted. "That is, if anybody can move."

The sore and tired Leafs had no choice but to move because Imlach put them through a brisk practice the next day, while Reay gave his troops the day off.

The wounded teams reconvened in the noisy confines of Chicago Stadium for Game 5 on the afternoon of April 15 as national television audiences tuned in on both sides of the 49th parallel.

Cigarette smoke, made more prominent by the heat and

humidity, hung in the air like fog as the squads took to the ice. In the Toronto net was the ageless wonder, Johnny Bower. Sawchuk had begged off from fatigue.

The Hawks looked at Bower as a cat to a canary.

"They've got old goaltenders! We were thinking that," Pierre recalled. "We knew that Sawchuk was tired and beat up. And Bower was what, 40? We knew that Bower was fresh, but if we could get him out of there and get Sawchuk back, we got 'em! We knew we could beat Sawchuk. We all thought he couldn't see the puck anymore."

With the backing of a boisterous hometown crowd, cheering wildly through the national anthems and the soaring Barton organ, the Hawks came out firing. They skated like the wind, but their lack of practice showed on the first couple of shifts as their passing game was a little off and though they seemed to take the game to the Leafs, they couldn't mount much of an attack. Then Dennis Hull took a penalty.

The Hawks defence managed to keep the Leafs from getting a single shot at DeJordy for the first minute of the Leafs power play but then Mike Walton connected from the slot at the 6:16 mark to put the Torontonians on the board.

Reay yelled at his troops and they turned it up a notch, immediately pressing into the Toronto zone.

As Bower attempted to clear the puck along the boards out of his end, Pierre intercepted it and fired the puck towards the empty Leafs net. His shot was deflected by Angotti into the Toronto cage to even the score. A minute and a half after their first goal, the Hawks swarmed towards him again. The goalie fumbled a Jarrett shot and the subsequent rebound was gobbled up by Hay, who fed Bobby Hull, who rifled the puck into the Leafs net. The Stadium exploded with euphoria.

Imlach didn't like what he was seeing from Bower. His veteran looked shaky, but Bower finished the period and Toronto even managed to tie it up courtesy of a Mahovlich goal. When Sawchuk started the second, the Hawks smiled to themselves. It was exactly the scenario they wanted. They were going to go at Sawchuk with everything they had.

Three minutes into the second period, referee Ashley called Stanley for charging.

At the puck drop, Mikita snared the puck and fed it to Pierre, who passed it back to Mikita, now in the right corner. Mikita circled back behind the net and fed a 30-foot pass to a charging Bobby Hull. The Golden Jet got the pass and in one fluid motion unleashed a bomb. The puck caught Sawchuk on his already tender left shoulder, bounced off his mask, and dropped him like he had been shot. The Leaf trainer came out to assess the fallen goaltender.

Hovering nearby, Pierre looked down at the fallen goaltender with a slight grin and said sarcastically, "Stay down, Ukey," meaning there was more to come. Sawchuk gave him a dirty look.

"There was some question whether he'd be able to get up in time to catch the plane back to Toronto," Magnus observed wryly.

After a few minutes Sawchuk stood to polite applause from the crowd, rubbed his tender left shoulder, and skated slowly around for a long time. He eventually reached for his gloves and stick and indicated he would continue. The Hawks thought they had him right where they wanted him.

The Hawks threw everything they had at him. For the duration of the Stanley penalty and later during a penalty to right-winger Pappin, the Hawks swirled around his net and peppered Sawchuk with shots that seemed like sure goals.

"I remember breaking in towards Sawchuk and throwing the puck back out to Bobby [Hull] for what I thought was a sure goal, as I braced for and took a hit," recalled Pierre. "I expected to get up to celebrate a goal. There was no goal! I couldn't believe the puck was not in the net!"

In that second period, the Leafs defence tightened up as the Hawks threw 15 shots at the Leafs net, to no avail. Sawchuk's saves on Mikita and Mohns had the crowd tied up in knots and the score was unchanged as the period ended.

"They mugged him unmercifully," Magnus wrote of Sawchuk's performance, "and he beat them every time with as fine a piece of goaltending as has been produced in the Stadium for years."

In their dressing room before that last period, the Hawks were still full of confidence. They were a scoring machine and had broken countless records that season. They were at their zenith, their most powerful. There was no reason to think that this game wasn't theirs for the taking.

On a faceoff in their own end, Reay sent out the line of Hull, Esposito, and Maki. From the puck drop, Hull drew the puck back, then he and Maki took off out of their end, but Pulford got to the puck first in the corner and fed a pass to Pappin. DeJordy stopped him but Stemkowski banged home the rebound to put Toronto ahead 3-2.

The play went back and forth and the Leafs defence threw a blanket around their goalie to protect him. The Leafs checked and checked and with time winding down, Chicago still had its chances.

"There was still time to get it done, six minutes left in the game, the Hawks down only one. Then from out of a big swirl at the net, Mohns suddenly showed up with the puck. He wasn't six feet from the net, nobody to stop him, and he walked right in on Sawchuk."

Mohns tried deking him but the weak shot that bounced off the goalie's pads took the life out of them. Chicago, who had thrown 20 third-period shots at Sawchuk to this point, managed only two more weak shots thereafter. Pappin put the final stake in the Hawks' heart to make it a 4-2 final.

Afterwards, the Hawks left the ice subdued and in total disbelief.

"We had our chances but [Sawchuk] beat us," Reay said after the game. "That's the best game I've seen him play in four years."

"He nearly gets his head torn off, and then comes back like

that," Pierre told Magnus in a quiet Hawks dressing room. "We kept shooting into the sand traps."

"[Sawchuk] was a man in a daze, soaked with fatigue, the nerves still screaming inside him, his face grey and drawn," wrote Jack Griffin eloquently. "'I don't know a thing about what went on out there. Not a thing.'"

Down 3-2, the Hawks had to regroup for the sixth game in Toronto. If they were panicking, they weren't showing it. When they arrived late in Toronto the day before Game 6, they passed up practising.

"We didn't need a workout anyways, because we had one yesterday," said Reay. "Besides, workouts are mainly to give the players something to do, and we're checking in pretty late this time."

At the hotel the players were devouring the local stories about the series.

"Hey look at this!" squealed Phil Esposito while reading the headline, "Terry and the Pirates Steal Another Game!"

When Pierre saw the headline "Get Pilote: Is the Cry!" he was not amused. The story alleged that he had speared Larry Jeffrey back in Chicago. He was having none of it.

"I didn't spear him!" he snapped at Magnus. "I was trying to freeze the puck in centre ice on the boards, and he came crashing into me. I don't know whether he was going for me or the puck, but all of a sudden he fell to the ice. He must have run into my stick, but I didn't shove it into his stomach. But if [the Leafs] want to get me, I'll be waiting!"

Reay was calm and confident going into the game. "I'm keeping our lines the way they've been. We played well Saturday, but not quite as well as some of you make out. After all, putting the puck in the net is part of the game—a pretty important part. Sure, Sawchuk played a whale of a game. He'd better have another one like that in his system. I told our players that we'd be back in the Stadium Thursday. We can still win this thing."

If the Hawks needed inspiration, the ever-game Hall provided it. His face and mouth still swollen from the vicious cut of a couple of days before, he heard Reay's rallying cry and was between the pipes for Game 6.

From the puck drop, the Hawks started off listlessly and at the five-minute mark, Brian Conacher rifled a bullet through Hall's legs to put the Leafs up by one. Hall had to come back and make great saves on Conacher again, Pappin, and Pulford to keep it close. The Hawks outshot the Leafs 15-14 in the first period, and they tied it up on Stapleton's long shot that was accidentally tipped into his own net by the Leafs' Tim Horton.

In the second period, the Leafs checked the Hawks at every turn and took the play to Hall, outshooting Chicago 14-10, but Mr. Goalie made great stops on Mahovlich, Pappin, Ellis, and Keon. The score remained 1-1 heading to the third period.

At the 4:47 mark of the third, Conacher put the Leafs ahead when his shot at the Chicago net hit something and got past Hall for the go-ahead goal. Then Stemkowski put the Leafs up 3-1 with just over 13 minutes gone in the third. The Leafs, smelling victory, threw a checking blanket on the Hawks for the duration of the game. As the horn sounded, the Leafs had beaten Chicago four games to two in one of the biggest upsets in hockey history.

"Terry, you son of a gun, you beat us!" Mikita said to Sawchuk during the post-series handshakes. The Toronto goalie was too tired to smile or respond. In the subdued Hawks dressing room, Reay was gracious in defeat.

"I'm a little one-sided so I think the best team lost," Reay said. "But Sawchuk stoned us and they outplayed us up the centre . . . but I've got no squawks. [The Hawks are] champions. . . . I'm happy with the year they gave me. . . . I'll be satisfied with one like it next year."

As the Hawks flew back to Chicago that night, the taste of another playoff disappointment was bitter. Pierre found little consolation in the fact that he had tied Bobby Hull in team scoring with two goals and four assists. It didn't matter. It was getting harder to lose, especially knowing that you could only have so many chances in a career.

He vented his frustration to reporter George Vass in Chicago a few days after the series. "You don't feel it for a couple of days, and then it hits you," he said. "I thought we were going to win—I was sure of it. You know who's going to take this even harder—my wife. The wives take it more to heart than the players. She's been more nervous than I. She's been with me for 14 years and it still bothers her.

"It's getting worse for me too, as I get older. Five or six years ago I'd play my game, figure I'd done my best. I could let it go at that. But the last couple of years, more and more, it's been getting to me. I carry the whole load on my shoulders, worry about everything. Both teams were a little tired, but I think if we could just have hit them then, got going more, we could have had it. We didn't play that badly, but we just couldn't come up with that something extra."

Vass asked him about Sawchuk.

"He played alright, but we didn't give him that many good shots. A lot of our chances came when we were falling down or weren't in good position. They kept checking us, kept us on the sides, away from the middle."

And he talked of Dave Keon. "He was checking all over . . . and on the power play, he'd rush, rush, and I couldn't move up on him. He kept us on the sides. Did you see that check Doug Jarrett put on Pete Stemkowski? I'm going to buy him a beer. It was a joy to see that . . .

"It has been a good season though. We did win first place—that's the big thing. What should I do now, go to Florida? Maybe just work around the backyard and get a tan that way. It's a lot cheaper!"

In the days after the ill-fated series, Pierre was selected to the NHL First All-Star team along with Harry Howell. With 52 points he was pleased with his season, the team's playoffs notwithstanding.

But uneasiness stirred within him and many others. NHL expansion, with six new teams—Los Angeles, Philadelphia, Pittsburgh,

Minnesota, St. Louis, and Oakland—meant that the Original Six clubs would only be able to protect so many players.

With only so many heads to protect from the underachieving team, who would Ivan cut loose and what kind of team would be left standing in Chicago after the expansion dust settled?

CHAPTER 20

The Defence Rests

The spring of 1967 was the most unsettled in the history of the NHL.

The Black Hawks landscape shifted, aided in large part by the actions of Phil Esposito at the wrap-up party. In his autobiography, *Thunder & Lightning*, Esposito described how he drunkenly walked over to where GM Tommy Ivan and Coach Billy Reay were seated and, in no uncertain terms, informed them that they were going to screw up their team, their potential dynasty. This, coupled with the fact that in the six playoff games against the Leafs, Esposito had gotten zero points, no doubt sealed his fate. The day after the party, when Esposito went to Ivan's office to collect his expense money, Ivan yelled through his secretary that if he ever saw Esposito again, it would be too soon.

"The problem with Phil at that time was that he couldn't get up for playoff games," recalled Bobby Hull. "I'd say, 'Phil, ya got to get going! Everyone else is moving and you have to too. You have to improve your game at least 10%!' He didn't flippin' care! His playoff stats always tailed off."

On May 16, Ivan made good on his threat and sent his smart-alecky centre to Boston along with Ken Hodge and Fred Stanfield in exchange for goalie Jack Norris, Pit Martin, and Gilles Marotte.

"Esposito is a big guy and so is Hodge," Boston GM Milt Schmidt excitedly told the press. "Chicago had so many good forwards. . . . Stanfield had a tough time trying to break into the lineup."

Stanfield had only played two games for the tribe, but Esposito had been their fourth-leading point-getter and Hodge had garnered 35 points. Martin had scored only 20 goals for the Bruins the previous season, and Norris played with the Los Angeles Blades in the WHL. The Hawks needed another defenceman like a hole in the head as they had Pierre, Pat Stapleton, Doug Jarrett, Matt Ravlich, and Ed Van Impe, though Ravlich was still recuperating from his broken leg and was a great unknown.

"They flippin' traded Phil Esposito, Kenny Hodge, Freddie Stanfield for 'Search and Destroy' Marotte, Jack Norris, a goaltender, which we needed like another asshole, and 'Pitiful' Pit Martin," recalled Bobby Hull with the same disdain and incredulity he felt the day he learned of the infamous trade. "That trade would make Boston and would weaken us equally! It ruined our team! I heard afterwards that they wanted to give us Gerry Cheevers and we refused. Can you believe that? That's how much Tommy Ivan knew about hockey! He couldn't coach a dog out of a storm with a T-bone steak!"

"The problem with Phil was that while he was not afraid, he was not a tough player with us," explained Pierre. "His points in a season were like the stock market—up and down. He'd get five or six goals then nothing for a quite a while. He was inconsistent. And on a line with Bobby, who was busy protecting himself, big Phil would get roughed up in front of the net. He had nobody to protect him like they would in Boston."

Ivan, like all Original Six teams' general managers, scrambled to set his protected lineup for the expansion draft on June 6, in Montreal. Each team could protect 11 skaters and one goalie.

The Hawks protected DeJordy, leaving the retired—again— Glenn Hall to be snapped up by the St. Louis Blues. The tribe also let go Lou Angotti, Van Impe, as well as the rights to retired players Moose Vasko and Billy Hay.

"I had the feeling I'd be protected, so I didn't really think about it too much," revealed Pierre. "The only surprises for me were Glenn Hall going to St. Louis and Ed Van Impe to Philly. They were big losses. They should have kept them, but then again, they couldn't keep everybody."

Another monumental shift in the NHL landscape was the impending formation of a revamped NHL Players' Association with a young, brazen Toronto lawyer named Alan Eagleson at the helm. The Golden Jet remembered the man the players eventually voted in to represent them.

"After asking this young Eagleson fella a couple of pertinent questions at an early meeting, he started hollering at me," angrily recalled Bobby Hull. "I said to everybody right there and then, 'This guy isn't for us! He's just for himself!' But Eagleson got some of our player reps all juiced up in some south sea island and they voted him in. I was against him from the beginning!"

Pierre was unsure but willing to give it all a try. "I had heard about him from the other players. 'Look, I want to talk to you,' he had said to me one night after a game in Toronto," remembered Pierre, the Chicago player representative. "We got a cab, and he says: 'Look, we're going to try to form a union or association. What do you think of it?' I told him our Chicago players were all for it. He says, 'We're going to get you all a better pension, and other things.' He looked very professional, well dressed and well-spoken. In retrospect, we should have been alarmed at who some of his good friends were in our group. What did we know? It all sounded good at the time."

The day after the draft, with the NHL world assembled in Montreal, Eagleson handled the negotiations for the players. The owners agreed to "officially" recognize the NHL Players' Association. It was a landmark decision announced by Charles Mulcahy, representing the NHL board of governors, namely the owners, and Eagleson, representing the players.

Neither Eagleson nor Mulcahy were talking. It was left to NHL president Clarence Campbell to boast self-servingly: "The league operated at 98% capacity in attendance last season and the players shared in a large piece of every dollar," he said with his poker face. "The average player salary in this league is $18,266 . . . and that compares favourably with any professional sport!" Average? Who really knew, but Terry Sawchuk, an 18-year veteran who had just led the Maple Leafs to the Stanley Cup over Montreal a few months before, was making less than that.

Campbell also knew that the days of skimpy contracts were coming to an end. Eagleson's negotiations with Boston for his new client, Bobby Orr, had made the rookie defenceman one of the highest paid players in the league two years before. Orr was one of the first players to have an agent.

The new NHL teams were signing players to larger contracts as Sawchuk signed with the Kings for $30,000 and Hall got more than $40,000 in St. Louis. Even minor leaguers, now finding themselves in the NHL, were getting more money than they'd ever dreamed of with the expansion teams.

Training camp at Chicago Stadium in fall 1967 was different.

"Gilles Marotte was built like a brick shithouse," recalled Pierre. "In training camp, his first big play was to knock out and separate Dennis Hull's shoulder. He hit him into the boards. 'Captain Crunch' must have weighed 220 pounds, could skate and shoot but had no hockey sense. He was like a loose cannon at camp!"

For Pierre, negotiations with Ivan started soon after the start of camp. As usual, they went back and forth but to show his resolve and dedication to the team, Pierre hit the ice for all of the practices before reaching a deal.

"Pierre Pilote, captain and player representative of the Black Hawks, yesterday signed for his 13th season in the NHL," reported Ted Damata on September 14. "The veteran All-Star defencemen, who will be 36 years old on December 11, came to terms after yesterday afternoon's drill in the Stadium. No figures were revealed by general manager Tommy Ivan."

In actuality, it was a two-year deal worth $40,000 per season.

Ken Wharram, Pat Stapleton, Martin, and DeJordy were still unsigned but, unlike Pierre, they refrained from practising, preferring to watch from the stands, to show their resolve and up the ante. DeJordy even stayed in Buffalo through it all, a tactic that would have been unheard of in the old days, but this was the new NHL.

The Hawks opened their season without DeJordy on October 11 against the Rangers and lost 6-3 with Dave Dryden in net. After a few games, DeJordy and the Hawks finally came to terms and he returned to the nets, but his presence wasn't much help: Chicago lost six games in a row, which included a 7-1 drubbing from the Bruins and their former teammates at the Stadium on October 18. Boos rained down from the gallery gods and many fans and players were looking back enviously at the trade with Boston.

"Just think, in Boston, Esposito was now on the first line with Wayne Cashman and Ken Hodge," recalled Bobby Hull. "Freddie Stanfield was on the second line with Johnny McKenzie and Johnny Bucyk, and Freddie was also on the power play with Bobby Orr. So the three guys that we sent to them were on their first two lines, and on the power play. What does that tell you about that trade?"

The tribe followed that forgettable game with further embarrassing losses to the expansion Penguins and Kings. It was clear that the Hawks were a diminished force that didn't get its act together until October 28, when they beat the Minnesota North Stars 4-2. After a loss to the Red Wings the next night, the Hawks regrouped, accumulating 27 wins, many at the expense of expansion teams, to take them to the All-Star break.

"They had to bring up a lot of new players for these new clubs, players that had played in the minor leagues. They were third-liners really in the NHL; it made it easier to play," recalled Pierre of his first impressions of NHL expansion. "When we went into Minnesota it wasn't tough, same with L.A., places like that. The toughest place was Philadelphia right from the get-go. Right away they had a good goaltender, a pretty good defence, and a couple of tough guys. St. Louis turned out to be pretty good too: they had Glenn Hall and Red Berenson, and he was hard to stop. The other teams were easier."

At this point in his career, Pilote continued to garner respect from his opponents, some of them new.

"He jumps at you," Noel Price of the Pittsburgh Penguins observed of the Hawk captain. "His favourite move is cutting across the rink, nailing a guy from the side. He once creamed Larry Jeffrey so hard I thought Jeffrey would never get up."

When defenceman Bobby Baun, now with Detroit, broke in and tried going around Pierre, the Hawk defenceman was ready with his famous Barilko Bump hip check. Baun's stick flew one way and his body crashed to the ice in a rolling heap.

"I like that kind of hitting. That is part of me!" Pierre later said with a smile.

Despite the fact that he was playing well, Hawks fans had started to turn on Pierre, booing him whenever he made a mistake.

"I can't understand it," Chicago hockey writer Dan Moulton would later say of this period in Pierre's career in Chicago. "I think Pierre's trouble is when he's having a bad night, he's *really bad*. But when he's on, nobody notices it."

At the halfway point, there seemed to be a bright future for the Hawks when Hull and Mikita were selected for the First All-Star Team and Pierre was placed on the Second Team. He received $250 for the honour.

As the league prepared for the short All-Star break, a tragic event marred the season when four minutes into a game between Minnesota and Oakland on January 13, Minnesota forward Bill Masterton was carrying the puck into the Seals zone. Shortly after completing a pass to teammate Wayne Connelly, he was hip checked by Oakland's Ron Harris and Larry Cahan, and fell to the ice head-first. Masterton lost consciousness immediately as blood gushed from his mouth and nose. He was rushed to hospital where he never recovered. He died two days later.

"It was a shocking event," recalled Pierre of Masterton's death. "I had got knocked out briefly before by Bob Pulford hitting me into the glass during the previous year's playoffs. Then the Masterton incident made me think twice and I thought it just made sense, to protect oneself. I told the trainer that I wanted a helmet. The first time I wore it was on the road in Montreal."

He joined the likes of Mikita, who had already been wearing one. Other players who would followe suit were Kenny Wharram and Doug Mohns.

"It was a big thing when you went onto the ice with a helmet," Pierre related. "I felt like everybody's eyes were on me because I didn't have an injury. I wasn't wearing it because I had an injury. It just made sense."

The 21st NHL All-Star Game in Toronto pitted the league's best against the champion Maple Leafs, and the All-Stars, including Pierre, won 4-3.

Reporter John Kuenster asked Pierre about the finicky Chicago fans who had taken to booing him, though he was not alone in receiving their wrath. "That's just the way fans are," Pierre shrugged. "They'll get on you for a while, and then, maybe, a game or so later, they'll be cheering for you."

Pierre told Kuenster that he felt that Detroit's Gordie Howe and Norm Ullman were toughest to take the puck from and Toronto's Ron Ellis and Dave Keon were the fastest players to defend against, and also told him that the most dangerous manoeuvre for any defenceman is to block slapshots.

"If you go down too soon," he said, "you worry about getting hit in the face."

As the Leafs enjoyed a pre-game skate at Chicago Stadium on the morning of February 6, Toronto's Jim Pappin skated up to Reay as the Chicago coach watched from the sidelines.

"How about making a deal for me?" Pappin joked to him half-seriously.

"I'd love to have you aboard," Reay answered.

The moment, unnoticed by all but a few, would have repercussions for the Hawks and Pierre, who was getting mixed signals that his Chicago playing days might be numbered.

"Tommy Ivan called me into the office one day, asking me what my plans were after hockey," recalled Pierre. "I had thought that I might be interested in coaching but then he talked about having to start at the bottom, like St. Catharines. I asked him how much a coach made in St. Catharines. When he told me, I knew I wouldn't be going into coaching. I wasn't about to starve my family. But that talk gave me an inkling that they no longer saw me on the ice with them in the future."

Then the booing got worse.

"It changed so suddenly, and then I couldn't do anything right," Pierre later told Toronto reporter Jim Proudfoot. "You'd like to think you could ignore the booing but you can't."

The Hawks limped towards the playoffs.

"Despite a fourth-place finish, the Hawks should give a good account of themselves in the playoffs if Bobby Hull and goalie Denis DeJordy are up to par physically," wrote Kuenster. "Still, prospects of the Hawks winning the Stanley Cup this season aren't too bright simply because they don't have enough depth."

Meanwhile Boston made the playoffs for the first time in a decade, led by Esposito's league-leading 84 points. The only bright spot for the Hawks was that centre Mikita had won another Art Ross as the league scoring champ, as well as the Hart as MVP and the Lady Byng for sportsmanship. While he and Bobby Hull had made the First All-Star Team, Reay's penchant for splitting up his two superstars worked against Chicago, as far as one of them was concerned.

"Pound for pound Stan Mikita was one of the greatest players of all time," recalled Hull. "If I could have only played with Stan more I would have scored 2,018 goals, not 1,018! Generally when I look back over the years, your best player on a team played with the next two best. Howe played with Lindsay and Abel; the Rocket played with the Pocket and Moore; Geoffrion played with Béliveau and Olmstead; Bathgate played with Prentice and Popie. Your best player played with the next two best—except in Chicago!"

The year-end All-Star team selections marked the first time Pierre had been left off in 11 years. The Hawk captain turned his attention to the upcoming playoffs and the second-place Rangers.

The series opened in Madison Square Garden, where the home team beat the visitors two straight. As the series shifted to Chicago, the assassination of Dr. Martin Luther King in Memphis on Thursday, April 4, 1968, put many American cities at the centre of the racial firestorm. Chicago was front and centre on the eve of the game, as race riots and looting broke out throughout the city, especially along Homan, Kedzie, and Madison avenues.

"I remember going to the Stadium with Mom and Dad and seeing police, soldiers, and army vehicles everywhere," said Pierre's son David. "That made quite an impact on a little five-year-old."

Against this backdrop, the tribe roared back and won the next two at home. In one game in Chicago, Rod Gilbert intercepted one of Pierre's passes and went in and scored. The boos rained down on him. The Hawks kept up the pressure and won the next two games to eliminate the plucky New Yorkers.

"We were lucky to knock them out," recalled Pierre of that series. "It was really unbelievable. Vic Hadfield played so well there. We were lucky to beat them."

Luck would be needed in their next series against the first-place Canadiens. The tribe got pounded 9-2 in the opening game at the Forum, in a game best summarized by coach Reay: "They were ready and we weren't."

Though the games were close, the Habs wound up allowing the Hawks only a fourth-game 2-1 victory, to eliminate them in five games. It had been a tough series for Pierre in many ways. He wasn't playing the power play as often as he had in the past, and yet the press noted that he had rebounded to play very well.

An idea floated in print on May 21 claimed that Pierre might be traded along with Dave Dryden to the L.A. Kings for Gord

Labossiere and Bob Wall. It was also claimed that the Leafs were interested in Pilote. Another scenario had him as the playing-coach with Chicago's Western League team in Denver.

To Pierre, it was all background noise that he didn't take seriously. His off-season focus was now on a car dealership, which he'd started in 1964, and his laundromat back in St. Catharines.

While on a business trip to Maywood, Illinois, on May 24, Pierre was reached by phone early in the morning by Red Burnett, a Toronto sports reporter.

"Hi Red, you've really tracked me down. What's up?"

"I'm calling to get your reaction to the trade."

"Trade? What trade?" Pierre asked.

"Oh, so you haven't heard?"

"Heard what? Who's been traded?"

"You have! You've been traded to Toronto . . . for Jim Pappin."

"You have to be kidding? Stop putting me on!"

"Sorry, Pierre. I'm not putting you on. Any comment?"

"Holy shit!" was all he could muster as he collected his thoughts. "You're sure about this?"

"Absolutely. I wouldn't call to joke about something like this."

"No, I guess not," Pierre said softly. He collected his thoughts.

"This is quite a shock," Pierre finally told him after a long pause. "But it's typical; the player is the last to know when a deal has been made. What can I say? Not that I didn't think about it, though. I have to admit I could feel it coming this past season. I was benched in spots in favour of younger players." Then he thought some more and added, "I'll give it my best as a Leaf. I hope I can fit the pattern and have a good season."

When he got off the phone, he began to wonder, you'd think the Hawks would have told me first. His business done, he drove home to tell Annie. She cried. Why hadn't the Hawks called? Weren't they like family?

An hour later the phone rang. It was Don Murphy, from public relations.

"Hey, I'm glad you're home, I've been trying to get you all day."

"Oh really? That's funny, Don, my wife has been here all day," Pierre answered sarcastically.

"Look, Pierre, I have bad news for you. You've been . . ."

"Traded? Yeah, I know," Pierre answered. "Red Burnett called me from Toronto asking for my reaction."

"I'm sorry, Pierre, but . . ."

"Goodbye, Don!" Pierre said angrily as he hung up. He couldn't believe he had been traded and even more, the manner in which it all went down.

"That was the biggest disappointment, the way I heard about it," he recalled sadly. "I had been the captain all those years. I thought I had a good relationship with Tommy and Billy. I had been loyal to the team, gone above and beyond the call of duty. But to hear it from Don Murphy, and not either of them, well, that was just so bush league. I just never thought I'd ever be traded like that!"

As he contemplated his life and new situation that afternoon, he became even angrier. After all that he had done for the Hawks, to be treated like this in the end? It was enough to make his blood boil. Toronto was on the way down. After winning the Cup in '67 they couldn't even make the playoffs this past season.

He contemplated not going, but he kept that to himself. Though Pierre didn't hear from anybody in the Leafs organization, there was plenty of print about the deal.

"We hated to part with Pilote," said Reay. "He was a great hockey player for us for 13 years, a tremendously loyal man, and a fine team captain. But I think the switch to Toronto will be good for him. The change of atmosphere should help. . . . There's no reason, though, that he couldn't work for us when he does decide to quit. He was a Black Hawk from his toes up and you can't forget that kind of loyalty."

When a reporter remarked to Toronto coach Punch Imlach that

he had given up youth in the 27-year-old Pappin for age and a high salary in the trade, Imlach balked.

"Pilote is not old!" Imlach crowed. "He's only 36—two years younger than Tim Horton, our best defenceman. I have said before I'm not interested in age or salary, just ability. I rate Pilote in the league's first eight—make that seven—defencemen. I think Pilote will have at least three good seasons with us. He was a little off last term, but still better than a number we had around. He could slip a little more and still be an improvement on our defence. He can move the puck out of his own zone and play the point on the power play. We need a man who can play that right point."

He was asked about Pilote making more mistakes and being booed by the Chicago fans. "You don't judge a player of Pilote's calibre on the basis of one season," said Imlach. "The fact they booed him might be a plus for me. He's got pride. He'll want to show a few people. He still got more points than any defenceman on my team last season. He was good enough to get on the Second All-Star Team at midseason. The change might give his glands an extra go. He knows that with us his age won't be any problem. We throw birth certificates in the waste basket. If I can get three more years out of Pilote I'll be happy."

As spring turned into summer, only Pierre knew that he had had enough.

He was going to retire.

CHAPTER 21

The Last Punch

"I wasn't going to Toronto! I was going to quit," recalled Pierre of those dark days after the trade. "Hockey had been my life and now I had to decide what else to do. The kids were still in school. I needed to find work. I still had my green card, so I wondered if I should just stay in the Chicago area to find work.

"I had a good friend named Albert Dick who owned a copying machine company and I went to see him. I was still torn up about the trade. I spent some time with him and he then sent me to see his sales manager. I thought maybe they were going to hire me or something, but no, this fella was like a counsellor of some kind. We talked and talked. At the end of our chat, he gave me these 45 LP records to listen to. Perhaps he could tell I was still torn about staying in hockey, about going to Toronto, even though my mind was made up. He said, 'Listen to these records before you truly make up your mind.'

"I went home and listened to those records, titled *Lead the Field*, by a motivational speaker named Earl Nightingale, who talked about life, about being upbeat, about making life decisions, about standing in front of a forest and not being able to see the trees. I listened and listened and most importantly, this speaker said it was important in life to recognize your strengths, to recognize your strong suits, and that it was important to go with your own flow, to use and stay with your natural God-given abilities.

"After listening to these records, I had second thoughts. Finally, I decided to stick with hockey. Annie, I, and the kids, we'd go to Toronto and make a go of it. And Annie was so devoted to me all the time. Going to Toronto was not a big thing for her at the end of the day. She was so used packing to go back to Fort Erie at the end of each season.

"It was hard for us to leave Chicago, of course—we had bought a house there and we had some friends, but we didn't have any sisters, brothers, or family to keep us there. And well, at the end of the day, we were coming back closer to home, to Fort Erie. I still had the car dealership, the laundromat, and I still had some buildings there. Toronto was closer. The longer I thought about it, the more it made sense. Now, if Chicago had traded me to Los Angeles that would have been a different story. It would have been in the wrong direction. In the end, Toronto made sense."

Pierre next turned his attention to his various enterprises: his hunting dogs, the car dealership, the laundromat, and his public relations firm, H-P-H. But the latter was now really just the "P."

"Glenn really didn't like public relations, going out and meeting people. That had never been his cup of tea," recalled Pierre. "And the Golden Jet was out flying on his own, doing his own thing, so I bought the two of them out." The company had other stars on board like baseball great Ferguson Jenkins and skier Jean Claude Killy.

After the kids finished school, the Pilotes said goodbye to friends, and adios to Chicago for the last time. They weren't back in Fort Erie long before they were relaxing at Cameron Lake again, swimming and fishing.

Pierre's tranquillity was broken by the letter that arrived in early August. It was a weird feeling to see letterhead with Maple Leaf Gardens instead of the head of Chief Black Hawk.

"We will start our training camp on Monday, September 16, at

Peterborough, Ontario. Headquarters will be the Empress Hotel," read the impersonal form letter from Leafs GM and coach, Punch Imlach. "You are to bring a pair of running shoes and gym shorts as you will be taking physical education starting Tuesday at 8:30 a.m. and every day during camp, by professional instructors from RMC [Royal Military College]. . . . I strongly suggest you report to camp in the best physical condition. No arrangements have been made for golf. You can use your car at any time. No wives are permitted at training camp."

What was different for Pierre was the physical conditioning. It was something that Billy Reay would never have had in Chicago, but Pierre knew Punch's penchant for hard work, especially for the veterans. It kept them young, Punch believed. It was his first actual contact from the Leafs organization.

"I never heard a word from them. Not a call, letter, hello, nothing!" recalled Pierre. Just before camp, Mike Pelyk was the first representative of the Leafs to meet Pilote in person. "Before training camp, Mike came riding in on his motorcycle to visit me," said Pierre. "We talked and became good friends. It made me feel a little better as training camp loomed."

Just as the school year was about to commence in September, the Pilotes settled into a nice bungalow in the Port Credit part of Mississauga, to the west of Toronto.

New York hockey writer Stan Fischler penned a piece on Pierre and wondered whether he'd make it as a Leaf. In the article, Fischler went over Pierre's stellar career as one of the NHL's best defencemen, his tough but now more refined play, and his diminishing penchant for the rough stuff.

"Those who personally know Pilote believe there's plenty of dynamism left in the body to produce a winner," wrote Fischler. "Whether or not Pilote will help the Leafs—and vice versa— remains to be seen, but this much is certain . . . the flame burning inside Pierre will push him to exert every ounce of energy at his command. And he'll fight if he has to, whether it's against the new boys or the old. It's a part of him."

At camp, the 36-year-old Pilote had aged company in a defence corps that featured Tim Horton, 38, Marcel Pronovost, 37, and goalie Johnny Bower, 43. His $42,500 per season contract from Chicago was carried over.

Interestingly, many miles away from Peterborough, Reay was having trouble appointing a new Hawks captain. Knowing he couldn't choose Bobby Hull over Stan Mikita or vice versa, he suggested that he may not appoint one in Pilote's absence: "There is no rule that says a team has to have one," he said. It spoke volumes about Pierre's missing leadership.

"I was sorry to see Pierre go to Toronto," Bobby Hull was quoted as saying at the time. "People were getting on Pierre's back in Chicago. They soon forgot all those years when he was the best defencemen in hockey. I hope he has a big year in Toronto!"

The Leafs were getting a sound Pierre Pilote. "I can't understand how Chicago let such a healthy specimen get away," said Dr. Hugh Smythe, shaking his head as he patted Pierre on the shoulder after the customary physical exam.

"Thanks, doc," Pierre answered nasally. "But I need something for this hay fever."

The doctor wrote him a prescription and Pierre headed to trainer Tommy Naylor's room, to get skates and sticks. After fitting him for new blades, Pierre had to contend with using Mike Walton's sticks until Naylor could get some of his from Chicago.

"It's strange walking in here after 14 seasons with the Black Hawks," Pierre told writer Red Burnett. "In Chicago, training camp was like returning home. You knew everyone. Here, everything is new. [Chicago] was a small camp. Here, there's a young army. How do you get to know everybody? I guess it will take time to break old habits.

"I expect to have a few good seasons with this club. I've been pretty lucky in life. There's usually something better for me around the corner."

Due to his stardom and newcomer status, Pierre was often sought out by the press but he was finding it hard to remember that he was now a Maple Leaf.

"You know, when you look at things, they weren't that bad a hockey team in fact," Pierre told the *Globe and Mail* before realizing his mistake and stopping. "Whoa! I should say 'we' weren't that bad a hockey team. You know it's going to take a while . . . when you've worn that red uniform for so many years it's going to be funny putting on the blue. I'll probably walk into the wrong room when we go to Chicago!"

When he was told that the Leafs had seven Sunday nights off this season, Pierre's smile broadened. "Home on a Sunday night? Really? I can't believe it!"

As for how well Chicago might do, he grinned and replied, "No comment!"

After four days of practising and land training, Pierre was feeling his age.

"This camp is a much tougher camp than in Chicago," he admitted to reporter Don Edwards. "There are a lot more fellows trying out for this team and there are so many good young players. This is my fourth day of training and I'm no kid anymore.

"If all goes well I could have three or four good years of hockey left. In any event, I'll be giving it my best for the Leafs and I just can't see this team missing the playoffs this year. I'm sure this team will be in top shape by the time the opening game rolls around."

Though it seemed the Leafs were happy to have Pierre on board, the ex-Hawk soon found out that he wasn't completely welcomed by all his new teammates.

"In Chicago, my play was to pass the puck to the winger, then I'd step into a hole and he'd give it back to me. Classic give-and-go, right?" Pierre recalled. "In my first exhibition game with Toronto, I passed it to Mike Walton and I took off but he passed it behind me.

The other team picked up the puck, went in, and scored. Okay, so the next time, I don't take off, I make the pass and stay right where I was. Well, guess what? He passed the puck ahead to where I should have been! Right then and there I thought, 'Oh boy, the old animosities are coming back to haunt me. It'll take quite a while to be accepted!'

"I had not been the easiest player to play against, and especially against Toronto, I had never taken any prisoners, so I came in being very disliked by some players. You just don't change that overnight—if ever."

What also alienated Pierre to a certain extent was his habit of driving back to his trailer in Fenelon Falls each evening instead of going out for a few beers with the boys. He would return to the Empress Hotel to sleep, before curfew. Besides, he wasn't too crazy about his roommate.

"I was rooming with Bob Pulford. I swear he was spying on me for Punch," Pierre said. "Thank God I only had to room with him during training camp. That didn't help my impression of Toronto."

He had to give up his familiar sweater no. 3, as it belonged to Pronovost, who was entering his fourth campaign as a Leaf. "There was nothing said, but it was just understood," recalled Pierre. "I was just handed no. 2."

Pierre had some early crow to eat as his former teammates beat the Leafs 2-1 at the Gardens on a Saturday night before the two teams returned to the Stadium the following day. For Pierre, the visit was disconcerting to say the least.

"The first game we played in Chicago, I took the faceoff against Pit Martin in our end and little Pit made me look silly," Pierre grimaced. "I thought he would drag the puck back, but no, he pushed it ahead through me, stepped around me, and got a clean shot away. I didn't feel too good about that and the fans razzed me good."

Despite the early mistake, Pierre enacted some revenge by helping his team defeat the Hawks 3-1 and got something back against Martin.

"Former Hawks defenceman Pierre Pilote has been Leafs best blueliner during the pre-season games and was sharp against his former teammates," wrote the *Globe and Mail*'s Louis Cauz. "He was especially good at separating Hull and Stan Mikita from the puck. Pilote also dealt the hardest bodycheck when he belted centre Pit Martin."

"I knew what he was going to do," explained Pilote.

As the new NHL season dawned, the pundits gave their predictions of the various teams. St. Louis Blues managing director Lynn Patrick picked the Canadiens with their deep talent pool to end up on top in the East, but predicted the Maple Leafs would end up in second place.

"Patrick feels Leafs assured themselves of a playoff berth when they acquired defenceman Pierre Pilote from Chicago," wrote Red Burnett in the *Toronto Star*. "'Toss out his form of last season with Hawks,' Patrick commented. 'That Chicago crowd killed him. I predict he'll duel Boston's Bobby Orr for the best defenceman award. Pilote will be the best point-man Leafs have had since Max Bentley.'"

Pierre himself wasn't so sure. He found the adjustment difficult.

"I had a hard time the first weeks and months with Toronto. I would pass the puck, and yell to get it back but the puck would go somewhere else and then I'd be caught out of position. I had to change my style, so I had a hard time. Maybe the old animosities. Who knew?"

It was tough to come to a team of wily veterans against whom he had waged war all those years. But there was no animosity with his new defence partner and roommate.

"Mike Pelyk and I got along good and he became a good friend of mine," recalled Pierre. "Pat Quinn was friendly. I had a lot of fun with Jim Dorey. Marcel Pronovost was quiet, kept to himself. Tim Horton was busy doing his own business. Ullman was a quiet guy. Ron Ellis was just starting out. It was a real different mix of players and personalities."

The Leafs stormed out of the gate, winning five of their first six games and allowing only 13 goals against, but they sputtered in their next two at home, losing 5-0 against the Canadiens and 3-2 versus the Philadelphia Flyers, losses attributed to goofs on the blue line.

"It takes awhile," Pierre explained to *Toronto Star* reporter Jim Crerar after a Leafs practice at the Tam O'Shanter Arena. "I used to be paired with Elmer Vasko. I knew exactly what Elmer would do. That's the whole secret. The key is knowing how to cover up the mistakes. We've made a couple of obvious ones, but as long as Mike [Pelyk] works for me and I work for him, we'll be okay. We're getting closer, and closer, although we haven't quite reached the point where we make our moves automatically. It will be soon enough.

"I like breaking in the young guys. They're eager and want to learn. By helping them I'm helping myself. After all, I'm only as good as the man I'm working with."

A week later, Pierre's students had to fly on their own when Pierre suffered strained knee ligaments in a 1-1 tie against the Bruins on November 13 that laid him up for over a week.

Pierre and his clan were settling nicely into their new life with the Leafs and Pierre was finding their Mississauga home convenient for both the airport and to drive into Toronto for games and practices. The yard was large enough to accommodate their 22-foot trailer and he found the area quaint and quiet enough to build a dog kennel for Trophy and his newest acquisition, "Hobby," a name given by Annie because she ended up caring for the puppy, even though the dog was supposed to be "Pierre's Hobby."

"My dogs had been staying with a professional dog trainer and I was running them in the field trial circuit there, but when I came to Toronto, I took my dogs with me," recalled Pierre. "I used to train them in Mississauga in a big empty field where there were a lot of pheasant and I trained them to hunt."

The kids had their own hobbies as well. Denise, now 13, was taking figure skating lessons, 11-year-old Pierre Jr. was taking piano lessons, while eight-year-old Renee was taking dance lessons. It meant Annie spent a lot of time as the family taxi, Pierre helping where he could. Annie had also lately been actively seeking a new local stable to continue horseback riding and jumping, using the new saddle Pierre had surprised her with the previous Christmas.

"I get very sentimental on Tuesday and Friday mornings, since those were the days when I used to go horseback riding in Chicago," Annie said in an edition of the *Maple Leafs Official Program*. Ironically, that night the Leafs were hosting the Black Hawks. Writer Margaret Scott asked her about her husband's trade.

"I feel we were part of a great rebuilding process," Annie said. "[Chicago] grew stronger as individual stars emerged and tickets were at a premium by the time we left. Players come to expect [being traded] almost every year. One begins to see the hand-writing on the wall and there's an instinctive warning that it's time for a change. I learned to enjoy Chicago and I felt sad when we left our friends, but one cannot dwell on the past. I'm already used to Toronto and I like it so much we bought a house in Port Credit before the season started."

"Anne, who located a babysitter almost as soon as they settled in their new home, likes to leave for the Gardens at 6:15 with her husband," concluded the article. "She still likes Pierre's former teammates but won't feel particularly sentimental when Chicago meets the Leafs tonight. When she had a telephone chat with Mrs. Jean Wharram a few weeks ago she issued this soft-hearted warning, 'You'd better look out, because we're going to smear you!'"

The Leafs, without Pierre, handily beat the tribe 3-1 to move four points ahead of the fifth-place Hawks. Pierre returned four games later, and potted his first two goals of the season against the Pittsburgh Penguins, 4-1, on December 8.

Like his teammate Tim Horton, Pierre's attention was shifting more and more to other businesses. "Pierre Pilote's profession is hockey. His sideline is collecting and investing in successful busi-nesses," wrote Louis Cauz. Pierre told the reporter the importance of having a successful business was choosing a knowledgeable busi-ness partner. "Basically, I'm a hockey player. What do I know about running a car dealership? So I get myself a guy who knows the business; a good, willing, honest partner. Somebody who owns a restaurant would look silly trying to compete with me on the ice, wouldn't he?"

Alienated on a team he found difficult to fit in with, Pierre felt he was still viewed as a Black Hawk and the dressing room got quiet when he was there. As a social personality, he found the misgivings hard to take. Still, he gave his all while enjoying teaching Pelyk the finer points of defence and helping catapult the Leafs to an amazing streak where they picked up 15 of 16 points in their next eight games, ending with a loss to the Red Wings on December 22.

Pierre found a new business that he viewed as a money maker. While Horton peddled coffee and doughnuts, Pierre was looking at luggage.

He saw an ad in the business section of a Toronto newspaper; Tony Waszczuk, an Englishman of Polish descent, was seeking an investor for his small luggage company located in the High Park district of Toronto.

"Tony was in his fifties and he'd been in the luggage business for quite a while," recalled Pierre. "Before I knew it, as Christmas of 1969 approached, I was really into the luggage and bag business, but secretly. I didn't tell a soul, only Annie. It was a challenge and I always loved a challenge—while still playing hockey for the Leafs, which was also a challenge."

A new tradition at home was started—Christmas lights on the new house. Having always rented in Chicago, Christmas lights were just something he never had to contend with, but this was his new life in the land of ice and snow. The lights were put up.

Pierre's present was a Christmas Day Leafs win in Chicago, 4-3.

"I didn't talk very much to anyone. It was a hard year. Davey Keon was a hard egg to figure out and Mike Walton kept trying to make me look bad," confessed Pierre. "Tim Horton was having a hell of a year, his best ever. It was great to see. Pat Quinn was playing in his first year and we got along great, but by Christmas my mind was way off playing. I was trying to start this luggage business and I wasn't talking to anybody about it, not even Mike Pelyk, who I got along great with. On the road, he could never figure out why I kept shopping at all these luggage stores and he'd ask me why I was buying all these bags and I'd answer that Annie loved bags. He never caught on."

Imlach suspended Mike Walton towards the end of the season. "Mike Walton was really disruptive to the team," Pierre recalled. "He caused a lot of grief particularly for Punch Imlach. Mike had a lot of ability, but he never really played up to his potential. He was not a great backchecker either and this and his lack of effort really made Punch crazy. But he was a tough guy; he could throw the punches."

The Leafs played only .500 hockey down the stretch to finish the season in fourth place with 85 points, making the playoffs while the Hawks finished dead last with 77 points. Toronto would face second-place Boston.

"The year after we traded Pierre away, the Leafs made the play-offs and we didn't," lamented Bobby Hull. "What does that tell you about that trade, eh? That pretty well sums it all up right there. That goes to show you what Pierre had meant to our team!"

Pierre's record for single-season points by a defenceman was toppled on March 16, when Bobby Orr got his 60th point. Pierre, who got 21 points in 69 games, his lowest point total since his first full year in the league, could only watch in admiration.

"When Orr came towards you with the puck, you had to think quickly, start backpedalling and fast," noted Pierre. "If you didn't, he was by you in a flash. You couldn't skate backwards in defending against him—he'd be by you! Not too many guys could get by me like that but he could!"

The Bruins gave the Leafs a 10-0 walloping in the first game, a wild affair where Quinn decked Orr and Boston goalie Gerry Cheevers fought with Forbes Kennedy.

"It was an awful game," Pierre recalled. "Quinn hit Orr right about 10 feet inside the blue line and that was it. What little flame we had just got blown out. Nobody wanted to go over the boards after that. From that point, we were getting physically beaten, bullied, it was just awful. Boston was coming on, they had some pretty tough guys and they came back hard. Punch had to push our guys out, except Forbes, he was not afraid of anything. I think he got into four fights that night and hit a linesman. But Boston had talent."

In the second game in Boston, the Leafs were hammered 7–0, and then swept away at home at the Gardens. After the last game, Leafs owner Stafford Smythe wasted no time in firing Imlach. It was the end of an era.

As the players left the rink that night, little did anyone know that another remarkable era was drawing to a close. Pierre had decided to retire. He had had enough. It didn't matter that when the Leafs left him unprotected, he was picked up by the AHL Buffalo Bisons for $15,000. He was retiring. Or so he planned.

Emile Francis, general manager of the New York Rangers, called him one day requesting a meeting. Pierre wondered what was up the Cat's sleeve.

"Emile asked me to lunch at the Royal York Hotel," Pierre remembered. "It became clear that he had engineered the Bisons to draft me as he was tied into Buffalo."

"Pierre, I want you to come to New York. I want you to sign a two-way contract so that you can come to New York and work with my young defencemen. Pierre you could teach them so much. I can offer you more money than you've ever made."

To Pierre, money was never the issue.

"Cat, I'm sorry, I'm retiring. My heart is not in it anymore. It wasn't this year at all," Pierre told him. "I would be stealing your money. I wouldn't be able to give you 100% and that wouldn't be fair to you. I've started a travelware and luggage company and my heart is in that. That's my future."

Francis tried for over an hour to get Pierre to change his mind—to no avail. Without any hoopla, or announcements, the storied career of one of the greatest defencemen of all time was over.

Pierre Pilote had walked out of the game he loved.

CHAPTER 22

Where Have You Gone, Pierre Pilote?

"Hello, International Travelware, Pierre Pilote speaking," was the greeting at his new venture.

Unlike a lot of retiring NHLers who had to deal with the sudden changes in their lifestyle, finances, and state of mind, 38-year-old Pierre Pilote always had a plan and he hit his retirement running. There was no fanfare, no teary-eyed press conference, and no goodbyes. One morning he simply got up and instead of going to the rink, he headed to his luggage factory, just like that. And Annie knew better than to think that she would have him around the house.

Like everything he did in his life, Pierre brought his enthusiasm and determination to his travelware company. His notoriety helped build up a business that soon had 30 employees making luggage bags in a 20,000 square-foot Toronto factory, but it only went so far.

"Sure my name opened doors but then you've got to produce, and we produced," he told writer Barry Conn Hughes. "We finish our products well here. I'm a rookie right now but I wanna be the Tote Bag King of Canada!"

Like his early hockey career, he learned from his mistakes about a business he knew little about. But one thing was typical Pilote: he wanted to be different and he wanted to be the best.

After researching and talking to experts in the business he

developed his own vinyl line, with his own colours and piping, which he sold to the Whitmore Luggage Company store near Maple Leaf Gardens. Most importantly, he used his contacts at Simpsons-Sears from the Sports Advisory Council to secure a meeting.

"We went and presented our products to Sears and they took it," Pierre recalled. "We were just rolling our line out and they sold like crazy. I found it financially tough as my partner made the bags, he knew nothing about costs, and I was backing the operation, as well as being the designer, the salesman, the cost accountant, and I wrote the cheques! Whew!"

Hockey wasn't completely out of his system. After turning down an offer to play for Canada's national team, feeling he couldn't devote the time to get into shape, he instructed players on Pierre Jr.'s Toronto Olympic Elks minor bantam team and then later, his Dixie Beehive midget team.

At the beginning of the 1969–70 NHL season, the media seemed to hardly notice that Pierre had retired. Louis Cauz of the *Globe and Mail* figured it out and cornered Pierre in December 1969 for his first interview since leaving the game.

"I'm settled here in Toronto now. . . . The trade proved to me one thing," Pierre told Cauz. "When you're no longer an asset, it is goodbye Charlie. My only knock against the Hawks is that they didn't come to my rescue when I was booed by the fans. I tried to help Dennis Hull when they got on him. I told them to get off his butt and get on me, I'm used to it. But nobody helped me.

"My wife tells me that when I get up to go to work now, I'm like a rookie. As far as I'm concerned, I'm a minor leaguer until I build this business up. Funny, most wives complain about their husbands being away so much when they're playing hockey. Now I spend more time away than when I was playing. But I've retired. I came into the NHL quietly and I've left the same way."

With his company rolling along, Pierre and Annie bought a 90-acre farm on the 4th line of Halton Hills, north of Milton, Ontario, in August 1973, and settled into rural living. It had an eight-sided gazebo barn to store farm equipment. Now Annie was able to ride her horse to her heart's content.

Another challenge was the restoration of the 10-room farm house, which would become Pierre's pride and joy after he returned it to its turn-of-the-century glory. The farm also enabled him to properly kennel his dogs and thus expand his participation in field trials. Pierre also became a director of the German Short-Haired Pointers Club of Ontario.

On June 8, 1975, it was announced that Pierre Pilote would be inducted into the Hockey Hall of Fame alongside George Armstrong and Glenn Hall. The ceremony took place on August 28 of that year.

"Making the Hall of Fame was the biggest hockey thrill," he said in a story about him in a 1977 edition of *Maple Leaf Magazine*. "I'm proud of that. . . . Loyalty in hockey doesn't mean a thing, but I don't carry a grudge. It was a fair exchange. I gave everything I had to the game and it gave me everything. Hockey owes me nothing. I owe it nothing."

In January 1981, Fort Erie inducted him into its Sports Hall of Fame and many of his old baseball and hockey buddies were in attendance. Thirty years later, the Chicago Sports Hall of Fame followed suit.

The first Original Six Old-Timer Tournament was held in Markham, Ontario, in summer 1981. Answering the call to play, Pierre dusted off the skates and was chosen captain of the Black Hawk team that included the likes of Pat Stapleton, Bill White, Stan Mikita, Dennis Hull, Keith Magnusson, Jim Pappin, Gerry Desjardins, and Gary Smith. Old rivalries never die, and the Hawks played hard in defeating the Canadiens old-timers 1-0 in the championship game to win a trip to the Caribbean. From the tournament, writer Ross Brewitt organized the "Old Stars" to play a series of exhibition games throughout Canada to raise funds for various causes. Pierre joined the group and for three years, they played in venues from Amherst, Nova Scotia, to Kamloops, British Columbia, averaging 35 games a season.

The NHL brought him back into the spotlight in spring 1982 when he was asked to attend an awards ceremony in Montreal, where he presented the Norris Trophy for best defenceman to Doug Wilson of the Hawks. Pierre's presence excited Wilson almost as much as the trophy.

Having already sold the car dealership, Pierre next sold the laundromat, H-P-H, and the luggage company, and, as of 1986, he did nothing. He did try his hand at a Tim Hortons restaurant franchise for a few years, but that didn't pan out.

Wherever he went, the fans still remembered him and never hesitated to tell him how much they loved—or hated—watching him play. Whenever people commented that the new hockey was "not as good as in the old days," he was always careful in his response, but he never hesitated to say that the fans were the most important part of the game and should never be forgotten.

"They have to reach a point where they have to say no [to higher salaries] because what's important is the fan," he told writer Ronald Zajac around this time.

When Belleville honoured local hero Bobby Hull shortly after his retirement, they invited his former teammates to play in an exhibition game. Pierre went but, having been off skates for too long, had his son Pierre Jr. play for him.

"After the game, we all went back to the hotel to get ready to go out for dinner," recalled Pierre Jr. "We never got to go out because all the players started to gather in Mom and Dad's room. It was packed. The drinks started flowing, the stories were flying, and oh the laughter! What a night that was!

"But what stood out to me the most was how much Dad was the centre of attention and how much they adored my mom. They all told me, increasingly as the night went on, that Dad was their leader, he was 'the guy,' the 'heart of the Black Hawks.' To hear and witness that first-hand was inspiring and made me so proud."

In the early 1990s, Pierre put the skates on again, playing with the "Heroes of Hockey" and he and Annie were regular guests at the NHL All-Star Games and attended the Hockey Hall of Fame ceremonies every year, something he thoroughly enjoyed.

His requests for appearances picked up as the millennium approached and he attended many celebrity events and golf tournaments. In the late 1990s, with the kids all grown up and gone, he and Annie sold the farm and settled down in a new home in the small northern hamlet of Wyevale, Ontario, in Simcoe County, to be near some of the family.

In 1998, *The Hockey News* published its top 100 list of all-time greats. Pierre was listed as number 59. Years later *The Hockey News* published its 20 all-time list of players at each position. Amongst defencemen, Pierre was listed as 19th, prompting his old buddy Glenn Hall to call and tell him, "Pierre, you should have been much higher!"

In 2005, Canada Post selected Pierre to be honoured on a series of six postage stamps, alongside Grant Fuhr, Henri Richard, Allan Stanley, Johnny Bucyk, and Bryan Trottier. He made several appearances at autograph sessions promoting the stamps.

That same year, with the NHL lockout having wiped out the previous season, the Stanley Cup had no victors to parade it around. The Hockey Hall of Fame allowed some of the old-timers who had won it but never got to bring Stanley home for a day, as is now the custom, to do so. Pierre was on the list.

Thirty years to the day of his induction to the Hockey Hall of Fame, Pierre and Annie hosted the Stanley Cup at a nearby hall and invited the community to come and see it through the afternoon of August 28, 2005. That evening they hosted a special supper for family and friends. It was a special night too because Pierre and Annie turned it into a mini 50th wedding anniversary gathering, with Stanley as the special guest!

"We hope that the heritage of the Stanley Cup has made your day as special as it has been for our family," Pierre started. Then he turned his thoughts to the player lockout.

"I see the players are now going back to work," he continued.

"As far as I'm concerned, the players make way too much money. I'm not mad at them—no sir! In fact, I'm mad at my mother! She should have had me later in life. Then maybe I could have earned that same kind of money. Man, would we have a party then!"

He thanked his family and friends for sharing this special day with them, but he saved the warmest words in thanking his wonderful wife, Annie, for all her support in the past 50 years.

"If it weren't for Annie," he said with a smirk, "I'd've gone through life thinking I had no faults!" Nobody laughed harder than the former Teepees fan from St. Catharines.

His biggest fan, Annie Greshchyshyn, passed away in May 2012. As he told friends and family the day of her Celebration of Life: "One cannot accomplish anything in life, without the support of family. I was fortunate all these years to have somebody supporting me and understanding me, like Annie. She allowed me to concentrate on being the best I could be. I will miss Anne the person but I am very fortunate that there is a lot of Anne's DNA in our four children, Denise, Pierre, Renee, and David, and also in our 10 beautiful grandchildren. They have been my greatest support. I love you all very much and when I am with you, I am still with her . . .

"Thank you, Annie. I will always love you!"

"Mom had been the glue at home," recalled daughter Denise. "She was our taxi everywhere when Dad was away and made sure things ran smoothly. She made sure that we were dressed properly and when she went out she always looked so beautiful. We had our chores and Dad did too when he would come back from a road trip. He might have been the captain of the Hawks, but she was the captain at home! But there was so much love. Dad wasn't the warm, fuzzy type but Mom made up for that.

"How well we turned out was directly attributable to the love, security, and support of our parents! And we were so proud of them."

Pierre and Annie raised a fine family.

The oldest, Denise, studied to be a dental hygienist and eventually became an office manager. She has two children and married Doug Worsley. (No relation to the Gumper.)

Pierre Jr. got into the media business as a production assistant but now owns his own catering business. He has three children with wife Anita.

Daughter Renee became a registered nurse and has one child with husband Dr. William Bateman.

"What can I say about my mom and dad?" said Renee. "They were just so supportive, especially my mother. She drove me to all my practices and competitions! They taught us a lot about life. And I've always been so proud of what my dad accomplished."

The youngest, David, also became a media technician. He is married to Charlene and they have four children.

"My parents raised us to be sensible and that gave us all a good base from which to grow. And Dad was a great listener and knew how to pick someone's brain to get new knowledge. He taught us to always learn something new each and every day. Great advice."

For many years in Chicago, former players—even those with their numbers retired to the rafters of the United Center—felt ostracized. All that changed in fall 2007, when long-time Hawks president "Dollar Bill" Wirtz passed away. When his son Rocky took over, he moved immediately to rebuild the franchise. His first order of business was reassigning long-time Hawks vice-president and general manager Bob Pulford, who had often been seen as a disruptive force around the team, and brought in former Chicago Cubs executive John McDonough.

"Before this franchise can move forward," McDonough said, "we have to step backward and extend ourselves to the Golden Era, and Bobby Hull and Stan Mikita are pillars of that era."

The two men were made Hawks ambassadors and put on the payroll to help bring back enthusiasm from the fan base, new and old. Another part of that mission was to extend an olive branch to other stars such as Glenn Hall, Tony Esposito, and Denis Savard, who had been recognized and had their numbers retired. But there was a big piece of the puzzle still missing: Pierre Pilote, whose number should have been retired long ago but wouldn't have been with Pulford around.

Along with other current and past players, Pierre was invited to a Blackhawks convention intended to reinvigorate the organization and its fan base.

In summer 2008, the Hawks held their first "Hawkfest" weekend at the Chicago Hilton. McDonough announced that the Hawks would be retiring no. 3 to the rafters of the United Center that fall in honour of Pierre and the late Keith Magnusson.

"I think because he waited so long for the jersey's retirement, it'll really be huge," commented Glenn Hall. "He was a great player and he's earned this honour."

It was the concluding chapter on a fabulous and unparalleled career: 498 points, 890 games played, five First All-Star Teams, three Second All-Star Teams, single season points record for a defenceman (pre-1967 expansion), three Norris Trophies as best defenceman, three Norris runner-ups, playoff point leader (1961), and induction into the Hockey Hall of Fame.

The ceremony honouring two captains, Pilote and Magnusson, took place prior to the Chicago-Boston game on November 12, 2008. Pierre, Annie, and their children were brought out on a red carpet to centre ice, as was the Magnusson family.

"Tonight, we welcome two of the Blackhawks' greatest defencemen into the pantheon of the Blackhawks family: Pierre Pilote and Keith Magnusson," began Chairman Rocky Wirtz. "Pierre, you inspired an entire generation of defencemen who watched you play and tried to copy your style and, most importantly, you brought the Stanley Cup to Chicago. Pierre, thanks for all you've done for the Blackhawks and this great city."

For Pierre, the moment was surreal as he stepped up to the microphone to address the crowd, surrounded by some of his former teammates and past Hawks.

"I can't tell you what a special evening this has truly been. It reminds me of the importance of teammates, friends, and most of all, family. To my own family, my wife, Anne, my confidante and best friend; thank you for sharing my highs and lows, in my pursuit of being the best hockey player I could be. I love you. To my four children, Denise, Pierre, Renee, and David, I am so proud to share this night with you. I feel very blessed these many years later, that on this night, I am able to share this with my grandchildren."

When he was almost out of breath in rhyming off the names of all 10, the crowd laughed and cheered. He thanked his brothers and sisters, his coaches, his teammates Hull, Mikita, Wharram, and Hall, who he called, "the best goaltender that I ever saw." Then there was the late Elmer Vasko: "Because he was the ultimate, steady defenceman, Moose allowed me to be who I was. Thank you, Moose. This night I share with you!

"All these people have taught me that when you win and do great things, you do it as a family, we do it together. A team is family. The fans are family. The old Chicago Stadium and that fabulous atmosphere, all this was part of my family.

"To all of you here, my Chicago family, from the bottom of my heart, thank you! It is wonderful to be back in this great city, a city that holds a special place for me. A part of my heart will always be here. So tonight, I stand proudly with Keith, who is surely with us, and we say thank you. Thank you, Chicago!"

PIERRE PILOTE'S CAREER STATISTICS

Season	Team	League	No.	GP	G	A	P	PIM	GP	G	A	P	PIM
				REGULAR SEASON					**PLAYOFFS**				
1949-1950	Niagara Falls Cataracts	OHA-JR. B		--	--	--	--	--	--	--	--	--	--
1950-1951	St. Catharines Teepees	OHA-JR A	5	54	13	14	27	230	9	2	2	4	23
1951-1952	St. Catharines Teepees	OHA-JR A	5	52	21	32	53	139	14	3	12	15	50
	Buffalo Bisons	AHL		2	0	1	1	4	--	--	--	--	--
1952-1953	Buffalo Bisons	AHL	15	61	2	14	16	85	--	--	--	--	--
1953-1954	Buffalo Bisons	AHL	4	67	2	28	30	108	3	0	0	0	6
1954-1955	Buffalo Bisons	AHL	4	63	10	28	38	120	10	0	4	4	18
1955-1956	Chicago Black Hawks	NHL	21	20	3	5	8	34	--	--	--	--	--
	Buffalo Bisons	AHL	4	43	0	11	11	118	5	0	2	2	4
1956-1957	Chicago Black Hawks	NHL	21	70	3	14	17	117	--	--	--	--	--
1957-1958	Chicago Black Hawks	NHL	21	70	6	24	30	91	--	--	--	--	--
1958-1959	Chicago Black Hawks	NHL	3	70	7	30	37	79	6	0	2	2	10
1959-1960	Chicago Black Hawks	NHL	3	70	7	38	45	100	4	0	1	1	8
1960-1961	Chicago Black Hawks	NHL	3	70	6	29	35	165	12	3	12	15	8
1961-1962	Chicago Black Hawks	NHL	3	59	7	35	42	97	12	0	7	7	8
1962-1963	Chicago Black Hawks	NHL	3	59	8	18	26	57	6	0	8	8	8
1963-1964	Chicago Black Hawks	NHL	3	70	7	46	53	84	7	2	6	8	6
1964-1965	Chicago Black Hawks	NHL	3	68	14	45	59	162	12	0	7	7	22
1965-1966	Chicago Black Hawks	NHL	3	51	2	34	36	60	6	0	2	2	10
1966-1967	Chicago Black Hawks	NHL	3	70	6	46	52	90	6	2	4	6	6
1967-1968	Chicago Black Hawks	NHL	3	74	1	36	37	69	11	1	3	4	12
1968-1969	Toronto Maple Leafs	NHL	2	69	3	18	21	46	4	0	1	1	4
	TOTALS			1232	128	546	674	2055	127	13	73	86	203
	NHL TOTALS			890	80	418	498	1251	86	8	53	61	102

(Courtesy of the Society for International Hockey Research. For more information, visit sihrhockey.org.)

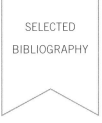
In addition to the extremely useful periodicals *Hockey Illustrated*, *Star Weekly*, *Blackhawks Magazine*, *Chicago Stadium Review*, and the Blackhawks yearbook and the DVD recording *The Forgotten Champs: The Story of the 1961 Stanley Cup Champion Chicago Black Hawks* (Sundown Entertainment, 2006), the following books were valuable references during the creation of *Heart of the Blackhawks*.

Adrahtas, Tom. *Glenn Hall: The Man They Call Mr. Goalie*. Douglas & McIntyre, 2003.

Béliveau, Jean, with Chrys Goyens and Allan Turowetz. *Jean Béliveau: My Life in Hockey*. Greystone Books, 2005.

Brown, William. *Doug: The Doug Harvey Story*. Vehicule Press, 2002.

Cole, Stephen. *The Last Hurrah: A Celebration of Hockey's Greatest Season '66–'67*. Penguin Canada, 1996.

Coleman, Charles L. *Trail of the Stanley Cup Volume 3: 1947–1967*. NHL, 1976.

Dupuis, David Michael. *Sawchuk: The Troubles and Triumphs of the World's Greatest Goalie*. Stoddart, 1998.

Esposito, Phil, and Peter Golenbock. *Thunder and Lightning: A No-B.S. Hockey Memoir*. McClelland & Stewart, 2004.

Ferguson, John, with Stan and Shirley Ferguson. *Thunder and Lightning*. Prentice Hall, 1989.

Fisher, Red. *Hockey, Heroes and Me*. McClelland & Stewart, 1994.

Geoffrion, Bernard, and Stan Fischler. *Boom Boom: The Life and Times of Bernard Geoffrion*. McGraw-Hill Ryerson, 1972.

Hewitt, John. *Garden City Hockey Heroes* (*Hewitt on Hockey Volume 1*). Mr. Books, 2008.

Hull, Bobby, and Bob Verdi. *The Golden Jet.* Triumph Books, 2010.

Jenish, D'Arcy. *Montreal Canadiens: 100 Years of Glory.* Anchor Canada, 2009.

McFarlane, Brian. *The Blackhawks: Brian McFarlane's Original Six.* Stoddart, 2001.

Mikita, Stan, and Bob Verdi. *Forever a Blackhawk.* Triumph Books, 2011.

Pfeiffer, Gerald L. *Chicago Blackhawks: A Sixty-Year History 1926–1986.* Windy City, 1987.

Storey, Red, and Brodie Snyder. *Red's Story.* Seal Books, 1995.

Vass, George. *The Chicago Black Hawks Story.* Follett Publishing Company, 1970.

Warchocki, Tim. *Before the Blade: The Complete History of the Buffalo Bisons.* RAMA Publishing, 1999.

Wittenberg, Harvey, and Bruce Wolf. *Tales from the Chicago Blackhawks Locker Room: A Collection of the Greatest Blackhawks Stories Ever Told.* Sports Publishing, 2012.

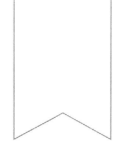

Acknowledgements

After many years of trying to get our good friend Pierre to tell his remarkable story, we have finally collaborated on just that. It goes without saying that it took much more than the three of us to bring this book together.

We thank Annie for her kindness, generosity, friendship, memories, and insight in helping us tell her husband's story. She was proud of being involved and she was as proud of Pierre as he was of her. Her collection of newspaper articles about her husband's career enabled us to tell their story as completely as possible. It was a pleasure and honour knowing her. We are sorry she never got to see the finished product but we hope that she will, somehow.

As well, we owe a big thank you to their children: Denise, Pierre Jr., Renee, and David for their friendship, insights, and observations of their parents. We know that your parents are very proud of you. To Al Arbour, Ray Gariepy, Dollard St. Laurent, Bobby Hull, Stan Mikita, John Kuentser, Ron Ellis, Red Fisher, and Ferguson Jenkins for sharing your memories of Pierre.

We would like to thank Jack David and Michael Holmes at ECW Press for believing in the project from the outset. Thanks to Greg Oliver for his great editing and assistance as well as Crissy Boylan, Carolyn McNeillie, and Erin Creasey.

We thank Anne Gagné and Tanis Dupuis for their French translations, MPP Garfield Dunlop for his great support, the Penetanguishene Sports Hall of Fame, Craig Campbell and Phil Pritchard at the Hockey Hall of Fame, Joe Rizzoto, Peter Hassen and the Chicago Blackhawks organization for use of their photos, Bob Crawford and his grandfather Tommy Ivan for use of his archival material, and Carl Kovacs for his time and support.

Hockey research and writing a book is not possible without the work of journalists who covered the game in Pierre's time and recorded his and his teammates' and opponents' feats for posterity. Thanks to the following writers for making our work easier and more complete: Chuck Wurzer, Cy Kritzer, *Buffalo Evening News*; Jack Laing, *Buffalo Courier Express*; Jack Griffin, Becky Blum, Dick Hackenberg, *Chicago Sun Times*; John Kuenster, *Chicago Daily News*; Charles Bartlett, *Chicago Tribune*; Marcel Bourassa, *Le Soleil*; Jacque Beauchamp, *Montreal Matin*; Scott Young, Jim Coleman, Louis Gauz, the *Globe and Mail*; Red Fisher, *Montreal Star*; Janet Garth, *Niagara Falls Evening Review*; Jim Proudfoot, Red Burnett, Jim Crerar, the *Toronto Star*; Dave Anderson, *Saturday Evening Post*; Dan Moulton, Chip Magnus, Bill Gleason, the Chicago *American*; Jim Hunt, *Toronto Star Weekly*; Dink Carroll, the *Montreal Gazette*; Jim Coleman, *Hamilton Spectator*; Ken McKenzie, Milt Dunnell, Dink Carroll, *The Hockey News*; W.R. Wheatley, Canadian Press; Harry Molter, *Hockey Pictorial*; Dan Parker, *Sports Illustrated*; Stan Fischler, *Sports Magazine*; Margaret Scott, *Maple Leaf Official Program*; Joe Mooshil, the Associated Press; Bud Booth, CBS.

Other writers whose work helped our research immensely included: Tom Wurzer, Jack Horrigan, Rex MacLeod, Charley Barton, Ted Damata, Marvin Weinstein, George Langford, Robert Markus, George Vass, Don Edwards, Ross Brewitt, Ronal Zazac, and Gene Gasiorowski.

Last but not least, David and Waxy thank the ever gracious

and incomparable Pierre Pilote for his trust, enthusiasm, generosity, insight, patience, memories, and most of all friendship. Our sojourn through this entire process has been unforgettable, funny, and always inspiring. Pierre, thank you for saying "YES"!

At ECW Press, we want you to enjoy this book in whatever format you like, whenever you like. Leave your print book at home and take the eBook to go! Purchase the print edition and receive the eBook free. Just send an email to ebook@ecwpress.com and include:

- the book title
- the name of the store where you purchased it
- your receipt number
- your preference of file type: PDF or ePub?

A real person will respond to your email with your eBook attached. And thanks for supporting an independently owned Canadian publisher with your purchase!